# TECHNIQUES OF CRIME SCENE INVESTIGATION

### FIFTH EDITION

SERIES IN FORENSIC AND POLICE SCIENCE
BARRY A.J. FISHER, EDITOR

TECHNIQUES OF CRIME SCENE INVESTIGATION,
Fifth Edition
Barry A.J. Fisher

SCIENTIFIC EXAMINATION OF QUESTIONED
DOCUMENTS
Ordway Hilton

INSTRUMENTAL DATA FOR DRUG ANALYSIS,
Second Edition, Vols. 1-5
Terry Mills III, et al.

INSTRUMENTAL DATA FOR DRUG ANALYSIS,
Second Edition, Vol. 5 (includes Index)
Terry Mills III, et al.

ADVANCES IN FINGERPRINT TECHNOLOGY
Henry C. Lee and R.E. Gaensslen

# TECHNIQUES
# OF CRIME SCENE
# INVESTIGATION

## FIFTH EDITION

## BARRY A.J. FISHER

Director, Scientific Services Bureau
Los Angeles County Sheriff's Department
Los Angeles, California

*with a Foreword by*

## SHERMAN BLOCK

Sheriff, Los Angeles County Sheriff's Department
Los Angeles, California

CRC Press
Boca Raton   Ann Arbor   London   Tokyo

**Library of Congress Cataloging-in-Publication Data**

Catalog record is available from the Library of Congress.

© 1992 by Elsevier Science Publishing Co. Inc.
© 1993 by CRC Press, Inc.

No claim to original U.S. Government works
International Standard Book Number 0-8493-9506-2
Printed in the United States of America      7  8  9  0
Printed on acid-free paper

This book is dedicated to
the men and women of the
Scientific Services Bureau,
Los Angeles County Sheriff's Department

# CONTENTS

# 7

## TRACE EVIDENCE AND MISCELLANEOUS MATERIAL / 159

# 8

## BLOOD AND OTHER BIOLOGICAL EVIDENCE / 217

# 9

## IMPRESSION EVIDENCE / 241

# 10

## FIREARMS EXAMINATION / 271

# 15

# 16

# FOREWORD

Each day law enforcement practitioners are called to crime scenes to decipher visible and often unseen clues. If properly recognized and interpreted, these leads may determine the identity of a victim or suspect. Serious consequences occur when the investigator fails to identify physical evidence. Such occurrences can be minimized when investigators are familiar with evidence-gathering techniques and procedures.

Those who have chosen to be forensic specialists shoulder a formidable burden. They must use their scientific and technical expertise to interpret evidence to help the trier of fact determine innocence or guilt. However, technical skills alone are not the true measure of one's abilities. Today's forensic science practitioner must have a sincere devotion to duty, justice, and virtue—in other words, he or she must possess integrity and professional ethics. All else is secondary.

Once again, Barry A. J. Fisher, Director of the Scientific Services Bureau for the Los Angeles County Sheriff's Department, has presented a wealth of personal experience and reference material applicable to a myriad of crime scene investigations. Many hours were spent creating this textbook for use in the classroom and library, and as a reference at the side of the investigator. The fifth edition of *Techniques of Crime Scene Investigation* updates some of the newer techniques in forensic science, including forensic DNA typing, latent fingerprint developing, automated fingerprint identification classification systems, and others.

The Los Angeles County Sheriff's Department is fortunate to have as a staff member a man worthy of being described as a true professional. Barry Fisher's accomplishments as a forensic scientist have brought him and the department worldwide recognition as leaders in the field.

Sherman Block
Sheriff of Los Angeles County

# PREFACE

The beginning of a police investigation, more likely than not, starts off at the scene of the crime. Crime scenes are exciting places. They hold the physical evidence that often provides detectives with information about the criminal, as well as the clues that, at some point, can help to solve the crime. A crime scene can be packed with details to aid in reconstructing the crime, in identifying the criminal and the victim. Yet often those details are hidden or not always obvious.

The key to unlocking the vast amount of information and physical evidence present at the crime scene is knowledge and understanding of crime scene investigation. Scrutinizing the scene, searching for clues, identifying, collecting and preserving physical evidence are all facets of a specialty requiring extensive study and training.

In 1981 I undertook a revision of Svensson and Wendel's classic text, *Techniques of Crime Scene Investigation,* and published a third edition. This writing is the fifth edition. As in previous editions, I have tried to address the nontechnical reader who uses this book as a textbook or as a reference work. *Techniques of Crime Scene Investigation* is not a technical treatise nor a step by step "how-to" book on the subject. The scope of the material contained herein is simply too broad to go into that much depth. Rather, my aim is to introduce the reader to some of the concepts, procedures, and technical information concerning crime scene investigations, awaken an interest in the subject, and spur a desire to pursue the technicalities further.

Readers of earlier editions have noted that one of the strong points of the book is the many photographs depicting examples of actual cases.

Some of the photos have not been of the best quality, and I have been trying to upgrade the selections with each edition. In addition to keeping up with new developments that readers will find useful, I have also been working on rewriting parts of the book into standard American English. The book was originally translated from Swedish, and some of the text was tedious to read.

Throughout the editions of this book that I have worked on, I have tried to focus on several notions about crime scene investigation. Investigation of criminal activities is a complex undertaking. A great number of people are involved: detectives, crime scene specialists, and forensic scientists, to name just a few. As in any complicated undertaking, teamwork and cooperation are essential to the task at hand.

I have included in this latest edition a prologue. During the past few years, concerns about professional ethics and integrity have come to the fore. I felt it important to spell out to those beginning their careers in forensic science and crime scene work just what their role in the criminal system entails.

Forensic science is an important component in the investigation and solution of serious crimes. Clues found at a crime scene often result in the solution of the case and frequently play a role in the prosecution of the criminal. Police investigators and prosecutors who fully utilize the talents of forensic scientists and technicians in their jurisdictions achieve more for their efforts. They are able to clear more cases and successfully prosecute a greater number of criminals.

# ACKNOWLEDGMENTS

In preparation of this fifth edition, I contacted many colleagues and requested that they share interesting cases for inclusion in this book. Although I was not able to use all of the submissions, I would like to thank those who responded to my request: Joseph Almog, Ph. D., Director, Division of Identification and Forensic Science, Israel National Police, Jersulalem, Israel; Gary B. Backos, Forensic Laboratory, El Cajon Police Department, El Cajon, California; Chris W. Beheim, Criminalist IV, Scientific Crime Detection Laboratory, Department of Public Safety, State of Alaska, Anchorage, Alaska; Arne Bergh, Ph. D., Director, Crime Laboratory, Ventura County Sheriff's Department, Ventura, California; Richard A. Bergman, Director, Forensic Laboratory Services, Royal Canadian Mounted Police, Ottawa, Ontario, Canada; Richard Bingle, Chief Forensic Chemist, S.I.D., Los Angeles Police Department, Los Angeles, California; George E. Burgman, D.D.S., Forensic Odontology Consultant, Niagara Falls, Ontario, Canada; Lt. Ken Chausee and the staff of the Los Angeles County Sheriff's Department, Arson-Explosives Detail; Vivian Emerson, Director, Central Research Establishment, Home Office Forensic Science Service, Aldermaston, Reading, Berkshire, United Kingdom; Robert Hawkins, Firearms Examiner, Deputy Sheriff (Retired), Scientific Services Bureau, Los Angeles County Sheriff's Department, Los Angeles, California; Ed Hueske, Supervising Criminalist, Northern Regional Crime Laboratory, Arizona Department of Public Safety, Flagstaff, Arizona; Robert Horn, Director, New York State Police Laboratories, Albany, New York; Ross James, M.D., Forensic Science Center, Adelaide, South Australia,

xviii   Acknowledgments

Australia; Kristine Jousimaa, Crime Laboratory, National Bureau of Investigation, Helsinki, Finland; James A. Njavro, Head, Forensic Photography and Support Services, Los Angeles County Department of the Coroner, Los Angeles, California; Peter W. Pfefferli, Ph. D., Head, Forensic Science Department, Zurich Cantonal Police, Zurich, Switzerland; Ray Prime, Ph. D., Section Head (Chemistry), The Centre of Forensic Sciences, Ministry of the Solicitor General, Toronto, Ontario, Canada; Gloria H. Reynolds, Third Deputy Chief, Commanding Officer, Crime Laboratory Section, Department of Police, Detroit, Michigan; LeRoy Riddick, M.D., State Medical Examiner, Alabama Department of Forensic Sciences, Mobile, Alabama; Norman D. Sperber, D.D.S., Forensic Odontologist, San Diego, California, and Detective Mike Howard, El Cajon Police Department, El Cajon, California; George M. Taft, Jr., Laboratory Director, Scientific Crime Detection Laboratory, Department of Public Safety, State of Alaska, Anchorage, Alaska; Fred Tulleners, Bureau of Forensic Services, California Department of Justice, Sacramento, California; Bruce Vander Kolk, Bureau Chief, Bureau of Forensic Sciences, Illinois State Police, Springfield, Illinois; Ted Van Dijk, Sergeant, Forensic Science Section, South Australian Police Department, Adelaide, South Australia, Australia; Deputy Ray Verdugo, Los Angeles County Sheriff's Department, Homicide Bureau; Michael H. West, D.S.D., Deputy Medical Examiner–Investigator, Forrest County, Hattiesburg, Mississippi; James White, Forensic Science Services, Orange County Sheriff–Corner's Department, Santa Ana, California; Xu Li Gen, Professor of Criminalists, Law Department, People's University, Beijing, People's Republic of China; and Ilya Zeldes, Ph.D., Director, Division of Criminal Investigation, State of Criminal Investigation, Office of the Attorney General, Pierre, South Dakota.

My thanks also to my wife, Susan, and to my children, David and Michael, for their support in this project. Without their encouragement, I would not have finished on schedule.

The following are earlier acknowledgments made in recognition of those who assisted in prior editions.

**From the fourth edition:** James Anderson and Sze-Ern Kuo, Scientific Investigative Division, Los Angeles Police Department, Los Angeles, California; James M. Bullock and Bruce R. Mackenzie, Forensic Science Division, Michigan State Police, Madison Heights, Michigan; Joseph H. Davis, M.D., Office of the Chief Medical Examiner, Metropolitan Dade County, Miami, Florida; Dr. James Donovan, Forensic Science Laboratory, Department of Justice, Dublin, Ireland; Richard S. Frank, Forensic Sciences Section, Office of Science and Technology, Drug Enforcement Administration, Washington, D.C.; Neil Holland, State Forensic Science Laboratory, Melbourne, Australia; Randy Hanzlick, M.D., Office of Fulton County Medical Examiner, Atlanta, Georgia; Robert W. Horn, New York State Police Laboratories, Albany, New York; Dr. Jia Jingtao, China Medical College, Shenyang, People's Republic of China; Kenneth F. Kowalski, Scientific Analysis Division, Arizona Department of Public Safety, Phoenix, Arizona; M. James Kreiser, Bureau of Forensic Sciences, Illinois Department of State Police, Springfield, Illinois; Henry Lee, Ph.D., Connecticut State Police Forensic Science Laboratory, Meriden, Connecticut; Douglas M. Lucas, The Centre of Forensic Sciences, Toronto, Ontario, Canada; Thomas J. Nasser, Forensic Science Division, Michigan State Police, Bridgeport, Michigan; Stephan M. Ojena, Kinderprint Company, Martinez, California; Nicholas Petraco, Police Laboratory, New York City Police Department, New York, N.Y.; Michael L. Rehberg, Division of Criminal Investigation, Iowa Department of Public Safety, Des Moines, Iowa; Roger S. Ritzlin, M.D., Forensic Science Division, Laboratory Medicine Consultants, Reno, Nevada; Harley M. Sagara and Gary P. Chasteen, Criminalistics Laboratory, Los Angeles County Sheriff's Department, Los Angeles, California; Nick F. Stames, Identification Division, FBI, Washington, D.C.; Capt. Robert Thibault, USAF, Directorate of Fraud and Criminal Investigations, Air Force Office of Special Investigations, Bolling Air Force Base, Washington, D.C.; Gerald L. Vale, D.D.S., Chief of Forensic Dentistry, LAC-USC Medical Center, Los Angeles, California; John D. Versailles, Forensic Science Division, Michigan State Police, East Lansing, Michigan; James White, Forensic Science Services, Orange County Sheriff–Coroner's Department, Santa Ana, California; Ray Williams, Ph.D., and Ann Priston, Ph.D., Metropolitan Police Forensic Science Laboratory, London, U.K.; Professor Xu Ligen, People's University School of Law, and Chen Jianhua, Beijing Forensic Science Research Institute, Beijing, People's Republic of China; Cecil Yates, Laboratory Division, FBI, Washington, D.C.; Ilya Zeldes, Ph.D., Forensic Laboratory, Office of the Attorney General, Pierre, South Dakota; Dr. Ronald Kornblum, Chief Medical Examiner-Coroner, Los Angeles County, California; James White, Orange County Sheriff-Coroner's Laboratory, Santa Ana, California; Donald A. Denison, Eddie Lu, John T. Cook, Kathrine R. Vukovich, and Harley M. Sagara, Scientific Services Bureau, Los Angeles County Sheriff's Department, Los Angeles, California.

**From the third edition:** Donald A. Motander, Eddie Lu, Paul Kayne, James G. Bailey, Keith E.P. Inman, Wayne G. Plumtree, Dr. Edward F. Rhodes II, Douglas A. Ridolfi, Harley M. Sagara, James R. Wells, Robert R. Christansen, James H. Warner, Herbert L. Campbell, Martin L. Kudell, Steven D. Frankel, Douglas L. Dunworth, Elizabeth Dickenson, and the Art Staff, Los Angeles County Sheriff's Department, Los Angeles, California; Douglas M. Lucas, The Centre of Forensic Sciences, Toronto, Ontario, Canada; Kenneth M. Betz, Director, Miami Valley Regional Crime Laboratory, Dayton, Ohio; San Diego County Sheriff's Regional Crime Laboratory, San Diego, California; U.S. Postal Service, Crime Laboratory, Western Region, San Bruno, California; Joseph V. Ambrozich, Crime Scene Technician, Department of Law Enforcement, State of Illinois, Bureau of Technical Field Services; James F. Cowger, Stephen M. Ojena, Gerald Mitosinka, Grady L. Goldman, John R. Patty, John Murdock, Contra Costa County Sheriff's Department, Crime Laboratory, Martinez, California; Polaroid Corporation, Cambridge, Massachusetts, Major Ronald A. Battelle, Executive Director, Division of Auxiliary Services, and Joseph Bono, Senior Forensic Scientist, St. Louis County Police Department, Crime Laboratory, Clayton, Missouri; Dr. Frank J. Kreysa, Chief, Scientific Services Division, U.S. Department of the Treasury, Bureau of Alcohol, Tobacco and Firearms, Washington, D.C.; C.D. Tiller, C/Supt., Assistant Director, Identification Services, Royal Canadian Mounted Police, Ottawa, Canada; Dr. Larry B. Howard, Director, Crime Laboratory, Georgia Bureau of Identification, State Crime Laboratory; Norman D. Sperber, D.D.S., Forensic Odontologist, San Diego, California; Gerald L. Vale, D.D.S., and Roger Ritzlin, M.D., Los Angeles County Department of Medical Examiner–Coroner, Los Angeles, California; Baltimore Police Department, Baltimore, Maryland; Tom Harless and Johnny Byrd, Firearms and Toolmarks Examiners, South West Regional Crime Laboratory, Parish of Calcasieu Sheriff's Department, Lake Charles, Louisiana; Carl H. Cloud, Assistant to the Director/Criminalistics, and Melvin R. Hett, Criminalist, Oklahoma State Bureau of Investigation; Sgt. Larry Michalscheck, Criminalistics Section, City of Albuquerque Police Department, Albuquerque, New Mexico; Richard S. Frank, Chief, Forensic Sciences Division, Office of Science and Technology, U.S. Department of Justice, Drug Enforcement Administration, Washington, D.C.; Robert R. Stoinoff, Jr., Supervising Criminalist, Santa Ana Police Department Crime Laboratory, Santa Ana, California; Capt. James G. Mitchell, Commander, Louisiana State Police Laboratory Services; Sgt. Don Garrett, Area II Laboratory Manager, Indiana State Police, Indianapolis, Indiana. S/Lieutenant R.F. Wilcox, Investigation Section, Ohio State Highway Patrol; William E. Alexander, D.M.D., Forensic Odontologist, Eugene, Oregon; Faye Springer, Criminalist, State of California, Department of Justice, Riverside, California; Mark E. Palenik, Walter C. McCrone Associates, Inc., Chicago, Illinois; John W. Beckstead, D.D.S., Chief Consultant to the District Attorney and Coroner, Alameda-County, California; Lt. James E. Nolan, Director, and

Corporal James E. Ross, Vermont State Police Crime Laboratory and Bureau of Identification; Ronald K. Wright, M.D., Deputy Chief Medical Examiner, and Joseph H. Davis, M.D., Chief Medical Examiner, Office of Medical Examiner, Metropolitan Dade County, Florida.

Barry A.J. Fisher

*Los Angeles, California*
*July 5, 1991*

# PROLOGUE

There are several elements of crime scene investigation techniques that must be discussed. These are far from the technical and "how to" aspects of the subject that are found in the text. Rather, they describe a philosophical approach to the subject and should be considered an integral part of one's work in forensic science.

Forensic scientists, crime scene specialists, latent fingerprint experts—men and women whose jobs are to apply science and technology to the solution of criminal acts—shoulder a weighty burden. Their skills and knowledge of science applied to criminal investigation and the law often result in establishing the innocence or guilt of a defendant. Many forensic specialists work for government law enforcement agencies that are responsible for the criminal investigation and/or prosecution of cases under forensic investigation. Some argue that this employment arrangement holds a potential for bias on the part of the forensic professional.

Government forensic scientists owe a duty to the truth. They may never be biased for or against a suspect in an investigation. The forensic practitioner's sole obligation is to serve the aims of justice. It is irrelevant whether or not a defendant is subsequently found guilty of the crime. What is important is that the forensic scientist or practitioner conduct the investigation in a thorough, competent fashion and submit the findings in reports and through testimony in a factual, unbiased manner.

Forensic practitioners have an obligation to neither overstate nor understate their scientific findings. Their positions within the criminal justice system places them in positions of authority and responsibility. Because of their education, training, experience, and skills, their opinions on technical matters often carry considerable importance.

Scientific and technological information is growing at an incredible rate. New techniques, methods, and procedures are constantly being developed and incorporated within forensic science and in other technical areas. Practitioners have an obligation to keep up with these new developments. They must maintain their abilities by attending continuing education programs, going to technical conferences and seminars, reading the technical and scientific literature, and supporting professional organizations in their own areas of expertise.

Forensic science administrators have a responsibility to foster high standards of practice and ethical conduct. Beyond the application of sound scientific procedures, there must be a recognition of the role of forensic science in the overall process of justice. The public's confidence in the various parts that make up the criminal justice system is equally important.

Modern Western society is built on the pillars of democratic institutions and the rule of law. The individual, not the state, is paramount. Personal rights usually take precedence over what may be in the best interest of society. In the United States, for example, there is a tension between the law and the state, which provides numerous checks and balances to safeguard individual liberties.

Forensic science provides one of many checks and balances critical to the administration of justice. Judges and juries require experts to explain technical matters that are beyond the knowledge or understanding of lay people. Courts have also recognized imperfections in our legal system. For instance, facts presented are not always what they seem. Experience has shown that abuse of authority, improper and sometimes unlawful police procedures have occurred in the course of criminal investigations. In addition, eyewitness testimony is not as certain as some believe. Juries, too, recognize the impartial scientific evaluation of physical evidence clarifies issues and frequently corroborates other evidence presented to the trier of fact.

For forensic science practitioners to perform their function properly within the legal system, they must exercise independence and integrity. Stated simply, forensic scientists cannot be biased for or against an investigation in which they are involved. The job of each practitioner is to champion his or her expert opinion based on accepted, properly performed scientific inquiry. Forensic scientists who understand their roles in a democratic criminal justice arena help to protect individual rights and freedoms while ensuring that justice is delivered.

The ethical practices of all practitioners, forensic science managers, crime scene investigators—of law enforcement in general—are a matter of concern. In 1986 the American Society of Crime Laboratory Directors adopted the document *Guidelines for Forensic Laboratory Management Practices.* In an introduction, these guidelines suggest:

> The following questions requiring individual judgment are offered to help laboratory managers comply with the general guidelines in this document. In evaluating the propriety of a proposed act, the manager should ask:
>
> Is anyone's life, health, safety, or good name endangered by this action?
>
> Is my action legal? If legal, is it ethical?
>
> Does my action comply with laboratory policy and approved practice?
>
> Will this action be handled honestly and impartially in every respect?
>
> Would I be compromised if this act were known by my supervisor, fellow employees, subordinates, or other professional colleagues?
>
> Could I defend this act before my supervisor, fellow employees, the courts, professional forensic science organizations, and the general public?
>
> The guiding principle should be that the end does not justify the means; the means must always be in keeping with the law and with good scientific practice.

Finally, teamwork is essential. The full investigation of criminal acts involves scores of people who may work in many different organizations. This system was purposefully designed so that no one person or entity can operate independently. There will always be "turf" issues that arise—"This is my responsibility; you're not allowed to do that." As larger and more complex criminal justice systems evolve, it is likely that many of us will be dealing with "faceless voices" at the end of a telephone line. Yet, for the success of any complex system, teamwork is of the utmost importance. Each entity—the uniformed officer, the detective, the crime scene specialist, the criminalist, the coroner, the forensic pathologist, the photographer, the prosecutor, the defense attorney, and all the other vital players in the "system"—have to work cooperatively to make the entire process work.

No one element or person is necessarily more important than any other person or element. Each has a vital role to play and each must be accomplished in a responsible, professional, and timely manner for the system to function properly. Each one working on a case should feel that he or she is important to the successful completion of an investigation. Each must feel empowered to do what needs to be done for the sake of justice.

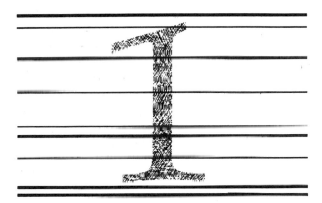

# INTRODUCTION

2

Charlie Richardson[1] was a 30-year-old student completing his final year at medical school and preparing to intern. The victim, Maria Richardson, was the defendant's wife of several years. The defendant and Maria had a marital relationship that appeared normal to those who knew them. On the morning of December 30, 1988, the defendant drove Maria to her workplace, a laboratory located in El Cajon, California. While they were alone at the laboratory, an argument ensued and Charlie strangled Maria with a ligature. After killing Maria, he scattered and misplaced laboratory specimens and the contents of Maria's purse to make it appear that a burglar had committed the murder (Figs. 1.1 to 1.3). Charlie then drove from the laboratory to the University of California, San Diego, medical school library to study for an upcoming exam.

Later in the morning one of Maria's co-workers found her dead in the laboratory. The police arrived and began an investigation. Meanwhile,

**FIGURE 1.1.** Victim Maria Richardson at the scene of her murder. Note the proximity of the telephone cord to her head. (*Norman D. Sperber, D.D.S., San Diego, California, and El Cajon Police Department, El Cajon, California.*)

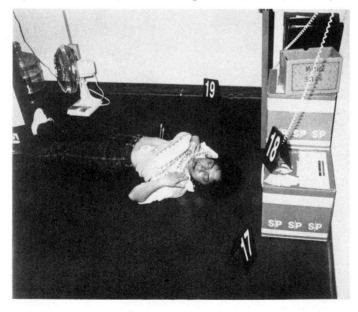

[1] This case was submitted by Norman D. Sperber, D.D.S., San Diego, California, and Detective Mike Howard, El Cajon Police Department, El Cajon, California.

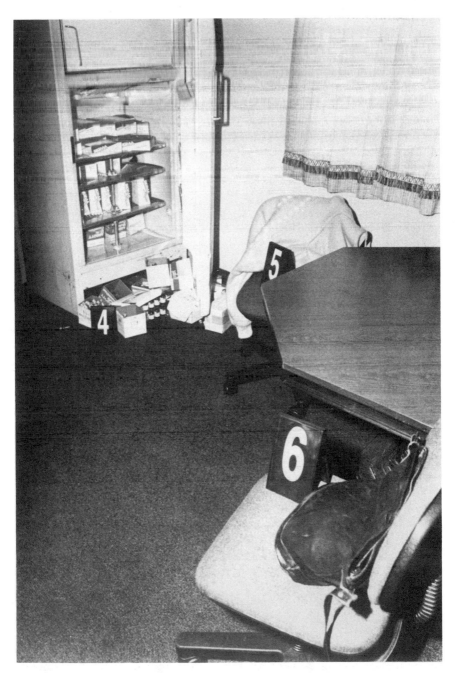

**FIGURE 1.2.** The killer's attempt at making the crime scene look as though there had been a burglary attempt. (*Norman D. Sperber, D.D.S., San Diego, California, and El Cajon Police Department, El Cajon, California.*)

the defendant went to several locations in the San Diego area and purchased several items, including roses for his wife. At noon he returned to the laboratory under the pretense of having lunch with Maria. He wondered why he was not allowed to see his wife and why there were detectives around the lab. Charlie was told of Maria's death and was then asked for background information about her. Charlie related his actions of the morning, explained how he left his wife at work and then went to the library to study. He told investigators that he planned to meet Maria for lunch and produced time-stamped receipts from various locations.

The victim had ligature marks around her neck and chin. Several items that could have been used as the ligature were collected, including a long telephone cord that was attached to a wall phone. During the investigation, a small crescent-shaped abrasion was noted on the edge of Charlie's right pinky finger (Fig. 1.4). Charlie, now a suspect, was read his *Miranda* rights. He explained the abrasion as a burn received while he was cooking. He was, however, unable to explain a very small, less visible matching abrasion along the edge of the left pinky finger. Charlie Richardson was arrested for the murder of his wife Maria. Dr. Norman D. ("Skip") Sperber was called into the investigation. Sperber, a forensic odontologist, made castings and took photographs of the suspect's fingers and of the ligature marks on the victim's neck (Figs. 1.5 and 1.6). The castings and photographs were compared with the wall telephone cord from the scene. In this case, the cord became critical evidence (Fig. 1.7). A search of the suspect's home yielded evidence of disharmony in the marriage. Investigators also found writings by Maria that stated that she was afraid of Charlie.

Although the defense tried to suppress the evidence in pretrial motions, it was admitted in a jury trial. After considering all factors in the case, including the damaging evidence to be presented by Dr. Sperber, the defense offered to plead to a charge of involuntary manslaughter on condition that Charlie would take the stand and tell the jury what actually happened. The defendant took the witness stand and told how he strangled Maria with the telephone cord during the course of a heated argument.

The dictionary defines evidence as "something legally submitted to a competent tribunal as a means of ascertaining the truth of any alleged matter of fact under investigation before it."

Police officers deal with evidence on a daily basis. The ability to recognize, collect, and use evidence in criminal investigations determines to a large degree the success of the officers as investigators.

Evidence can be divided into two types: testimonial and real, or physical, evidence. Testimonial evidence is evidence given in the form

A

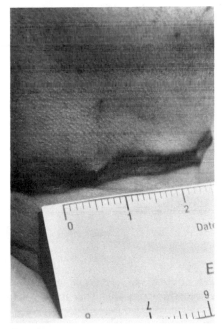

B

**FIGURE 1.3**
(A) The wall telephone and cord presumed to have been used to strangle Maria; (B) a close-up of the ligature marks on the victim's neck; (C) marks presumably made from the telephone cord on the victim's chin. (*Norman D. Sperber, D.D.S., San Diego, California, and El Cajon Police Department, El Cajon, California.*)

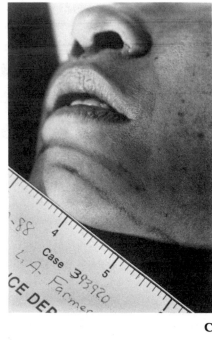

C

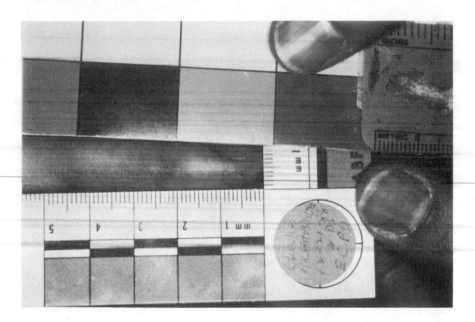

**FIGURE 1.4.** The abrasion on Charlie Richardson's right little finger, which the defendant explained was due to a burn received while he was cooking. He was unable to explain another less visible one on his left little finger. (*Norman D. Sperber, D.D.S., San Diego, California, and El Cajon Police Department, El Cajon, California.*)

**FIGURE 1.5.** Dr. Norman Sperber making castings of the defendant's left and right little fingers. (*Norman D. Sperber, D.D.S., San Diego, California, and El Cajon Police Department, El Cajon, California.*)

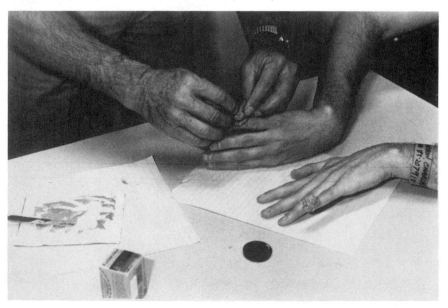

A

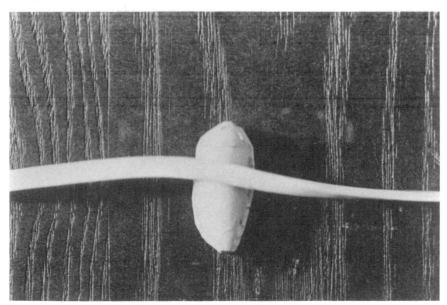

B

FIGURE 1.6. (A) The telephone cord fitted into a casting of the ligature mark on the victim's neck; (B) the telephone cord fitted onto a casting of one of the defendant's pinkies. (*Norman D. Sperber, D.D.S., San Diego, California, and El Cajon Police Department, El Cajon, California.*)

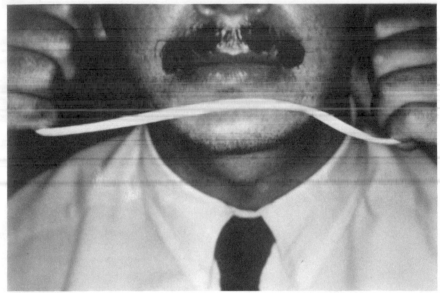

A

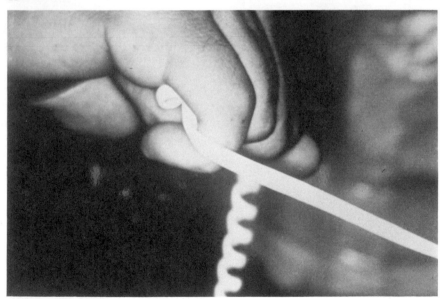

B

FIGURE 1.7. (A,B) Two illustrations of how the markings on the defendant's pinkies and on the victim's chin might have occurred; (C) a close-up illustration of how the markings on the defendant's little finger occurred. (*Norman D. Sperber, D.D.S., San Diego, California, and El Cajon Police Department, El Cajon, California.*)

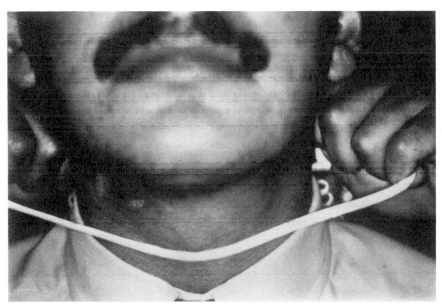

**FIGURE 1.7.** (*continued*)                                                                    **C**

of a statement made under oath, usually in response to questioning. Physical evidence is any type of evidence having an objective existence, that is, anything with size, shape, and dimension.

Physical evidence can take almost any form. It can be as large as a residence or as small as a fiber, as fleeting as an odor or as obvious as the scene of an explosion. Indeed, the variety of physical evidence that may be encountered by a police officer is enormous.

What is the value of physical evidence, and why should police investigators concern themselves with an understanding of the uses and ways to collect physical evidence?

1. Physical evidence can prove that a crime has been committed or establish key elements of a crime.

   | *Case* | Proof of rape requires a showing of nonconsenting sexual intercourse. In an alleged rape case, the victim's torn clothing and bruises were sufficient to prove nonconsent. |

   | *Case* | Arson investigators dispatched to the scene of a suspicious fire collected some burned carpeting. Later analysis revealed that gasoline was present in the carpet, proving that the fire was started intentionally and was, hence, the result of arson. |

2. Physical evidence can link a suspect with the victim or with the crime scene (Fig. 1.8).

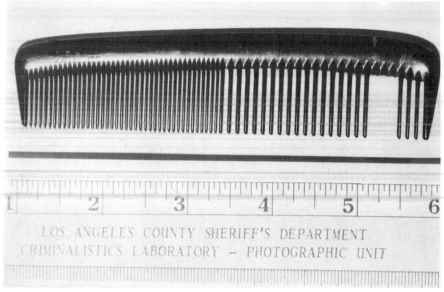

A

**FIGURE 1.8**
In this example of a physical match, a comb (A) with three missing teeth was found in the suspect's possession. Two plastic teeth (B) were found at the crime scene, which were fitted to the comb (C). The evidence placed the victim at a burglary. (*Los Angeles County Sheriff's Department.*)

B

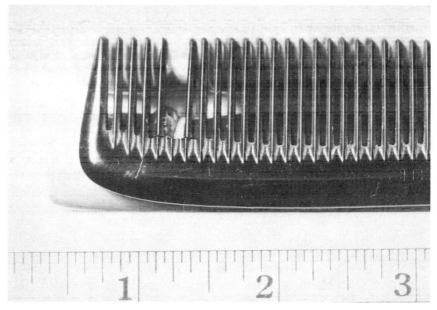

FIGURE **1.8.** (*continued*)                                                                                     **C**

---

*Case*  A suspect was apprehended shortly after an alleged rape
in the victim's home. Cat hair was found on the lower
portion of the suspect's trousers, which the suspect was at a loss to
explain. The victim owned two cats.

3. Physical evidence can establish the identity of persons associated
   with a crime.

   *Case*  Every burglar of a safe knows that fingerprints should not
   be left at a crime scene, so it was not surprising that
   rubber surgical gloves were found at the scene of a burgled safe. The
   identity of the burglar was established by developing the fingerprints found inside the rubber gloves.

   *Case*  In a series of rape cases in a major metropolitan area,
   DNA typing proved that a lone defendant was responsible for the rapes.

4. Physical evidence can exonerate the innocent.

   *Case*  An 8- and 9-year-old brother and sister accused an elderly
   man of child molestation. They claimed the man gave

them each pills that made them feel very drowsy and then molested them. The investigator had a physician examine the children. Urine specimens were collected for a toxicology screen. The results of the analyses were negative. When presented with this information, the children confessed that they had fabricated the entire story because they disliked the old man.

5. Physical evidence can corroborate the victim's testimony.

   *Case*    A female hitchhiker was picked up by a motorist. She claimed that he pulled a knife and attempted to rape her. During the struggle, the woman's thumb was cut before she managed to escape. She related her story to the police and the suspect was eventually arrested. During interrogation, the suspect steadfastly proclaimed his innocence. The investigator noted a small quantity of dried blood on the left lapel of the suspect's jacket. The suspect claimed that the blood was the result of a shaving mishap. The investigator submitted the jacket to the crime laboratory, along with blood samples from the suspect and the victim. Test results indicated that the blood on the jacket could not have come from the suspect, but could have come from the victim. This physical evidence was instrumental in obtaining a conviction for attempted rape.

6. A suspect confronted with physical evidence may make admissions or even confess.

   *Case*    High meat prices have led to an increase of cattle rustling cases. Blood found on a suspect's shirt was tested and determined to be bovine, that is, cow blood. The suspect, who first claimed the blood to be his own, made a full admission when confronted with the evidence.

7. Physical evidence is more reliable than eyewitnesses to crimes. Psychological experiments have shown that observations made by test subjects witnessing simulated violent crimes are inaccurate over a period of time after the event.

   Volunteers in a psychological test were witnesses to staged assaults. At the conclusion of the mock crimes, they were asked to detail their observations in writing. Over a period of several months, they repeatedly were asked to write down what they had observed.

   The study showed that people are likely to fill in gaps with details not observed. If a portion of an event was not seen or did not make sense, the subjects made up situations that seemed reasonable to explain the episode. This "fill in" behavior occurred subconsciously, and subjects were not even aware that it was happening. They simply reported what they believed they saw.

8. Court decisions have made physical evidence more important. The United States Supreme Court in a number of decisions, such as in the *Miranda* case, has limited the authority of the police to rely on statements and confessions made by defendants. These landmark cases have, in effect, shifted attention to physical evidence as proof in court cases.

9. Physical evidence is expected by juries in criminal cases. Two unrelated factors, television police shows and the technological orientation of our society, have biased the public's concept of the role of physical evidence in criminal cases. Jurors expect physical evidence in a trial; after all, that's the way it is on television. And if science and technology are used to scrutinize the evidence, so much the better.

10. Negative evidence, that is, the absence of physical evidence, may provide useful information and even stop defense arguments at the time of trial.

   Case    In an insurance fraud, the "victim" claimed his home was burglarized. No evidence of forced entry could be found, and eventually the fraud was discovered.

## Identification and Individualization of Physical Evidence

Many police investigators believe that any item of physical evidence can be directly related to a specific person, place, or thing. They expect a single strand of hair or a fiber to be associated with a unique source. Unfortunately, this is not generally possible.

There are actually only a few kinds of physical evidence that can be individualized. Individualization means that an item is unique. The item can be shown to be directly associated with a specific individual source. A broken piece of plastic physically fitted to reconstruct an item is an example of individualization. Other types of evidence such as fingerprints, tool marks, and fired bullets are also examples of evidence capable of being specifically associated with a unique source (Figs. 1.9 and 1.10).

Most evidence can, at best, be identified. Identification means that an item shares a common source. The item can be classified or placed into a group with all other items having the same properties (Figs. 1.11 and 1.12).

The difference between individualization and identification is a subtle one. Consider the following example. A blue-colored cotton fiber is found at the scene of a burglary. A suspect who is wearing a torn blue cotton shirt is apprehended. All the tests conducted by the crime laboratory on the evidence fiber and exemplar fibers show that they have identical physical properties. Can it be concluded that the blue cotton fiber found at the scene definitely came from the torn blue cotton shirt worn by the suspect?

No! The best that can be stated is that the fiber could have come from the shirt or any other source of similar blue cotton fibers. The item has been identified as a blue cotton fiber and can be placed into a class of all other similar blue cotton fibers. No matter how much testing is done on that evidence, the conclusion will always be the same.

Contrast the fiber with a fingerprint. The fingerprint may be identified. It can be placed into a group, e.g., a whorl or loop. However, fingerprint evidence can go beyond identification; fingerprints can be

FIGURE **1.9.** The victim in this case was raped and strangled in her home in a suburb of Beijing. The criminal tried to disguise the crime scene by tying an electrical desk lamp cord around the victim's neck and making the death appear as a suicide. A latent fingerprint was discovered on the base of the lamp using super glue. The case was solved when the latent print was matched to a youth who lived in the neighborhood and who claimed never to have been in the victim's house. (*Institute of Forensic Science, Beijing, China.*)

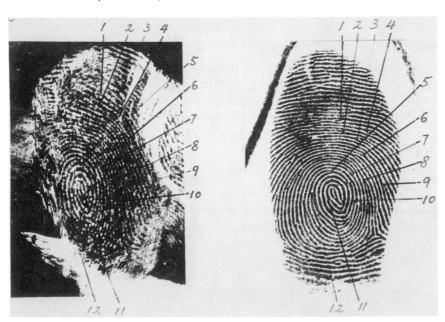

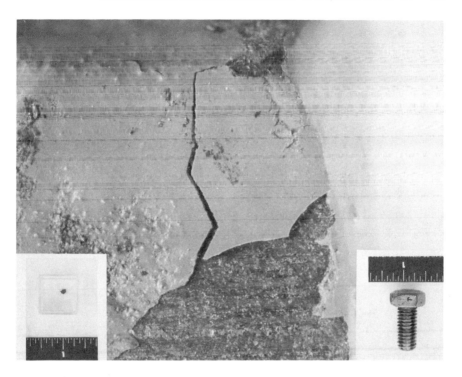

**FIGURE 1.10.** Physical matches are another example of individual characteristics. The tiny paint chip in the evidence container on the left was removed from the suspect's wrench, and a physical match was made to an area on the bolt (bottom right insert) from a safe. The photograph is a close-up of the physical match. (*Illinois State Police.*)

shown to be unique. They can come only from a single person; that is, they can be individualized (Fig. 1.13).

Most physical evidence cannot definitely connect a suspect to a crime as can fingerprint evidence. This should not diminish the usefulness of that evidence. Physical evidence that is identified can corroborate testimony, place a subject at a scene, and be useful as an interrogation tool.

## Case

A robbery[2] of a Ventura, California, cocktail lounge occurred wherein a lone gunman tied the manager—hand and foot—with lengths of white plastic

---

[2] This case was submitted by Dr. Arne Bergh, Ventura County Sheriff's Crime Laboratory, Ventura, California.

FIGURE 1.11. Class characteristics place an item of evidence in a given class or group. These items depict an example of class characteristics. The upper two strap segments in the photograph were found in a murder suspect's van. The lower strap is of similar manufacture, design, and content. It was from a similarly designed and manufactured swimsuit reported to have been worn by the victim. (*Los Angeles County Sheriff's Department.*)

clothesline. Later, another robbery occurred at a cocktail lounge approximately 20 miles north of Ventura, during which the manager was bound with white plastic clothesline in the same fashion. This time, however, the victim was also shot and killed by a single .45 caliber bullet fired into the back of his head.

An intensive investigation led to a suspect, a middle-aged part-time cook who resided in Van Nuys, immediately northwest of Los Angeles. A search of his car led to the discovery of a 24-foot length of white plastic clothesline in the trunk and two lengths of clothesline—each about 40 inches long—under the driver's seat.

Laboratory examinations revealed that the sections of clothesline from the three sources all bore the same class characteristics, including the physical and chemical composition of the plastic components. The components consisted of 121 interior filaments of nine different plastic types and one metallic filament, all contained in a white plastic cover. The outer covers or sheaths were approximately one-quarter inch in diameter. Examination of the interior portion of the sheaths showed that the perimeter filaments left their impressions permanently in the interior of the sheaths as a result of the manufacturing process. In

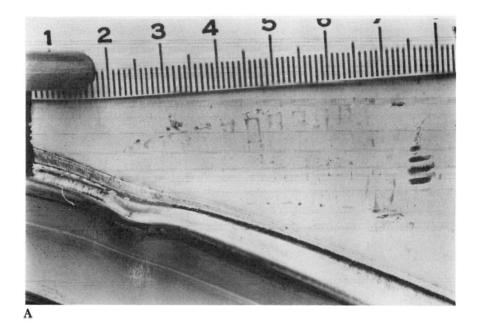

**A**

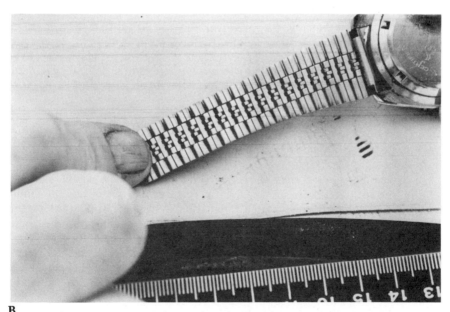

**B**

FIGURE **1.12.** These items provide an unusual example of class characteristics. The body of a hit-and-run victim was found next to a major highway. A suspect vehicle was located with an unusual impression (A) that matched the pedestrian's wristwatch band (B). (*Division of Identification and Forensic Science, Israel National Police.*)

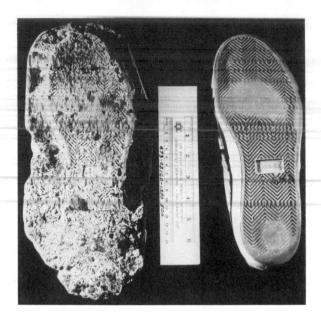

**FIGURE 1.13.** Sometimes class characteristics may be unusual enough to permit the inference that a certain item of evidence came from a single source. This illustration shows a plaster cast (left) from a burglary and the suspect's shoe (right). The cast is shown photographically reversed in order to orient the two items the same. Note that the tread on the sole and that on the plaster cast have the same design and similar wear pattern. The staple in the sole, also found in the cast, is convincing evidence that this shoe made the impression. (*Los Angeles County Sheriff's Department.*)

this process the filaments constituting the core are pulled through white PVC melt and extruded to produce the white outer cover.

Experiments showed that successive cross-section cuts along a single clothesline section, one-quarter inch apart, resulted in quite noticeable differences because the filaments varied in position from point to point along the clothesline (Fig. 1.14). By virtue of this highly individual characteristic, these filament impressions constituted the strongest single feature of identification. Through this means the Ventura robbery was tied conclusively to the suspect. On the other hand, the robbery/murder case was not connected conclusively through the clotheslines. There was no matching ends to tie the robbery/murder case to the first robbery or to the car.

Measurements of all of the clothesline sections, collectively, indicated that less than one complete clothesline was present. There was a shortage of about 10 feet. Such a portion of the clothesline, or parts of it, may be lying on a police property room shelf somewhere—perhaps to link another crime someday. In any event, the accused person was convicted of robbery and murder, based on the plastic clothesline and other physical evidence (Fig. 1.15).

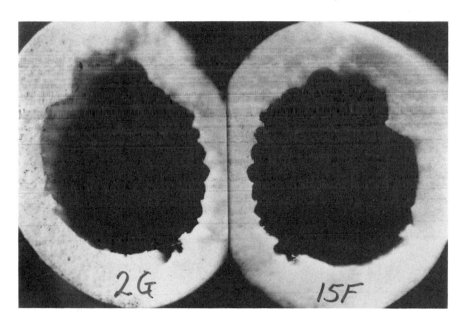

FIGURE **1.14.** Cross-sections of the clothesline showing similarities. (*Ventura County Sheriff's Department, Ventura, California.*)

## Collection and Preservation of Physical Evidence

Two major areas must be considered in a discussion of collection and preservation of physical evidence: the legal and the scientific.

*Laws* regarding physical evidence vary among jurisdictions; however, there are many similarities. Before evidence is seized, the need for a *search warrant* or court order should be considered. Case law in many jurisdictions is constantly changing, and investigators should keep themselves abreast of developments. Court orders may be required for blood samples, hair specimens, medical tests, teeth impressions, and the like. The prosecutor's office should be consulted when there is any doubt. Failure to secure a search warrant may result in the physical evidence seized at a crime scene being inadmissible in court. Further, under the so-called "fruit of the poison tree doctrine," any subsequent information derived from illegally seized physical evidence may also be inadmissible in court.

The idea of *chain of custody* or chain of evidence is important. The court will require proof that the evidence collected at the crime scene and that being presented in court is the same.

To prove that the integrity of the evidence has been maintained, a chain of custody must be demonstrated. This "chain" shows who had contact with the evidence, at what time, under what circumstances, and what, if any, changes were made to the evidence.

20

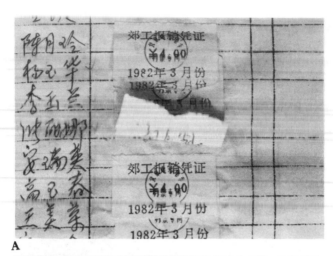

A

B

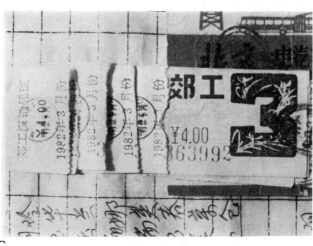

C

Typically, evidence is put into a container or tagged, and certain information is written on the container or tag as well as in reports and logs to establish the chain. Police department policy may dictate which information is required, but usually the following are needed on the tag or container:

1. Name or initials of the individual collecting the evidence and each person subsequently having custody of it.
2. Dates the item was collected and transferred.
3. Agency, case number, and type of crime.
4. Victim's or suspect's name.
5. Brief description of the item.

This information serves to prove the chain of custody to the court and assists in admitting the items into evidence.

*Storage* of physical evidence has legal implications. Evidence must be held in a secured area prior to transportation to court. Evidence that reasonably may be assumed to have been tampered with by unauthorized persons because it was held in an unsecured storage area may be inadmissible in court. Evidence should be stored in a specific locked area, with access kept to a limited number of authorized persons.

Several scientific aspects of proper collection and preservation of evidence require discussion.

*Sufficient samples* should be collected. Judging the amount of specimen to obtain is largely a matter of experience. As a general rule, however, as much material as is reasonably possible to collect should be taken. It is often impractical and sometimes impossible to return to a crime scene at a later time if more physical evidence is needed.

*Known or control samples* are needed for comparative laboratory analyses. For example, if a bloodstained shirt is submitted to a crime laboratory, the blood-typing results have to be compared with something to be useful. A known sample of the victim's and/or suspect's blood is needed. Similarly, if an automobile paint specimen is sent for analysis, a known sample of paint from the vehicle in question needs to be submitted for comparison.

*Blank samples* may be important. Consider a bloodstained carpet. In collecting the bloodstain, a segment of unstained carpet should be collected next to the stained area. This is a blank sample. A blank

---

FIGURE 1.15. In this example of individualization, a receipt for payment of a monthly bus ticket (A) purchased by a murder victim was compared with a ticket found in the suspect's home (B). The two pieces were originally part of the same ticket (C). (*Institute of Forensic Science, Beijing, China.*)

sample is needed for testing to verify that the sample alone does not interfere with the analysis.

*Physical evidence* should be handled as little as possible. Too much handling may obliterate fingerprints; dislodge minute trace evidence such as hair, fibers, and debris; break brittle evidence; or contaminate serological evidence. Forceps, rubber gloves, and special containers may be necessary for handling physical evidence.

Crime scene investigators should have on hand an assortment of envelopes, containers, and packaging to properly collect and preserve physical evidence. Generally, plastic bags should be avoided. This is especially true when preserving biological evidence such as bloodstained articles. Plastic bags accelerate deterioration of biological evidence.

Airtight containers are desirable for volatile materials such as gasoline. Clean glass jars with screw-cap lids or metal paint cans with widemouthed openings make excellent containers for arson evidence. Burned debris that has to be checked for accelerants should never be packaged in plastic bags or plastic jars. Volatile evidence will evaporate.

It is good practice to double-wrap very small items such as hair, fibers, or glass fragments. These items should first be folded up in a sheet of paper and then placed in an envelope. Careful packaging of minute items of evidence will assure their not being lost.

*Contamination* is a concern for proper preservation of evidence. Items of evidence should be packaged separately in individual containers. Each piece of evidence should be completely segregated from other evidence.

---

## Case

A burglary suspect was apprehended near a residential tract. He had broken into a house through the rear door. The arresting officer observed splinters, paint, and other building material on the suspect's jacket. Samples from around the point of entry were collected for comparison and submitted with the jacket to the crime laboratory. All the evidence was packaged together in a paper bag. When it arrived at the laboratory, it was not possible to tell whether the debris on the jacket was from the crime scene or from the known samples placed in the bag.

---

Microscopic or *trace evidence* presents unique collection problems. There are a number of techniques available to collect this type of evidence.

Vacuum cleaners specially equipped with traps can be used to collect trace evidence such as hairs, fibers, glass fragments, and so on. Evidence collection vacuums are available commercially, and regular household vacuum cleaners can be modified to collect trace evidence.

Another method for collecting trace evidence consists of simply shaking or swooping an item, such as clothing, and letting the trace material fall onto a clean sheet of paper.

Yet another suggestion is the use of cellophane tape. A 4-inch length of tape is pressed onto suspected areas and then placed sticky side down on a microscope slide. Each of these techniques has advantages and disadvantages.

Physical evidence collected at crime scenes is usually examined at forensic science or crime laboratories by specially trained personnel such as forensic scientists, criminalists, forensic technicians, identification technicians, and so forth. What makes these practitioners unique is that they must also prepare reports and testify in court as expert witnesses. Because scientific evidence is often beyond the knowledge of lay people, courts permit persons with specialized training and skills to appear in court to explain and interpret scientific evidence to juries. Expert witnesses can be used when the subject of the testimony, e.g., scientific tests and conclusions made on physical evidence, is beyond the experience and knowledge of ordinary lay people and about which the expert has sufficient skills, knowledge, or experience in his or her field to aid the trier of fact in determining the truth.

Those entrusted with the investigation of criminal activity carry a heavy burden. Although the ultimate solution of the crime is a primary goal, one cannot forget that all activity surrounding the investigation will eventually be scrutinized at a later time. Actions taken during the investigative phase, e.g., interviews, collecting and preserving physical evidence, documenting the crime scene, and so forth, must all be done in the proper legal fashion so that evidence can be admitted when the case goes to trial. Mistakes are often unforgiving, and there are scores of examples of unintentional errors that have resulted in evidence being declared inadmissible by the courts. The best advice is to consider all the ramifications before taking action.

This chapter has introduced some of the major concepts concerning physical evidence, including its definition, its value, the difference between identification and individualization, and a brief discussion of the collection and preservation of physical evidence. Subsequent chapters explore these topics in greater detail as they relate to specific types of evidence and investigations.

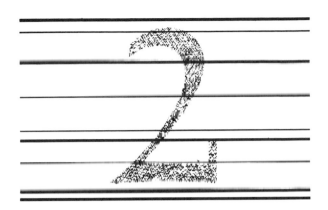

# THE
# FIRST OFFICER
# AT THE
# CRIME SCENE

Rock Valley College - ERC

The crime scene is a dynamic, rapidly changing place. The first officer to arrive at the scene of a crime must be concerned with a myriad of details. To a great extent, the very success of the investigation and, perhaps, the chance for a successful resolution of the case hinge upon the actions and steps taken by the first officer to arrive at the crime scene.

The crime scene is the place from which most physical evidence associated with the crime will be obtained. It provides the investigating officer with a starting point, a beginning of the investigation to determine the identities of the suspect and victim and to piece together the circumstances of what happened during the crime. Physical evidence found at the crime scene can be the key to the solution of a crime. The first officer's most important task at the scene is to prevent the destruction or the diminished utility of potential evidence that may lead to the apprehension of the criminal and the solution of the crime.

No matter what the rank of the first officer to arrive at the crime scene, the duties are always the same. The duties remain the same regardless of the seriousness of the crime. The first officer, upon arrival at the scene, must assume that the criminal has left physical evidence at the scene. It is the first officer's duty not to destroy or change anything at the scene for the simple reason that information developed from that evidence may serve to reconstruct the crime or in some way prove the identity of the suspect. Further, the first officer must not inadvertently add material that may later be misleading to the investigators.

Common sense explains why the scene of the crime can yield so much useful information. It is simply impossible for anyone to enter a location without changing it in some way, either by bringing something to it or taking something away. Although these changes may sometimes be exceedingly small, the course of the investigation often hinges on their detection. Therefore, the first officer's actions or inactions may well affect the future of the investigation.

The importance of detailed, meticulous note taking throughout all phases of the case cannot be overemphasized. Officers have numerous jobs to perform during the initial phases of the investigation. Furthermore, police handling many cases can find that one case blurs into another—a very human reaction. Thorough, detailed note taking, i.e., recording significant as well as mundane observations at the time they are noticed, is the most effective way to minimize loss of information.

Naturally, the general rule of protecting the crime scene cannot be applied to every case. The resources of the individual department as well as the nature of the crime must be taken into account. Petty thefts and like misdemeanors will obviously not receive the same in-depth investigation as a major crime such as murder or assault. Some departments may arbitrarily set a lower limit to property value lost in a burglary as a way to determine the scope of their investigation.

In certain relatively serious crimes, it may not be possible to preserve the crime scene because of its location. A street with heavy traffic is such an example where it may be impossible to properly protect a crime scene for a sufficient period of time. In situations like this, the deciding factor in safeguarding the crime scene is the likelihood that the criminal has left clues that can be recovered versus the negative factors. Each case must be decided on its own merits.

At first glance, the measures to be taken by the first officer on the scene may seem simple and not beyond the scope of routine police duties. Some further examination of these duties will show that this is not the case.

First of all, the officer must not approach the scene hastily. Rather, movements should be calm and deliberate. He or she should always expect the worst and, thus, take what may seem to be precautions too extensive for the conditions. Approaching the task with an open mind about the crime will help the officer to avoid carelessness and false moves that may prove disastrous.

Errors committed during the interrogation and other aspects of the preliminary investigation can perhaps be corrected, but errors committed in the protection and examination of the crime scene can never be rectified. The eventual success of the investigation can thus be completely dependent upon the preventative and preliminary measures taken by the officer who first arrives at the crime scene. Many examples can be given of how an omission or a mistake on the part of the first officer proved fatal to the investigation and resulted in an unsolved crime.

In difficult situations, the officer may be faced with a problem that requires quick analysis of the circumstances and appropriate steps to be taken. But if the basic rule of always anticipating the worst and taking extensive rather than minimal precautions is followed, the most serious errors can be avoided.

As conditions and situations can vary infinitely from one crime scene to another, it is not possible to lay down hard-and-fast rules. However, certain guidelines can be formulated. These are mainly applicable to cases of homicide and other serious crimes because it is in just these cases that the officer is faced with the most difficult tasks, and the actions taken have the most far-reaching consequences. These rules are also basically pertinent to less serious crimes.

## Recording the Time

Precise notations of the time are of great importance to the investigating officers. They are most important in checking a suspect's story, and can often be quite important in other connections. Therefore, the officer who first arrives at the scene should write down the times that may turn out to be important. Notation should be made of the time that the crime was committed, the time that the officer was first called, the time of arrival at the scene, and so on. Such notations lend precision and credibility to the officer's testimony should testifying in court about the investigation become necessary. Keeping track of the time spent at the scene also maintains a chronological record of the way things were done during the crime scene investigation. Such notes will prove invaluable should specifics about the investigation be needed several years after the actual event.

## Entering the Scene Proper

When entering the scene, the officer should, as quickly as possible, try to form an estimate of the situation. This estimate is the basis for any appropriate action. When entering the scene proper, or the focal point of events, the officer must proceed with extreme caution and concentrate attention on possible evidence that may be found on doors, doorknobs, light switches, floors, and the like.

An effort must be made to observe details, particularly those that are transient, and to make written notes on such points as the following:

*Doors*
   Open, closed, or locked?
   On which side was the key?
*Windows*
   Open or closed?
   Were they locked?
*Lights*
   On or off?
   Which lights were on?
*Shades or shutters*
   Open or closed?
*Odors*
   Was there an odor of cigarette smoke, gas, powder, perfume, etc.?
*Signs of activity*
   Meal preparation, dishes in sink, house clean or dirty, etc.?
*Date and time indicators*
   Mail, newspapers, dates on milk cartons.
   Stopped clocks.
   Spoiled foods.
   Items that should have been hot or cold but are at room temperature.

Nothing at the crime scene should be moved initially unless absolutely necessary. The crime scene should remain as close as possible to its original condition when the investigating officers arrive. If it becomes necessary to remove any object because it may be disturbed by others, the officer should consider the possibility that the item holds fingerprints. Before any object is moved, its location should be noted. The exact position of an object at a scene may become critically important later in the case. Its position should be noted in a report, outlined in chalk, sketched, photographed, or videotaped. Under no circumstances should the officer wander about the crime scene simply to satisfy his or her curiosity or pick up and handle items. Unfortunately, there have been many disturbing situations where the first officer arrived at the scene and toured it, leaving fingerprints on a variety of objects. Such carelessness cannot be tolerated.

Personnel at the crime scene should never use the toilet, turn on water, drink out of glasses or cups located at the scene, smoke, or use towels at the scene of the crime. The criminal may have used any of these objects. A towel could have been used to wipe a bloodstained weapon. There is even the possibility of evidence being caught in the sink trap. The rule is quite simple. *The first officer at the crime scene should touch nothing unless absolutely necessary or unless he is charged with the responsibility of processing the scene for physical evidence.* Most officers consider it quite embarrassing to have their fingerprints found and identified at the crime scene (Fig. 2.1).

The first officer should clearly understand that he or she may be called on later by the investigator or detective to account for every movement made at the crime scene. This may be necessary in order for the investigating officer to get a clearer picture of the original condition of the crime scene proper or to explain seemingly out-of-place items at the scene.

On occasion, the victim or a relative of the victim may attempt to clean the scene. Such persons would like everything to be in proper order when the police arrive. They may be trying to conceal something, or simply cleaning out of a psychological desire to put everything in order. If such a cleanup is in progress when the officer arrives, it should be stopped. If the cleanup has been completed or the officer suspects that such is the case, a detailed inquiry should be made to determine the original condition of the scene. It may be possible to recover material or undamaged items that were thrown out.

## Protecting the Scene

As soon as possible after arriving at the scene, the officer should take steps to protect the scene from everyone not directly involved with the investigation, including other officers, the press, curiosity seekers, and

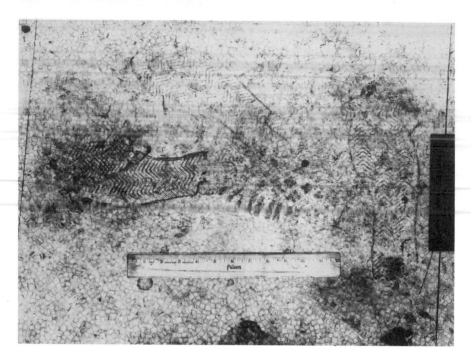

FIGURE **2.1.** Uniformed officers must take care when securing the scene. This officer did not and consequently superimposed his shoe prints over those of the suspect. (*Los Angeles County Sheriff's Department.*)

family members. Sometimes some ingenuity may have to be used since sufficient personnel may not be available to accomplish this task.

The crime scene can be secured by simply locking a door or stringing rope or tape around the perimeter. If these measures do not suffice, officers may resort to using vehicles, boards, or pieces of furniture gathered from someplace away from the scene to keep curiosity seekers out. Even with devices such as police barricades, yellow crime-scene tape, and ropes, an officer may still be needed to take an active role in keeping people away.

The extent of any protective measures must be decided on a case-by-case basis. As a general rule, *if the scene is indoors, the barricade should include the central scene and, where possible, the probable entry and exit paths used by the criminal.* In this connection, it is important to focus attention on potential evidence on the ground outside a window, in rooms through which the criminal had to pass, in stairways, or in entrances. *If the location is outdoors, an ample area should be roped off to include the path taken by the criminal to and from the central scene.* Sometimes critical evidence may be found on or near a route leading to or away from the scene. It is especially important to search these paths carefully when the crime scene proper has been trampled by onlookers before the arrival of the police, and when the search for evidence at the scene proves fruitless.

In open spaces, a reliable barricade can be set up only if an officer is stationed outside the perimeter. The protection of the scene in this instance merely requires that the officer should not walk around aimlessly inside or immediately outside the roped-off area. Limiting movements enables later accountability for the officer's own tracks.

The officer should remain at the scene whenever possible and should send others to call headquarters or detective personnel. Leaving the supervision of the crime scene to persons other than police officers should be done only in exceptional circumstances.

Protective measures at the scene should be taken as early as possible to prevent valuable or even vital evidence from being destroyed. It is also important that barricades be sufficiently extensive from the start of the investigation. Experience has shown that often a sufficient area around the crime scene was not protected soon enough.

When large outdoor areas are to be protected, officers may take the initiative by enlisting the aid of reliable local citizens such as police reserves or other persons who can be trusted to assume responsibility for protecting the scene.

## Injured Person on the Scene

If an injured person is on the scene, first aid should be administered immediately even though valuable evidence may be unavoidably lost or destroyed. Saving lives takes precedence over all other considerations. If first aid to the injured is not immediately essential, the officer should note the victim's position on a simple sketch, by marking the floor, or by forming a mental picture of the position. The officer should note how the victim is lying or sitting, the position of the hands, arms, and legs, the condition of clothes, and so on. It is also important to note whether the victim's hands have anything in them such as hairs, fibers, and the like.

When paramedic or emergency medical personnel arrive, the officer should—without interfering in their work—instruct them how to enter the scene so as not to disturb it needlessly. Further observing the actions of the medical personnel and noting what objects they moved, and where they walked, is necessary.

If the injured person is moved by nonpolice, emergency medical personnel, a police officer should accompany the victim. An alert investigator may hear an important word or accusation or what might be equivalent to a dying declaration that may be the key to the entire case.

In one instance, a dying woman was supposed to have said something—possibly named her assailant—only to have her words fall on the untrained, inattentive ears of civilian emergency medical personnel. No amount of interviewing could sharpen their recall.

The officer should arrange for the correct removal and custody of the clothing of the victim. All too often, when the hospital or mortuary is contacted for the purpose of obtaining the victim's garments, they may have been incinerated or at best wadded into an almost hopeless mess after being cut or ripped from the body. It would be helpful if investigative agencies would make periodic visits to local hospitals to instruct medical personnel in the proper handling of evidence. The medical profession's prevalent lack of interest in and knowledge of evidence are surprising, considering the otherwise broad scope of their training.

## Dead Person on the Scene

If the first officer on the scene is able to establish certain signs of death, i.e., marked rigor mortis, odor, lividity, beginning decomposition, etc., the rule is not to touch or remove the body until a detailed examination can be made.

Once the first officer at the crime scene has established that the victim is dead and has made cursory inspection of the crime scene, superiors must be notified regarding the nature of the case. A telephone should be used for this purpose rather than a police radio as it is not uncommon for the press and other news sources to monitor police radio frequencies.

## Summoning the Coroner

Whether the medical examiner or the coroner should be contacted at this point of the investigation is a matter of local custom. Many agencies wait first for the investigating officers to arrive and begin their investigation before notifying the coronor's office. Policies should be arranged with the local medical examiner's office on call-out matters.

It should be noted that the medical examiner-coroner's office generally has jurisdiction over the body. Where this jurisdiction is in effect, the body may not be moved or searched without the prior consent of the medical examiner-coroner.

On rare occasions, it happens that the first officer must take immediate steps for the removal of the body. In such situations, the officer must see to it that the deceased is placed on the stretcher in the same position in which the body was discovered, provided that circumstances permit. Limbs fixed in certain positions should not be straightened. If the victim is found face down, the body must remain in that position because lividity may change position and appearance, trickles of blood may change direction, and so on.

If the rigidity must be broken in order to transport the body properly, the officer should make notes thereof and preferably make a sketch or take photographs showing the original position. Before the body is moved, its position must be marked on the floor or on a sketch. It is important that the position of the head, arms, hands, knees, and feet be indicated on the sketch. The officer should also note the condition of the clothes and any tracks of blood that may be present. The latter can become extremely important in answering the question of whether the body had previously been moved. Blood may also run while the body is being removed, and a question may later arise as to how and where this secondary flow of blood occurred.

---

## Suspicious Death

A woman was found dead on the floor in her bedroom. The officer who was called made a superficial examination of the scene. Some of the deceased's relatives stated that the woman had been very ill. The officer had the body removed from the scene without examining it and mistakenly concluded that the woman had died of natural causes. After the deceased was removed, it was discovered that she had died of strangulation. A scarf had been tightly wound around the neck three times and was knotted at the throat. A trickle of blood had run over one cheek from the mouth in an upward direction in relation to the position of the head at the time of the brief examination. The continued investigation of the case became very complicated and, in some respects, impossible because of the officer's premature decision in allowing the body to be removed. It could never be established whether the blood had flowed during the transportation or before.

---

In cases of strangulation or hanging where unmistakable signs of death are observed, the officer should do nothing with the body. If there is a danger that the rope might break, the officer should attempt to support the corpse but not cut it down. If obvious signs of death are not present, the officer must, of course, try to save the person's life. In such cases, the knot should not be untied, if possible. The knot may be of a special kind typical of a certain occupation. The noose may be cut and the loose ends labeled so as not to be mixed up. An alternative to labeling is to tie the ends back together with string or thread. If these materials are not available, the noose or rope should be placed so that the officer can later remember which ends belong together. In emergencies, the knot may be loosened somewhat and the noose pulled over the victim's head. It is also important to remember which end of the rope had been anchored to a fixed object or pulled over a branch or beam. The direction of distorted surface fibers on the rope may indicate whether the victim was pulled up. It is always possible that a hanging had been arranged to cover up a murder.

## Firearms and Ammunition on the Scene

The general rule is that firearms and ammunition should be left untouched until investigating personnel arrive. It can happen, however, that recovery of weapons and ammunition is essential (Figs. 2.2 and 2.3). If such objects may be inadvertently moved or lost during the removal of an injured person, or if conditions are such that the officer cannot effectively protect the scene alone and bystanders might disturb the evidence, then the evidence may be removed. When weapons are recov-

FIGURE 2.2. A suspect discharged a weapon in a Fairbanks, Alaska, nightclub and subsequently fled, discarding the gun in the snow. A previously convicted felon was interviewed about the crime and denied any knowledge or ownership of a weapon. A latent print was developed using cyanoacrylate ester and photographed using direct reflective lighting. The felon's prints were compared with a latent print on the trigger and identified. He was charged with Felon in Possession of a Firearm. (*State of Alaska Scientific Crime Detection Laboratory, Latent Print Section.*)

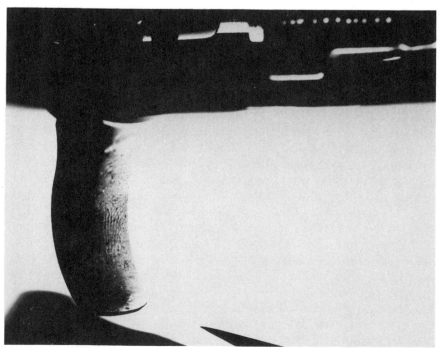

ered, the officer should concentrate on the possibility that valuable evidence may be found on cartridge cases as well as on weapons. If there is reason to believe that plastic fingerprints are present in oil or grease on a weapon found at a crime scene outdoors in cold weather, the weapon should not be moved to a heated room. The heat may destroy such valuable evidence. In picking up pistols and revolvers, *a pencil or a stick should never be inserted in the bore* in order to lift the weapon. Dust, blood, particles of tissue, and the like may be present in the barrel and could easily be destroyed. Instead, the weapon should be lifted by grasping with two fingers the checkered surface of the grips on which fingerprints cannot be deposited. If the butt is provided with a lanyard ring, the weapon may be lifted by it. Before the weapon is recovered, its position should, of course, be marked on a sketch or on the floor. This marking is very important. There may also be a mark in the floor under the weapon, indicating that the gun fell from the hand of a suicide victim; the position of bullets and cartridge cases may reveal the direction of the shot and possibly the location of an assailant. The position of hammer and safeties should be noted.

FIGURE **2.3.** This latent print was developed with cyanoacrylate fuming. The 30.30 caliber bullet was recovered from inside a loaded rifle magazine. The crime involved the shooting death of an elderly white male. The photographic technique employed "shadow" photography and inner negative reversal of the ridge color. The reader is referred to the article on shadow photography in the *Journal of Forensic Identification* 38,(5) September/October, 1989. (*State of Alaska Scientific Crime Detection Laboratory, Latent Print Section.*)

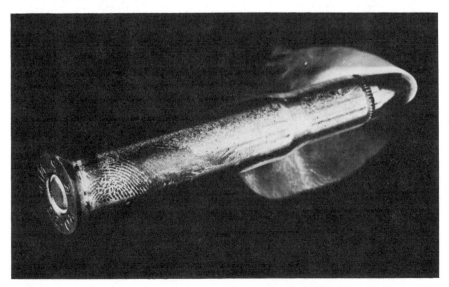

*Suspicious Death*

A dying man with a bullet wound in his head was found in his apartment. A police officer and emergency medical personnel arrived and took the man to a hospital, where he was pronounced dead on arrival. The officer accompanied the injured person to the hospital, a move that lengthened and complicated the investigation. Because the first officer did not communicate any information, detectives immediately began an investigation of the apartment.

A bullet and a cartridge case were found in the room where the victim had apparently been shot, but a weapon was not located. However, an automatic pistol was found on a shelf in the hallway and appeared to have been recently fired. A suspicion of murder arose immediately, as the injured man could not have placed the gun there himself. Thus began a thorough and time-consuming examination of the apartment. After the first officer who had gone to the hospital was questioned, the case was reduced to an ordinary suicide. The first officer had found the gun beside the victim and, without thinking of the consequences, examined it and placed it on the shelf before leaving the apartment. Had the investigators known the facts from the first witness—the first officer—much time and effort could have been saved. Certainly, the detectives acted properly by assuming the worst; however, the first officer at the scene failed in his responsibility to brief the investigators adequately.

If a weapon is found, it should be delivered, in its original condition at the time of recovery, to a firearms examiner for examination. When the firearm is packaged for submission as evidence, a detailed description of what, if anything, was done to it may be prepared and sent to the crime laboratory. The first officer should not pull the slide back on a pistol, nor turn the cylinder of a revolver, nor touch the trigger or the safety catch. The only acceptable changes to the weapon would be the removal of a cartridge from the chamber or the marking of the position of the cylinder. However, these things should be done only by an experienced detective or crime scene investigators.

## When a Suspect Is Found at the Scene

The first officer to arrive at a crime scene is sometimes faced with the necessity of arresting or holding a suspect. In such situations, the rule of doing the most important duties first must be followed. The police officer must use common sense in taking whatever measures are available in order to protect the scene. If it is not possible to hold the suspect at the scene or in the police vehicle, a possible alternative is to find a reliable civilian to protect the scene until other officers arrive. The first officer must instruct such a person on how to guard the premises, as the task is likely to be unusual for him or her.

The first officer should also be aware that the longer the suspect remains in the crime scene, the greater becomes the possibility of changing or contaminating the crime scene. The suspect could, for example, remove evidence, leave new evidence, or even gain information by being allowed an opportunity to observe the scene in detail. The suspect should be searched and removed from the location as soon as possible.

## What to Do Until the Investigating Personnel Arrive

While waiting for the investigators to arrive, the officer should attend to the following:

1. *Write down names of witnesses and other persons who are known to have entered the scene.* This is important for the subsequent sorting of fingerprints and other clues found at the scene.
2. *Who was at the scene when the officer arrived?* This information can become particularly important if the crime has just occurred.
3. *Establish the basic facts.* A factual account of what happened is of great assistance to the investigators when they arrive because it helps them decide on the next move. However, the officer should *under no circumstances* undertake lengthy and detailed interrogations that may damage later questioning or give rise to misleading suggestions in the statements of witnesses. Furthermore, the officer cannot properly guard the scene if occupied with interrogations.
4. *Keep suspect and witnesses separated wherever possible.* If suspect and witnesses are allowed to talk, it may interfere with later questioning. Family members may be left in the care of neighbors when necessary, taking care that no alcoholic drinks or sedatives are administered. Remember that the dramatically grieving relative may be the prime suspect.
5. *Instruct witnesses not to discuss the events.* This can prevent distortion by suggestion. If possible, the principal witnesses should be separated. In relating events to each other, the witnesses may distort each other's impressions to the point where they believe that they saw things that they really did not see or that never happened.
6. *Do not discuss the crime with witnesses or bystanders.* This is also intended to prevent suggestion and distortion. Furthermore, circulating details of the crime may hinder the investigation.
7. *Listen attentively but unobtrusively.* An alert officer can often pick up information of vital importance to the investigation simply by being a good listener.
8. *Protect evidence that is in danger of being destroyed.* During rain or snow, divert water and cover tracks with boxes, cardboard, and the like. If the crowd of onlookers becomes large, it may become necessary to expand the protective measures at a given location to prevent the trampling of evidence.

When the investigating officers arrive, the first officer should report all that has been learned and observed and the actions taken (Fig. 2.4). This is of great importance to the evaluation and planning of the crime scene investigation. It is particularly important that reports be given of the extent to which the scene has been altered, and whether objects have been disturbed or moved.

## The Continued Protection of the Scene

In protecting the scene after the investigators have arrived, the officers detailed to guard the scene should act only on order from the detective in charge. During the technical examination of the scene, it is the crime scene investigator who is in charge of the officers on guard duty as well as of the scene proper.

FIGURE 2.4. The suspect stated that he had never been in the murder victim's house in Ninilchik, Alaska. Trash from the victim's wastebaskets was examined for latent prints. A print was developed on the ring tab of a beer can, using cyanoacrylate ester fuming. The latent print was compared and identified with the suspect in the case. (*State of Alaska Scientific Crime Detection Laboratory, Latent Print Section.*)

No one should be allowed access to the crime scene without the investigator's permission, not even other investigators or superior officers. Command officers would render a fine service to their investigators if they would preserve the integrity of the crime scene with a passion and set an example for other officers by keeping out of the crime scene. Those allowed on the scene must move with their *hands in their pockets* so as not to touch anything. Through carelessness or without even being aware of it, they may touch objects on the scene. The explanation might be that a desire to do something prompts them to touch objects that should not be touched before they have been examined. The wearing of gloves should not be permitted on the crime scene (except in cases where quantities of blood or other biological fluid is present and AIDS is a concern). People wearing gloves are more likely to become careless and touch objects bearing fingerprints and thereby destroy or wipe them out.

Unfortunately, there are countless instances of police officers on sightseeing tours through crime scenes. Sometimes they destroy more evidence than any group of lay people could. At one crime scene, it was reported that the presence of one more police official would have threatened the collapse of the building. Even experienced investigators are guilty of allowing such tours, especially in cases of murder and other serious crimes.

*News reporters* sometimes arrive at the scene before the officers who are to examine it. They are usually called by people in the neighborhood, or they may have heard a call on the police radio. The first officers on the scene should not, under any circumstances, give information about the case to reporters. To inform the press is the responsibility of the police chief, sheriff, or officers designated by them. Officers should not favor one reporter or news agency by giving out information that may not be available to the competitors through prescribed channels. In dealing with reporters officers should be firm, not curt or nonchalant, even when the reporters are persistent. The officer should remember that reporters often give invaluable help in the investigation of major crimes. *Press passes should be disregarded during the protection of a crime scene.*

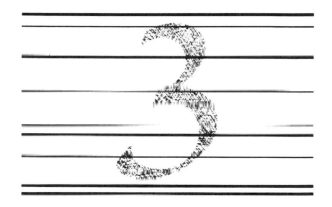

# THE
# CRIME SCENE
# INVESTIGATOR

Most police departments today make use of uniformed or patrol divisions and detectives in crime scene processing. The patrol officer is the first officer at the crime scene and the detective, who arrives later, is responsible for the investigation and processing of the crime scene. This division of labor by function is useful in that it allows for a certain degree of specialization and hence the likelihood of a better performance in the respective responsibilities. Although patrol and detective personnel are usually used for crime scene processing in serious crimes, some agencies delegate responsibility for the crime scene search, and collection and preservation of physical evidence, to the patrol or uniformed officer in less serious crimes. It is, therefore, not unreasonable for a uniformed officer to respond to the scene of a residential burglary, take a report, photograph the crime scene, dust for latent fingerprints, and collect evidence, all without calling a detective or using specialized personnel such as crime scene evidence technicians.

The rules are the same no matter who is responsible for the crime scene. The crime scene contains important information that, if sought in a systematic, legal, and scientific way, can help the investigator determine what happened and who was involved. Law enforcement personnel involved in criminal investigations must be able to derive the most information possible from the crime scene.

The objectives of a crime scene investigation are as follows:

To reconstruct the incident.

To ascertain the sequence of events.

To determine the mode of operation.

To disclose the motive.

To determine what property was stolen.

To find out all the criminal may have done.

To recover physical evidence of the crime.

In some cases, the investigation yields results that point directly to a culprit and provide solid evidence against him or her, even before the offender becomes a suspect. Generally this happens when the perpetrator's fingerprints are found at the scene and the prints are already on file. Such cases, unfortunately, happen less frequently than anyone would like, but the advent of automated fingerprint identification systems has greatly improved the chances of identifying a criminal.

The task of crime scene investigators[1] is sometimes thankless. Often police officers and the public think of them as modern day Sherlock Holmeses and believe that they are capable of magically providing complete information about the identity of a criminal. When a crime scene investigator does not succeed in doing just that, he or she is considered to have failed. This attitude is, of course, absurd. It is the duty of investigators and detectives to pursue and apprehend the criminal. The duty of the crime scene investigator is to gather all evidence available at the scene. For the investigative process to function best, the detective and crime scene investigator need to work cooperatively. Each must consider the other as part of a team.

Crime scene investigators know that criminals always leave trace evidence behind or take away minute material from the scene and/or victim. The crime scene investigator's job is to find these traces and preserve them. Such evidence may be used in the reconstruction of the crime or as proof that the suspect committed some unlawful act. The value of a given item to a criminal investigation should not be overlooked. An apparently unimportant object or fact may turn out to be extremely important later in the investigation. No item, however small, should be overlooked.

The crime scene investigator's job at the scene is similar to that of the first police officer to arrive there. Each must proceed calmly and deliberately. The crime scene investigator should not approach his or her task with preconceived ideas nor draw premature conclusions. Investigators should scrutinize the scene with eyes open for details. Experience teaches them to suspect the worst and to be more thorough than superficial. Better to have processed the scene more carefully than needed. The alternative may be that a critical piece of evidence in the investigation is overlooked. A complete investigation may produce information corroborating a confession or refuting a defense contention raised at the trial. *Mistakes made during the investigation may never be rectified.*

The crime scene investigator cannot allow superiors or coroner's investigators to influence calm deliberation on the case before or during the actual examination. The investigation should not be rushed on their account. They will have to wait; *the investigator is personally responsible for his or her mistakes and, therefore, has the right to determine personal actions at the scene.*

---

[1] The term *crime scene investigator* used in this chapter and elsewhere refers either to a specialist whose principal job it is to identify, collect, and retrieve physical evidence from the crime scene or to the detective or investigating officer who has the collateral duty of collecting and preserving physical evidence.

An experienced crime scene investigator asked to explain how he or she proceeds at a scene may be hard put to formulate a general rule. Each crime scene is different. It is therefore not possible to lay down absolute rules for conducting an investigation. At best, a general outline of the process can be made to suit an infinitely varying number of conditions. No matter how experienced the investigator is, there will always be new situations to be faced and completely unfamiliar problems to master. The best advice to an investigator in out-of-the-ordinary situations is to be calm, adaptable, and flexible. The basic qualities of a good crime scene investigator are *intuition* and an *eye for what needs to be done* in each individual case—both in addition to a thorough knowledge of the methods of locating and preserving physical evidence.

Before any actual work at the scene begins, the investigator should stand at an appropriate vantage point on the periphery of the scene and formulate a systematic plan: geometry of search, location of photographs, possible sources of clues, and so forth. Then the crime scene investigation can begin.

The investigation of the scene can be divided into the following functions:

FIGURE 3.1.   A team of arson investigators and crime laboratory personnel examine the scene of the Universal Studios fire (note the use of the video recorder to document the crime scene). (*Los Angeles County Sheriff's Department.*)

1. Photography and/or videotaping (overall views) (see Fig. 3.1).
2. The investigation of the crime scene proper (when needed, combined with photography and videotaping—detailed views).
3. Sketching[2] (combined with 1 and 2—detailed sketches may be required during the investigation) (see Fig. 3.2).
4. Note taking (to be done all during the investigation—constant interruptions for notes are the rule).

Note taking at a crime scene is essential. Good, contemporaneous written notes are invaluable later in the investigation and especially at the time of trial. It is frustrating for the officer who is assigned an old open case to find inadequate notes of an original investigator's initial observations. There are no substitutes for good note taking at all phases of an investigation.

The order of work to be done at a scene is not sacrosanct. Sometimes, immediately on arrival at the scene, the investigator must examine a detailed part of a scene or make a sketch of an object that had to be moved. *Consequently, the order of the various phases of processing a crime scene must be decided on a case-by-case basis.*

The investigator needs to be *extremely curious* about everything at the crime scene, even the smallest item. The perpetrator may have forgotten or dropped something. A seemingly innocuous object may later become the decisive piece of evidence. The investigator should maintain a healthy skepticism. Things may not be what they seem. He or she should take a critical attitude and not accept conditions or appearances without first questioning them. There are many examples of simulated crimes or accidents that are really cover-ups for criminal activity.

## Actual Examination of the Scene

Throughout the examination, the investigator should attempt to think through and reconstruct the actions of the criminal. If the reconstruction does not make sense or if there are inconsistencies, it is necessary to go back to the beginning and reevaluate the sequence of events. One method is to proceed by elimination while reasoning, "It could not have been done this way," and continuing until only one or two possibilities remain.

A helpful suggestion is to carry a few pieces of chalk in a crime scene

---

[2] At this writing, the use of computer aided design or CAD software is just beginning to be used. This software has the additional ability to be used to reconstruct the crime, depict perspective views from various sites within the crime scene and be used in court to help juries better understand the scene.

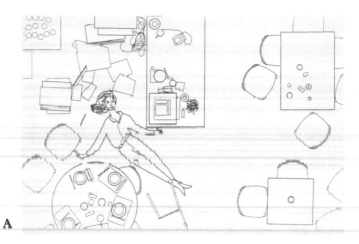

A

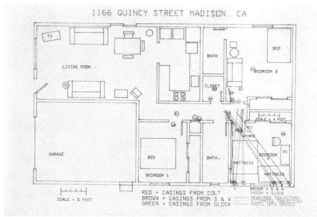

1166 QUINCY STREET MADISON, CA

B

SCALE = 5 FEET

RED = CASINGS FROM COLT
BROWN = CASINGS FROM S & V
GREEN = CASINGS FROM GLOCK

C

**FIGURE 3.2.** Various types of computer-aided design (CAD) software are being used to document crime scenes. (*Zurich Cantonal Police Forensic Science Laboratory (A) and the California Department of Justice, Bureau of Forensic Services (B and C).*)

equipment kit. If a certain object must be moved, the object's location may be marked with the chalk or, if no chalk is available, with a pencil or crayon.

Unless it is absolutely necessary, *do not examine a nighttime, outdoor crime scene until daylight.* If for some reason the investigation must be done outdoors under artificial lighting, the scene should be kept intact as long as possible for a final search in daylight. No matter how powerful the lighting equipment, daylight is better. Experience shows that *certain evidence that can be missed in artificial light will show easily in daylight.*

Do not start to search the crime scene if it is clear from the beginning that specialized personnel will be called in to take over the job. The crime scene specialist's task is complicated enough. It need not be made more difficult by having to finish what someone else has begun. The specialist should be permitted to take charge of the intact crime scene. This guarantees the best possible results.

Two crime scene investigators constitute the most effective staffing level to use to search most major crime scenes. Certainly, one could carry out the investigation but two are best, partly because their later testimony will be more reliable. There are cases, however, when this recommendation may be abandoned. The crime scene investigator may call on an officer who is an experienced photographer to photograph the scene and take on full responsibility for the photographic job. Similarly, the investigator may use temporary assistance in the developing and preservation of fingerprints, sketching, packaging of evidence, and the like. This assistance should be employed only on the condition that the helpers are given detailed instructions and are closely supervised.

The two crime scene investigators should be accustomed to working together on crime scenes. In any case, they should be able to cooperate. While at the scene *they should not work on separate tasks but as a team.* One way of dividing the work is for one investigator to do the actual examination while the other keeps notes and assists by making personal observations and by helping to examine a particular area. Two persons working together are able to observe not twice as much as a single person, but many times more. Whatever one of the investigators discovers should immediately be reported to the partner. They should also discuss the different possibilities of how a certain clue might have been caused, how the criminal proceeded, and so forth. What might not occur to one person might well occur to the other.

In cases of homicide and other serious crimes, it is important that *the crime scene specialists have no other investigative duties.* They should devote their full attention to the scene to get the most out of it. If crime scene work and the detective functions are paired, one of the tasks, typically the crime scene duties, will usually suffer. Specialized personnel assigned to crime scene duties should, of course, cooperate closely with the investigating officers. This division of tasks between specialized personnel may not always be possible because of a lack of sufficient personnel. However, the two types of work should be separated wherever feasible.

On arriving at the scene, the crime scene investigator should first obtain the basic facts from the officers already present. It is important that the investigator be as well briefed as possible about the case before undertaking the examination of the scene. Arrival time and weather conditions should be noted. Another detail that requires immediate attention is the determination of which persons had prior access to the scene and whether they caused any changes in the original conditions there.

*When entering the actual scene,* the investigator should proceed cautiously, keeping in mind potential clues on floors, doorknobs, light switches, and other areas that the criminal may have touched. Even in cases where chances are slight that evidence may be found, the investigator should not exclude the possibility at this stage. The investigator should not walk around the crime scene aimlessly. Exercise the same caution that would be expected of inexperienced personnel. Watch where you put your feet, even if a great many persons have already trampled the scene. Although it might be excusable for untrained officers to destroy evidence inadvertently by handling items or stepping on surfaces, it is never excusable for the crime scene investigator.

Before beginning the examination, the investigator should stop *to consider the crime scene thoroughly.* This is very important because a very significant circumstance may be overlooked by starting without first having evaluated the situation thoroughly. The investigator should make a complete and systematic survey of the actual scene as well as of the immediate surroundings, indoors and outdoors. Attempt to reconstruct the actions of the criminal and constantly ask "why?" Why did the criminal do this, how was the building entered, how was this mark made? Nothing should be allowed to interfere with the investigator's initial reconstruction of the case, which is essential to planning the investigation intelligently and getting the most out of the scene.

Everything the investigator learns during the investigation should be taken down in writing. Notes should be taken all during the progress of the examination, and constant interruptions should be made for this purpose. The position of an object should be measured and recorded in the notes, along with a description of the object, before it is moved or examined in detail. In some cases, it might be necessary to make a detailed sketch or a close-up photograph of the object before moving it.

The record of the examination should not be edited at the crime scene, but the notes should be made in the order of the various phases of the work. The editing and report writing must be left for completion later. The extent of the notes must, of course, be somewhat proportionate to the seriousness of the crime. A burglary does not require as detailed notes as a murder. In a murder case, however, *the notes must be sufficiently complete that a full reconstruction of the case could be made even 15 to 20 years later.* All objects and details pertinent to a description of the scene must be noted. The report of the investigation of a major crime can never be too detailed. The completeness of the report is especially important in those crimes that are not solved within a reasonable time. Rough notes and sketches made at the scene must not be discarded. They should properly be placed in a separate envelope included with the case file.

With respect to news reporters, the same rules apply to the crime scene investigator as to the first officer at the scene. In major or sensational crimes, reporters often try to photograph the crime scene, preferably including the officers working there. Do not pose for such pictures unless ordered by a superior officer or when it cannot be reasonably avoided. A police officer who poses for photographs at a crime scene usually looks ridiculous and only serves the doubtful purpose of satisfying the public's desire for sensation. News photographers should not be permitted to photograph the actual crime scene without express permission from the officer in charge.

*The investigator should also see to it that reporters do not learn of specific clues or conditions at the crime scene that may be essential to the solution of the crime.* As a rule, only the criminal profits from detailed accounts of discoveries made by the police. Such information should be given to the press only if it would assist the investigation, and only the investigating officer in charge may give permission for its release.

If paramedics have been called, they must be allowed to enter the crime scene whenever an injured person is present or when death has not been established with certainty. The crime scene investigator should nevertheless see to it that the paramedics do not needlessly destroy clues.

When unmistakable signs of death (rigidity, lividity, odor, beginning decomposition, etc.) are present, paramedics need not be called. Once the first phase of the investigation has been completed, the coroner may be called. The investigator should cultivate good cooperation with the coroner's representative. Smooth cooperation between the two is a requirement for successful completion of the investigation.

A crime scene investigation is characterized by *organization, thoroughness,* and *caution,* three essential conditions for success.

After the "mental reconstruction" of the case, the investigator's first task normally should be to take overall photographs of the central crime scene. When this is finished, the actual investigation should, as a rule, begin with the central scene, unless the initial survey showed that traces are likely to be found along *the criminal's route* and these traces cannot effectively be protected. If such is the case, these clues should be examined and recovered first. The search of the criminal's route should, however, always start from the central scene.

The central crime scene, or the area where the actual crime took place, can be searched beginning with the floor or a certain area of the floor, followed by the rest of the room with a door as starting point. The investigator should attempt to work according to a system that does not vary much from case to case, thereby running the least risk of overlooking something. A trace or object, no matter how insignificant it may seem, can be overlooked. The perpetrator may have forgotten or dropped something.

When a dead person is still at the crime scene, the investigator should not begin with a detailed examination of the body. Doing so might cause other aspects of the scene to be set aside that require earlier attention. Also, the examination of the body might not be as thorough as it would be if the investigator had formed a clear picture of what happened by first examining the whole scene. *Let the detailed examination of the body wait until the basic examination of the scene has been completed.* Important clues may be destroyed if the body is moved before this phase has been completed. If the rest of the scene is examined before the body, the body might yield more valuable information than if the order is reversed. During the initial examination of the scene, the investigator may be able to discover facts that were not previously known and that may be of great value in relation to findings on the body. This does not mean, however, that an examination of the body sufficient to suggest the mode of death should not precede the crime scene search. Obviously, knowing that the deceased has a gunshot wound would indicate that bullets or cartridges should be sought. Likewise, if considerable time will be consumed in the crime scene search, it would be important to determine body temperature and other factors indicative of the time of death.

In many cases, it may be helpful to leave the most important objects in their original positions during the investigation. This is important for the reconstruction of the crime, because sometimes a question is raised about a certain item during the reconstruction of events or the logical steps of the reconstruction do not mesh. When this happens, it is helpful to be able to start all over and retrace one's steps. If it seems necessary to the reconstruction of the crime, the body should not be removed in haste, but should be left in the original position until a satisfactory record and study have been made. In some instances, it would be ideal to leave the deceased even overnight. However, consideration should be given to the availability of a pathologist. If an autopsy can be performed immediately, it should take place as soon as possible after the deceased's position has been recorded. However, if the only purpose for moving the body is to place it in storage in a mortuary, this would be a serious error. *Mere consideration of the dead should not influence this decision.* The initial examination by the pathologist can be superficial, and a closer examination made at a later time.

At the very start, the investigator should select a place as a "trash pile" where things may be put that should not be lying about the scene. A certain amount of waste normally accumulates during the use of film packs, blood-testing materials, and the like. A work area is needed for filling out evidence tags, developing fingerprints on small objects, handling casting material, and so on. Although it is not proper to smoke at a crime scene, the rule is not inflexible, particularly where the investigator is forced to work for a long period of time. Such a trash collection point should be located as far as possible from the central crime scene. It might be started by spreading a newspaper or using a paper trash bag and marking it accordingly.

As to the special methods of detecting, preserving, and evaluating evidence found at the crime scene, the reader is referred to subsequent chapters that deal with methods used at different kinds of crime scenes.

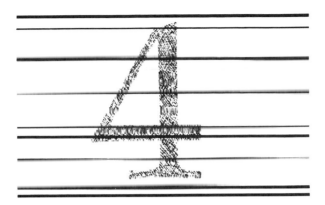

# SPECIALIZED PERSONNEL AT THE CRIME SCENE

On June 6, 1988,[1] a 9-year-old white female was abducted while riding her bicycle. Later that same day, a 26-year-old white male was arrested for theft involving a 1976 GMC vehicle that had been stolen from the sheriff's impound lot the previous day. The individual arrested, who had a previous conviction for abduction and sexual assault of his 16-year-old cousin, immediately became a suspect in the little girl's disappearance.

After the arrest, the vehicle was examined for trace evidence and latent fingerprints, and an inventory of items in the vehicle was made. The found items included a wrapped cigar, a cigar wrapper, rubber bands, a case of miniature Suntory Vodka bottles with two missing, a green blanket, fake-wool front seat covers, floor mats, and numerous food and clothing items (Figs. 4.1 and 4.2). The significance of some of these items did not become apparent until some time later. The suspect's clothing was collected and submitted to the crime lab for analysis.

On June 25, 3 weeks after the child's disappearance, two hikers located some little girl's clothing on the top of a cinder hill in the vicinity of where the victim had last been seen. The police department responded and shortly thereafter located the victim's body under a pile of brush under a pinyon pine tree. The body was nude, with her hands tied behind her back with a shoestring. There were extensive head injuries. Near the body was an unwrapped cigar. On one of the branches covering the body was a rubber band, and elsewhere in the pine tree was an empty plastic bag. Approximately 20 yards from the body, under another tree, was found an empty miniature Suntory Vodka bottle.

Near a crude road on top of the hill was found a small piece of metal, a lock of hair, two clumps of fibers, and a large number of rubber bands. The victim's clothing had been strewn down the side of the hill, and rubber bands were found along with the clothing. A second empty Suntory bottle was found on the road leading to the top of the hill. With these discoveries, items found in the suspect's vehicle took on new importance to the case.

Upon examination of the suspect's clothing, human bloodstains were identified on both the shirt and the blue jeans (Fig. 4.3). The shirt exhibited a medium velocity impact spatter pattern on the right upper back and shoulder area. Two small spots of blood were found on the blue jeans.

Since at the time of the identification of human bloodstains on the

[1] I am indebted to Ed Hueske, Benita Harwood, Bob Burris, and Bob Blackett, of the Arizona Department of Public Safety Laboratory in Flagstaff for sharing this case.

FIGURE **4.1**
(A) "Mini" bottle of Suntory
Vodka; (B) clump of hair
matching the victim's.

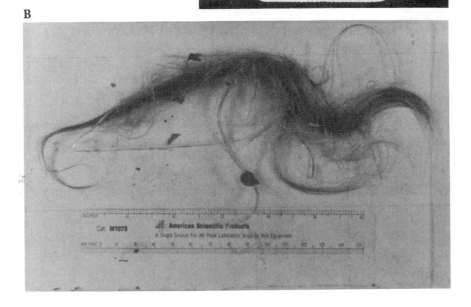

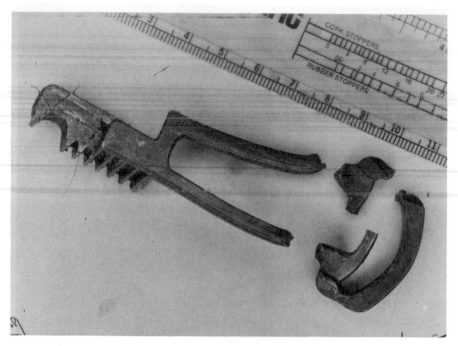

**FIGURE 4.2.** Portions of an ignition actuator rack.

suspect's clothing the victim's body had not yet been recovered, blood samples were obtained from the parents of the victim and from the suspect for comparison purposes.

PGM subtyping of the bloodstain found on the suspect's shirt showed the enzyme type 2+. The victim's parents were PGM type 2+1+ and 2+1−, and the suspect was type 1+. This enzyme grouping and subsequent additional enzyme grouping showed that the blood on the shirt could have originated from an offspring of the victim's parents, but not from the suspect.

Once the victim's body was recovered, muscle tissue samples were used to determine the victim's PGM enzyme type. They were found to be the same as those on the suspect's shirt.

The bloodstains, muscle tissue, and blood standards were later submitted to a private laboratory for DNA analysis. This analysis confirmed that the blood on the suspect's shirt could have originated from the victim. This was the first time DNA evidence was admitted in a criminal proceeding in Arizona courts.

The vehicle involved in this case was originally stolen from a carrier for the *Arizona Republic* newspaper. At the time it was stolen it was believed to have contained a one-pound plastic bag of rubber bands of

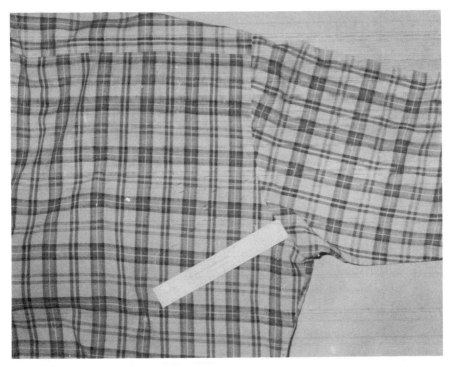

FIGURE **4.3.** Suspect's shirt with blood spatters on the back right shoulder.

the type commonly used for wrapping newspapers. When the vehicle was recovered, shortly after the little girl's disappearance, the plastic bag and all but a few of the rubber bands were missing (Fig. 4.4).

Examination of the plastic bag and rubber bands revealed two facts:

1. The rubber bands remaining in the vehicle were similar to those found at the crime scene.
2. The plastic bag and rubber bands from the crime scene and vehicle were similar to the type used by *Arizona Republic* newspaper carriers.

To make a valid comparison, a known one-pound plastic bag of rubber bands was obtained from the *Arizona Republic*. A sample of these was aged for 3 weeks under similar conditions to those at the crime scene. Both the crime scene and vehicle rubber bands and known rubber bands were found to match well with respect to physical characteristics such as dimensions, degree of weathering, visual/microscopic appearance, and "elasticity." Dimensions were measured with a micrometer and ruler, and other features were observed visually and under

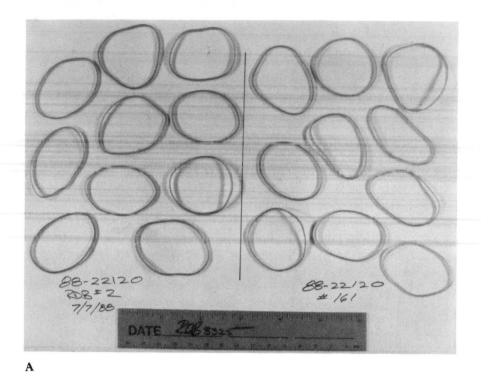

A

B

**FIGURE 4.4.** (A) Rubber bands from the crime scene (left) and rubber bands from the *Arizona Republic* newspaper; (B) plastic bags (left) for rubber bands from *Arizona Republic* newspaper and (right) found at the crime scene near the body.

FIGURE **4.5.** Photomicrograph of victim's hair found on the suspect's clothing (note cut end).

low-power magnification (approximately 10—15×). The elasticity of the rubber bands was measured by placing a weight on a balance, attaching a rubber band to the weight, and stretching the rubber band to a specified distance. The difference in weight (at rest and with the rubber band in place) was recorded as the "grams per inch of stretch."

Chemical analysis was conducted on the rubber bands, but was found to be of little value in discriminating between different brands of similarly colored rubber bands.

The plastic bags were likewise compared and found to be of consistent construction and composition (Fig. 4.4).

The "similar to and could have come from" conclusions of hair and fiber analysis were given much greater significance in this case by unusual characteristics.

A lock of victim-matching head hairs found near the victim's body had no roots; rather, they exhibited a peculiar combination of cutting and tearing at the lower end. Nearly 100 other victim-matching head hairs of similar length were recovered from the suspect's clothing (particularly the felt lining of his jean jacket) and vehicle (particularly the fake-wool front seat covers). Most of these hairs also showed this cut/torn end (Fig. 4.5). When arrested, the suspect had two pocket knives in his possession, and experimentation with a variety of cutting instruments showed that cutting hair with a sharp blade of a similar knife could produce the cut/torn combination.

Mixed with the lock of cut/torn victim-matching head hair was a single suspect-matching pubic hair. An attempt to DNA-type the single root sheath failed.

Two fiber matches were given added weight by combinations of matching fibers:

1. As mentioned above, the well-worn and deteriorating vehicle front seat covers were of fake wool, actually mostly white acrylic. Trace amounts of yellow acrylic, white polyester, and white wool fibers were noted. Two patches of fibers from the crime scene were similarly of white acrylic with occasional yellow acrylic, white polyester, and white wool.
2. A green blanket recovered from the suspect's vehicle was a green wool/green rayon combination. Both green wool and green rayon fibers matching those of the blanket were recovered from the brush used to hide the victim's body.

The cigar found next to the body was compared with a similar cigar found in the console of the suspect's vehicle (Fig. 4.6). Similar breaks

FIGURE 4.6. Cigars: (top) Dutch Masters Cigar Standard, (middle) cigar and wrapper from the suspect's vehicle, and (bottom) cigar found next to the victim's body.

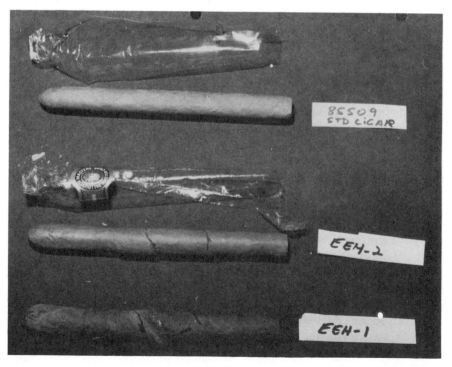

were noted in both cigars. These breaks were suggestive of both cigars having once lain side by side in the bottom of the console with something heavy, such as the box of vodka bottles, on top of them.

The cigar found next to the body was unwrapped but unsmoked. A cigar wrapper was looked for and found in the ashtray of the suspect's vehicle. Likewise, the suspect's shirt pockets were examined for the presence of cigar tobacco particles. Several tobacco particles were found.

All of the tobacco-related items of evidence were sent to the Bureau of Alcohol, Tobacco, and Firearms Laboratory in Rockville, Maryland, for physical comparison and elemental analysis. The two cigars were subsequently identified as Dutch Masters brand with no distinguishable differences in elemental composition. The tobacco found in the suspect's shirt pocket was found to be consistent with having come from a cigar such as a Dutch Masters.

The wrapper found in the ashtray was found to be consistent with a Dutch Masters wrapper. No fingerprints were found on any of the items. Nor was there any indication of saliva found on the cigar next to the body.

The vodka bottle found near the body was compared with the remaining vodka bottles from the suspect's vehicle. The bottles were all found to be indistinguishable from one another with respect to all physical characteristics. No fingerprints were found on any of the bottles or the plastic case. A second vodka bottle, like the others, was later found near the crime scene on a road leading out of the area. It, too, failed to have any fingerprints. Likewise, no indications of saliva were found on either of the two empty bottles.

During the initial search of the suspect's vehicle, it was noted that the steering column had been sawed open in order to compromise the steering wheel lock/ignition system. During the search of the crime scene, a small metal fragment was found on the trail near the body. Subsequently, the vehicle steering column was removed and disassembled to reveal a broken ignition actuator rack with at least one missing piece. The metal piece from the crime scene proved to be one of the missing pieces.

In an effort to account for the remaining piece(s) of the rack still missing, a search was made of several areas in which the suspect's vehicle was believed to have stopped either before or after the crime. The third and final piece needed to complete the broken ignition rack was located at one of these locations.

Although there were no witnesses or fingerprints to connect the suspect to the murder, the preponderance of physical evidence linking him to both the crime scene and the victim resulted in the jury's finding the suspect guilty and sentencing him to death.

The patrol officer and investigating officer or detective may not possess the special skills and expertise needed to process the entire crime scene. Specialized support personnel can provide these talents when called to a crime scene investigation. Sometimes a particularly serious case may warrant outside assistance, such as hazardous material specialists in clandestine drug laboratory cases, or federal authorities (e.g., Federal Bureau of Investigation, Bureau of Alcohol, Tobacco, and Firearms, or Drug Enforcement Administration) in investigations of mass disasters, bombings, or major fires.

*Crime scene investigation (CSI) officers* and evidence technicians are police and civilian personnel specially trained to process a crime scene. These persons are equipped to collect and preserve physical evidence at a crime scene. They arrive at the scene with evidence collection kits and all tools and equipment needed to thoroughly conduct the crime scene search and collect the evidence.

Other police agencies employ *identification (ID) officers*. ID officers photograph the crime scene and search for latent fingerprints. They may not be responsible for collecting other types of physical evidence at the crime scene. ID officers are generally experts in fingerprint comparison. They may be subpoenaed as expert witnesses to establish the identity of the suspect by comparison of latent fingerprints with inked prints.

Some cases may require an accurate pictorial rendition of the crime scene. A *forensic surveyor* is used for this purpose. Relying on accurate measurements, notes, sketches, and photographs, the surveyor produces an architectural drawing of the crime scene for use at the trial. In some instances, three-dimensional models of the scene may be prepared to better assist the prosecution in presenting the case (Fig. 4.7). Personnel also use computer-aided design or CAD programs to render crime scenes.

*Photographers* are used for specialized photography. Aerial photographs may be needed to illustrate outdoor crime scenes. Unusual photographic problems such as low levels of light, infrared photography, or aerial infrared photography may require their expertise.

Videotaping is currently used by some law enforcement agencies as a means of recording crime scenes. Another new technology is still video photography to capture images at the scene. Specialists trained in these areas are required to operate and maintain the sophisticated equipment necessary to produce quality crime scene videotapes.

The *criminalist,* or forensic scientist, has special training and education in the recognition, identification, collection, and preservation of physical evidence. Criminalists are most often called upon to assist in more serious criminal investigations such as homicide, assaults, bombings, and arson. A criminalist's special area of expertise in these cases is

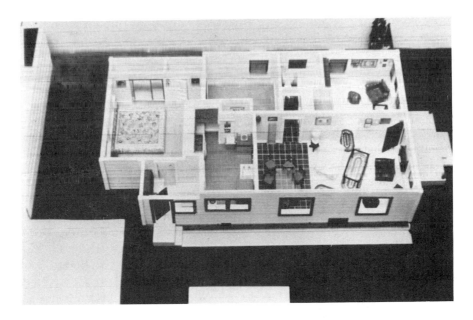

FIGURE **4.7.** Three-dimensional mock-up of one of the crime scenes from the infamous Hillside Strangler cases in Los Angeles, California.

trace evidence, serological evidence, and crime scene reconstruction. In addition to assisting at the crime scene, criminalists conduct laboratory tests on the evidence, prepare reports, and testify as expert witnesses on their findings.

Most large cities have replaced the use of a coroner with the *medical examiner-coroner* system. The purpose of the medical examiner-coroner is twofold: to determine the cause of death and to identify the deceased.

The *forensic pathologist,* or a trained investigator from the medical examiner's office, should be called to the scene of a homicide as soon as the police investigator has completed the initial examination of the scene. It is the medical examiner's responsibility to identify the deceased, determine the approximate time of death, and take custody of the remains. Ideally, the forensic pathologist or coroner's investigator should be present at the crime scene to conduct an initial examination.

*Hospital emergency room personnel* may play an important role in gathering evidence in a criminal investigation. Doctors and nurses who treat rape or assault victims are often required to collect physical evidence relating to the assault. Hospital emergency room personnel may not know which evidence is important or the legal requirements of evidence. The first officer to arrive at the scene of, for example, a rape may be required to inform the emergency room physician what evidence needs to be collected.

The *district attorney* may sometimes become a member of the crime scene investigation team. The district attorney may be called upon to obtain a search warrant for a location under investigation or a court order to obtain known specimens from a defendant.

In special cases, a *forensic odontologist* may be called to a scene. Mass disasters such as plane crashes or a scene where charred remains are discovered require the expertise of forensic dentists to assist in identification by means of dental remains. They also may be called upon to collect and preserve bite mark evidence on a victim or on foodstuff.

If the crime scene is a burial site, the assistance of a *forensic anthropologist* may prove valuable. The evaluation of skeletal remains at the scene is important in some instances. In addition, excavating a grave site requires skill, and experts with such experience can be helpful.

*Forensic psychologists* are available to assist in evaluating a crime scene. The FBI, through its VICAP program, is in the forefront in the use of psychological profiling techniques. Evaluation of the crime and crime scene can be used to classify murderers into two general categories: organized and disorganized. Although this technique is still in its infancy, further study and experience may well prove useful in some cases.

*Forensic engineers* may play a role in studying the structural integrity of a building or other structures in accident investigations. Sometimes an item of building material may require engineering tests to determine whether it was tampered with.

*Forensic audio specialists* may be required to evaluate recordings or assist in reconstructing events by means of studying sound recordings of an event. Sometimes echoes can be used to pinpoint where a weapon was fired.

*Forensic toxicologists* may become involved in product tampering cases to determine the nature of the adulterant in the foodstuff or consumer product. Using sophisticated laboratory instruments, they may be able to examine products for unknown poisons or other contaminants.

*Firearms specialists* may be called to assist in a crime scene, to recover spent bullets and assess the trajectory of fired weapons. They may also assist in determining whether a shooting could have been an accident or was more likely to have been intentional.

Police investigation is a team approach. Professionals with multidisciplinary expertise may be brought together to solve crimes. It is not possible for a police investigator to have a detailed knowledge of the law, forensic science, forensic medicine, and all the other training

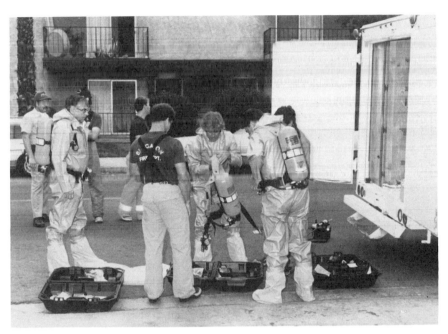

FIGURE **4.8.** Hazardous material gear was worn before going into a murder-suicide crime scene involving hydrogen cyanide gas. (*El Cajon Police Department Crime Laboratory, El Cajon, California.*)

specialties needed to completely process a crime scene and investigate a crime. A listing of local experts who can be readily mobilized to assist the investigator in a case should be available and is a major asset to successful police work (Fig. 4.8).

The importance of teamwork cannot be overemphasized. During the investigation phase of the case, the detective in charge is responsible for pulling together information from many sources. Leadership skills are needed to glean the maximum amount of information from the many forensic experts who may be associated with a major case, at the crime scene and later as the case is coming together. Investigators who take time to work closely with experts and maintain close liaison with them will often be rewarded by the extra effort.

Because many of the experts police investigators must work with do not come from police backgrounds, interpersonal skills are vital. Most experts, including those who routinely work for law enforcement as well as those who only occasionally do so, are eager to help. Police investigators, however, should remember that they are working with people from a variety of backgrounds. Working with these people in a spirit of mutual cooperation and respect and in a professional manner will aid in achieving successful outcomes to investigations.

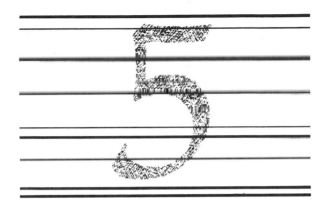

# PROCESSING
# THE
# CRIME SCENE

C hapter 3 briefly outlined some of the measures necessary for a proper crime scene search. The purpose of this chapter is to develop these concepts more thoroughly into a plan for processing the crime scene.

## Plan of Action

Processing the crime scene—which includes careful examination, note taking, sketching, photography, and collecting physical evidence—requires a plan of attack. The crime scene must be approached in a systematic, methodical way. Certain steps must be performed before others. Considerations about legal and scientific matters must be made when searching a crime scene. All of these details require a plan or a method of approach.

The plan of action should be readily available to investigators. It should be defined as a departmental procedure, outlining what should be done and in what order. It is, of course, impossible to foresee every single detail in a crime scene investigation; however, certain ground rules should be set forth to direct the officer to a specific goal.

## Note Taking

Of all the many duties and responsibilities of the officer conducting the crime scene search, perhaps the most important is note taking. Note taking is important for several reasons. It forces investigators to commit their observations to writing. It enables them to keep a detailed record of everything they see and do. It is not infrequent to find some seemingly insignificant item in an investigator's notes become a key in an investigation at some later time.

Notes should be taken in chronological order. They should detail, step by step, each and every action the officer makes. Notes should be complete and thorough. They should be written in a clear and legible fashion. Sloppy notes or those that do not clearly state what the investigator means can be misinterpreted later. Negative or unexpected conditions, such as the absence of bloodstains at a location or a light found lit, should be noted. Vague statements such as "near" or "to the left of" should be avoided. The writer should be as specific as possible. If an item of evidence is to be located, a description such as "on the living room floor, 6 inches east of the west wall and 3 feet south of the north wall . . ." should be used. Any notes, sketches, tape recordings, negatives, and like objects should never be discarded. They should be put into a case folder and retained for as long as the department's policy indicates.

The investigating officer is responsible for the crime scene. Upon arrival at the location, a brief statement must be obtained from the first officer at the scene about what has transpired. The investigating officer should gather as much information, facts, and opinions from those officers first present at the crime scene as is needed to obtain an understanding of the case. The crime scene can then be approached. The investigating officer's first contact with the scene should be a cursory one, and extreme care should be exercised not to disturb the scene in any way. Items of evidence at this point in the investigation should not be moved or touched until properly noted, measured, sketched, photographed, and fingerprinted. The investigator must begin to assimilate information obtained from the first officer to arrive at the scene, statements from witnesses, victims, and suspects, and the overall appearance of the crime scene. This information is used to formulate a plan by which the crime scene will be thoroughly processed.

*Protection of the crime scene* will be a continuous problem for the investigator. Uniformed personnel should remain posted at the scene to keep members of the public, members of the victim's family, and the press away from the crime scene. The presence of other officers is generally a more serious problem. In highly publicized crimes, the presence of superior officers may present difficulties in preserving the crime scene. One suggestion is to set up a command post with a pot of coffee to help keep unnecessary persons away. Another possibility for discouraging officers who visit a scene is to give them an assignment and require them to file a written report. Sometimes it may be necessary for the investigator in charge of the crime scene to politely inform the superiors that the scene is still active and their presence on the scene might compromise the finding and collecting of physical evidence.

Some investigators prefer to use a tape recorder or a pocket dictating device for note taking. Although a tape recorder makes it easy to take down information that can later be transcribed, the investigator should remember that anything done at the crime scene has the potential of being used as evidence in court. Statements on the tape, particularly those made by officers who do not know a recording is being made, can later prove embarrassing in court. Video recording creates a similar problem.

The following is an outline of some of the information that should be included in notes made at the crime scene:

1. The date and time the crime was first reported to the police.
2. The type of crime.
3. The location of the crime scene and a brief description of the area.
4. A brief description of the crime or event that led to the investigation.

5. The name of the person who ordered the crime scene investigation.
6. The names of all officers, witnesses, investigators, and special personnel at the crime scene.
7. The names of the persons who conducted the crime scene search and who took the photographs, fingerprints, sketches, etc.
8. The weather and lighting conditions at the time of the investigation.
9. A description of the location of the scene including the surrounding houses, streets, community, etc.
10. A description of the interior and exterior of the crime scene including the type of residence, number of rooms, windows, and the like, and of the outside of the location including the terrain, type of plants, soil, etc.
11. A description of the primary crime scene, i.e., the location of the body and accompanying detailed description.
12. The location of any evidence found during the investigation and the names of those who collected it, and the results of a search for fingerprints and other trace evidence.
13. The date and time the crime scene investigation was concluded.

These particulars represent some of the many pieces of information that should be included in the investigator's notes. They do not, however, include all the possible information. The officer, relying on personal experience and skills, should use this list as a guide. Attention to detail in note taking—as in the entire investigation—is the key to effective crime scene investigation.

## Crime Scene Search

Once the investigating officer has gathered as much information as possible and made a quick survey of the location, the actual crime scene search should begin. The crime scene search consists of several parts: surveying the crime scene, recording the crime scene through photographs and sketches, mapping location by measurement and documentation of all physical evidence, and searching for fingerprints.

A general rule can be stated at this point: *Evidence and information of a fragile nature should be collected before material that is less likely to be lost or destroyed.* Thus, photography and crime scene sketches of the location should be done early because the crime scene will change with passing time and the investigator's objective is to make a record of the scene as close to its original condition as is possible.

The search of the crime scene should be conducted in a systematic way. Criminal investigation texts recommend a variety of search patterns: the lane search, grid search, spiral search, wheel search, and so on. Some search patterns lend themselves to outdoor areas, whereas others are more appropriate for indoor crime scenes. The important idea to remember is that thoroughness is the goal of any search plan.

Anyone who has ever been present at crime scene searches has probably encountered another search method: the "mill around" method. In this method, the officer, by use of a pen or pencil (for indoor crime scenes) or a stick (for outdoor ones), randomly pokes around, pushing aside objects and picking up items that look interesting. *This is not the proper way to conduct a search!*

The *indoor crime scene search* should be done with two persons (Fig. 5.1). One easy way of accomplishing a search is to divide the room in

FIGURE **5.1.** A workable pattern for conducting a crime scene search should be formulated and used. Several typical patterns are shown here. The specific case will dictate which search pattern is used.

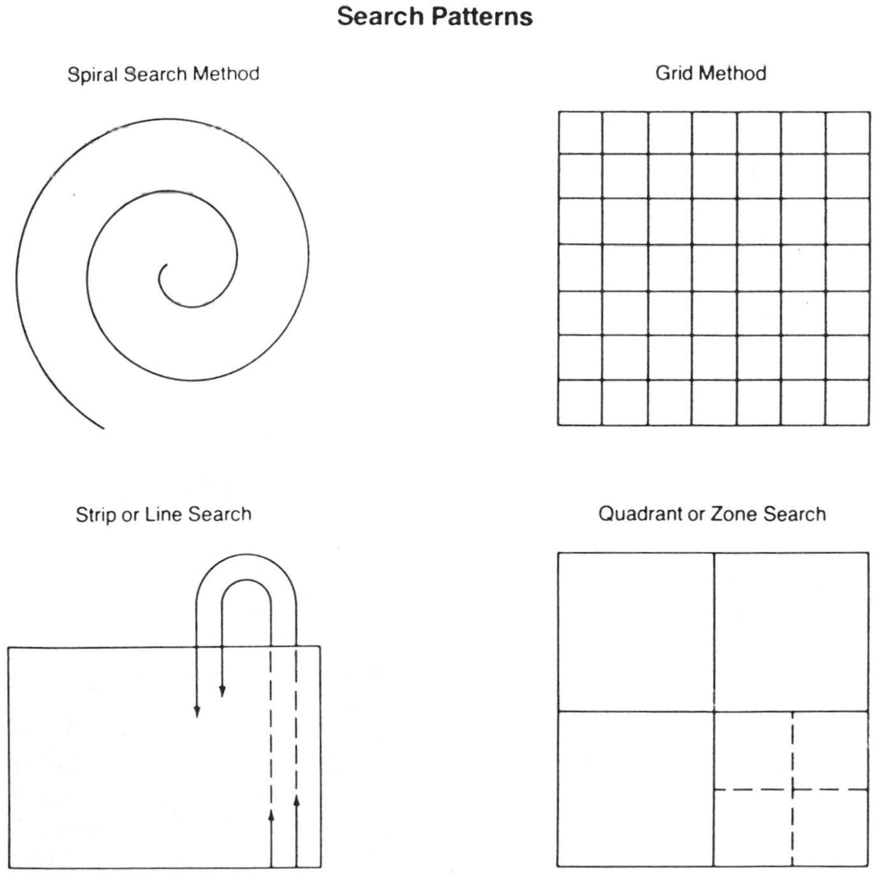

## Search Patterns

Spiral Search Method

Grid Method

Strip or Line Search

Quadrant or Zone Search

72

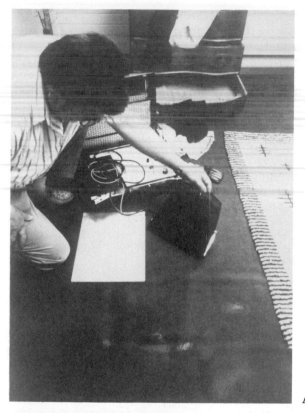

FIGURE 5.2
Crime scene
investigator lifting a
foil film (A) to collect
a footprint using static
electricity. (B) The lift
is shown next to a
photograph of the
shoe's sole. (*Zurich
Cantonal Police
Forensic Science
Laboratory.*)

A

B

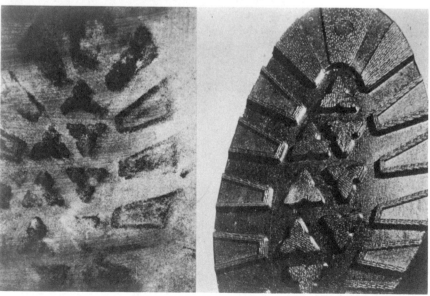

half and have each investigator search one half. After they have done as detailed a search as possible, they switch halves. The search is thus repeated by a different investigator.

*Outdoor searches* often cover greater areas than indoor searches. For this reason, more searchers may be required. Again a systematic method should be used. The area can be roped off into a grid, each square representing a given search area. Areas several feet square, e.g., 6 by 6 feet, afford a reasonable size for a detailed and comprehensive search. As in the indoor search, each area should be double-checked to ensure thoroughness.

*Don't forget to look up!* Often, when going through a crime scene search, investigators concentrate on what is on the floor or at eye level. Frequently, there may be useful evidence above their heads such as on ceilings or caught on tree branches.

*Before walking into a room,* the investigator will find it worthwhile to consider the possibility of shoeprints being present in dirt or perhaps floor wax (Fig. 5.2). If many officers have walked through the room already, the opportunity of finding these impressions is gone. If no one has gone into a room, a simple technique is suggested. Using a flashlight at an oblique angle to the floor, observe for the presence of footwear prints in a darkened room. If any are present, an attempt to photograph them with a camera on a tripod using side lighting should be made. After the photographing, the print may be lifted with large rubber-backed lifting tape, which is commercially available from police supply firms.

*Nighttime outdoor crime scene searches* present difficult problems. If at all possible, the search should be put off until daylight hours. If waiting is not possible, the next best solution is the use of high-intensity lighting supplied by portable generators brought to the crime scene.

*Vehicle searches* demand the same degree of care as indoor or outdoor searches. The type of crime under investigation determines the location to be searched. Thus, in hit-and-run investigations, the search concentrates on the exterior and undercarriage of the vehicle, whereas the interior is examined more carefully in a rape or murder case.

In most cases, the vehicle examination begins with an examination of the exterior. In the case of a hit-and-run, the examination focuses on areas likely to have struck the victim: bumper, grill, and so on. Dents, broken headlamps, damaged paint, and fabric impressions should be looked for. Also present may be blood, hair, torn pieces of clothing or fibers, and the like (Fig. 5.3). Broken and missing pieces from the vehicle should be carefully documented. The undercarriage should also be carefully inspected for evidence. Using a hydraulic lift for this purpose is helpful. Items of evidence noted should be photographed and sketched.

FIGURE **5.3.** The vinyl seat of a car with distinctive gang-style writing (the "187" refers to the California Penal Code section for murder). (*Los Angeles County Sheriff's Department.*)

Fingerprints should be searched for in likely areas such as door handles, outside mirrors, and so forth.

The interior of the vehicle should be searched for fingerprints. A systematic approach should be taken, such as dividing the interior into sections: front right, front left, and so on. Before entering the vehicle, vacuum sweepings should be taken to minimize the likelihood of contaminating the vehicle with foreign material possibly brought by the investigator. Only after trace evidence is collected will a fingerprint examination be conducted. (*Note:* a more detailed procedure for vehicle searches is given in Chapter 15.)

## Crime Scene Photography

The well-worn saying "One picture is worth a thousand words" certainly holds true with crime scene photography. No matter how well an investigator can verbally describe a crime scene, photographs can tell the same story better and more easily. The following is not intended to make the reader an expert in photography, but merely to discuss certain issues that relate to photography in general and crime scene photography in particular.

Before a detailed examination of the crime scene is made and before any items are moved or even touched, the crime scene should be photographed. The photographs should be taken to clearly and accurately depict the scene as it was found, the path taken by the criminal to the scene, the point of entry, the exit, and the escape route. Detailed photographs should be taken to show items of physical evidence in the condition in which they were found by the investigator prior to their removal.

## Types of Cameras

Many types of cameras are available for use in crime scene photography. Generally, a large format camera, such as a 4 by 5 or 120, is desired. The reason for this is that as a rule, the larger the negative, the greater the clarity when enlarging the photograph. For example, if two identical scenes are photographed with a 4 by 5 camera and a 35-mm camera with the same type of film and enlargements are made from each, the photograph taken with the larger format camera, i.e., the 4 by 5, will have greater resolution, and very small objects will be easier to pick out.

The use of 35-mm format cameras should not be quickly dismissed. Of all cameras, the 35-mm single-lens reflex camera offers the greatest versatility of any camera. Many police departments choose this camera for routine crime scene work.

Other cameras such as Instamatics and Polaroids are useful for specific applications. The Instamatic variety are very inexpensive, take tolerable pictures, and are useful for officers without much training in photography. The Polaroid camera is useful for identification photographs, such as in those instances when a deceased needs to be identified.

## Types of Film

Numerous types of film are available today. Color negative film has become standard in most police departments. With speeds as high as ASA 1000 and good color rendition, color photography presents few problems in either indoor or outdoor crime scenes. Black and white film, however, should not be completely dismissed. It is considerably less expensive than color film. In situations where relationships of items are more important than actual appearance, black and white film should be considered.

## Number of Photographs

"How many pictures should be shot?" This is a common question in any discussion about crime scene photography. There is no firm answer

A

B

**FIGURE 5.4.** Photographs of a crime scene serve to depict its nature and extent. Photograph (A) is a view from one perspective; the aerial view (B) provides a picture of the total scene. (*Los Angeles County Sheriff's Department.*)

to this question. As a general rule, however, it is better to overshoot a crime scene (i.e., take more photographs than are necessary) than to try to economize. Time, of course, is a concern. Certain evidence needs to be collected as quickly as possible. In the final analysis, it is the experience of the crime scene photographer that best answers the question of the quantity of photos.

Photographs serve a number of purposes. They aid in refreshing the memories of witnesses and investigators. They also show the relationships of items of evidence at the crime scene. A very important purpose of crime scene photographs, and one that is frequently forgotten, is that they help to convey the crime scene and the circumstances of the crime to the jury. In light of these purposes, a number of important photographs should be made in most every crime scene:

1. *Location.* Photographs of the location of the crime scene should be taken (Fig. 5.4). In the case of a residence, for example, the exterior of the dwelling should be photographed, including the locations of doors and windows. Photographs of surrounding areas of the house should be included, such as the front and back yards and views in each direction (i.e., looking north, south, east, and west). In some cases, an aerial photograph is useful to depict the location of the residence and other areas of interest in proximity to the primary crime scene.

2. *Witness photographs.* Witness photographs are overall photos of the crime scene. They depict the scene as observed by a witness. In the case of a murder crime scene in a house, such photographs might depict the victim lying on the floor as viewed from a number of locations in the room. These photographs are designed to tell a story, to relate what the location looked like to someone who was not present. To accomplish this task, several overlapping photographs should be made. In addition, long-range and intermediate-range photographs should be taken to show both perspective and the relative positions of different items found at the crime scene.

3. *Close-up photographs.* In addition to long- and intermediate-range photos, close-up pictures should also be taken to further clarify the scene (Fig. 5.5). Two photographs of an item should be routinely taken: 1) as the item actually appears and 2) the same photograph with a scale such as a 6-inch ruler included. It is important that the film plane be parallel to the plane of the object. The scale and the parallel film plane ensure the ability later to produce good quality enlargements or 1:1 photographs of the evidence.

4. *Evidence photographs.* Photographs of every item of evidence should be made prior to removing the item or changing it in any way. Photographs should be made of shoe imprints, fingerprints,

bloodstains, weapons, defense wounds, and so on. Additional photo-graphs should be taken during the crime scene search when new items of evidence are discovered as a result of moving items at the crime scene.

When taking photographs, a *photo log* is recommended. Some police agencies use preprinted forms and others keep track of photo-graphs by different means. A typical log might include the case number, date, photographer's name, type of camera, lens, film, and a listing of each photograph. The list may include the shutter speed, *f*-stop, and a very brief description of the location of the evidence.

Normally, photographs should be taken at eye level to give the proper perspective of the scene. If the photo is taken from a different perspective, it should be noted in the log.

The type of lens used also affects the perspective of the scene. Typically, a normal lens should be used, such as a 50-mm lens in the 35-mm photographic format. If the crime scene is indoors with cramped quarters, medium-wide-angle lenses may be used; however, the lens change should be noted in the photo log.

In low-light situations, flash photography is recommended even though high-speed film may handle these situations. Most shooting is hand held, but for exposures less than 1/60 of a second, a tripod should be used to ensure sharp photographs.

Photographs accurately represent the crime scene as seen by the

FIGURE 5.5. A bearded victim was shot in the face with a shotgun. A small fragment of beard hair and skin spattered back onto the suspect's corduroy coat. (*Los Angeles County Sheriff's Department.*)

witness or investigator. They should be clear and sharp. Subjects and items extraneous to the crime scene do not belong in the photographs. Thus, crime scene equipment and personnel should not be present in evidence photography.

Posed photographs that locate where a witness was standing when first entering the crime scene may be taken. A photograph should then be taken from that location to show the appearance of the crime scene from that point of observation.

This section on crime scene photography is not meant to be an all-encompassing guide to the subject, but rather to present some important points for consideration. Several worthwhile classes in general photography are offered in colleges and adult education programs that give the beginning crime scene photographer the basics on the subject of photography. The *Kodak Master Film Guide*, available in most photographic shops, is a valuable pocket reference that can be carried in a field kit for ready information. Finally, Nikon offers a one-and-a-half-day photography school on basic 35-mm photography at locations around the country, which is an exellent program for individuals reasonably familiar with general photography who wish to improve their capabilities (Fig. 5.6).

FIGURE **5.6.** These playing cards look perfectly normal under ordinary room light. They are obviously marked, as shown when viewed and photographed under reflective infrared lighting. (*Los Angeles County Sheriff's Department.*)

## Admissibility of Photographs

For a photograph to be admissible in court, the investigator must be able to testify that the photograph accurately depicts the area shown. For it to be accurate, it must represent the subject matter properly in terms of color, scale, and form. Further, the photograph must be in focus and should show the relationships and distances between objects. Crime scene sketches (which are discussed later) also assist in depicting the crime scene.

All negatives from crime scene photographs should be retained. They are important to demonstrate that the pictures have not been altered. Negatives are also important if blowups of certain areas of the crime scene are needed to better depict parts of a photograph.

It is worthwhile to reiterate the importance of scales or rulers in photographs. These are useful to show the actual size of the object in question. Some courts do not allow even minor modifications of photographs; therefore, it is necessary to take duplicate photographs, one showing the scene as is and the second with the scale.

## Videotape

Before leaving the area of crime scene photography, it is necessary to mention another method of recording the crime scene: videotape. Today's lightweight, portable, low-light video cameras are ideal for gathering a pictorial rendition of the crime scene. Video photography does not do away with the need for crime scene photographs; it has the advantage of depicting the scene more graphically.

When videotaping a scene, it is suggested that the investigator first take the video operator through the location. The filming should begin outside an indoor crime scene or with an overall shot of an outdoor location. The investigator should narrate the videotape by recording the audio portion as the videotape is being taken. The narration should include the name of the speaker, time, date, location, case number, and other pertinent identifying information.

Videotapes should not be edited or erased. The entire tape must be in its original condition if it is to be admissible as evidence. It has been noted that some agencies have edited videos as a means of refreshing the memories of investigators. Courts may or may not admit these tapes for the jury's consideration. As with most generalizations on the legal aspects of crime scenes, it is worthwhile to check with local authorities to determine what will be acceptable to the prosecution and to the court. Better to find out in advance than to assume the practice is okay, only to find out that a key piece of evidence is excluded for some legal reason not considered by the investigator.

While the scene is being recorded, other personnel at the location should be silent since their voices can be picked up. Such conversations may prove distracting and sometimes embarrassing if recorded.

As with photographs, close-up videotape recordings of small items of evidence should contain a scale to show the actual size of the item. Additionally, the relative location should be shown by panning the area and zooming in on the item.

Some courts may be reluctant to admit videotape recordings of certain crime scenes because of their concern of prejudicing the jury. However, with more widespread use of this technique, the procedure will eventually be fully accepted.

## Sketching the Crime Scene

Photographs alone are not sufficient for recording a crime scene adequately. A crime scene sketch should also be routinely made, and the two should be used to complement each other to adequately and properly depict the crime scene. Sketches clarify the appearance of the crime scene and make the scene easier to comprehend. It is, therefore, important for investigators to develop the ability to make good crime scene sketches.

A crime scene sketch is not considered an architectural drawing such as one drawn by an artist or forensic surveyor. It is simply an illustrative diagram or drawing that accurately depicts the appearance of the crime scene.

Sketching the crime scene requires some skill on the part of the investigator. Generally, it requires more than one person to draw the diagram. One person may be responsible for the actual drawing and the second person for taking measurements.

Sketches may sometimes leave out important information or be subject to error. Yet despite these drawbacks and problems with crime scene sketches, they do yield valuable information and, if done properly, are very useful in criminal investigations. Sketches help investigators recall details of the crime scene. They also help persons who were not present, such as prosecutors, courts, and juries, to better understand what the scene looked like.

Sketches offer a permanent record of the relationship of items at the scene to each other and help supplement photographs. They depict the overall layout of the location more easily than can be accomplished by a single photograph. Sketches also allow for selectivity. The sketch may be drawn purposely to leave out extraneous and confusing details that would be recorded in a photograph.

Crime scene sketches can provide a record of conditions that are not readily recorded by other means. Distances can be shown over large areas and topography can be easily illustrated. Paths taken by subjects or vehicles can be demonstrated on drawings more easily than on photographs. Drawings may be used to aid in questioning suspects and witnesses of crimes and to corroborate testimony of witnesses. Sketches combine the best features of photographs and crime scene notes.

### Information Included in Crime Scene Sketches

What information should be present on a sketch? Information placed on a sketch is used to make the drawing understandable and admissible into evidence. Like all evidence, it should contain case-identifying information: case number, name of suspect, victim, investigator, person drawing the diagram, and date and time the sketch was made. It should contain a scale, if required, and distance measurements between items present on the sketch. The location of the drawing should be included, as well as reference points to located items. A legend may be helpful to identify and clarify portions of the drawing.

### Equipment

Writing materials are, of course, required. Although pens may be used, lead pencils are easier to work with, especially if erasures are made. Colored pencils are also useful to outline important items. Graph paper is best to use, although blank paper will do. Graph paper simplifies scale drawings and provides guidelines for line measurements. Some sort of drawing surface, such as a clipboard, is helpful.

Measuring devices such as rulers and tapes are required. A 50- or 100-foot surveyor's tape is especially useful to measure longer distances. A folding 6-foot carpenter's ruler is also a useful piece of measuring equipment. Finally, a compass is helpful in determining directions.

### Types of Sketches

Different types of crime scene locations, both indoors and outdoors, present different types of problems in sketching. To best represent the scene, it may be necessary to rely on different types of crime scene sketches. The type of sketch chosen by the investigator is not especially important. What is important is that the resulting drawing best and most easily depict the crime scene.

The *overview, floor plan, or bird's-eye view* sketch is the simplest and most commonly used in diagramming crime scenes. It may be used in nearly all crime scene situations where the items of interest are located in one plane. Because of its simplicity, it is the easiest for lay people, such as jury members, to comprehend.

Another type of crime scene sketch is the *elevation drawing*. This type of sketch is used when the vertical, rather than the horizontal plane is of interest. Thus, if bloodstains were present on a wall of a house, the elevation drawing of the wall would be used to depict this scene.

The *cross projection*, or *exploded view*, is a combination of the preceding two types. It is similar to the floor-plan sketch, except that the walls have been folded down into the same plane as the floor.

The *perspective drawing* is another type of sketch that depicts a three-dimensional view of the scene. Although the final drawing will be very clear if done properly, this type of sketch requires a fair amount of artistic skill and, therefore, is generally not recommended.

## Locating Objects in the Sketch

Once the drawing has been made and the relative locations of the items have been sketched in, it is necessary to locate them in the sketch. *Location* is defined as the actual position in the crime scene where the object is located. A position on a flat surface may be defined by two measurements. That is to say, if a knife is located on the floor of a room, it will require two measurements from two fixed points to accurately locate the true position of the knife. Therefore, a measurement could be taken from the north wall and the east wall (e.g., 3 feet from the north wall and 6 feet 7 inches from the east wall).

Although perpendicular measurements are the easiest to use, they may be impossible in outdoor crime scenes. In those situations it is necessary to find fixed points to locate the item in question. This can be done by using telephone poles, fire hydrants, trees, the exterior corner of a building, and so on. Whatever the item of reference used it must be permanent and identifiable. Examples such as the number on a telephone pole, a street address, or a roadside marker may be used as a point of reference to locate an object.

## Admissibility of Sketches

As with photographs, a sketch may be entered into evidence only by someone competent to testify as to its authenticity. The qualified individual must be able to testify that the sketch is a true and accurate representation of the original scene.

Crime scene diagrams are extremely useful in court presentations. Frequently in major crime cases the original crime scene sketch is used as the basis of a finished drawing made by an artist. In some instances where the scene is particularly complex, an architectural model may prove useful to detail the crime scene.

## Computer-Aided Design (CAD)

Computer software is available to render drawings of crime scenes in two and three dimensions. Beyond the ability to draw crime scenes to scale, CAD programs have been used to depict trajectories in shooting scenes and reconstruct crime scenes. Some of the advanced programs are able to depict the scene in three dimensions on a video display terminal and take a viewer through the scene by means of computer graphics. Such a system could be used in the courtroom by means of a video projector coupled to the output of a computer to explain to a jury the sequence of events in a crime scene. The software can be used to present the crime scene as seen by the victim and the subject and show in pictorial form what each saw.

## Collection of Evidence

Following the initial search, photography, and sketching of the crime scene, physical evidence may be collected. It is useful to set priorities as to which evidence to collect first. The most fragile evidence must have first priority. Therefore, search for fingerprints first. After fingerprints (a detailed examination of fingerprint evidence is covered in Chapter 6), collect other fragile evidence such as blood and trace evidence. Once the evidence has been collected (see the appropriate sections of the text for specific methods of evidence collection), it is important to search the crime scene carefully a second time to make certain that no items of potential evidence were overlooked.

Evidence that is to be sent to the crime laboratory should be packaged in such a way as to prevent breakage, spoilage, or contamination that can destroy its value. Containers should be sealed and, depending on the nature of the evidence, strong enough that they will not break in transit.

Evidence that consists of several objects should be packaged in separate containers or wrapped individually. Each object should be clearly marked as to contents and then packed in a shipping container. In some cases, it may be necessary to fix articles to the container separately so as to make sure that they will not come in contact with each other. Bottles and other glass containers that contain liquid should not be packaged with other evidence, since they may break and contaminate the other material.

If Styrofoam or other packing material is used for cushioning, all

A

B

**FIGURE 5.7**
Occasionally a criminal leaves
behind an item that at first
glance may not seem
important to the case. This
flashlight was left at a murder
scene. Fingerprints developed
on one of the batteries led to a
suspect in the case. (*Los
Angeles County Sheriff's
Department.*)

that might be altered by contact with such packing material be separated and tightly wrapped.

n though objects may have individually identifying markings, such as serial numbers, they *should be marked with the recovering officer's initials* and the date so that the identity of a given object cannot be questioned. The markings may be placed either directly on the object, on a tag attached to the object, or, when this is not practical, on the sealed container of the object. It is also useful to place a seal on the final package so that the shipment reaches the laboratory expert intact.

*A complete inventory of the items submitted and a request of examinations to be performed* should be included with each shipment. The inventory enables the expert to check the contents so that a small object among many items is not lost or overlooked. The request for specific examinations enables the laboratory to begin examinations, even though the official written request has not yet arrived.

The official written request to the laboratory should always contain as complete information as possible about the case (sequence of events, statements of the suspect, the victim, witnesses, etc.). This facilitates the expert's evaluation of the extent of necessary examinations and of the techniques required. Such information may also provide answers to questions that come up as a result of the laboratory's findings or provide confirmation of findings that necessarily went beyond those specifically requested. It is helpful to include copies of pertinent police reports or interrogations.

The following is a brief description of packaging instructions for certain items of evidence:

Objects bearing *fingerprints or glove prints* should be packed so that they do not come in contact with each other or the package sides.

*Original tool marks* should be protected from contamination and moisture. Marks may be protected from rust by a light film of oil if transfer of trace material is not indicated.

Clothing containing dry *stains of blood, seminal fluid,* and so on should be wrapped separately and in such a way that the stains are not broken or rubbed off. The part of the garment that is stained may be attached to a piece of cardboard that is then fixed to the bottom of a cardboard container. If several garments are submitted, they may be fixed separately in compartments built inside the container.

In crimes of contact, the *victim's clothing* must not be packaged or come in contact with that of the suspect's.

Garments bearing *hair* should not be allowed to come in contact with other garments that may contain hair.

*Firearms* should be rigidly fixed inside a wooden container without further wrapping. Postal regulations should be consulted before mailing firearms.

*Cartridge cases and bullets* should be packed separately and with soft cushioning material.

*Loaded cartridges and other explosives* should be packed to protect fingerprints and shipped by a parcel carrier.

*Stomach contents or other organs* for toxicological examination should be placed in tightly sealed glass jars that are packed in cushioning material. The containers should be of a size proportionate to the amount of fluid, so that volatile agents do not evaporate.

*Pills and capsules* and the like should be tightly cushioned in vials or pillboxes so that they will not break. Absorbent cotton should be used.

*Charred paper* should be packed in strong boxes and supported on all sides with absorbent cotton. The container should preferably not be shipped, but hand-carried to the laboratory. It is also possible to place the charred paper in a large plastic bag that is blown up and sealed tightly.

The actions taken by the crime scene investigator often have a significant effect on the subsequent investigation. The care and detail with which activities relating to processing the crime scene are conducted may be the key to the solution of a case.

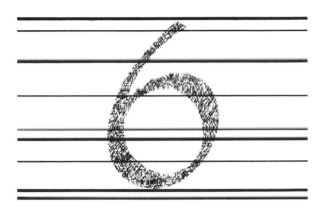

# ESTABLISHING
# IDENTITY

One of the most important purposes of physical evidence is to establish the identity of the suspect or victim. This is possible through a variety of methods discussed in this chapter. Fingerprints are usually thought of first when considering methods of identifying individuals.[1] However, techniques such as handwriting examination, forensic anthropology, forensic odontology, and other methodologies are also important and should be considered. (See Figs. 6.1 to 6.3.)

## Fingerprints and Palm Prints

Among the most valuable clues at the scene of a crime are fingerprints and palm prints (barefoot prints occasionally play a role, too). Such prints are decisive evidence. The report made by the expert after examination either contains the finding that the print *was* or *was not* made by the suspect, or the statement that the print is *not indentifiable.* The value of fingerprints is greatly increased by the possibility of tracing a criminal by searching through the single fingerprint file.

In this section, the term *fingerprints* includes all types of prints of friction ridges. Prints of the palm of the hand and of the sole of the foot are made under the same conditions as fingerprints, and are preserved in the same manner. It is often difficult to decide whether a print has been left by a finger, the palm of a hand, or the sole of a foot (see Fig. 6.4). For this reason, in ordinary speech, the term *fingerprints* has come to include also prints of the palms or feet.

### How Do Fingerprints Occur?

When criminals work, they cannot avoid leaving clues in the form of fingerprints unless their hands are covered with gloves or some other form of protection. Prints may be produced when they take hold of an object or support themselves with their hands. Generally, prints are formed from the friction ridges, which deposit grease and perspiration on the object touched. It may also happen that the fingers are contaminated with foreign matter, e.g., dust, blood, and so on, or they may press against some plastic material and produce a negative impression of the pattern of the friction ridges.

---

[1] Professional organizations in the forensic sciences play an important role for practitioners who need to stay current on new technologies. The most well known association dealing with forensic identification matters, e.g., fingerprints, is the International Association for Identification. Information about this important organization can be obtained by writing to the Secretary-Treasurer, International Association for Identification, P.O. Box 2423, Alameda, CA 94501.

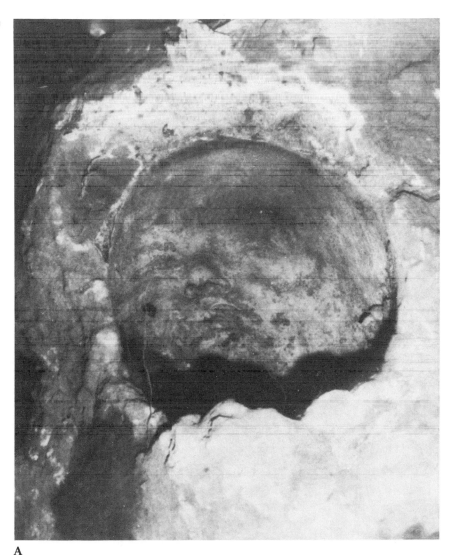

A

FIGURE **6.1.** The Case of the Lady in Cement. On December 19, 1987, the skeletal remains of a middle-aged woman, unceremoniously labeled Jane Doe No. 9, were found buried in the foundation of a residence in the Pacific Area of the City of Los Angeles. Examination indicated she had died of multiple stab wounds.

The upper portion of her body was encased in cement, a factor that led to her identification through a variety of unusual scientific measures. The wet cement that flowed over her body settled in a vivid outline of her skull (A). This allowed the composite artist of the Los Angeles Police Department,

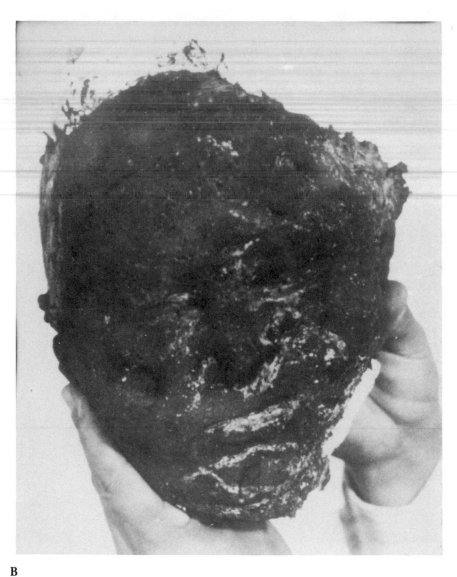

**B**

FIGURE **6.1.** (*continued*) Scientific Investigation Division, to cast a death mask (B) of the victim. The mask and artist's rendering (C) presented a startling likeness to the victim, who was ultimately identified.

C

## Where to Look for Fingerprints

In a case of burglary, the investigation should commence at the place of entry of the criminal. Generally it is possible at that point to determine whether the burglar worked with protected or unprotected hands. In the instance of a door that has been broken open, prints are looked for on the lock or its immediate surroundings or at any place where entry was forced. With regard to windows, special attention should be given to

FIGURE 6.2.  When the drawing appeared on TV, a citizen produced a photograph of a woman resembling the drawing. This led to the possible name of Adrienne Piraino. A fingerprint card was found on file because she had been fingerprinted as a job applicant.

Her arms, crossed over her body, left tell-tale finger holes in the cement where her hands had rested. Portions of the cement were surprisingly smooth textured, leading to speculation that the preservation of fingerprint evidence might be possible.

After experimenting with various substances, the Latent Print Section determined that rubber silicone was superior because of its high tensile strength and other properties necessary for detail enhancement. Silicone was carefully poured into each hand mold, allowed to dry, and the cast painstakingly removed from the mold. The silicone casts bore ridge detail on the fingers and palm that enabled the Latent Print Section to make positive identification of the victim as Piraino. Just as dramatic, the casts clearly defined additional cuts and stab wounds on her hands and finger, probably as the result of defending herself at the time she was attacked by her killer.

searching for pieces of broken glass. The method of breaking in through a window is generally by knocking a small hole in a pane of glass so that it cracks, after which the criminals break away pieces of glass with their fingers until they have succeeded in making an opening large enough to enable them to reach the window latch. Almost always on the broken pieces of glass there are prints either of fingers or of gloves or other protection. The broken pieces do not always lie just inside the window—the criminal often throws them away or conceals them.

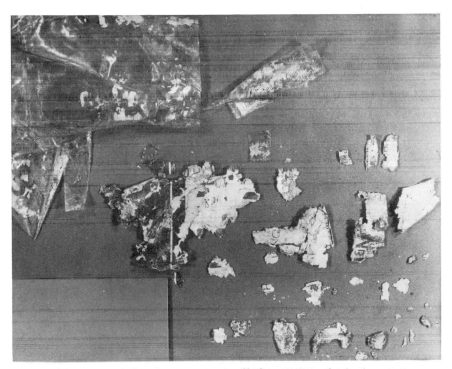

**FIGURE 6.3.** Meanwhile, the concrete-walled grave in which the victim was found was also found to contain items of clothing and other artifacts. The Comparative Analysis Unit was able to pin down a meaningful estimate of an entombment date to provide detectives with a time frame in which to target their investigation. They determined that the most likely item found with the body for dating was a partly deteriorated cigarette package. The name of the manufacturer, Liggett & Meyers (L&M), was discernible. A partial reconstruction of the deteriorated package was necessary to determine additional package characteristics, such as the style, color, location and content of the imprinted information, tax seal dimensions, and package components. Detailed photographs were taken to record the pertinent information.

In working with a Liggett & Meyers representative, it was learned that the package was a L&M Menthol Long, soft pack, which had been introduced as part of a test market in March 1974 in their Western Region, which included California, Arizona, New Mexico, Colorado, Nevada, Idaho, Montana, Wyoming, North and South Dakota, Washington, Oregon, and Utah. The product was withdrawn in March 1975 and the L&M packaging was changed. Furthermore, the tax-stamp dimensions, affixed to a package by the local wholesaler, were consistent with the type used in California.

This narrow time frame of one year—bracketed by March 1974 and March 1975—in which the cigarette package was marketed and probably purchased, helped detectives target a suspect who had access to the house during that time span.

Although other items of evidence were available and dramatically important in this particular case, the cigarette package clearly demonstrated the hidden potential of physical evidence. Murder charges have been filed against the suspect. (*Los Angeles Police Department.*)

A

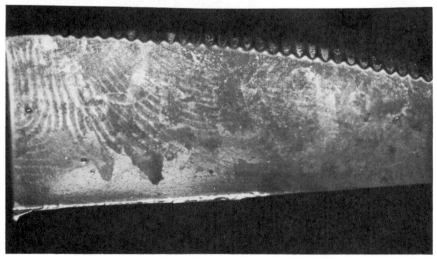

B

FIGURE 6.4. The suspect went into a convenience store in Kodiak, Alaska, where he robbed the clerk, hit her in the head with a gun, and took her into the back room, where he tied her up with an electrical extension cord and tried to rape her. The police developed a good suspect, but the clerk was unable to identify him. Inked finger and palm prints were submitted, and an identification was made from the latent developed on the plug (A and B) of the extension cord to the prints of the suspect (C and D). (*Alaska Department of Public Safety, Scientific Crime Detection Laboratory, Latent Print Section.*)

C

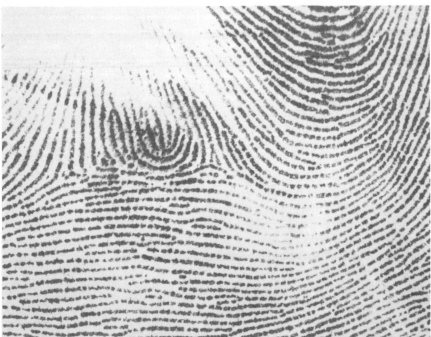

D

When the burglar is climbing in through the window, fingerprints are left on the inside of the window sill, the frame, and jamb, resulting from a firm grip on these parts.

A good rule for the police officer is to search for fingerprints as quickly as possible at places where a burglar may have taken food or drink. Fingerprints on glass or china are generally good ones. If the criminal has discovered and drunk liquor, a satisfactory result may be expected from the search. There have been cases of breaking in where the burglars had their hands protected at the start, but gradually became intoxicated, forgot all caution, and took off their hand coverings. If bottles of liquor have been taken away from the place, prints may be found on glass or china that has been moved out of the way or on bottles that have been examined by the thief.

Electric light switches, circuit breakers, and fuses should always be examined, as well as any light bulbs that have been loosened or removed.

If it is possible at an early stage to decide that the criminal's hands were protected, special care should be taken at places where the burglar's activity would be such that a hand covering would be a hindrance, for example, when opening a case or drawers with stiff locks, searching in the drawers of a bureau, and so on. It is a common weakness of thieves that they generally remove their hand coverings too early after leaving the scene of the crime and leave fingerprints, for example, on the banisters. If the thief has used the toilet, inconvenient hand coverings may have been removed. Fingerprints should, therefore, be looked for on the handle of the toilet, on the lock of the door, on the roll of toilet paper, etc. On objects that the criminal has brought and forgotten, there are good prospects of finding fingerprints, e.g., paper used for wrapping tools, flashlights (including batteries), and the like.

All smooth surfaces on which prints could be left should be examined. The best prints are found on glass or china, objects with polished, painted, or otherwise smooth surfaces, and smooth cartons and paper. Under favorable conditions, a print may be found on rough surfaces, starched collars, cuffs, newspapers, etc. When examining furniture, one should not overlook places the criminal may have touched when pulling out drawers, moving furniture, and so on. Even if the thief worked with protected hands, prints may have been left when, for example, a heavy piece of furniture was moved. The gloves may have slipped, or they may have been so open at the wrist that a small part of the palm left a print.

In looking for fingerprints a flashlight may be used as fingerprints can be seen in obliquely falling light. Using a flashlight on some surfaces does not work and, if it is expected that prints should be found at a certain place and they are not discovered, the place must be examined by special methods described in the section "Latent Fingerprint Developing Techniques."

During the investigation, police officers should not wear gloves, but must become accustomed to working in such a way that they do not leave their own prints. If they wear gloves, there is always the risk that they may become careless and destroy prints left by the criminal. Further, it may happen that the scene has to be reexamined by police officers who are more familiar with such matters and, if the latter find glove prints that were made in the first investigation, they may easily be misled.

Should an officer accidentally deposit fingerprints, this fact should be recorded so that they may later be eliminated from the relevant prints.

*All* prints at the scene of a crime should be preserved, even if they can be assumed to belong to the people of the house.

## Different Types of Fingerprints

Fingerprints[2] can be divided into three main groups: 1) plastic fingerprints, 2) prints of fingers contaminated with some foreign matter, or "visible prints," and 3) latent fingerprints.

1. *Plastic fingerprints.* These occur when fingers touch or press against a plastic material in such a way that a negative impression of the friction ridge pattern is produced (see Fig. 6.5). Such a print may be found in paint on a newly painted object, in the gum on envelopes and stamps, on substances that melt easily or soften when they are held in the hand (e.g., chocolate), on adhesive tape, in thick layers of dust, plastic explosives, putty that has not hardened, wax that has run from a candle, sealing wax, in edible fats, flour, soap, thick and sticky oil films, grease, pitch, tar, resin, clay, etc.
2. *Prints of fingers contaminated with foreign matter.* The commonest type is the dust print. When a finger is pressed in a thin layer of dust, some of the dust sticks on the friction ridges. When the finger is subsequently placed against a clean surface, a fingerprint results which in a favorable case is fully identifiable and may even be so

---

[2] A considerable number of advances in fingerprint technology have occurred in the last decade. Many new techniques have been developed for visualizing prints. Most of the new techniques involve chemical reagents that react with materials present in components which make up the print or contaminants. Cooperation between forensic chemists and forensic identification specialists has made such techniques possible. Continued collaborative efforts between persons expert in fingerprint identification and chemists should be encouraged in forensic science laboratories. Forensic chemists and criminalists should be assigned to identification units within laboratories to assist fingerprint and identification specialists develop and use newer print visualization techniques.

**FIGURE 6.5.** A plastic fingerprint in putty is sometimes found at burglary crime scenes. (*Los Angeles County Sheriff's Department.*)

clear that it may be searched in a single fingerprint file. Similarly, a print can be left when a finger is contaminated with other substances, for example, pigments, ink, soot, flour, face powder, oils, certain types of safe insulation, etc. Fingerprints in blood are sometimes indistinct and less usable for identification purposes.

3. *Latent fingerprints.* This type results from small amounts of grease, sweat, and dirt being deposited on the object touched from every detail in the friction ridge pattern on the tip of the finger (see Fig. 6.6). The skin inside the hands and soles of the feet has no oil glands. The grease found on the inside of the fingers comes mostly from other parts of the body that are continually touched by the hands. The secretion from the friction skin contains 98.5 to 99.5% water and 0.5 to B5% organic and inorganic components. If the hands are cold, practically no liquid is secreted; when they become warm, this secretion returns to normal.

"Latent prints" thus include not only those invisible to the naked eye but also all that are in any way visible or distinguishable but that can be examined properly only after development.

Latent prints are usually found on objects with polished or smooth surfaces and on paper; however, under favorable conditions they also appear on rough surfaces, starched fabric, etc.

## Latent Fingerprint Developing Techniques

There are many procedures available to develop latent fingerprints.[3] Those listed below are most of the standard procedures in use. It is important to understand that practical experience with these procedures is needed to use them effectively. Certain of the methods work better than others for certain types of materials. The sequence of use in the procedures is also important as it is possible to use multiple procedures, one following the other to search for prints. Some of the procedures have an adverse effect on other classifications of evidence. For example, some solvents may cause inks to run on documents or render biological evidence unsuitable for typing. *Latent fingerprint examiners are well advised to make certain they understand these techniques before trying them on actual casework.*

We also strongly recommend that latent print examiners consider formation of regional user groups to help keep up with a very rapidly changing technology. Such groups are made up of local practitioners who meet informally monthly to share technical experiences with other practitioners. These users or study groups are especially helpful in small indentification sections with one or two examiners who have little opportunity to attend technical conferences.

*1. Development with powders.* This is done by brushing fingerprint powder over a latent print. The substances that form the print show up and the print becomes fully visible. The choice of powder depends partly on the kind of surface on which the print is found, and partly on how it is intended to be preserved. If the latent print is of high quality, the choice of material for development is not especially important. There are several types of commercially available fingerprint powders: black, white, colored, aluminum, copper, fluorescent, and magnetic powder. The type used is determined by the color of the background and

---

[3] At this writing, the definitive single reference on latent fingerprint development techniques is the *Manual of Fingerprint Development Techniques* and its abridged companion work, *Scene of Crime Handbook of Fingerprint Development Techniques*. These fine books can be purchased from the Publications Officer, Home Office Library, Room 1001, Home Office, Queen Anne's Gate, London SW1H 9AT, United Kingdom. The FBI has also published an important reference work on the subject *Proceedings of the International Forensic Symposium on Latent Prints*, July, 1987. It is for sale and available by writing to the Superintendent of Documents, U.S. Government Printing Office, Washington, D.C. 20402, International Standard Book No. 0-932115-080X; Library of Congress No. 87-619890.

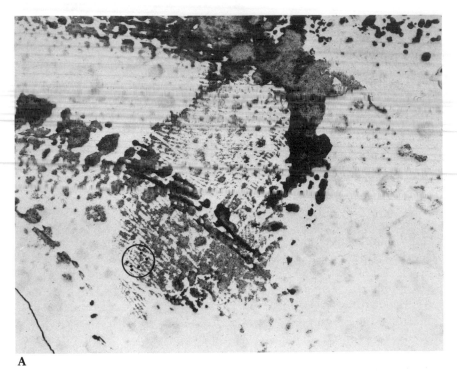

A

FIGURE **6.6.** A suspect stabbed a victim to death in Juneau, Alaska, and left a bloody latent print (A) on a sheetrock wall inside the front door where the attack took place. Subsequent investigation lead to suspects.

the nature of the surface (i.e., magnetic powder cannot be used on ferrous materials).

There is little safety information about fingerprint powder. Common sense suggests that long-term exposure to fine particulate matter may cause respiratory problems. Dust masks can be worn by persons who routinely use fingerprint powders to minimize the amount they breathe in.

A fiberglass, animal hair, or synthetic or natural fiber brush may be used to develop fingerprints. If the brush is damp or oily, it is useless. The brush is first dipped lightly into the powder and then tapped with the finger so that only a small amount of powder is left on the brush. The object is then brushed lightly, in curved strokes. The particles of powder stick to all places where there is grease or dirt. If there are fingerprints on the object, they show up more or less clearly.

When brushing, powder should *not* be sprinkled over or tapped onto the object. This technique can destroy prints made by sweaty or dirty fingers or produced by such a firm grip on an object that friction ridges

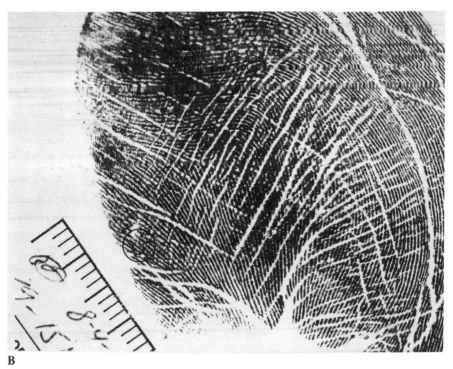

B

FIGURE 6.6. (*continued*) One (B) suspect's prints matched the bloody print left at the crime scene. (The circle shown on the latent and inked prints is a starting point for comparison.) (*Alaska Department of Public Safety, Scientific Crime Detection Laboratory, Latent Print Section.*)

have spread out and almost filled up the spaces between them. If too much powder is put onto a print, it can be "washed" by pressing a fingerprint lifter against it. If the lifter is then drawn off, generally the spaces between the friction ridges are almost free from powder. If necessary, the latent print can be reprocessed to get a favorable result.

Many fingerprint examiners use black fingerprint powder as a universal developer on smooth, nonporous surfaces. On dark surfaces like furniture and firearms, colored powders such as those mentioned previously have application, especially if the print is to be photographed before being lifted. With the use of aluminum powder, it should be remembered that the lifted print will appear as the reverse of a print developed with black fingerprint powder.

Perspiration and grease that form a fingerprint on paper will soon disappear from the surface and penetrate into the paper, after which they will not react to the mechanical powder method. If the print being sought is supposed to have been made a long time before the examination, it is of little use to treat it with powder. In such a case, some other medium of development should be used, such as iodine, ninhydrin, physical developer, or silver nitrate treatment.

Another aid to fingerprint development, the Magna-Brush, uses magnetic powders and a magnetic applicator (see Fig. 6.7). Streamers of magnetized powder are brought in contact with the suspected surface. Powder adheres to the latent print, and the excess is removed by the magnet. This method has the advantage of not leaving excess powder on the object and the surrounding area. Because of the nature of the process, it can be used effectively only on nonmagnetic surfaces.

Fluorescent powders are yet another type that may be used in some special cases. These powders, available in both powder and aerosol form, are used to dust paper currency and documents and are sprayed in areas where recurring thefts take place. They are technically not fingerprint powders in that they are used prior to the prints' being deposited. After the suspect has handled the money or touched the dusted area, the area is examined with ultraviolet (UV) light. The latent fingerprint is easily visualized by UV light and may be photographed using proper photographic techniques.

FIGURE 6.7.  Magnetic fingerprint powders work well on some items. Only the rays of powder come in contact with the surface, as in this example on a plastic bag. (*Los Angeles County Sheriff's Department.*)

2. *Amido Black.* This is a protein stain that turns proteins present in blood to a blue-black color. It does not react with any of the normal components of fingerprints and should be used in conjunction with other developing techniques. Other more sensitive stains, such as Coomassasie Blue, a general protein stain used in forensic serology, may also be considered.[4] Benzidine and o-tolidine are recognized carcinogens and should be avoided. Fingerprint specialists should consult a forensic serologist before using any protein stains on bloodly fingerprints as some stains may cause difficulties in blood typing.

3. *DFO (1, 8-diazafluoren-9-one).* DFO is a ninhydrin analogue. It reacts with proteins to give a highly fluorescent red-colored product that is more sensitive than ninhydrin. Although some prints developed using DFO will be visible to the naked eye, illumination with high intensity light improves the sensitivity. However, interference may become a problem with certain colors of inks and papers that fluoresce. Longer-wavelength light sources, e.g., mercury vapor lamps at 546 nm, lessen the interference. Ninhydrin may be used in conjunction with DFO; however, DFO must be used first.

4. *Fluorescence examination.* Using lasers, alternative light sources, or ultraviolet lamps on untreated substrates sometimes yields prints (Figs. 6.8 and 6.9). Various naturally occurring chemicals and contaminants present in latent prints fluoresce even without treatment with laser-sensitive dyes. Although the chances of finding autofluorescent latent prints is small, the ease of the procedure recommends its use. The use of laser-sensitive dyes and powders in conjunction with other techniques is discussed later in this chapter.

5. *Gentian violet or crystal violet.* These substances stain fatty components of latent prints and are especially effective when used on adhesive tape sticky surfaces (Fig. 6.10). This material is toxic and appropriate laboratory precautions must be taken. The dye produces a purple color. The sensitivity of the procedure is increased by using a laser. A yellow-orange light source yields the best results, e.g., a copper vapor laser at the 578 nm line. An alternative dye, basic fuchin, yields good results with green excitation and has an absorption maximum at about 500 nm.

---

[4] The FBI's Latent Fingerprint Section (LFPS) Research Team has been working on new procedures involving BBD (7-benzylamino-4-nitrobenz-2-oxa-1,3-diazole) and MBD (7-[p-methoxybenzylamino-4-nitrobenz-2-oxa-1,3-diazole]) in conjunction with a monochromatic light source. For the latest information, practitioners may wish to contact the FBI, Identification Division, Latent Fingerprint Section, 10th Street and Pennsylvania Avenue N.W., Washington, DC 20537.

A

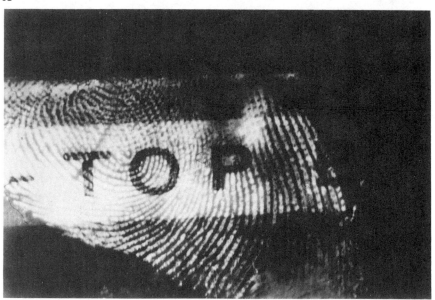

B

FIGURE 6.8. Latent prints can be developed using a combination of cyanoacrylate, or superglue, and fluorescent powders or dyes that can be visualized under ultraviolet light, laser, or alternative light sources. These examples (A and B) are latent prints developed on multicolored, glossy coated papers (*Zurich Cantonal Police, Forensic Science Department.*)

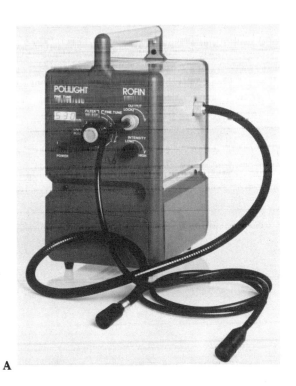

A

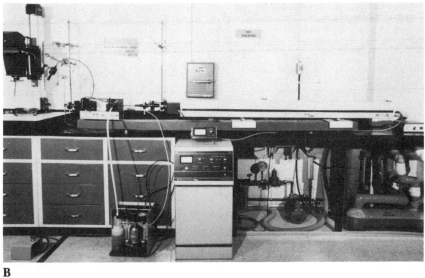

B

FIGURE 6.9. The Polylight, one of several alternate light sources (A) (*Kinderprint Company, Martinez, California*) and the laser (B) (*Federal Bureau of Investigation*) are in use in many modern law enforcement agencies.

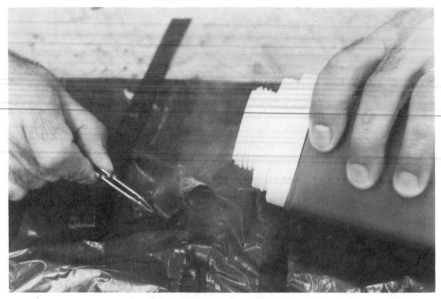

A

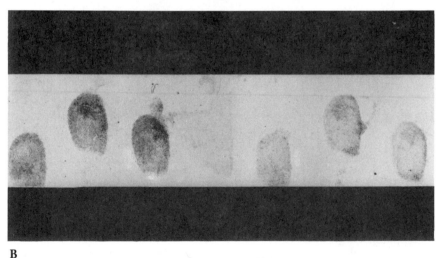

B

FIGURE **6.10.** (A) Adhesive-backed tapes are an excellent substrate on which to locate fingerprints. The difficulty is removing the sticky tape from surfaces. Denis E. Kebabjian, a forensic scientist with the New York State Police laboratories, developed a simple technique for removal by using liquid nitrogen. (*New York State Police, Albany, New York.*) (B) Gentian violet is a technique sometimes used to visualize latent prints on the sticky side of adhesive tapes. (*Zurich Cantonal Police, Forensic Science Department.*)

6. *Iodine.* Iodine is one of the oldest agents used to visualize latent prints on porous and nonporous substrates. The technique is simple to use; however, iodine vapors are toxic and corrosive and the reaction is not permanent. Methods have been introduced for fixing prints developed by iodine fuming, e.g., 7,8-benzoflavone, which also increases sensitivity.

7. *Ninhydrin solution.* Ninhydrin is another technique used with porous surfaces, e.g., paper, cardboard, wall board, and raw wood. Ninhydrin reacts with amino acids to form a purple-colored compound called "Ruhemann's purple." The reaction is speeded up by means of humidity and elevated temperatures. Sensitivity of the technique is improved by treating with zinc chloride solution and viewing with a laser. Background fluorescence may be overcome by using cadmium nitrate solution cooled to liquid nitrogen temperatures and viewed with a laser. Modifications to the chemical structure of ninhydrin have been synthesized and are useful under certain conditions. The importance of these analogues is that they fluoresce at different wavelengths and provide a way to overcome background interference from certain substrates.

8. *Physical developer (PD).* Also called stabilized physical developer (SPD), PD is a silver-based solution used as a substitute for the conventional latent print silver nitrate procedure. PD is useful in detecting latent prints on porous surfaces that are wet or have been wet, e.g., paper, cardboard, and raw wood. The technique may be used following the use of ninhydrin. PD reacts with components of sweat and appears in shades of gray to almost black. PD-developed prints are preserved by photography.

9. *Silver nitrate.* This substance reacts with chlorides in prints, but with the advent of Physical Developer, it is not in widespread use. It may have some application on raw wood; however, the background staining of the substrate may cause problems in photography.

10. *Small particle reagent (SPR).* This is a wet process for developing latent prints. The reagent is a suspension of molybdenum disulfide particles prepared in a detergent solution. Molybdenum adheres to lipids found in prints and grey deposit. The process works well on nonporous surfaces (e.g., plastic bags, wax paper, glass, painted surfaces) and may be used effectively on water-soaked firearms. Visible prints may be lifted and/or photographed.

11. *Sudan black.* This is used on nonporous articles, e.g., glass, plastics, and metal. Usually less sensitive than Small Particle Reagent, it may be the method of choice if the substrate is oily or greasy. Sudan black lipid components of prints blue-black and is messy to use. It is not effective on dark-colored objects.

12. *Superglue or cyanoacrylate fuming.* Superglue is used on nonporous surfaces to produce visible prints that appear white (Fig. 6.11). The visible prints may be dusted with powder, photographed, and lifted, or washed with laser-sensitive dyes such as Rhodamine 6G and others and viewed with lasers or alternative light sources. The superglue procedure is one of the easier to use; however, in some instances other latent print visualization techniques may yield superior results.

13. *Vacuum metal deposition.* This method is reported to be the most effective technique to use on most smooth, nonporous surfaces, e.g., plastic bags, plastic packaging material, and other smooth surfaces. The major drawbacks to vacuum metal deposition are that the equipment is somewhat expensive and the sample chamber of the vacuum coater is not very large. The procedure evaporates gold or zinc in a

FIGURE **6.11.** Latent prints developed using cyanoacrylate or superglue on a pistol. (*Los Angeles County Sheriff's Department.*)

vacuum chamber, and a very thin film of the metal is deposited onto the latent print, making it visible.

## Lasers and Alternative Light Sources

The word *laser* is an acronym for *light amplification by stimulated emission of radiation*. The use of lasers and other alternative light sources has grown to become an important adjunct to locating and visualizing latent fingerprints, as well as other types of physical evidence such as trace evidence and certain types of biological evidence.

There are several types of lasers and so-called alternative light sources (high-intensity arc lamps) in current use. There is no one "best" light available and, hence, there are several factors that need to be considered in choosing the type of high-intensity light most suitable in a forensic laboratory: cost, wavelength(s) or color of light, power output or light intensity, portability, safety, and its application for other forensic uses.

Cost is an important factor, as none of the devices on the market is inexpensive. Some require special setups and work space remodeling, e.g., darkened work areas for photography, laboratory sinks and a fume hood to handle light-sensitive dyes, power requirements, plumbed-in water to cool the unit or additional units to cool and recirculate coolant for the laser, liquid nitrogen for use in certain laser procedures—the list can be long and must be considered when budgeting for a unit. Other costs include maintenance and purchase of the component parts that must be replaced from time to time.

Not all lasers are suitable for forensic latent-print work. The color or wavelength of the output, as well as the light intensity or power output, are important. Initial studies of lasers in latent fingerprint detection used an argon-ion laser and, later, copper-vapor and portable neodymium:yttrium aluminum garnet (Nd:YAG) lasers. The working frequency of these lasers determined the laser dyes and visualization techniques that were first developed. Alternative light sources such as xenon arc lamps seem to produce comparable results and have become more widely available. Some lamps have broad light frequencies (250–1100 nm), although their light intensities are not as great as those of some lasers. Alternative light sources have the additional benfits of being less costly than some lasers, more compact, and thus more portable.

Safety is a concern with the use of lasers and alternative light sources. The high intensity of the light sources can cause eye damage and eye fatigue. Persons working with these tools should be required to wear appropriate eye protection to minimize the possibility of such damage.

## Image Processing

Space age technology is being used to enhance latent prints that heretofore were of insufficient quality to be used. Although image processing has been used for some time, the high cost of computers precluded the use of such technology in most crime laboratories. Major advances in the microchip industry and the resulting proliferation of relatively inexpensive microcomputers have placed image processing technology within the budgets of many laboratories.

Latent prints are examined by means of a video camera, the video output signal of which is digitized and fed into a computer. Unlike the human eye, the computer is capable of distinguishing between hundreds of shades of gray, which show up as varying degrees of density captured in the video image. The computer in turn can process the digital image in several ways. The image can be shown in reverse video (equivalent to a photographic reversal or negative) or with a color TV monitor, highlighted in different colors. This is particularly advantageous if the print is on a textured surface that makes it difficult to examine because of the background pattern interfering with the ridge detail of the print.

The technology works well with the other methods of latent print visualization, including laser. Although the procedure is still relatively new and in use in only a small number of forensic science laboratories, it promises to be a significant addition to the identification technician's arsenal of techniques over the next few years.

## Automated Fingerprint Identification Systems

Automated fingerprint identification systems (AFIS) represent the single largest advance in fingerprint identification technology. Heretofore, the ability to compare a latent fingerprint discovered at a crime scene with a criminal fingerprint data base was, for all intents and purposes, impossible. The amount of human effort to compare a latent print with several million inked prints on file was astronomical and simply out of the question.

Today, cold searches, i.e., searching a data base of several million prints against a single latent print, is done every day on hundreds of latents found at crime scenes. Even more unbelievable, a search of the prints on file of a data base can take about 10 minutes.

AFIS is causing a revolution in the way police departments approach latent prints. Dusting for prints at a crime scene was once seen more as a public relations effort than effort well spent. Crime scene investigators would dust crime scenes almost out of a belief that crime victims wanted something done. The effort put into dusting a scene gave the victim a good feeling. Only in a small percentage of cases would dusting produce latent prints that were used to identify a criminal. Some police administrators questioned the value of even trying to locate finger-prints in certain crimes against property, such as residential burglaries and automobile burglaries. AFIS has completely changed that way of thinking. Simply put, the more usable latent prints collected at crime scenes, the larger number of criminals identified by automated finger-print identification systems.

There are several AFIS technologies in use today. The main drawback at present is that they cannot "talk" to one another. Prints stored electronically in one region's AFIS cannot be searched by a system designed by a different vendor. The only way around this problem at present is to input the latent (or a copy of the latent) into the other system. The development of computer software and hardware to bridge that gap will improve the utility of AFIS technology.

In computer jargon, there is a saying: "GIGO" or "garbage in, garbage out." Simply put, if the quality of the inked fingerprint cards is poor, or if the cards are inputted into the AFIS data base improperly, the ability to search for and find a print decreases. Quality control of the fingerprint-taking process and in AFIS data entry process becomes very important. A new alternative to taking inked prints is an electronic technique whose generic name is "livescan." Livescan technology produces high quality print cards without the need to take inked prints. Each finger is inserted into a reader and its fingerprint is captured. At the end of the process, a standard print card is produced. The next step of the process (at this writing, still to be accomplished) is to input the electronically captured prints directly into the AFIS data base.

## Preservation of Fingerprints

*Preservation by photography.* Fingerprints found at the scene of a crime should be preserved by photography when possible. This procedure has many advantages. Photography leaves the object intact so that further photos can be taken if the first are unsuccessful. It also makes it easier to produce the evidence in court. If prints are lifted, the object on which they were discovered can be seen in the picture.

The photography of fingerprints and other evidence differs from ordinary picture taking. The photographer must be skilled in photographic techniques and understand how to obtain a reproduction of a finger-print as accurate and true to the original as possible. Additionally, a knowledge of the principles of fingerprint comparison is helpful to appreciate what the person making the print identification requires. The finished photograph should be either white on a black background or black on a white background. The ratio should be 1 : 1 (or in the actual size) and a ruler should be included in the photograph to allow for the printing to be 1 : 1. The person taking the photograph should advise the person making the fingerprint comparison as to whether the print is a direct or a mirror image, and a positive or negative image.

If the print is visible without development, it should be photographed as found, in view of the possibility that any measures taken for development might destroy it. This can generally be done by a suitable arrangement of lighting. An attempt can then be made to make the print clearer—for example, by treatment with powders—after which more photographs can be taken.

A number of companies have produced special "fingerprint cameras" or close-up cameras with built-in light sources that work rather well. Polaroid has a fixed-focus close-up camera with a ring light attachment that gives excellent results, as does the Kodak Ektagraphic EF Visualmaker unit. The latter has built-in batteries, whereas the former comes with a portable battery pack. These cameras are intended for close-up photography only and cannot be used for routine crime scene photographic work.

An alternative to the fixed-focus camera is the 35-mm camera with close-up lens, extension tubes, or a bellows attachment. The 35-mm camera provides the added benefit of focusing on a ground glass screen rather than through a view finder. The camera can be placed on a tripod or hand held, depending on the lighting conditions. Fingerprints should be photographed with a scale in the picture if 1 : 1 enlargement is desired.

*Preservation of plastic fingerprints.* When a fingerprint has been left in material that has hardened or is able to withstand transport, and when it is on an object that is small and easily transportable, it may be sent directly to the crime laboratory. If removing the plastic print poses some special problem, it should be photographed using oblique light to bring out as much detail as possible. The fingerprint impression may then be preserved by an appropriate casting material. (*Note:* see Chapter 9, which deals with impression evidence, for information on casting materials.)

*Preservation with fingerprint lifters.* Frequently, curved surfaces, such as doorknobs, with latent fingerprints present are difficult to photograph or do not lend themselves to the use of cellophane lifting tape. For such surfaces, elastic or rubber lifter material works well. Rubber lifters are commercially available items made of a thin, rubbery material coated with an adhesive. The adhesive is protected by a transparent celluloid material removed prior to use and replaced onto the lifter after use. The color of the lifter is either black or white for use with different fingerprint powders

To use, the latent fingerprint is first dusted with an appropriate-colored fingerprint powder. The protective covering of the lifter is pulled away and the sticky surface is pressed against the print and then pulled away. Part of the powder sticks to the lifter and gives the mirror image of the print. After collecting the print, the protective covering is carefully replaced on the lifter.

The lifter comes in different sizes and can be cut for a specific use. It is useful for picking up footprints in the dust as well as fingerprints. The lifting method is simple and easy to master. It requires no knowledge of photography and no photographic equipment. Its use, however, requires greater accuracy in specifying the position of the print. Carelessness in this respect can have disastrous results.

*Preservation with fingerprint lifting tape.* The most common method of collecting latent fingerprint evidence today is by special transparent cellophane tape. The material is supplied in rolls and is usually 1 or 2 inches wide. After the surface is dusted with fingerprint powder, the tape is placed over the print. Care must be taken to prevent any air pockets. The tape is smoothed down over the print with the aid of a finger and then drawn off. Particles of fingerprint powder adhere to the sticky surface of the tape and thereby transfer the fingerprint pattern. The tape is finally placed onto a card of suitable color, contrasting with the powder used.

## How Long Does a Fingerprint Remain on an Object?

*Plastic prints* remain for any length of time provided that the object on which they are left or the substance in which they are formed is itself stable. In investigations, it sometimes happens that police officers find fingerprints that give the impression of having been made in dust, but on closer examination are found to be dust-filled plastic prints in oil paint made years earlier.

*Prints that have resulted from contamination of the fingers* with soot, flour, face powder, or safe fillings are soon destroyed. Prints of fingers contaminated with blood, pigments, ink, and oil are more resistant and can be kept for a long time under favorable conditions.

*Latent prints* on glass, china, and other smooth objects can remain for years if they are in a well-protected location. On objects in the open air, prints can be developed several months after they are made. Fingerprints on paper are very stable and will last for years provided the paper does not become wet and deteriorate.

## The Effect of Temperature Conditions on the Possibility of Developing Fingerprints

When objects on which there may be fingerprints are found outdoors in ice or snow, they must be thawed slowly and placed so that the thawed water does not run over and destroy the prints. A suitable method of treating is to scrape away as much snow and ice as possible, with the greatest care, before the object is brought to a warm place. Only when the object is dry should the print be developed.

When plastic fingerprints are present in oil or grease, the thawing must be allowed to proceed slowly and under close scrutiny since the print may easily be destroyed by heat. Such prints should be photographed when they appear.

Damp objects should be dried in a room at ordinary room temperature. As a general rule, never examine cold objects, especially metal, until they have been kept for at least some hours at room temperature. In indoor investigations in a cold house, the rooms should first be heated. The heating should be done slowly so that water from thawing does not run off frosted objects or places.

## Examination of Developed Fingerprints

The officer who investigates the crime scene should only search for, develop, and preserve the fingerprints. Unless specially qualified by training and experience in the identification of fingerprints, the officer cannot be expected to carry out the continued examination of the developed prints.

A detailed account of fingerprint identification is omitted here, partly because it lies outside the scope of crime scene investigation, and partly because it is a vast and specialized subject. Several comprehensive works on this subject are available.

The officer examining the scene should preserve *all* developed fingerprints. Even small, fragmentary prints that might seem insignificant to a nonspecialist may turn out to be very valuable when examined by an expert. Large fingerprints are not necessarily more valuable than small ones. It happens frequently that the larger print is usable only for comparison with a suspect's fingerprints; it is useless for searching in a single fingerprint file. The smaller print, however, may be usable for both purposes.

## Palm Prints

On the inside of the hand there are patterns of friction skin just as there are on the fingers, and they are of equal value as evidence. When part of a palm print is found, the area involved can often be deduced from the position of the print or from other parts of the hand and possible fingers having left marks in the form of "smears" or portions of print. If the position of the hand represented by the fragment can be estimated, a simple sketch of the inside of a hand greatly facilitates the work of the expert.

## Prints of Friction Ridge Patterns from the Sole of the Foot

On the soles of the feet, there are friction ridges with the same evidential value as fingerprints; they are developed and preserved in the same way. There have been cases in which burglars lacking gloves or other protection for their hands have taken off their socks and put the socks on their hands, not thinking that their unprotected soles would leave a print!

## Packing of Objects on Which Prints Are Found

For the transport of objects to be examined for fingerprints, the police officer must decide on the most suitable method of packing for each particular case. Under no circumstance should the object be wrapped directly in paper, cloth, or plastic bags, since this would destroy the print. If possible, the object should be wedged firmly in a strong box in such a way that the surface is not touched by the packing. Since a rigid suspension can cause breakage or other damage to an object in transit, the box must be wrapped in a sufficient quantity of soft material such as cotton, corrugated paper, crumpled newspaper, and the like. If nails are used to fix the object in the box or to secure the lid, they should not be hammered completely in; the heads should be left free so that they can be pulled out without using much force.

## Taking Fingerprints for Elimination

As a rule, it can be expected that the majority of fingerprints found and developed at the crime scene have been deposited by persons who have had legitimate access to the premises. It is of great importance that these fingerprints be eliminated so that the continued examination may be concentrated on the remaining prints—presumably those of the perpetrator. The investigating officer should, therefore, always take elimination prints of all persons on the premises. These should be submitted to the fingerprint examiner together with the crime scene prints.

As the identification of legitimate fingerprints is as critical as the identification of the criminal's prints, the elimination prints should be as clear as the recorded criminal's prints for filing purposes. Elimination prints should therefore be taken with printer's ink or specially prepared ink pads. It is not required, however, that they be recorded on standard fingerprint forms as long as they are clearly marked as being for elimination purposes.

A large proportion of the latent prints developed at a crime scene are palm prints. *Elimination palm prints* should, therefore, be taken in addition to the elimination fingerprints. Inked palm prints require special care for them to be useful for comparison purposes. The palm should be inked with a roller to ensure that all parts of it are inked. The prints should be made on a sheet of white paper. Place the inked palm flat on the paper and press on the center of the top of the hand.

## Prints of Gloves

The general knowledge of the great value of fingerprints as evidence has resulted in criminals' using gloves as the most usual protective measure. In many cases, "glove smears" are found in a search for fingerprints, and all too often little attention is paid to them. The search is concentrated at places where it may be expected that the individual would have been compelled to work with bare hands or to use a good deal of force, whereby the hand coverings would slip so that the wrist or a part of the palm near the wrist would be exposed and leave an imprint. Prints of gloves, however, may be just as valuable as fingerprints so that it is advisable always to examine and preserve them for closer investigation, as long as they are not typical "smears" formed by the glove-covered hand slipping against a surface (Fig. 6.12).

The leather of a glove often shows a very characteristic surface pattern. It may show furrows in a more or less definite pattern, or be perforated in a fairly regular manner. It is much the same with fabric gloves. The surface pattern varies according to the method of manufacture and the yarn or material used. It is the wrinkled or textured surface pattern of leather gloves that can make identification possible. In contrast, the surface pattern of fabric gloves is regular for each type so that, in general, identification cannot be based merely on this. Characteristic and, from the point of view of identification, very valuable formations in the seams may be present, especially at the tips of the fingers.

After they have been worn for some time, both leather and fabric gloves become shaped to the hands, and typical wrinkle formations often are produced in the leather of the fingers, at the seams, or at places where the gloves do not fit the fingers properly. These wrinkle formations and injuries in the form of tears or holes or, in the case of leather gloves, cracks in the surface of the skin generally show in the print and are most valuable. In rare cases, it is even possible to find fragments of a

A

FIGURE **6.12**
Animal hide, like friction-
ridged and smooth human
skin, is individual in its
minute characteristics
and can be conclusively
identified. The latent glove
print (A) was compared
with the test print (B) on
the basis of the size, shape,
orientation, and
interrelationship of "plateau"
areas delineated by tension
lines in the leather. Three
areas have been darkened to
serve as a starting point in
the comparison. (*Contra
Costa County Sheriff's
Department, Criminalistics
Laboratory, Martinez,
California.*)

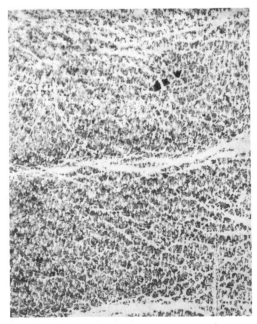

B

fingerprint within a glove print. This can occur when the gloves have such large holes that some part of a finger is exposed and leaves a print at the same time as the print of the glove. If prints of gloves and friction ridges appear together, it may be difficult to distinguish the difference without closer examination. At first glance, the print gives the impression of being blurred or of being composed of two glove prints within each other. On closer examination, however, the glove print is distinguished by its regular lines that lack the detailed pattern of the friction ridges.

Glove prints are always formed best on smooth surfaces. Their development requires great care since the prints are not as strong as fingerprints and, therefore, are easily destroyed if too much powder is used. To be sure of not destroying any such prints that may be present at the scene of the crime, the area should not be "painted" vaguely. A systematic search may be made with the aid of a lamp and then cautious brushing. On the other hand, there is the prospect of finding glove prints at conspicuous and easily accessible places, since in most cases the criminals abandon all caution and, believing that they are fully protected by their gloves, use their hands freely.

In developing prints, white or black powder may be used. The developed print can be taken off on a fingerprint lifter, but it is better to take possession of the object on which the print is found so that it can be compared directly with prints from the gloves of a suspect.

A print can be produced by leather or fabric gloves. With the former, the leather itself contains some fat, and both leather and fabric gloves become contaminated with dirt, skin grease, and the like after being in use for some time. In addition, at least with fabric gloves, the warm and moist secretion from the skin of the hands plays an important part.

Comparison prints from the gloves of a suspect are best made on glass, which is generally the most convenient even when the original prints are on furniture. In certain special cases, however, it may be necessary to form a print on the same kind of material as that which was at the scene of the crime. Where possible, such material should always be enclosed when a print and gloves from a suspect are sent for examination. Comparison prints should be made in a manner similar to the original ones. Thus if it is possible, in view of the placing of the original, to decide, for example, how the hand of the suspect gripped when making the grip, this information should be communicated to the expert so that the same grip can be used for the comparison print. Consideration must also be given to the degree of pressure that may have been used in forming the original print, and statements forming a guide for judging the pressure should also be submitted. It is of great importance that neither too great nor too small a pressure should be used in making the comparison prints since their appearance is greatly affected by pressure.

It is often difficult to make clear prints with a glove, but the operation may be assisted by breathing slightly on the finger of the glove. In certain instances, it may be treated with powder, fat, or the like; however, there is a risk of destroying any characteristic details.

## Prints of Other Coverings

In place of gloves, perpetrators may sometimes use socks, towels, handkerchiefs, or other such items as protection for the hands. It has also happened that individuals have protected the insides of their hands with adhesive tape to prevent the formation of fingerprints.

In most cases, when using the first-mentioned objects, prints are left only if the material is thin, dirty, or somewhat damp. If, however, it is thick, dry, or relatively clean, it leaves no prints.

Prints of such hand coverings rarely have any value from the point of view of identification. Only in cases where the material used has a characteristic surface pattern and shows typical injuries, unusual seams, or characteristic crease formations, which are reproduced in the print, is identification possible. In such a case, the investigation is tedious because the extent of the edges of the protective medium is not definitely fixed as it would be in the case of a glove and, therefore, it must be searched for before a direct comparison can be undertaken.

Although the possibility of identification of hand coverings in such cases is not great, the print should still be given some attention, since the method of operation may be typical for a particular individual or gang who have perhaps carried out other crimes in the same or another area.

### Latent Fingerprints on Human Skin

Techniques for developing latent fingerprints on human skin have been devised, but have been successful only in rare instances. They may be attempted in certain cases. The procedures are simple to use, inexpensive, and can be accomplished by evidence technicians. The procedures work on both living and deceased subjects (Fig. 6.13).

The first technique is the *Kromekote Lift Technique*. The equipment needed includes a fiberglass filament brush, fingerprint powder, and Kromekote cards. Kromekote cards are approximately 5-by-7-inch, high-gloss, 80-lb paper similar in appearance to photographic paper. Kromekote is manufactured by the Champion Paper Company in Hamilton, Ohio, and is generally available locally from paper suppliers.

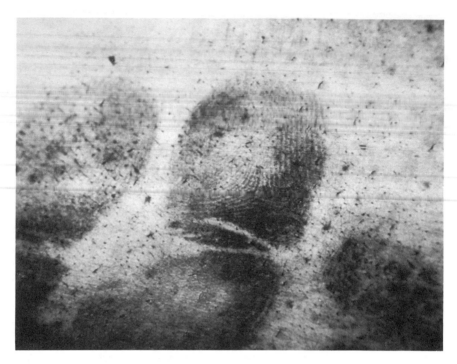

FIGURE 6.13. Prints developed from a body by dusting the surface using the Magna Brush and photography. (*Metropolitan Dade County Office of Medical Examiner, Miami, Florida.*)

The Kromekote card is used to lift the print from the skin surface by placing the card over the skin in the suspected area and applying pressure for about 3 seconds. The card is carefully removed and then dusted with black fingerprint powder to develop the print transferred onto the card. The fingerprint obtained is the mirror image of a normal print, which can be reversed through photography.

After the Kromekote technique is used, fingerprint powder can be applied directly to the skin to develop prints. The literature reports that the Magna-Brush gives results superior to a fiberglass filament brush. If a print is developed by this method, it must be photographed and then may be lifted using cellophane lifting tape.

Fingerprints on skin surfaces appear to last about 1½ hours on living victims. Deceased victims should be examined for latent prints on the skin as soon as possible. The technique is still somewhat experimental, but the simplicity and ease of use of the methods will result in greater use through experience on the part of investigators.

Obtaining latent prints from skin is still in an experimental stage and with continued research may one day prove to be routine procedure.

## Handwriting Examination

Handwriting is another means of establishing identity. Like finger-prints, it offers the investigator the ability to establish conclusively the identity of an individual. Handwriting characteristics are of two types: style characteristics and personal characteristics. *Style characteristics* constitute the general type to which cursive writing belongs. This general type is learned in school and is used by almost everyone. *Personal characteristics* are changes both intentionally and unconsciously made by the writer in the general style characteristics. Personal characteristics are those used to establish the identity of the writer.

Handwriting examination can be used to answer two questions: 1) was a signature or document a forgery, and 2) were two writings made by the same person? To answer these questions, the document examiner makes a careful examination of the questioned writing and known exemplar writings. Factors such as the relative size of letters, their slope, spacing, the way letters are formed, and other personal characteristics are used to make a determination.

Written documents occur in every facet of today's society. Daily business transactions include the use of checks, credit card receipts, money orders, purchase receipts, and so forth. Writings may occur on paper such as letters and notes, and may also be present on desks, table tops, walls, floors, doors, and even on dead bodies. Wherever they occur, they should not be overlooked.

Once a document is discovered, it must be properly handled and preserved. Failure to do so may result in its inadmissibility as evidence. Excessive handling may damage the document and smudge or obscure important writing characteristics, which may preclude any possibility of identification and eliminate latent fingerprints. The document should be preserved in the same condition as it is found. Generally, this is best accomplished by placing it in a clear plastic envelope or sheet protector. This keeps the document clean, preserves fingerprints, and prevents damage or destruction of minute identifying details. If the document is wet or soaked with blood, it should first be allowed to air dry at room temperature and then be placed in a cardboard box for delivery to the laboratory. Documents should be handled with forceps so as not to leave prints that may confuse subsequent tests for finger-prints.

Documents should not be altered in any way. They should not be folded or creased. If a document is damaged or torn, no attempt should be made to repair it. The investigator should not write on the document to identify it. Documents should not be stapled together or to reports. If a document is stapled, the staple should be removed slowly and care-fully so as not to tear the paper. A staple remover should not be used, nor should a paper punch be used on a document. Documents should not be left under paper on which the investigator may be writing, because indentations may damage the identifying characteristics on the writing in question. Indented writing should not be "brought out" by rubbing the side of a lead pencil across the document. Stickers or gummed labels should not be affixed to the document. The document should never be handled by the suspect during the course of the investigation.

If chemical processing to develop fingerprints on documents is used, the document should first be photographed with a scale present. After the chemical processing is completed, the paper should not come into contact with other papers because the stain can transfer. Paper should not be handled because additional fingerprints and smudges can easily be deposited onto the paper. Chemically processed documents should be kept in clear plastic envelopes or sheet protectors.

Documents damaged by fire could contain valuable information to the investigation. Arson has long been used in insurance fraud or to conceal another crime. If possible, burned documents should be left in their container and handled as gently as possible. (Refer to Chapter 7 on trace evidence for a more detailed discussion of preserving burned documents.)

If questioned writings are found on a wall or on a body in a homicide case, it is advisable to contact a document examiner for possible assistance at the crime scene. If this is not possible, photographs of the area should be taken. Writings on walls, desk tops, mirrors, and other surfaces should be photographed with a scale present (Fig. 6.14). If possible, the item containing the writing should be removed and submitted to the laboratory. If the writing is confined to a relatively small area, such as on a part of a wall, and circumstances justify it, the section should be cut out and taken to the laboratory.

Marking documents that may later be entered into evidence during presentation of a court case is necessary. The best place to mark a document is usually on the back. It should be done inconspicuously with initials and date and as far away from other writings as possible. In the event that this is not possible, the best solution is to use a pen with an obviously different color ink so that the marking cannot be confused with the questioned writing. (Red ink should be avoided because it does not survive well when ninhydrin is used to develop latent fingerprints unless freon is also used.) Extraneous markings and writings should never be placed on the document. If additional information beyond the investigator's initials and the date is necessary, it should be recorded in the officer's notes.

It is generally necessary to store documents for varying lengths of

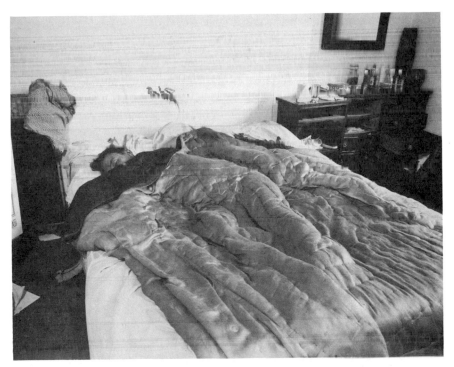

**FIGURE 6.14.** Before dying, a murder victim wrote the name of his assailant using his own blood. (*Metropolitan Police, Forensic Science Laboratory, London.*)

time, sometimes several years, pending final disposition of the case. The documents can be stored in protective plastic envelopes or sheet protectors and filed in folders or envelopes large enough to keep them flat. With such care, they will remain in good condition for long periods of time. Photographs can be kept in flat folders or envelopes. Documents that have been processed for fingerprints with ninhydrin or other chemicals must be enclosed in clear plastic envelopes or sheet protectors. Documents should be stored in an area with a relatively cool, dry temperature and away from excessive heat or direct sunlight.

Once the questioned documents have been discovered and received as evidence, having been properly handled and marked for identification, exemplar writings must be obtained. *Exemplar writings* are known specimens from the suspect and/or victim. Exemplars are extremely important and are necessary to connect the suspect or victim to the document. Like the questioned document, exemplars must be properly identified and cared for. They should not be stapled, folded, rolled up, torn, punched, smeared with fingerprints, or otherwise damaged if they are to be acceptable as evidence (Fig. 6.15).

The purpose of exemplars is to give the examiner of the document in question a known specimen of the subject's writing. The exemplar provides a source of the writer's individual writing habits and personal style characteristics.

There are two general types of handwriting exemplars: informal and formal. Informal exemplars are also referred to as *nonrequest writing*. These include writings produced in the routine, normal course of business, such as letters, application forms, business records, checks, and the like. These documents are sometimes difficult to admit as evidence

**FIGURE 6.15.** Reconstructing shredded documents in a bookmaking investigation is very time-consuming, but is an integral part of the prosecution's evidence. (*State Forensic Science Laboratory, Melbourne, Australia.*)

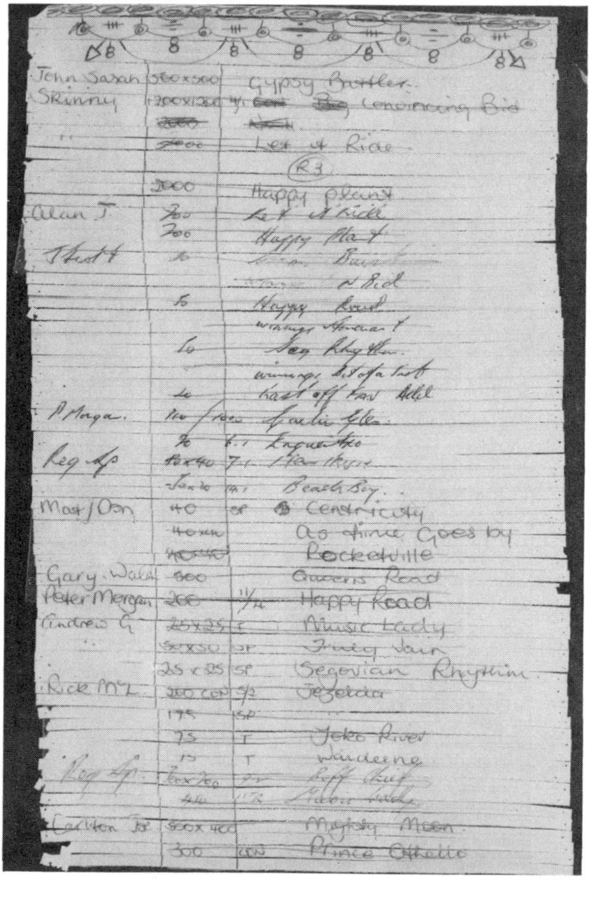

since there may be a question of their authenticity. They are, however, the best examples of normal or natural handwriting.

Formal or *request writing* exemplars are prepared by the subject at the request of another person, usually the investigator. The format generally used is a handwriting exemplar card designated for that purpose. In addition to an exemplar card, fingerprint cards, booking slips, and, at times, tablet paper may be used to obtain miscellaneous or specific exemplar writing samples. These writings will be witnessed by the investigating officer.

There are several helpful suggestions the investigator should keep in mind when obtaining request exemplars. It is useful to study and become familiar with the questioned document, paying close attention to names, specific words, spellings, and other unusual features of the document. The writing instrument should be in good working order. It is preferable to use a ballpoint pen with blue or black ink. A felt-tip pen or pencil should be avoided unless it is the type of writing instrument used in the questioned writing.

The writer should be provided with a comfortable writing area. Generally, exemplars written in the back seat of a police car en route to the station are worthless. The investigator should actually be present to observe the writing since the investigator will be called upon in court to testify to this fact. Only like materials can be compared, that is, cursive writing must be compared with cursive, printing with printing, block letters with block letters, and so forth.

In addition to the exemplar card, specific writing specimens should be requested. This includes material contained in the questioned document. The wording of the questioned document should be dictated to the subject; the actual document should not be placed before the writer from which to copy. The writing instrument should be similar to the one used on the questioned document, and the paper should be of a similar type with respect to size, style, whether it is plain, ruled, etc. Several specimens should be obtained as long as the subject is willing to cooperate.

If the writer is trying to disguise the writing, it is best to interrupt the period of writing with conversation and fresh paper from time to time (Fig. 6.16). This procedure makes it difficult for the subject to maintain a consistent alteration of natural writing habits. In the event that there is wide variation or difference in the questioned writing and the exemplar, it may be useful to have the writer provide additional exemplars with the other hand.

Narcotic addicts may produce writing that varies from time to time. It may be necessary to obtain writing exemplars at different time intervals, sometimes several days apart. Handwriting reflects the effects of age, illness, injuries, and mental state. It is sometimes necessary for the

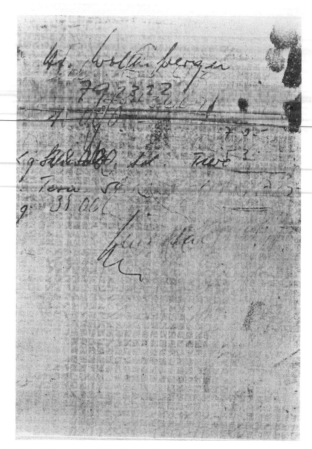

**FIGURE 6.16.** Visualization of indented writing using ESDA, the Electrostatic Detection Apparatus. (*Zurich Cantonal Police, Forensic Science Department.*)

investigator to obtain additional exemplars of the individual's writing by obtaining informal exemplars.

## Identification of Human Remains

The fields of forensic anthropology and forensic odontology (dentistry) have made major contributions over the past decades in the identification of human remains. An in-depth examination is beyond the scope of this book; however, it is worthwhile for the investigator to be aware of some of the information that can be gleaned from semiskeletal remains. Forensic anthropology and odontology techniques are useful in cases where normal methods of identification, such as facial photographs, fingerprints, physical description, blood grouping, markings on the body, and the like, are not available for use (Fig. 6.17). Such cases may

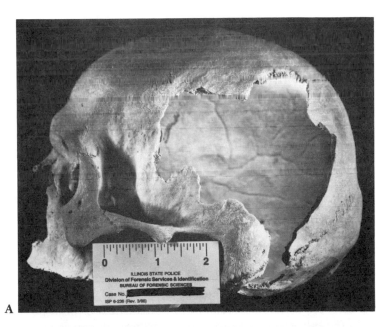

A

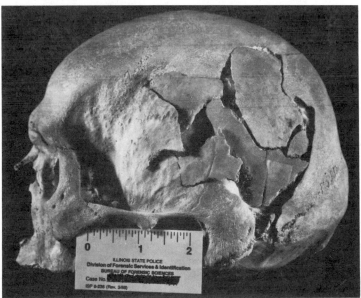

B

FIGURE 6.17. Suspected of being killed with a hammer blow on Christmas Eve, the victim's body surfaced in a nearby pond nine months after the murder. The body had been tied to stones and cement rocks with a torn-up sheet. The laboratory was asked to determine if a certain hammer left any unique markings on the skull. The illustration shows (A) the skull and (B) the skull with bone fragments in place. It was not possible in this case to match the hammer to the damage. (*Illinois State Police, Bureau of Forensic Sciences.*)

involve discovery of buried bodies, badly burned bodies, skeletal remains, major disasters, and so on.

It is possible to determine two types of information from remains. The first is physical characteristics such as sex, ethnicity, approximate age, stature, certain disease states, old injuries, and the like. The second and far more important for forensic purposes is the actual identification of the individual (Fig. 6.18). To accomplish this identification, adequate records indicating the deceased's physical characteristics must be available as a basis for comparison with the data collected from the examination.

Personal identification is one of the most important functions of an investigation. The identity of a living person at a crime scene establishes a strong link between the suspect and the crime. Likewise, the identity, or nonidentity, of a dead person sets the investigation in motion. Because the vast majority of homicide victims are killed by relatives or acquaintances, knowing the identity of the victim provides a starting point. In conjunction with the identity, the character of the victim suggests possible suspects. Although not a responsibility of criminal investigations, the identity of a noncriminal dead person enables the deceased's relatives to collect insurance, settle estates, and provide for the welfare of dependents.

When police are called to a case of death, the identity of the body is generally established by relatives or acquaintances of the dead person or from documents or possessions found on the body. Caution should, however, always be exercised in making a decision about identity merely because documents concerning a certain person are found on the body—such documents may be stolen, false, or "planted." Furthermore, the body itself may be "planted" to permit someone to disappear. Substitute bodies have been discovered when the dead man's measurements did not agree with those of the alleged victim.

It cannot always be assumed that a relative or acquaintance is competent to identify the body. There have been instances, owing to the state of the body, when even a spouse has made a mistake as to identity. It is necessary, therefore, to be careful in establishing the identity of a body, even though its identity can be determined with a fair degree of probability. These precautions consist of taking the fingerprints, photographing the body, noting the description (including the dental data), and examining and describing in detail the clothing and objects found on the body. Blood typing may sometimes also prove to be of assistance.

Sometimes when the body of an unknown person is found, it is better to postpone a definite conclusion for a few days until the discovery has become generally known through publicity in local papers and/or the national press. Most unknown bodies are identified by relatives or acquaintances of missing persons who read or hear of the discovery and

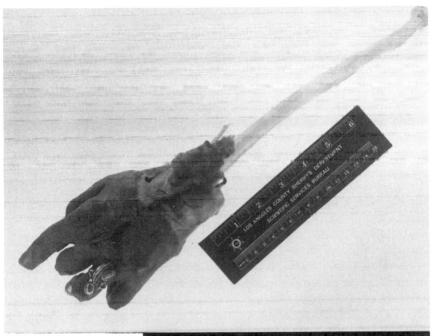

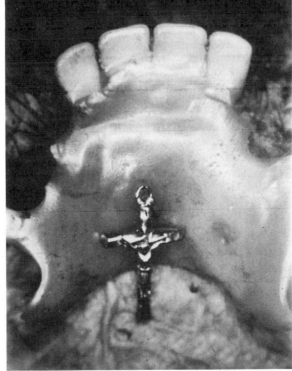

**FIGURE 6.18.**
Unusual jewelry may play a part in identifying a deceased person. A distinctive ring found on the hand of a badly decomposed body (Los Angeles County Sheriff's Department) or a gold crucifix attached to the dentures of an unknown person may provide useful identifying information. (*George E. Burgman, DDS, Forensic Odontologist, Niagara Falls, Ontario, Canada.*)

communicate with the police. The examination by the pathologist at the autopsy of the body will assist greatly in its description, particularly if the body is in an advanced state of decomposition. The pathologist will be able to give such details as apparent age, height, build, weight, and presence of scars (including surgical scars).

If, however, all this information, general examination, and publicity fail to establish the identity of the dead person, and the body has to be buried as that of an unknown individual, it is most important that everything that may be a guide to identification later, including the belongings of the deceased, be preserved for possible future use. Further samples should be taken of hair from the different parts of the body, and blood group and dental data should be recorded.

In the identification of unknown deceased persons, the police officer may have to work with bodies in varying states of decomposition. The most frequent case is that of a body found in water, which can be considered as the most repugnant and difficult since at quite an early stage—in summer, only a few days after death—the body swells up and the skin becomes almost black. More rarely, a mummified or petrified body is under inquiry. A dead body may become mummified when it lies in a dry place exposed to sun and air, the tissues not putrefying but gradually drying up. Under certain conditions, a body can become petrified: the external parts become as if calcified, owing to formation of adipocere, and the body resembles a marble statue. Formation of adipocere occurs chiefly in bodies that lie in very damp places. It also may be necessary to identify a greatly changed or mutilated body or one of which only the skeleton or certain portions remain.

The deceased may be a murder victim. Therefore, before an attempt at identification, the work should be carefully planned. It must be decided to what extent a search of pockets and other articles for identifying documents can be permitted without destroying other important evidence. It may be necessary to move the body or other form of remains to a mortuary where a careful examination can be conducted.

Generally, the first measure is a preliminary investigation of the pockets of the clothes. If any documents or other material that can be a guide to identification are found, careful note should be taken with a view to publication. If this does not lead to any result, the work of identification is continued by taking photographs and fingerprints, preparing an accurate description, and making a detailed investigation and description of clothes and belongings. The discovery of the body may then be published in a police bulletin for distribution to other agencies and to the general press.

A form of identification work that requires exceptional organization is the identification of victims of a catastrophe. dure for this type of identification is described later in this c...

## Taking of Fingerprints

Even if an individual is not on record in the fingerprint file, there is a good possibility of identifying the body through fingerprints. There are often cases in which there is reason to assume that a body is that of a certain missing person, but even near relatives are unable to identify it because it has altered so much. Under these conditions, fingerprints are taken in order to compare them with latent prints in the home of the individual or at the place of employment. Such investigation often gives a positive result.

There is no special difficulty in taking fingerprints from a body after the rigidity has relaxed or when rigidity has developed to only a small extent and the body has not undergone any considerable change. If there is rigidity in the fingers, the joints should be bent several times until they are sufficiently flexible. The tips of the fingers are then inked, using a rubber roller and printing ink or commercially available inking materials, and the prints are taken on small pieces of thin card that are pressed against the papillary pattern on the tip of the finger. The finger should not be rolled against the card because the print will inevitably suffer from slipping. With some practice, the card may instead be rolled around the fingertip for satisfactory results. A number of prints of the same finger are taken so that the best results can be selected. When a sufficient number of prints have been taken from one finger, each piece of card is marked to show to which finger it corresponds. When prints have been taken from all the fingers, the best are selected from each and stuck on the respective sections of a fingerprint card. It is important to be careful not to get the fingers mixed up when sticking on the prints; if prints of two fingers do happen to get interchanged, then a search in the register will probably be fruitless. It is best to make up two cards, one to be sent to the state or federal file and the other filed with the records. If suitable thin cards cannot be obtained, ordinary glazed writing paper can be used. In such a case, the taking of the prints is facilitated by using a piece of wood or sheet metal cut to a form fitting the finger. The pieces of paper are placed on this and fixed or held fast on it when taking the prints.

When the rigidity of the body is complete, it is difficult to take fingerprints because the fingers are bent toward the palm of the hand and are so stiff that they can hardly be straightened. There is no point in trying to extend such a finger. In such a case, it is sometimes suggested to cut certain tendons in the fingers so that they can be straightened. Certainly, this method is quite effective, but it is not necessary to go so far. It is simpler to bend the hand backward at the wrist to a right or acute angle against the forearm, whereby the fingers straighten out themselves. It is then possible to hold a finger firmly and lift it up to make the print, the bend at the wrist becoming slightly reduced. If this should also be found difficult, then the wrist is bent down again and the required finger is pressed down toward the palm, which makes it accessible from below.

Difficulty is often experienced when the body is considerably decomposed. The changes in the fingers consist either of their drying up and becoming horny and hard, or of the tissues becoming loose and filled with liquid and the epidermis becoming fragile and puckered ("dishpan hands"). The first occurs generally when the body has lain in a dry place; the second when it has been in water.

When the fingers have shriveled and dried up, fingerprints cannot be taken by the method just described, and other methods must be employed. For example, the prints may be read directly from the fingers and classified without taking impressions. It is necessary to be very careful and, if possible, to do ridge counting and ridge tracing also on those fingers that are not necessary for the classification formulae. A selection is then made of the finger or fingers most suitable for recording with printing ink. When this has been done, a proper search can be made in the fingerprint file. This method can, however, be applied only by persons with great experience in fingerprint classification, and is not suitable for a police officer who seldom or never has anything to do with fingerprint identification. When reading a pattern directly from a finger, it must be remembered that the print is seen reversed as in a mirror.

The police officer who is unfamiliar with fingerprint classification can use a very simple method of casting with the aid of dental casting material. The material usually consists of a cream and catalyst that are mixed together and applied to the fingertip. After a material has set, it can be removed and classified by a qualified expert. The cast also serves as a permanent record of the print.

Another method of recording fingerprints of deceased persons is photography. This method is rather tedious and difficult to carry out. If the fingers are stiff and bent, it is necessary to photograph each finger separately.

Frequently, fingertips are so dried out and wrinkled that the friction ridge pattern cannot be read from directly or cast because important parts are concealed in hard folds of the skin. The pattern may be obtained by thin layer casting as just described, or the fingers may be removed by cutting so that the skin can be softened. The pathologist should have an opportunity to view the deceased before this step is taken. The fingers should be cut at the second or middle joint and placed in individual bottles, each labeled according to the hand and finger. This operation should be done only by a pathologist or other competent person, but the police officer should be present to check that the different fingers do not get mixed up. The simplest method of softening the fingertips is then to leave them in water or Eastman Kodak Photo-Flo 200 for 1 or 2 days, after which they are kneaded cautiously until sufficiently soft. A print can then be taken with the aid of printing ink. Should there still be difficulties, the prints must be photographed.

The taking of fingerprints from a corpse removed from water is generally very difficult because of the effect of the alterations in the body. In general, these changes may be divided into three stages: 1) the epidermis of the fingertips becomes loose and coarsely ridged, 2) the epidermis is loose everywhere and can be removed, and 3) the epidermis is missing entirely.

In the first stage, the fingertips must be washed and dried, preferably with cotton or a soft towel, this operation must be done with great care and without rubbing so that none of the skin is torn off. Fingerprints are then taken in the way described for a body that has not undergone any appreciable amount of change. When the skin is wrinkled and granulated, water must first be injected into the upper joint of the finger so that the creases and granulations are smoothed out. For this purpose, a 10-ml hypodermic syringe with a fine needle is used. The needle is inserted approximately at the center of the inside of the center joint and is brought close to the bone in the upper joint, after which water is injected until the skin appears hard and tense. The point must not be allowed to come too near the skin since the pressure might be sufficient to break the skin, and the needle should not be put in the outer joint or too near it since in such a case the return path would be so short that the water would run out again. After the needle has been removed, the print is taken in the usual way. In earlier technical literature, an injection of glycerin, paraffin, or melted tallow was recommended. There is, however, no doubt that a properly performed injection with water gives better results and is easier to carry out.

In the second stage, when the epidermis has loosened, it is easier to take fingerprints. The loose skin (finger stalls) of the tip is pulled or cut off from the fingertips, that from each finger being placed in a labeled test tube filled with water. The finger stalls should not be put in an envelope or other paper wrapping since after time they will dry up and stick to the paper. When they have been removed this way, the finger stalls may be sent to the fingerprint unit for examination.

The best procedure is to place the skin from each finger separately between two glass plates where they are easier to handle and photograph. To do this, the fingerprint pattern is cut out of the finger stalls. Since the cut-out pieces of skin are then convex, they easily split when flattened between the glass. This splitting is unavoidable, and it is necessary to make cuts in the edges so that the splits do not occur in parts of the fingerprint pattern that are needed for the purpose of classification. When placing them between the glass plates, a small piece of paper or card, carrying the name of the finger, is placed near the top of the sample to indicate that the print is being viewed from the correct side. There is not much risk of any such piece of skin being the wrong side since the inside is lighter, smoother, and more glossy than the outside. If, however, in a particular case there should be some doubt as to which is the inside, this can be determined by taking out the piece of skin and seeing which side is concave. The glass plates are bound together with tape. The fingerprint patterns should be photographed by transmitted light, and the lines will show up very distinctly.

Prints may also be taken with the aid of printing ink. After careful cleaning and drying, the pattern area is coated with printing ink in the usual way and pressed against a piece of paper. The method is difficult to carry out since the skin is generally so fragile that the print can be destroyed by the slightest carelessness. Occasionally, the finger stalls are so strong that they can be picked up on a finger, and the print can be taken as it would be from a living person. But it is only in rare cases that the skin on all 10 digits is in such good condition that this method can be adopted.

It often happens that large portions of the epidermis become loose, but small parts remain so firmly attached that the finger stalls cannot be removed whole. Sometimes cautious scraping of the attached tissues will loosen the tips in a comparatively whole condition. If this is impossible, the part of the underlying tissues to which the finger stalls are attached is cut off, and the whole is mounted on a piece of plasticine. The fingerprint can be then taken with printing ink or photographed.

It is far more difficult to take a fingerprint from a dead person when the epidermis of the fingers has become loose and fallen away and cannot be found. This occurs generally with bodies that have been in water for a long time. Sometimes it is possible to make out the fingerprint pattern in the remaining underskin. Only rarely is it possible to take these fingerprints with printing ink, owing to the ridges in the pattern being so low. The only possible method is to photograph the pattern. In general, however, it can be assumed that the fingerprint pattern will have disappeared entirely, owing to the loosening of the skin.

It is difficult to take a palm print from a dead body, even in a case where the body has undergone little or no change. There is hardly any hope of taking a complete palm print and it is, therefore, necessary to take portions of the print on small pieces of paper or card. To simplify the identification of these prints, each piece of paper should have outlined on it a hand on which the part corresponding to the palm print is marked in.

In taking fingerprints and palm prints from bodies, printing ink is the best medium since the impressions can be mounted directly on a fingerprint card or other suitable form. These forms can later be filed with other cards. However, an alternate method may be used that employs black fingerprint powder. In some cases the results of the latter method may be superior to those using printing ink.

The finger or palm is lightly coated with the black powder, using a brush. The impression is then obtained by lifting with transparent fingerprint tape. The pieces of tape are then mounted directly on a fingerprint card or on paper that is cut up into squares for attachment to the card. In the case of palms, pieces of tape should be laid lengthwise over the whole palm area and removed one at a time. The pieces are then mounted on a card or paper. This method is somewhat more difficult than the inking method, but it is superior in that a full impression is obtained. A condition for successful lifting is that two persons are available: one to hold the hand and one to manipulate the tape.

## Photographing

In photographing an unknown body, a full-face and a right-profile face are always taken. If necessary, further pictures should be taken, including a whole view, left profile—especially with a view to identification from the ears—and detail pictures of scars, injuries, teeth, tattooings, clothes, and so on. It is good practice to ensure that an unknown body is not buried before it is photographed. It is always important to photograph the body early, before putrefaction sets in and swells or discolors the features. With regard to a body that has undergone some degree of change, although it may be considered that a photograph of the face will be quite meaningless, it should still be taken. It should also be remembered that the individual may be identified after burial and that the relatives may ask to see the photograph of the face. In taking a full-face picture, the body should be laid on its back with the face turned upward. When the body is in a mortuary a wooden rack or other structure is generally under the head. This should be removed in the photograph. The lower jaw may sometimes show a tendency to drop and the mouth to open, so that it is best to prop up the jaw with a peg or other object that will not be too conspicuous in the photograph. The camera is placed vertically above the face. The background should be chosen so that the outer contour of the head is well defined against it. Often the simplest way is to spread a towel under the head. When profile portraits are taken, the body should be raised so that the camera can be placed at the side of the head. A suitable background is also required for this exposure so that the profile shows up distinctly. The head should not be turned to one side to make it easier to photograph, as this might cause a considerable alteration in appearance owing to the position of the camera.

In photographing whole-face pictures, the camera is placed high above the body. If this is not possible because of a low roof, then the body can be turned somewhat to one side, but the procedure must be previously thought out in view of the possibility of any blood running down or other conditions of the body being altered. Under no circumstances should the body be tied or suspended in a leaning position. In photographing scars, injuries, tattooings, and details of clothing, a measuring tape or ruler should always be placed on or by the side of the object.

Photographs are best taken using color film. In certain instances, however, where tattoos or other marks present on the body are poorly contrasted, appropriate filters or black and white photography may be helpful (Fig. 6.19).

Even at such an early stage when the changes in the body are limited to rigidity and livid stains, it may be difficult to distinguish scars, strawberry marks, and birthmarks from livid stains, discolorations of the skin, and wrinkles. The further the deterioration has proceeded, the greater the difficulties. Blue tattooing is sometimes barely perceptible since the skin becomes dark-colored and blistery. Under such conditions, the police officer must not rely on personal judgment, but must consult the pathologist. Any special characteristics are described in essentially the same way as for living persons, except in one respect. In the case of a description of a living person with a large number of tattooings,[5] only those that are characteristic or unusual (names, dates,

---

[5] Asian gang members often have elaborate tattooing, frequently depicting dragons and other animals. Such tattooing on an oriental decedent may be suggestive of gang membership.

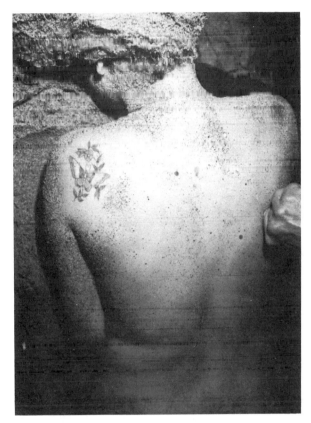

FIGURE 6.19. The body of a nude female was found on a beach in Los Angeles County. A butterfly was tattooed on the left shoulder. (*Los Angeles County Sheriff's Department.*)

emblems, etc.) are described. With unknown bodies, however, all tattooings should be described, including those of a very common type (Fig. 6.20). It is of great importance that all tattooings and other special characteristics be described accurately in a recognized manner with respect to kind, form, size, and position.

Ultraviolet photography and ultraviolet video imaging techniques are useful methods for studying and recording injuries on human skin, such as bite marks and ligature marks, including fluorescent UV photography, reflective long-wavelength UV photography, and short-wavelength UV photography (Fig. 6.21). Taking UV photographs is a cumbersome procedure in that it is difficult to focus UV images because they cannot be seen. A new procedure involves using an ultraviolet

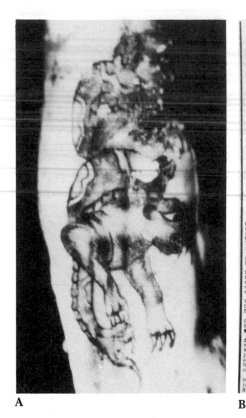

A        B

FIGURE **6.20.** Using reflected infrared photography, a photograph of a tattoo (A) was made from a badly decomposed body. The tattoo depicts a black panther encircled by a snake. A police artist copied the tattoo and it was published in newspapers (B). (*State Forensic Science Laboratory, Melbourne, Australia.*)

image intensifier. One unit marketed by Hamamatsu has the appearance of an infrared "night scope" and can be used coupled to a camera or a video unit or by viewing through an eye-piece in the unit. It allows for quick and easy viewing of trauma and even some latent fingerprints on surfaces, when using ultraviolet lighting.

Many people are X-rayed for the purpose of diagnosing an ailment or for detecting tooth decay. These films are often retained in medical files for many years. Before an unknown body is autopsied or buried, dental and body X-rays should be taken. Not only will they provide a means for definite identification, but they might also provide information as to the cause of death.

## Marks of Trades or Occupations

Marks of trades are nowadays less common than in the past, owing to the mechanization of work and the use of modern machine tools. However, marks that are the result of a characteristic manner of working are still found in certain trades.

Clerk, draftsman: hardening of the last joint of the right middle finger at the point where the pen rests when writing or drawing; a draftsman also has a hardening on the part of the ball of the right little finger that lies nearest the wrist.

Baker: hardening on thumb and index fingers of both hands, resulting from handling the edges of hot pans and plates.

Engraver, jeweler: wear of nail of right thumb.

Tailor, dressmaker: marks and scars of needle punctures in the tip of left index finger.

Shoemaker, upholsterer: round hollows in front teeth from biting the thread; shoemakers also show wear on left thumbnail.

FIGURE 6.21. Ultraviolet photography is useful in visualizing ligature marks as depicted in this case, one of the Hillside Strangler murders in Los Angeles. (*Los Angeles County Sheriff's Department.*)

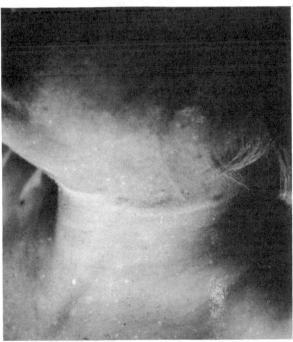

*Glazier:* hardening between middle and index fingers, arising from handle of diamond being held between these fingers.

*Dyer, photographer, chemist:* nails dry, brittle, and often discolored.

*Butcher:* callouses and hardening on inner joints of fingers and on neighboring parts of palm of the hand that holds knives.

*Bricklayer, stonemason:* hardening of right hand from grip around trowel or hammer; skin of left hand worn very thin from holding bricks or stone.

*Carpenter, joiner:* hardening in ball of thumb of right hand from grip on plane; unusual number of injuries and scars on left index finger.

*Painter:* callouses and hardening between right index and middle fingers from grip on handle of brush.

If evidence of repeat operations is observed, this should be noted, sketched, and photographed. It may take imagination, ingenuity, and some practical research to connect these callouses to an occupation, hobby, or sport.

## Making a Description

Making a satisfactory description of a dead body often takes a lot of time and is difficult, especially if the body has begun to decompose. In compiling descriptions, it is, therefore, best to avoid using too definite expressions when describing details for which there is some doubt as to the most suitable choice of words. In case of difficulty, the pathologist should be consulted. The body may conveniently be described in the following order: estimated age, length, build, shape of face, neck, hair, beard or mustache, forehead, eyes, eyebrows, nose, base of nose, mouth, teeth, chin, ears, hands, feet, and special characteristics.

If the body has undergone a certain amount of change it is often nearly impossible to decide the age, and even a trained pathologist will often avoid making any definite statement. In many cases, the age can be determined only by postmortem examination.

The length of the body is measured with the body stretched out on its back, the measurement being taken from heel to crown of head. It is often difficult to describe the build. In the case of a swollen body taken out of water, there is often a temptation to write "powerful" or "heavyset," which may be quite wrong. The form and profile of the face can usually be described quite satisfactorily, but the fullness of the face cannot be specified in the case of a body that has undergone change. The color of the hair also may change some time after death. When a body has lain in dry earth or in a dry place, the hair often becomes reddish; however, in one taken from water, hair color does not as a rule undergo any appreciable change.

In describing the hair, it should be noted whether it has been well cared for, how it is parted, and the like. Samples of hair should be taken from bodies that cannot be identified. There possibly may be a question of comparison with hair found in the house or workplace of a missing person, e.g., on a comb or brush. In describing facial hair, one is often tempted to say "unshaven," which may be quite wrong since stubble on the face often arises from the hair roots, which lying originally at an angle to the skin, straighten up after death because of drying and shrinking of the skin. The story that hair and beard grow after death is quite erroneous.

It is often difficult to judge correctly the color of the eyes of a dead person since at an early stage the eyes undergo considerable alteration. Special attention should be given to the presence of artificial eyes. The forehead is not liable to change much with respect to form. It is difficult to judge the form and size of the nose since it swells up considerably. On a body that has not undergone any considerable amount of change, the profile of the nose can still have altered considerably owing to the tissues in the tip of the nose having shrunk. For this reason, a nose that in life was concave may become straight after death, and a straight one may become convex. It is usually impossible to decide the size of the mouth since the lips undergo great change even at a very early stage.

The ears may undergo minor changes with respect to size and form, but even in cases where the body has become completely unrecognizable, the ears may be found relatively normal. Therefore, it is important that both ears should be photographed so that a comparison with a photograph of a missing person can be made at some future date.

In the case of hands, the care taken of the nails should be described. If necessary, dirt under the nails should be kept since this sometimes gives information about the trade or occupation. When an unknown body is found without shoes, the foot should be measured for probable shoe size. The pathologist concerned should be reminded to take a blood sample from the body. There may possibly be a question of a comparison with, for example, bloodstained clothing found in the home of a missing person, or a statement of the individual's blood group may be available. Although an individual cannot be identified by blood type, this material may be valuable for excluding possible identities. Typing of putrefied blood is difficult and generally unreliable.

## Deceased's Clothing

The visible clothing of the deceased is described first, including accurate indications of the type of material, quality, color, buttons, any damage and, if possible, how the damage is thought to have occurred, stains of dust and dirt, and so forth. A preliminary examination is made of the pockets and other areas of the clothing, e.g., between the clothing and the lining where objects may be found that can be a guide for identification. Garments should be taken off one by one, placed on clean paper, and allowed to air dry at room temperature. If at all possible the clothing should not be removed by cutting or tearing, but removed carefully in the normal manner. The person undressing the corpse should remember that microscopic trace evidence may be present on the clothing and should, therefore, exercise appropriate care so as not to lose this useful evidence. If the clothing must be cut off the body, care must be taken to avoid cutting through areas with bullet holes or knife cuts since these areas will be examined at a later time.

After the garment is removed and air dried, it should be packaged and sent to the crime laboratory for careful examination for debris, trace evidence, and marks of identification such as laundry marks, monograms, manufacturer's markings, and dry cleaning tags.

Shoe size, color, make, and style should be noted. If the size cannot be determined, it is possible to determine the approximate shoe size by the length of the shoe. Repairs, degree of wear, defects, and the like may also be used as a possible means of identification. Shoes should be submitted to the laboratory to be examined for the presence of soil, debris, and other trace evidence that may be helpful in determining identity.

Garments should not be laundered until after they have been carefully examined for trace material and photographed. After these procedures, the garments can be laundered so that clear identification photographs can be made of the clothing and laundry marks can be searched for.

Articles of clothing should be repackaged following examination and retained until after adjudication of the case. Under no circumstance should these or any other items of evidence be destroyed until after all legal proceedings have been completed. This allows the investigator to reexamine the clothing at a later time if new questions arise.

## Laundry Marks and the Like

In searching for laundry marks on clothing, it must be remembered that they may be invisible. Many large laundries now stamp all incoming laundry with a colorless dye that is quite invisible to the unaided eye, but which fluoresces strongly in filtered ultraviolet light. The mark usually comprises both the identification mark of the laundry and the number given to the customer. The identification mark sometimes consists of the first letters of the firm's name. The number of the customer is registered with the laundry. The marks are almost indelible and remain even after many washings. When the garment is marked by the laundry, a search is first made for old laundry marks that are crossed out with invisible ink before the new mark is put on. In this way, a garment may have several laundry marks, which greatly facilitates identification.

It is a common practice in the cleaning and laundry industry to identify garments by a paper tag clipped to the article. Unless this tag is attached in an obscure place, the customer usually removes it before wearing the garment.

A good lead for identification can be obtained from monograms, maker's marks, firm's marks, stamp numbers, sewn-on initials, and markings made with marking ink. In the case of more valuable garments such as fur coats, overcoats, and suits, it is important to look for marks or alterations that careful owners often place on parts turned toward the inside with the idea that the garment may be stolen and that the thief would remove the usual marks. Such identification marks may consist of seams sewn with a different thread, small cuts or pieces cut out of the cloth or lining, threads sewn in, and so on.

## Watchmaker's Marks

If a watch is found on an unknown dead body, it should be examined for any marks or figures that might aid in the identification. Usually the serial number of a watch is stamped inside the case. Certain watchmakers mark watches sold by them with letters or signs that indicate their watchmakers' society, together with a figure that is their membership number. When a sale is made, it may be recommended to the customer to take out insurance on the watch, in which case the purchaser's name and the serial number on the watch are registered by the watchmaker. Some watchmakers mark the date of sale on the inside of the case.

When a watch is taken in for repair, it is usual for the watchmaker to scratch on the inside of the case certain letters or marks and figures that are partly special marks of the individual watchmaker and partly a repair number. The latter is recorded together with the serial number of the watch, name of the owner, and kind of repair. The watchmaker's own mark generally consists of one or more initials, but may also be formed of a monogram, Greek letters, or other characters, shorthand signs, punctuation marks, private marks, lines, figures, or mathematical signs. In the United States, investigative agencies may send descriptions of marks, together with a description of the watch, to the National Watch Mark Identification Bureau, American Watchmakers Institute, 3700 Harrison Avenue, Cincinnati, OH 45211. Any matching marks are communicated to the submitting agency. Unknown marks are circulated in the trade journal.

## Jewelry

Finger rings usually remain on a body even though it has decomposed to a considerable extent, and they can, therefore, be a guide for identification. Inscriptions may often be found inside engagement, wedding, and other commemorative rings, while signet rings may carry initials, insignia, seals, crests, or other distinctive markings. In a number of countries, special rings are worn by graduates of universities, while orders, societies, and associations may use rings as marks of membership.

Although not often used, systems have been reported for the identification of precious gems. These systems are based on macroscopic and microscopic imperfections in any gemstone that are not likely to be found in their entire combination in any similar gem. All jewelry, cheap or expensive, should be photographed.

## Eyeglasses

Eyeglasses discovered on or near a dead body may provide a means of identification. If the name of the optometrist is present on the eyeglass case, it may be possible to determine the victim's name from the doctor's records. Even if the identity of an individual cannot be determined from a prescription, eyeglasses may be useful. Friends or relatives of the victim may be able to identify the eyeglasses as being similar to those worn by the victim.

## Teeth

Information of special value for identification can be obtained from the investigation of the teeth of a dead person because these are often characteristic in many respects. This applies not only to a case in which the appearance of the dead person has not altered to any appreciable extent, but also to greatly decomposed corpses, to badly mutilated victims of airplane accidents, explosions, and catastrophes, and also to burned bodies. The teeth are, in fact, very resistant not only to the normal changes undergone by the body, but also to fire and chemicals.

The examination of the teeth of an unknown dead person for identification is done by the pathologist, assisted if necessary by an expert in dentistry. The police officer in charge of the case will decide, according to its importance, to what degree it is necessary to have detailed information in connection with a particular case. In some cases, there may be an abundance of other information that will not necessitate basing an actual identity on the teeth alone.

When making an examination of the teeth, attention is always directed to the changes or injuries in the face of the dead person that may possibly interfere with the subsequent postmortem examination or identification. If a body is altered considerably, the tissues of the face may be missing or may fall apart if the lower jaw is moved out of its position. In such a case, photographing and examining the body should be done first. If for any reason a police officer has to make an examination of the teeth of a body before the arrival of the pathologist, it should be done in such a way that no marks of the flow of blood or injuries in the face are aggravated or changed, and particularly that the position of any object in the mouth is not changed. If there is any danger of anything of this kind occurring, the examination of the teeth must wait until the pathologist deals with the body.

The first note to make in connection with the teeth is how many are present. A note should be made as to which teeth are missing both in the upper and the lower jaw. This is most easily done by making a sketch of the teeth of each jaw. Special forms, sometimes used for this purpose, greatly facilitate the work. On these sketches or forms are marked both the position and size of any visible damage resulting from decay (caries) and pieces broken away, cracks, missing fillings, jackets and other crowns, bridge work, root fillings, and so on. The material used in crowns, fillings, and the like is also noted. Sometimes entire gold crowns melt when teeth are exposed to high temperatures from fire. This is apparent from the amalgam filling running out and around the mouth. Complete or partial dentures should be kept since the material used in them may possibly be a guide for identification. Dentures may have some identification inscribed or attached to them. It may be the inmate number, service serial number, doctor's identification, or the patient's name. A study of the style of the inscription will give some indication as to the probable source.

Further, all characteristics of the teeth should be noted carefully. The teeth can be very light (white) or dark (brown); the teeth of the upper and/or lower jaw may be directed inward or outward and the teeth may be widely spaced, close together, or wedged in against one another; exceptionally large spaces may be found between the middle front teeth (central incisors); and the central teeth in the upper jaw may be exceptionally powerful (wide), and the front teeth in the upper or lower jaw may have noticeably smooth, uneven, or inclined cutting surfaces.

Attention should also be given to the bite, that is, the relation between the teeth of the upper and lower jaw when they come together. In a normal bite, the lower edge of the front teeth of the upper jaw comes outside the front teeth of the lower jaw, and the outer chewing surfaces of the upper molars bite somewhat outside the corresponding teeth in the lower jaw. This is called normal occlusion. However, it can happen that in the bite the front teeth of the upper jaw come quite appreciably outside the front teeth of the lower jaw or inside them, or that the front and canine teeth in the upper jaw come alternately in front of and behind the corresponding teeth of the lower jaw.

When examining teeth, the assistance of a dentist should be obtained if possible. This is especially needed for root fillings and other work that may be difficult for the untrained individual to discover. A small mirror is a valuable help in the examination.

If dental work is found, there are possibilities of identification through a dentist by whom the patient was treated. Dentists generally keep records of the work on their patients. In an important case, an X-ray examination should be made. Any roots, root fillings, or the like remaining in the jawbones may have a characteristic appearance, and an X-ray photograph may agree exactly with one that a dentist has kept.

If teeth are wholly or partially missing from the body, there is reason to suspect that the individual used a full or partial denture. The latter may be found at the house of a missing person or with relatives, and it can then be fitted in the mouth of the dead person, whereby identity or nonidentity can be proved.

In addition to identification of a victim by means of X-rays of teeth compared with dental records, other useful information can be developed through dental examination. These data are useful in identifying the remains of a decomposed or skeletal body.

Age is one of the items of information that can be determined through dental examination. The ages for eruption of deciduous (baby) teeth and permanent teeth are fairly well established. X-rays of the jaw and examination of the mouth allow the forensic odontologist to make an age determination of the deceased.

Habits or occupation may be deduced through a dental examination. For example, a pipe smoker may have stained and worn surfaces on the teeth, and a tailor may have a groove on the surface of two opposing teeth caused by biting thread. Such changes, like those discussed earlier with regard to skin callouses on hands, may prove useful in certain cases.

The arrangement of teeth in the mouth can be useful for identification. Thus, crooked or "buck" teeth of a deceased may be used as a means of elimination or identification of a particular person. Similarly, disease states, missing teeth, chipped or broken teeth, and the like are all helpful for identification.

## Facial Reconstruction

Occasionally, the police investigator will want to obtain a photograph of the face of a mutilated victim. In instances where parts of the face are missing, it is possible to reconstruct the area with various types of mortuary supply materials and cosmetics to a point where a reasonable likeness of the deceased can be made. The procedure requires a fair amount of skill and workmanship, but is possible in instances where a reconstruction for identification is needed.

## Determination of Sex

For the determination of sex, the skeletal characteristics are as follows:

*Pelvis:* size and form are different for men and women. The preauricular notch and pubic curve are especially significant, and even small fragments can make a determination of sex possible.

*Cranium:* the walls of the cranium are normally thinner in men than in women. The angle of the root of the nose where it comes out from the forehead (frontal nose angle) is more pronounced in a man. The curve of the eyebrows is generally more rounded in a man than in a woman.

*Head of joint of upper arm:* this is generally larger in a man than in a woman. The size of the head of the joint, moreover, shrinks only slightly under the action of fire.

*Breastbone:* both size and form are significant for determination of sex.

*Thighbones and shinbones:* are also important from this point of view.

*Skeleton:* the whole of the female skeleton, with the exception of the pelvis, is in general more lightly constructed than that of a man.

*Teeth:* an important point for the determination of sex, in the case of the remains of a child, is the uninjured crown of the first permanent incisor of the upper jaw. In certain cases, these can show the sex according to whether their width is especially great (boy) or small (girl).

*Organs:* the uterus or the prostate gland may allow the determination of sex. The uterus, however, if exposed to decay, can become very fragile so that great care should be observed.

## Determination of Age

Teeth are especially significant in the determination of age, which is possible even when only one tooth is available; however, it is necessary to allow for a certain percentage of error in this case (according to some authorities, about 15 to 20%). If a number of teeth are found, the reliability of the determination is increased. The determination of age from teeth is based on the changes the teeth undergo with age. These changes are listed below:

1. Wearing down of chewing surfaces (abrasions).
2. Loosening (paradentosis), detected from changes in the attachment of the roots.
3. Formation of secondary dentin inside the pulp cavities (can also be formed as reaction to disease of the teeth).
4. Deposition of cement on and around points of the roots.
5. Degree of transparency of lowest parts of roots (root transparency).
6. Corrosion of root points (root resorption).
7. Closing of root openings—until the teeth are completely formed, the size of the root openings stands in direct relation to the age so that this is of special importance in young individuals.

If the body has been completely burned, the crowns of grown-out teeth break up but the roots often remain whole. Teeth of a child or young person, if they have not come through, do not get broken up. The discovery of such teeth that have not come through or of remains of deciduous teeth thus gives a direct indication of age.

In this connection, it is convenient to touch on the possibility of determining whether different teeth belong together, which may be important when there is any doubt as to whether the remains come from one or more individuals. Such an investigation can often be carried out with good results. It is based on microscopic appearance of the lines in the dentin that are characteristic of individuals, and with the aid of which it is possible to determine whether teeth come from the same individual or not.

The roof of the cranium gives information that is especially valuable for the determination of the age of an individual, the sutures (ossification lines) being extremely significant. With newborn babies and children up to 3 years of age the sutures are straight or slightly curved. After this, they begin to become saw-edged in form, passing over slowly into the forms typical of the adult. With increasing age, the sutures grow together more and more, finally disappearing entirely; those of a woman, however, join up considerably later than those of a man. The appearance and degree of fusion give an opportunity of estimating an age up to 50 years.

If the cranium is exposed to great heat, the sutures split up, but if they have grown together completely, the cracks resulting from the heat may take a new path. To some extent, this circumstance makes possible an estimation of age even from small portions of the roof of a cranium.

The thickness of the roof of the cranium as well as the character of the outside and inside parts of the walls and the intermediate parts give information that may be used as a guide for the determination of the age of an individual.

The form of the wedge bone part of the inner ear differs in children and adults. This part is already formed at the fifth month after conception.

The epiphyses at the ends of the long bones fuse with the diaphyses at rather fixed stages in the development of the skeleton. This occurs when the increase in length of the particular limb is complete. Therefore, it is important for the determination of age to note whether this calcification has occurred and to what extent.

### Length of Body

It is possible to determine the approximate body length of an individual from the skeleton or a part of it, assuming that some of the longer bones of the limbs (femur, fibula, tibia, humerus, radius, and ulna) are found. The length of some of these is measured, after which the body length is calculated with the aid of formulae and tables developed by anthropologists. The values given by the tables represent the length of the skeleton and should be increased by an inch or so to allow for other tissues and to give an approximately correct value for body height.

### Hair Color

The hair is very resistant to change provided that it is not exposed to fire, but it may often be difficult to find at the scene of a discovery when the body has changed greatly. Generally, it is only the hair of the head—more rarely hair from other parts of the body—that can be used as a basis for estimating hair color as required for a description. Great caution should, however, be exercised. There may be surprising changes in the color of hair after even a comparatively short time, depending on the character of the soil and other such factors.

*Blood Type*

Blood types are potential means of identification of both living and deceased subjects. Information obtained from blood grouping cannot conclusively identify an individual in the same way that a fingerprint can. However, it can certainly eliminate a person and can even add to other, less conclusive types of identity information to assist in forming an opinion about identity.

Blood taken from a deceased person is subject to decomposition and deterioration. The specimen of blood used for typing should be taken from the heart or major blood vessel rather than from the body cavity. Blood samples should be preserved in EDTA (ethylenediamine tetraacetic acid) preservative and not in sodium fluoride, which is a preservative used for toxicology testing.

Blood from deceased persons must be compared with hospital or military records. Red Cross records may also be sought. The investigator should be aware of possible errors in both hospital and military blood-typing records and not base the conclusion of identity solely on these documents.

Only the ABO and Rh blood grouping systems are available in hospital and military records for use in identity determination. An additional series of blood groups (which are discussed under forensic serology in Chapter 8) are not of use for identification purposes. If the victim received a transfusion prior to death, that information should be made known to the serologist performing the blood typing.

## Identification in Catastrophes

In occurrences of a catastrophic nature in which a number of people are killed, such as rail and airplane accidents, big fires and explosions, the collapse of a building, and accidents at sea, the work of identification must be organized as quickly as possible and carried out in such a way that there is no danger of faulty identification of the bodies. It is not only for sentimental considerations that accurate identification is essential; the legal requirements for proof of death must be satisfied in the case of each victim. A great deal more than mere satisfaction at having made a correct identification is involved. Questions of pension rights, the payment of insurance, and so forth are some of the ancillary matters that depend on a correct analysis.

It is essential to obtain as quickly as possible a list showing all persons who may have been killed. In some commercial transportation accidents, this can be obtained from the passenger list (Fig. 6.22). When the information is available, the task of identification is easy, so long as the victims are not badly mutilated or burned or the bodies have not undergone any considerable amount of decomposition.

The work of identification should preferably be done by a special group, which may consist of a pathologist, a dentist, and two police officers with experience in the identification of dead bodies. The group also needs assistants, varying in number for each particular case. The identification group should be present when the first measures of rescue and clearance are started at the scene of the catastrophe, and as bodies are found they should take charge of them. If the group cannot be organized or does not reach the scene in time, a suitable police officer should be detailed to take the first steps in securing the bodies.

A preliminary sketch should be made of the site, and the scene as a whole should be photographed, the position of the camera and direction of the different exposures being marked on a sketch. The record is made during the course of the work. When the body of a victim is found, it is given a number that may be written on a piece of card tied to the body. Any objects found beside the body that may be supposed to be personal belongings are collected in a bag that is given a number. When possible, each victim and object should be provided with a label giving more detailed information, e.g., who found it, the time of discovery, and a statement of the nature of the location, preferably in the form of a simple sketch. The numbers are entered in the record in succession and in such a way that they can easily be referred to, and the position of each object in relation to a body is recorded. Photographing should be done thoroughly. The photographing and sketching must be considered rather as a precaution that may possibly be of use in the work of identification. The numbered places of discovery are also marked on the sketches. If parts of bodies are found, they are given new numbers and placed in strong bags. If a pathologist present confirms that a part belongs to a particular body, then the two are placed together, but this must be done only on the authority of a pathologist. As victims are found and the proper measures are taken, the bodies are wrapped in sheets or cloths so that loose objects cannot fall out and get lost. The bodies are then taken to a suitable place where the work of identification is to be done.

When the scene of a catastrophe is so large that the bodies can neither be collected by the identification group alone nor protected by police personnel working under the group, then the victims must first be brought to the identification point by suitable means. There each body is labeled with a number and an accurate statement of the position where it was discovered, time of handing over, and name of person who found and transported it. If possible, the stretcher bearers who collect the bodies should be given instructions as to their activities so as to avoid any mistakes.

Under all conditions, the scene of the catastrophe should be cordoned off as quickly as possible, and the guards should see that unattached persons do not take part in the rescue work. Stretcher bearer patrols

A

B

**FIGURE 6.22.** Mass disaster created special identification problems. A commercial airline crashed in Los Angeles. (A) An aerial photograph depicts the extent of the disaster. (B) and (C) show some of the scene at ground level and the extent

C

D

of manpower and equipment needed, as (D) the remains of one of the victims await removal to a temporary morgue where various specialists will try to make an identification. (*Los Angeles County Sheriff's Department.*)

should be under the command of a specially selected supervisor, preferably a police officer. Relatives of persons who are thought to have been killed should not be allowed to take part in this work because there is a risk that they may pick an unidentified body they think they can recognize, but which is possibly an entirely different individual. The presence of the relatives at or near the scene is, however, desirable, since they possibly can give information that can help in the rescue or identification.

When the scene has been cleared or thoroughly searched, all bodies and remains have been found, and all objects that can be assumed to belong to victims have been collected, the work of identification can be started. The record made during the first stage should be written up in a clean copy and the photographs arranged in order as quickly as possible so that they will be available for reference together with the sketches.

During the time taken for the rescue and clearing up, and before the actual identification is started, the police authorities concerned should obtain statements of the number of persons involved listing their names, occupations, and dates of birth. If it is to be anticipated that the identification will offer great difficulties, then the list of names must be supplemented by statements that can assist the identification. These are obtained from the relatives of the deceased or from persons who may be supposed to know them sufficiently well. In an especially difficult case, the following information should be obtained:

1. Description, preferably in the form normally used by the police.
2. Any illnesses, operations, or bone fractures (possibly X-ray photographs).
3. Fingerprints, if they have been taken for any reason.
4. Photographs (simple amateur pictures are better than retouched studio portraits).
5. Dental history or extract from it.
6. Description of garments and shoes (if possible, samples of cloth, statement of where bought, make, size, markings, repairs, etc.).
7. Description of personal belongings that might be expected to be in the deceased's clothes, together with rings, jewelry, and watch—in this connection, a statement may also be needed about what would have been near the deceased, e.g., briefcase, handbag, or traveling case.

Thus, when the work of identification is commenced, all the bodies, portions of bodies, and objects have been numbered in sequence. This numbering is preliminary and should be employed only as an aid to identification.

In the identification, a start is made with the least injured bodies or with those that offer the best possibilities of quick and satisfactory identification. One of the police officers in the identification group keeps the record. The bodies are renumbered in the order in which they are examined. In the work of identification, the bodies should lie on a suitable table or bench. All loose objects in or on the clothing or on the body are recorded and then placed in a bag. If any identifying documents are found on a body, such as a pass, visiting card, identification card, or other similar items, and this agrees with statements obtained regarding a certain person who is supposed to have been killed, then the identification may be considered complete. There have been cases where identifying documents have been found on a body belonging to another person who was killed at the same time, owing to the bodies having been thrown against one another so that the documents were transferred from the owner to another person. If statements regarding the dead person have been obtained, they must be compared with the body to confirm the identification. The first body examined is given the number 1, after which numbers are given to the bodies in succession as the corresponding measures of identification are taken. The bags containing the belongings are given the same numbers as the bodies to which they belong, and clothes are bundled together and given corresponding numbers. Regarding injuries and assumed cause of death, the report is made in the usual manner. The pathologist decides whether these statements should be made in a separate report or included in the report of the identification.

As the bodies are identified, they are put to one side. Clothes and belongings are placed at the sides of the bodies. It is safest not to allow any body to be taken away before all the others have been identified so that any mistake can be rectified in time. When the deceased are placed in coffins, the work should be supervised and controlled by at least two members of the identification group. The coffins are marked externally with number and name.

The work of identification then proceeds to the more difficult cases, and the identification group must rely more on and refer to the statements that have been obtained. In due course, it can become easier to work on the principle of elimination. However, this method cannot be employed except in cases where there is absolutely reliable information of the number of victims and their names, and the statements obtained are detailed and reliable. For the most difficult cases, the group must work according to the method described in the preceding section of this chapter. It is especially important that the dentist make a complete report of the teeth of each body.

Where there is a large number of victims, the police or other authorities should not allow the body of any victim to be removed before the identification group has been organized and has arrived at the scene. Even if at an early stage a particular body can be identified with absolute certainty, its removal should not be permitted. It is the identification group that has the responsibility of identifying all the victims. If this group were to deal only with the difficult cases, then it would naturally work under the suspicion that the bodies released might have been wrongly identified, and this can destroy the possibility of certain identification of the more difficult cases.

Establishing identity is one of the most important uses of physical evidence. The investigator should make maximum utilization of experts in various fields, such as fingerprints, handwriting, dentistry, anthropology, and so on, to assist in the identification of a subject.

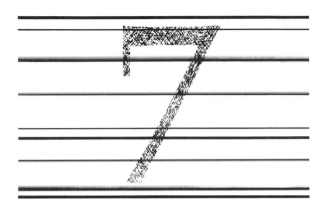

# TRACE EVIDENCE
# AND
# MISCELLANEOUS
# MATERIAL

On Saturday, September 19, 1987, the body of an 18-year-old was found on the side of a road near Porvoo (a small city about 50 km northeast of Helsinki, Finland).[1]

The deceased was completely naked from the waist down and the upper part of her body was clothed normally. The victim's jeans, stockings, and underwear were bundled on her chest. The technical research team took as samples the clothing of the deceased, fingernail scrapings, head hair and pubic hair combings, and known hair standards. Fiber evidence was found in the victim's hair (Fig. 7.1).

The autopsy determined that the cause of death was strangulation and that the victim had been raped. Semen was found in vaginal and rectal samples taken during the autopsy, and the victim's blood group was determined to be type A. The hope of solving the case centered on the fiber evidence, and an initial hypothesis was made that the fibers must have had something to do with the crime.

Eleven brown uniform and multicolor acrylic fibers were found in the combed hair samples. Similar fibers were searched from tape-lifted samples taken from the clothes of the victim. About 200 fibers were found in the clothes. With the help of reference samples, it was deduced

A

[1] This case was submitted by Kristine Jousimaa, National Bureau of Investigation, Crime Laboratory, Helsinki, Finland.

B

C

FIGURE **7.1.** (A) The roadside near Porvoo where the body was discovered. (B) The body was discovered partially clothed. (C) A closeup of the victim.

that these fibers most probably originated from the seat cover of a car. The police were advised that the laboratory was especially interested in brown automobile seat covers made from a pile-type material. Police were asked to give special attention to red textiles while searching cars.

From the samples combed from the head and pubic hair, two- and three-thick viscose fibers were found respectively which were unusual in their color and dying. Twenty-eight similar fibers were found in the victim's clothes. In the combed samples an orange-red woolen fiber was found which was about 3 cm long. Thirteen similar fibers were found in the clothes.

Because of the number of red-colored fibers found, it was possible to think of primary transfer. Because neither of the fiber types belonged to typical cloth textile types, it was assumed that the origin of the fibers must have been a textile other than clothes worn by the subject.

The technical research team examined 12 cars during a period of 2 months. The possible seat covers were collected, hairs and fibers were picked, the seats were taped, and fingerprints of the victim were searched for. The fiber samples taken from the victim did not match the samples taken from these cars. Clothes of the victim were white and light blue and made mainly of cotton, therefore it was pointless even to try to collect these types of fibers.

The thirteenth car to be examined belonged to a person who had been charged with rape 9 years earlier but released because of insufficient evidence (Fig. 7.2). The suspect was also a type A secretor. The seat cover material of his car matched the acrylic fibers from the hair and clothes of the victim. In addition, the samples taped from the seat covers contained similar red-colored viscose and woolen fibers found in the samples taken from the victim.

Thirty-nine samples were taken from the interior furnishing textiles of the suspect's residence and from his clothes. The red viscose fibers proved to be the same as the cloth fibers of the pillowcase found on the sofa in the living room of the suspect's residence. The red woolen fibers were the same as fibers from a blanket also found on the sofa.

The fiber research was continued by comparing the samples taken from the victim's hair, pubic hair, fingernail scrapings, and clothes, with the samples taken from the furnishing textile materials from the suspect's residence and his clothes.

Thirteen dark-blue cotton fibers were found in the victim's hair, and one of the same type in her fingernail scrapings. These fibers could not be differentiated from the fibers taken from the suspect's blue trousers.

In the clothes of the victim, three thick, yellow-brownish V-shaped viscose fibers were found which were cut in the head. Their color, quality, thickness, shape, and size were the same as plush fibers found on a velvet cover of the sofa in the suspect's residence (Fig. 7.3).

FIGURE 7.2. (A) The police eventually located the suspect's car, partly because of leads the laboratory was able to provide them about the seat coverings.

The sixth fiber similarity between the samples taken from the victim and samples taken from the suspect's residence was seen in pink acrylic fibers, of which three were found in the victim's clothes and were similar to the fibers of a sweater in the suspect's residence.

All of the different types of fibers were found in the suspect's car seat cover and his clothing. During the investigation, it was concluded that the victim had not been to the suspect's residence but that the suspect's untidy habits had transferred the fibers from his residence to his car, which was a secondary transfer.

None of these fibers were found at the victim's residence, in her clothes, or at her mother's home.

The fiber research was done using polarizing light microscopy, fluorescence microscopy, and microspectrophotometry. FTIR spectroscopy was used to investigate the brown acrylic fibers.

The accused did not confess to the crime but admitted that he alone used his car. He was convicted and sentenced to 10 years on the basis of evidence produced by the fiber investigation.

*Trace evidence* is a generic term for small, often microscopic material. Such evidence may easily be overlooked in crime scene investigations unless proper care is exercised in the search. The variety of trace evidence is almost endless. The purpose of this chapter is to examine some of the more common types of trace materials frequently encoun-

A

B

FIGURE 7.3. (A) A search of the suspect's home yielded other fibers similar to those found on the victim. (B) Fibers from the fabric on the couch and woolen blanket on the sofa proved important evidence in the criminal prosecution.

tcrcd in criminal investigations and to discuss concepts of collection, preservation, identification, and use of these materials.

When an individual comes into contact with a person or location, certain small, seemingly insignificant changes occur. Small items such as fibers, hairs, and assorted microscopic debris may be left by the person or picked up by that person by contact with the environment or another individual. In short, it is not possible to come in contact with an environment without changing it in some small way, whether by adding to it or taking something away. This concept of change is the so-called *Locard Exchange Principle* and is the basis for a study of trace evidence.

The importance of exchange evidence is that it links suspects to victims or locations. It is physical evidence of contact and, although microscopic, this evidence can become a significant part of an investigation.

## Sources of Trace Evidence

### Clothing

Clothing is an excellent source of trace evidence. Microscopic and macroscopic substances may cling to the clothing by static electricity or become caught in the fabric. Useful evidence is most likely to be found if the clothes are collected from the suspect or victim as soon after the crime as possible. Small items of evidence no bigger than a fiber may easily become dislodged from the clothing and lost.

After a suspect is apprehended, the subject's clothes should be cursorily inspected for obvious physical evidence connected with the crime. If evidence is observed, its location and description should be noted.

If possible, the suspect should be made to undress while standing on clean wrapping paper. The paper will catch any trace evidence that might fall from the clothing. The clothing should then be collected, tagged, or marked for chain of evidence purposes and packaged in paper bags. Plastic bags should not be used for packaging clothing because the clothes may mildew.

Care should be taken when placing the garments into paper bags. The clothes should not be shaken so as not to loosen or dislodge trace evidence. If the clothes are wet or bloodstained, they should first be allowed to air dry prior to packaging.

It is especially important to keep the suspect's clothing away from any sources of trace evidence located at the scene. If known samples from the scene have been collected as exemplars, they should never be packaged with the clothing.

*Case*

Police were called to the scene of a warehouse burglary. The suspects gained entrance by chopping a hole through the roof. Officers at the scene collected samples of roofing tar, wood, and plaster to be used as exemplars for any trace evidence that might be found on the suspects. The suspects were subsequently arrested a short distance from the scene of the crime. They were taken to the police station and their clothes were examined. Some building materials and tar-like material adhering to their pants in the knee area were noted. The clothes were packaged in paper bags along with known debris specimens collected from the crime scene.

When the evidence arrived at the crime laboratory and was opened, it was discovered that the known material had been thrown into the paper bag along with the clothes. Although building material was found on the pant legs of the suspects' clothing, it was not possible to determine whether the debris came from the crime scene or the exemplars submitted in the paper bag.

Similarly, a subject should not be brought to the crime scene while clothed in the same garments worn during the crime. This will stop the argument that any trace evidence found on the clothes was from the visit to the scene while in the custody of the police.

Once clothing has been collected and packaged in paper bags, it should be submitted to the crime laboratory for careful examination. Although some police agencies may have equipment to vacuum the garments and send the sweepings to the laboratory, it is preferable to allow the laboratory to conduct the search. It is in instances where extremely small items of evidence such as a single hair or fiber might be lost that evidence should be carefully packaged in a test tube, pillbox, or other appropriate container. Naturally, the location of this evidence should be noted and the items appropriately marked for identification.

Clothes from murder and assault victims pose other problems for consideration. As on a suspect's clothing, trace evidence may be present on a victim's clothes. These garments, however, may have been removed by other than law enforcement personnel who usually are not knowledgeable about proper collection and preservation of evidence. Problems invariably arise when clothing is removed during life-threatening emergencies by paramedics or hospital personnel. It is not uncommon for clothing to be cut off the victim with the aim of initiating emergency procedures. Often this results in cutting through bullet holes, tears caused by stabbing, and the like. Wet, bloodstained garments are often rolled up and packaged in a large plastic bag and tightly sealed.

In these instances of improper evidence handling by emergency medical personnel, police agencies can do little more than attempt to educate those groups and hope that the potential value of the evidence was not too greatly diminished. Crime laboratory personnel should be advised that the victim's clothing was cut off so that they can effectively interpret the information in their attempt to reconstruct the crime.

Clothing on deceased victims requires still other considerations. Before the victim is undressed, the body should be carefully examined for trace evidence by the investigator, criminalist, and/or pathologist. The clothing should be carefully removed and placed onto clean wrapping paper. In most instances of violent death, the clothes will be wet from blood. The garments should be air dried prior to packaging.

## Footwear

Shoes and other footwear are valuable items of evidence. There may be dust, soil, debris, vegetation, bloodstains, and the like on them. In addition, shoes and other footwear may yield useful shoe impression evidence (Fig. 7.4).

Shoes should be individually packaged to avoid cross-contamination. Particular care must be taken when packaging footwear evidence containing clumps of dried soil. Careful examination of the soil might lead to the determination of the path a suspect took. This possibility would be greatly lessened if the clumps of soil became dislodged and pulverized in transit to the laboratory.

## Evidence from the Body

Useful trace evidence may be discovered by a careful examination of the suspect's and/or victim's body. Injuries caused by a struggle between victim and suspect may be noted. Microscopic particles of gunshot residue are often present on the hands of a shooter following discharge of a firearm. Hair is sometimes found on the victim's body in rape cases. Bloodstains on a victim's or suspect's body are not uncommon in assault and murder cases. A close examination of the head, ears, fingernail scrappings, and hands may yield traces of debris from a burglary, assault, or other crime where there was contact between the subject and another person or the crime scene.

## Trace Metal Detection

The trace metal detection test (TMDT) has been in use with mixed results. The test involves the use of a 1 to 2% solution of a chemical, 8-hydroxyquinoline, which is prepared in isopropanol. The solution is sprayed on the subject's hands and observed under ultraviolet light. The

A

B

FIGURE 7.4
(A) Shoes seized from
a breaking-and-
entering suspect. (B) A
close-up of the crepe
sole of the left shoe
showing a piece of
glass from the crime
scene embedded in the
tear. (*Royal Canadian
Mounted Police,
Forensic Laboratory
Services.*)

presence of dark areas indicates the location of metal. Different metals give somewhat different colors.

The TMDT is usually used to test whether a subject has recently held a metal object such as a weapon. In the case of a handgun, it is sometimes possible to see the location of the trigger on the index finger and the location of the strap, the metal frame that touches the palm.

The problem with the test is that results are not always consistent or predictable. Since we live in a high technological society and come into contact with metal objects every day, there will always be present some amount of background trace metal on a suspect's hands. In addition, experiments with the method have shown that holding a handgun with a metal frame and test firing it does not always produce a positive trace metal result. Apparently, the amount of perspiration on an individual's hands will significantly change the results of the test. Moreover, if a suspect is in an environment where there is metal, the suspect may grasp an object, which will result in a positive test. Washing or any kind of mechanical motion of the hands naturally lowers the likelihood of a positive test result.

If the investigator's purpose in contemplating use of the TMDT is to determine whether a suspect has recently fired a weapon, he or she might consider the other available scientific test procedures that do not result in as much ambiguity. Gunshot residue (GSR) analysis is such a procedure.

## *Other Objects as Sources of Trace Evidence*

Trace evidence may be present on tools and weapons as well as other objects. Where possible, the items should be carefully wrapped to protect the material on them. This may be done best by placing a paper bag secured by cellophane tape over smaller objects.

If the instrument bears larger particles that may be lost, the particles should be carefully removed and placed in appropriately labeled containers.

Tools used in burglaries may contain traces of building material, metal shavings, paint, and so forth (Figs. 7.5 and 7.6). These items may be used to establish a connection between the tool and the location. Similarly, a weapon such as a knife may have present hairs or fibers that may prove to be useful evidence.

Larger items may be fruitful sources of trace evidence. A vehicle from a hit-and-run accident is such an example. Naturally, objects of this size cannot routinely be brought to the laboratory. However, a careful examination in the field can turn up hairs, fibers, skin, blood, and the like.

*Microscopic evidence* presents more a challenge than a problem to modern crime laboratories. Use of low-power and high-power light

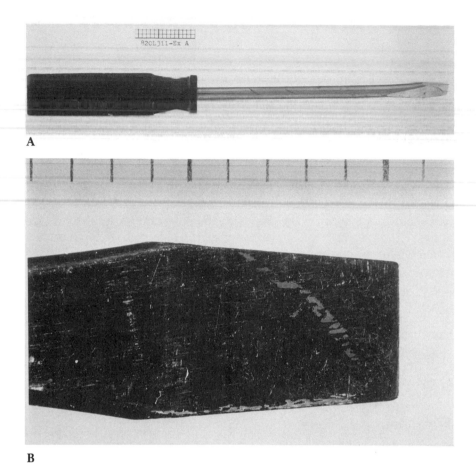

A

B

FIGURE 7.5. (A) A screwdriver seized from a suspect of a burglary case. (B) Close-up of the blade of the screwdriver showing paint transfer. The colors of the paint on this photo are red, green, and white. (*Royal Canadian Mounted Police, Forensic Laboratory Services.*)

microscopes and sophisticated instruments such as scanning electron microscopes and various types of spectrographic tools make commonplace the examination and characterization of minute items of evidence.

A far greater problem than size is *quantity of material*. Particles and material collected from vacuum sweepings and careful searches of evidence can yield thousands of microscopic items to be examined. Only patience and the examiner's expertise can ultimately determine the nature and utility of the collected items.

A

B

FIGURE 7.6. (A) Fragments of the window frame. (B) A close-up of the window frame fragment showing red, green, and white paint layers. Chemical analysis of the paint pigments and binders demonstrated that the paint on the tool was similar and enhanced the value of this associative evidence. (*Royal Canadian Mounted Police, Forensic Laboratory Services.*)

## Collection and Preservation of Trace Evidence

As with all evidence, the investigator or crime scene technician must be concerned with various legal and scientific aspects of the collection and preservation of trace materials. *Legally,* issues of chain of custody and the necessity of a search warrant or court order must always be considered. Case law has generally dictated what is necessary to fulfill the requirements of a chain of custody as well as the need for warrants. When in doubt, the investigator should contact the local district attorney or state attorney general's office for guidance.

*Scientific requirements* depend on the nature of the evidence being collected and the proximity of the laboratory conducting the examinations. It is obvious that if evidence needs to be mailed or sent by a parcel carrier, extraordinary care has to be taken to properly preserve fragile substances.

The question is sometimes asked, "Is it better to remove an item of trace material from a larger item or to leave it alone?" The answer is, "It depends!" If a hair, fiber, loose paint chip, or other very small and easily lost item of evidence can reasonably be expected to become dislodged or lost from the item to which it is attached, that smaller item should be removed. On the other hand, if in the investigator's opinion the smaller substance will not be lost, then it should not be handled. It is preferable to submit the entire item with trace evidence attached to it to the laboratory for an examination. Of course, in those instances in which the item is too large or inconvenient to transport, the trace material should be carefully removed, packaged, and sent to the laboratory for examination.

Small items of evidence should always be double-packaged. *Double-packaging* means that the evidence should be first placed in an appropriate container and secured. The first container should then be inserted into a larger container. Both containers should be appropriately marked to indicate the person performing the packaging, the date and time, the case number, and a very brief description of the evidence. Should the inner container inadvertently open, the outer one will be able to hold the evidence.

As an example of double-packaging, consider a hypothetical case. Suppose an investigator has observed a small fiber on the bumper of a car suspected in a hit-and-run accident. Bringing the car to the laboratory or a location where the vehicle could be raised for a thorough examination of the undercarriage would be the best way to conduct an examination. Assume that this is not possible. The detective still wants to collect the fiber for comparison with the victim's clothing. The fiber should be carefully removed and placed in a test tube, small envelope, pillbox, paper bindle, or any other appropriate package. The inner package would be marked with the detective's initials, date, time, case number, and so on, and would then be placed in a second or outer package. This outer package would also be appropriately marked.

*Control or known samples* are required in all cases. The investigator should make every attempt to collect a sufficient quantity of known material to be submitted with the items in question. The known exemplars must never be packaged with the questioned samples. This separation is necessary to avoid cross-contamination of the unknown by the known specimens.

Almost all classes of trace evidence are capable of being placed in a class or group, i.e., identified. Only in rare cases is trace evidence of the type discussed in this chapter capable of conclusively indicating a specific source or origin. A single fiber cannot be shown to have come from a unique garment, nor can a clump of dirt prove to be from a specific location. Does this mean that trace evidence is of no value? On the contrary! Trace evidence, because of its usefulness as circumstantial evidence, may often be the sole means of corroborating testimonial evidence in a case.

## Examples of Trace Evidence

### Building Materials

Building materials of a wide variety may be encountered in burglary cases. Materials such as stucco, cement, brick, mortar, plaster, plasterboard, wood, paint, and the like all constitute evidence generally considered as building materials. This type of evidence is most likely found on the clothing of burglary suspects, in their cuffs, pockets, and shoes. Another likely location for this type of debris is on tools used to break into a location.

Items suspected of containing building material debris should be carefully packaged, employing the considerations previously discussed and submitted along with appropriate exemplars to the crime laboratory.

The investigator should carefully examine the crime scene to ascertain the nature of the trace evidence. In cases of breaking and entering, the point of entry or any other location indicating damage should be examined and exemplars of building material collected.

If tool marks are present at the point of entry, known samples of building materials should *not* be collected from the area of the tool mark but rather adjacent to the mark. Further, if an area is to be cut out, particular care must be taken *not* to cut through the tool mark.

In cases where one type of building material shows indications of having been tampered with at several locations, it is necessary to collect known specimens of the material in question from each of the damaged areas. This is important since the composition of the building material may vary from location to location.

It must again be stressed that it is of the greatest importance to package each item of evidence separately and individually, to mark the package properly, and to note the location where the specimen was collected.

Tools may be useful sources of building material evidence. Bits of paint, plaster, wood, and sometimes glass may become attached to the tool. In addition to the debris they may contain, tools are useful for tool mark comparisons and physically matching broken pieces of the tool.

If building material is noticed at the end of a tool, the area should be carefully wrapped so as not to dislodge the evidence. In instances where the item is too large to be transported, the trace material can be carefully removed with a clean pocket knife or razor blade onto a clean sheet of paper. The paper is then folded and placed in an envelope. Both the paper and envelope should be properly marked.

Another area that should be searched for the presence of building materials is the suspect's vehicle. Building material debris may be present in the interior or in the trunk. Vacuum sweepings may be taken for a later search of debris.

Clothing is an especially good place to find building materials. The clothes should be collected from the suspect as promptly as possible to minimize any loss of evidence.

Building materials can be characterized by physical, chemical, and microscopic means. In most cases building material evidence can demonstrate only class characteristics and cannot be shown to be unique to a specific source. As with other evidence of this type, it is valuable as circumstantial evidence.

## Asbestos

Although asbestos is no longer permitted for use as insulation, it may be present in older buildings and in some safes. It can be identified microscopically.

## Safe Insulation

Various types of materials are used in fire-resistant safe walls to prevent the contents from burning. Some common materials are diatomaceous earth, vermiculite, and cement, to name a few. These materials may readily become deposited upon the burglar of a safe in the course of opening the safe. Examination of a suspect's clothing, shoes, and tools may yield safe insulation.

Safe insulation may be identified microscopically and chemically. Expertise in recognizing the types of insulation used by various manu facturers can allow the analyst to make an educated guess useful for an investigative lead.

## Paint

Paint evidence is frequently recovered in hit-and-run, burglary, and forced-entry cases. In some cases it is possible to show conclusively that the paint came from a specific location if the chips are large enough and the edges can be fitted together in jigsaw puzzle fashion (Fig. 7.7). In most instances, however, only class characteristics can be demonstrated.

Paint and other protective coatings such as lacquer, enamel, varnish, and so on can be identified by both physical and chemical properties. Physical characteristics such as color, layering, weathering, and texture

FIGURE 7.7. A person complained that his parked car had been struck by a hit-and-run vehicle. Police suspected that the complainant had struck a steel pole. Paint chips from the vehicle and base of the pole were examined. Not only did the paint from the pole match the transfer to the car, but a physical match was made of the chip (left) from the pole and the chip (right) from the car. (*Centre of Forensic Sciences, Toronto.*)

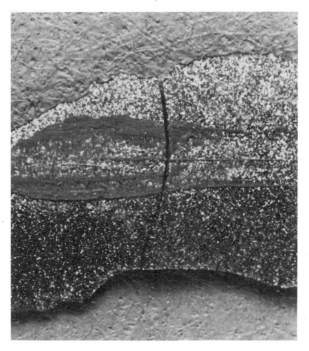

are useful in characterizing this evidence. Chemical properties such as solubilities and composition can indicate the type of paint and identify the type of pigmentation and fillers used in the manufacturing process.

In some cases involving automobile paints it is possible to determine the type of vehicle. The U.S. Bureau of Standards prepares automobile paint standard reference samples. The standards are available only for late model American-manufactured automobiles. This means that older vehicles and foreign cars are not represented in the collection.

Even if a vehicle cannot be identified as to manufacturer, known and questioned specimens can be compared by examination of chemical and physical properties. It should be understood that in any event, the best that can be stated in most cases is that the paint from the control and questioned sources could have come from the same or any similarly painted vehicle.

In some instances, vehicles and residences that have been painted and repainted many times may have so many layers of paint that upon examination, the probability is very high that the two specimens share a common source. This, however, will depend on the specific case as well as the expertise of the analyst.

When collecting standard specimens of paint from automobiles or a door or window in a forced-entry case, the specimen should be collected as close to the area of damage as possible to lessen the possibility that an area farther away from the location of interest was painted differently.

In burglary cases, it is particularly important *not* to collect a standard or control paint sample from the pry area. The specific area of the jimmy or pry will contain a tool mark that may be compared with a pry bar or another tool found at a later time in the investigation. (Tool marks are discussed in Chapter 9.)

When collecting paint samples in a hit-and-run investigation involving two vehicles, a total of four paint samples should be collected and separately packaged. From vehicle A, collect a sample from the point of impact that contains a paint transfer from the other vehicle (B). Also collect a standard paint sample that shows no damage but is adjacent to the damaged area. Similarly, two samples should be collected from vehicle B, one from the damaged area and a second specimen from the undamaged area to be used for a standard of the paint from vehicle B.

If dislodged paint chips are present in the damaged area of the vehicle, they should be carefully collected and packaged in such a way as to avoid breaking. They may be able to be fitted with other larger paint chips collected from the scene of the accident or from the second vehicle.

A known sample of paint can be collected by holding a folded piece of paper and tapping into the side of the vehicle, thus chipping some paint and allowing it to fall into the paper. A razor blade or pocket knife may be used; however, care should be taken not to separate the outer layer of paint from any undercoating. Cellophane tape should not be used in collecting paint samples.

When collecting paint samples, it is best to place the paint into folded paper or a small box with a good seal. Small envelopes are not advised for this type of evidence since the seams of the envelope located in the bottom corners are generally not sealed. Paint chips placed in envelopes usually fall out through the small, unsealed space. Small plastic bags should also be avoided. These containers have a static electric charge that makes it extremely difficult to remove the small paint chips once the evidence is received at the laboratory for examination.

Paint present on tools should not be removed. It is preferable to carefully wrap the end of the tool in such a way as not to dislodge the paint and submit the tool to the laboratory with the paint still intact.

## Rust

Rust stains may sometimes be confused with bloodstains. However, rust can easily be differentiated from blood by a simple chemical field test. Refer to the orthotolidine test in Chapter 8.

## Metals

Filings, shavings, and other metal particles can easily be identified chemically or spectrographically. It is possible to make a comparative analysis of a known and questioned metal sample that can show class characteristics.

Metal filings located in the jaws of pipe wrenches are fairly common sources of this type of evidence (Fig. 7.8). The wrench is used as a burglary tool by placing it onto a doorknob. Metal filings present in the teeth can be compared with the metal from the doorknob.

---

## Case

A thirteen-year-old boy,[2] evidently quite bright, decided to poison his mother slowly with mercury. He set out collecting mercury by breaking into a number of homes in the neighborhood with a seventeen-year-old friend and collecting the mercury contained in the thermostat switches of these homes. He may have read that mercury salts are highly toxic and mistook this to mean that elemental mercury and table salt together are highly toxic. Whatever the reason, he placed the mercury in glass salt shaker along with table salt, shook up the

---

[2] The case was submitted by Ray Prime, Ph.D., Centre of Forensic Sciences, Toronto, Ontario.

.ES COUNTY SHERIFF'S DEPARTMENT

CIENTIFIC SERVICES BUREAU

FIGURE 7.8. In the case of an alleged jail break attempt, the investigator wanted to know if an inmate had used a hacksaw blade on his leg chains. When the crime was reenacted, a magnet was able to pick up numerous metal particles from the clothing of the investigator, whose hand was also slightly injured from using the blade. None of this evidence was found on the inmate, calling into question the hypothesis that he had tried to escape on his own. (*Los Angeles County Sheriff's Department.*)

shaker to break the mercury into fine droplets, and left the shaker to be used by his mother (Fig. 7.9).

A request was made to the forensic science laboratory to show that the shaker had been used to dispense mercury. The lid of the shaker was examined using a scanning electron microscope (SEM) with an energy dispersive X-ray detector (EDX). This combination allowed the operator to magnify an image of an object and determine its elemental composition.

The lid of the salt shaker was made of plastic, coated with nickel and chromium to give it a shiny appearance. The area around the holes in the shaker's lid were examined for traces of mercury, and one fine droplet of elemental mercury clinging to the nickel plating at one of the holes was found using the SEM, and identified as mercury with the EDX.

## Textiles and Fibers

Fragments of cloth may become evidence in a wide variety of cases. Torn fabrics have been examined in murder cases where the victim was tied and gagged with torn fabric, in burglary cases where a suspect left a small torn piece of clothing caught at the point of entry, and in hit-and-run cases where torn clothing was left on the undercarriage of the suspect's vehicle.

Fragments of textile evidence may yield class as well as individual characteristics. A portion of fabric may be physically fitted into another piece of fabric, thereby proving a common source.

A number of physical, chemical, and microscopic characteristics of textiles can be used for comparison purposes. Properties such as color, type of cloth, dye, direction of fiber twist, thread count, and the like are all useful in characterizing the evidence.

When a fragment of fabric is found during the course of a crime scene search, its location should be noted, indicated in a crime scene diagram, and photographed. As with other items of trace evidence, it is preferable not to remove the fabric item from the object it is attached to (Fig. 7.10). If this is not possible, the fabric should be packaged in a clean, properly labeled container with the proper chain of custody information.

The location of the evidence at a point of entry or the physical appearance of the fabric may be useful in itself as an investigative lead. The detective may be able to theorize the location of a tear on an article of clothing or the type of cloth evidence that needs to be found for comparative purposes.

Fibers, as opposed to fabric evidence, are often overlooked by investigators because of their extremely small size (Figs. 7.11 to 7.13). Five types of textile fibers can be encountered as evidence: animal fibers such as wool; vegetable fibers such as cotton; synthetic fibers such as polyester, nylon, rayon, etc.; mineral fibers such as glass wool; and blends of synthetic and natural fibers, the most common being polyester and cotton.

Fiber evidence may be transferred as a result of contact by one person's clothing to another or from articles such as blankets, carpet, upholstery, and so forth. Fibers may be located on clothing, in fingernail scrapings, on hit-and-run vehicles, at points of entry, and on hair from subjects wearing knit hats.

Removal of fibers from other objects is best done at the crime laboratory. If this is not possible, fiber evidence can be removed by use of forceps, cellophane tape, or by vacuum sweeping. Of the three procedures, the tape method is probably the best. A length of tape about 4 inches long is taped end-to-end forming a cylinder with the sticky side of the tape on the outside. The hand is inserted into the center of the tape and the sticky side of the tape is pressed on the item of interest. After sampling, the tape is placed sticky side down on a microscope slide for submission to the laboratory. The procedure has its advantage in that it collects only surface material, whereas vacuum sweeping

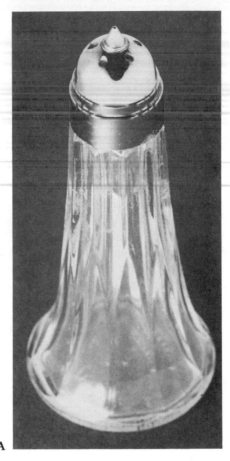

A

FIGURE 7.9. The glass salt shaker used in the attempt to poison the boy's mother (A). A photograph, using scanning electron microscopy, of one of the holes of the shaker (B) and magnification clearly showing the droplet of mercury (C). (*Centre of Forensic Sciences, Toronto.*)

collects huge quantities of debris and forceps may miss many items of trace evidence.

The laboratory will be able to tell the type of fiber and whether it is similar to the control fiber specimen. It is not possible with fiber evidence to state with complete certainty that it came from one and only one source. This is because most garments and textiles used today are mass produced. It is not possible to determine that a specific sample comes from a garment in question or any other garment of similar manufacture.

B

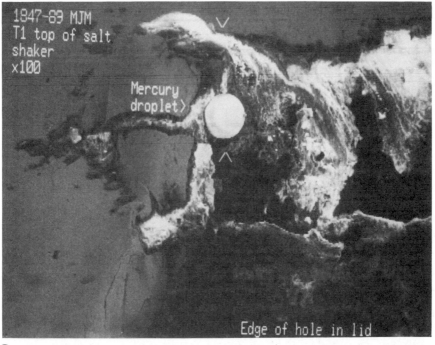

C

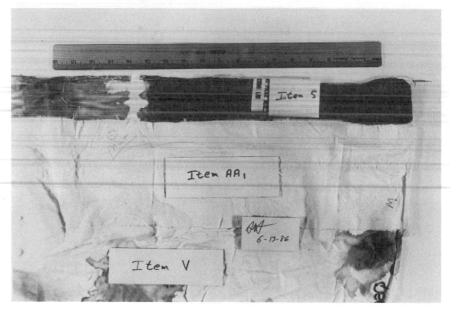

FIGURE **7.10.** Two teenage girls were discovered dead from multiple gunshot wounds. One of them was bound and gagged and covered with bedding. The bedding was a sheet with several strips of cloth missing. A search of the suspect's house was conducted, and several strips of cloth were found that matched the sheet from the scene. (*Detroit Police Department, Crime Laboratory Section, Detroit, Michigan.*)

## Buttons

Buttons come in a very wide range of sizes and patterns. Only in exceptional cases is it possible to identify a button with the buttons of a particular garment. In general, when a button is torn off, the thread and sometimes a piece of fabric may be present (Fig. 7.14.). If exemplars of the sewing thread and the garment are available for comparison, a more definitive conclusion about the source of the button may be made.

If a piece of broken button is discovered, it is possible to physically match the broken piece with another portion of the button. This type of evidence can lead to a conclusive statement about the source of the evidence.

## Cordage and Rope

Pieces of string or rope are sometimes found at crime scenes. If they were used to tie up a victim, the knots should not be untied; rather, the rope should be cut and tied back together with string. The knots present in the rope may prove to be useful evidence (Fig. 7.15).

A

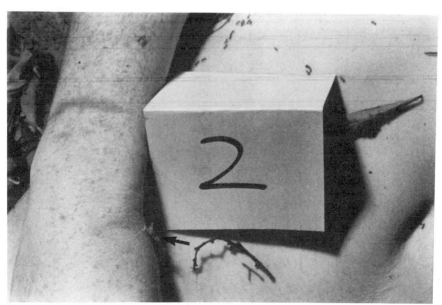

B

FIGURE 7.11. In a four-month period between October 1977 and February 1978, 10 nude bodies of girls and young women between the ages of 12 and 21 were found dumped on hillsides in Los Angeles County. All were raped, tortured, and strangled. One of the victims (A) found lying at the side of a road had a small tuft of fiber on her left wrist (B). (*Los Angeles County Sheriff's Department.*)

184

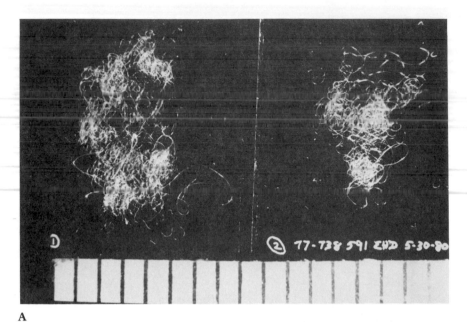

A

B

FIGURE 7.12. Fibers (A) were subsequently collected from a chair (B) found in the suspects' home almost 2 years after the murders and compared. The suspects, Angelo Buono, a 48-year-old auto upholsterer, and his cousin, a 32-year-old former security guard, Kenneth Bianchi, posed as police officers and "arrested" young women, who were then raped and sodomized, and sometimes tortured before being slowly strangled to death. (*Los Angeles County Sheriff's Department.*)

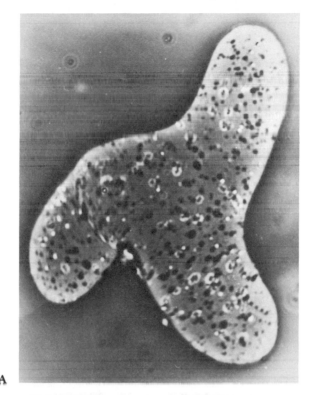

A

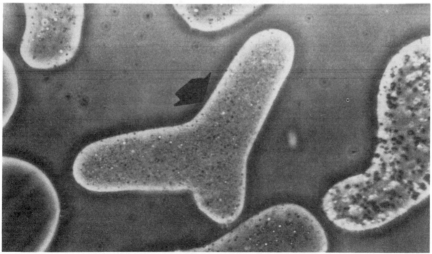

B

FIGURE **7.13.** Fibers from one of the cases linked the victim to the assailants' home. A Monsanto Cadon fiber (A) made only between 1968 and 1974 and a second rare "modified Y" fiber (B) produced by Rohm and Haas for a short period of time were important evidence in the trial. The defendants were found guilty of nine murder counts and sentenced to life imprisonment without the possibility of parole. (*Los Angeles County Sheriff's Department.*)

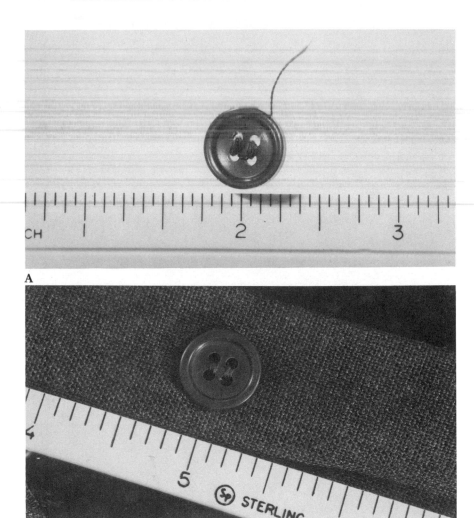

**FIGURE 7.14.** A button found at a burglary scene (A) is compared with one found on the suspect's jacket (B). A photomicrograph (C) shows the manufacturing marks indicating common class characteristics. (*Orange County Sheriff-Coroner, Santa Ana, California.*)

Rope and cordage evidence can be compared with exemplars for similarities. Properties that can be examined include the material from which the cordage is manufactured, the number of strands, direction of the twist in the rope, color, diameter, weight per unit of length, and so on. All of these properties taken together will allow the examiner to determine whether the material is of a similar manufacture. Only in very rare cases where a microscopic examination indicates that a cut

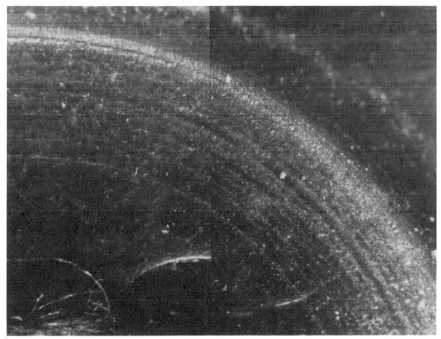

C

rope came from a specific exemplar can a conclusive statement of source be made.

In some cases rope and cordage evidence may have other trace evidence attached to it. In cases of strangulation it may be possible to identify epithelial (skin) cells attached to the cordage.

## Cigarettes and Tobacco

Cigarettes, cigarette butts, tobacco, and ash are frequently found at crime scenes and just as frequently overlooked as potential useful evidence. From the point of view of forensic science, very little work has been done in the identification of tobaccos. This does not lessen, however, the possible use of this type of evidence.

Several laboratories maintain cigarette libraries from which they can often identify the brand from a cigarette butt. In some cases information about the brand a subject smokes may be useful to the investigation.

Similarly, the appearance of the ash left at a location may indicate that a suspect smoked a pipe or cigar, which is useful in describing the habits of that individual.

Cigarette butts may be a useful source of other physical evidence. In

FIGURE 7.15. The body of a young male victim was discovered bound with a rope. The binding used was a white, nylon-braided rope with a highly unusual core consisting of 24 different types and/or colors of yarns and a total yarn count of 106. The yarns consisted of polyesters, rayons, polypropylenes, sarans, cotton, acetates, nylons, and monoacrylics. Similar rope of this very unusual type was found in the possession of a suspect who later, when presented with the evidence of the case, confessed to the murder. (*Federal Bureau of Investigation.*)

some cases latent fingerprints have been developed from cigarette butts by the ninhydrin process. It is also possible to determine the smoker's ABO blood group by typing the saliva left on the butt. Although latent prints and typing results are often inconclusive or negative, the fact that they do at times yield positive and useful information speaks for the utility of this type of evidence.

Empty cigarette packages are frequently found along with cigarettes. Besides identifying the brand and the possibility of determining fingerprints, a cigarette package sometimes offers the possibility of determining the general location of the sale of the cigarettes by the numbers located on the package. The ability to determine the area of sale will depend on whether the distributor kept records of these numbers.

## Matches

Matches found at a crime scene may have been left by smokers or suspects who used them to light their way. They are commonly found in burglary cases where the suspect lit several in order to find the way.

The surface of a single match is usually too small to find sufficient detail to identify a latent fingerprint. However, other useful bits of information may be determined from matches.

Matches may be of the wood or paper variety. Characteristics such as type of wood, microscopic appearance of the cardboard, color, dimension, shape, and the like are useful in comparing a burned match with some exemplars associated with the suspect.

Paper or cardboard matches are by far the most common kind found at crime scenes and offer the best chance of directly incriminating a suspect. To show a connection, it is necessary to find the book of unused matches on the suspect or at least at a location where this person's latent prints are present. Cardboard matches are made from wastepaper. As such, there is wide variability from book to book. It is possible to show a connection between the cardboard left in the matchbook and that of the match. In some instances it is possible to actually fit the match into the book by the appearance of the torn end of the match and the remaining end in the book.

Matches are sometimes used as toothpicks. If the end of the match appears to be chewed, it may be possible to determine the ABO blood group of the chewer by saliva typing.

## Burned Paper

Burned papers and charred documents are sometimes found in arson investigations or in instances where there was an attempt to destroy records by burning them.

Burned documents can be deciphered provided they are reasonably intact. If the paper has been reduced to ashes it is not possible to determine any writing on the paper. For this reason, it is particularly important to exercise extreme care when collecting, preserving, and transporting this type of evidence.

If burned paper is found in a metal file box, it should *not* be removed from the box. It should be transported in the receptacle in which it is discovered. If the documents are found in the open or if the files they are in cannot be taken to the laboratory, the paper should be carefully placed in rigid cardboard boxes. Charred papers can be picked up by gently sliding a flat piece of cardboard under them. Once picked up from the scene, they can gently be placed in boxes.

It is preferable to hand-carry the boxes to the laboratory because of the fragile nature of this evidence. If this is not possible, the paper must be packaged in such a way that it will not break up in transit. Cotton or any other similar material that will preserve the evidence can be layered in the cardboard boxes.

If the paper is burning when the investigator arrives at the scene, no attempt should be made to put out the fire. If the air supply can be shut off without handling the document, this is satisfactory. The paper should be allowed to burn completely.

If the burned material consists of a book, folded papers, or currency, no attempt should be made to separate the different layers of paper. The debris should be kept together and submitted to the laboratory in that state.

Chemical treatment, photography, and examination under ultraviolet and infrared light often makes the writing legible in charred documents. The documents must arrive intact, however, in order to conduct such examinations.

## Ash

The composition of ash can vary greatly depending on the source. It can sometimes be identified microscopically, chemically, or spectroscopically. However, the source of the ash may prove difficult to determine.

One type of ash common in arson cases is the residue of burned highway flares. This ash contains a significant level of strontium, which is responsible for the bright red color of the flare.

## Soil

Soil evidence may be encountered in a wide variety of criminal investigations. It may be found on shoes, clothing, or the underside of motor vehicles. It is useful in tying the suspect or victim to a location. A tire or footwear impression in soil makes it possible to prove that the subject was in fact present. (Chapter 9 discusses impression evidence.)

Soil is a mixture of decaying and weathered rock and decomposed organic material known as humus. Soil contains a wide variety of minerals such as quartz, feldspar, mica, and so on, and partially decomposed leaves, pine needles, pollen grains, and other plant fragments. As such it is easy to differentiate soils from various locations by microscopic examination of various components.

Known soil specimens from the crime scene are absolutely required for an analysis of the evidence sample. Samples should be collected from various locations at the specific location in question, several feet away from the location, and at other locations such as the subject's home and workplace for elimination purposes.

Known samples can be placed in individual small glass jars or metal cans. Clean baby food jars are useful for this purpose. Two or three tablespoons of topsoil is all that is usually required for known specimens. It is important not to dig deeper than an inch or so when collecting these specimens. The subsoil may have a significantly different composition from the topsoil and lead to confusing results. Again, the containers should be appropriately labeled and the location of each sample noted.

Soil specimens on shoes and other objects should be carefully handled. In certain instances, it may be possible to remove successive layers of the soil sample a bit at a time and reconstruct the activities of the subject based on the different types of soil present.

## Case

In a murder, the victim's home was entered through a bedroom window. Beneath the window was a somewhat muddy planting area. A poorly defined footprint, believed to be the suspect's, was found in the planting area.

A suspect was arrested a short time later. The police confiscated his muddy shoes. The suspect maintained that the mud was due to some gardening work he was doing at his home.

Soil specimens were submitted to the laboratory from several locations at the crime scene, the suspect's home, and two other locations where the suspect claimed to have been that day.

Examination of the evidence indicated that the soil on one shoe did not come from the suspect's home or either of the two other locations. The soil was consistent with the soil from the crime scene. The other shoe contained two different soils, one consistent with the suspect's home and the second consistent with the crime scene.

## Wood

Wood may be present as evidence in the form of sawdust, splinters, chips, larger pieces used as assault weapons, and the like. Evidence may be present at the crime scene, on a suspect's clothing, or in a wound. Wood may also bear tool marks.

Because of the wide variety of wood types and its extensive use in building, furniture, and hand tools, this kind of evidence is most valuable. It is possible to identify, compare, and match sources of wood evidence.

Wood may be divided into two types: hardwoods and softwoods. It is possible to determine the type of wood and often the type of tree from pieces the size of sawdust particles. The examination of wood is done microscopically.

If it is a question of *deciding whether two pieces of the stem of a tree originally belonged together*, the original external contour of the stem forms a good guide, if it is found in good condition. Moreover, cracks in the bark, structures and formations on the surface of bark, the position of the sawn surface in relation to the longitudinal axis of the trunk, together with the placing and general appearance of any felling cut, all have their own significance for the task of identification, which is simply a matter of seeing how the different pieces fit together. By matching them against one another it is frequently possible to determine the correspondence between two pieces of wood that are separated from each other in the longitudinal direction of the tree.

The annual rings of a tree are very characteristic; by making a transverse section of an object under investigation it is often possible to obtain a picture just as characteristic of the tree, within a limited region of the stem, as a fingerprint is of a person.

Bruises and decay in the wood are often characteristic in position and extent, and may assist in identification.

If an object under investigation is made of wood that has been worked in some way with tools (knife, plane, saw, or the like) or that has been painted or surface treated in any other way, then the possibility of identification is increased. Injuries in the edge of the knife or plane blade (including planing machines) leave characteristic marks in the wood that can possibly be found on both pieces of wood. Unplaned wood, when sawn in the direction of the grain, often shows marks of varying width and depth from the saw used. In the case of frame-sawn lumber, these marks arise during the upward and downward movements of the frame saw, and variations are caused by inequalities in the setting of the teeth and by variations in the pressure on the wood under the saw. The same conditions hold for wood cut with a circular saw, the marks being more or less curved depending on the diameter of the saw, and differing from the marks of a frame saw that are straight but may be more or less oblique with reference to the grain of the wood. These saw marks have special significance in the identification of pieces of wood separated from one another in the direction of the grain.

It can be more difficult to determine, solely with the aid of marks from the saw used, whether two cut-off pieces originally belonged together. If the cutting was done with a handsaw, identification is sometimes possible, since the marks of such a saw are often irregular and show characteristic formations. This is connected with the fact that changes in the position of the saw in relation to the piece of wood always occur on the forward and backward strokes of the sawing arm. In addition, after a pause in the sawing the saw never takes up exactly the same position again when sawing is restarted. In cutting with a machine saw, the marks are usually regular and meaningless and therefore cannot generally be used for identification. A transverse section of wood has, in fact, a lower potential for reproducing marks from a saw than a longitudinal section, owing to the difference in the structure.

If pieces of wood have been painted or surface treated in any way, then shades of color may be useful for identification. The pigment can be examined chemically and spectrographically to confirm the agreement or difference between the metallic constituents of the pigment. There may be several coats of paint, and agreement or difference in this respect may be noted.

Any knots, cracks, or the like in pieces of wood, as well as drill holes, nail holes, or screw holes, are significant when it is necessary to decide whether pieces of wood previously made a unit. It is sometimes possible, from nail or screw holes or remaining nails or screws, to determine whether a certain piece of wood was previously combined with another piece, formed part of a floor or wall, and so on.

If pieces of wood are separated from one another by a break running in the direction of the grain, then identity can be determined by fitting the pieces to one another. In the case of a break going across the grain there are certain difficulties in doing this, since the broken surfaces are often badly splintered and a number of fibers may have fallen away and been lost.

## Chips and Splinters of Wood

Considerable quantities of chips or splinters are often found at the scene of a forced entry, and they are usually examined routinely with a view to finding any marks from the tool used in making the entry. Chips of wood, however, can also be valuable for the direct identification of the tool in another way: among the chips from forced doors, windows, and the like there may be found a chip that has broken off the handle of a chisel, hammer, or other tool, so that this opportunity for identification should be kept in mind when examining the chips. There may perhaps be found later, at the house of a suspect, a tool with a damaged handle. A small chip from the scene of the crime may fit this and thus prove a connection. Chips of wood may be found to be painted, surface treated, or contaminated in the same way as the handle of the tool.

## Sawdust, Wood Meal, or Other Particles of Finely Powdered Wood

Particles of sawdust, wood meal, or finely powdered wood can sometimes be found in the pant cuffs, pockets, headwear, or gloves of a suspect, or detected in vacuuming the clothes of a suspect. Clues in the form of such particles may also be left behind at the scene if the clothes of the criminal were contaminated with them.

In some cases the species of tree can be determined simply by a microscopic examination, and the occurrence of any foreign bodies on or together with the particles can be confirmed. If, however, it is not possible to obtain a satisfactory result by microscopic examination, owing to the characteristic morphological structure not showing sufficiently clearly, the species can often be determined by a microscopic investigation of the ash picture (spodogram) obtained when the particles are burned. After the burning, which should be complete, the mineral substances (especially calcium oxalate and silica) in the wood are left behind in a form (silica skeleton) that is characteristic for different species of trees, and that can be observed by a microscopic examination of the ashed material. Such characteristic ash pictures are obtained not only from wood, but also from particles derived from other parts of plants (stem, root, leaf, fruit, etc.) and preparations of these, so that this method of investigation may also be applied to such evidence.

*Carbonized Wood*

In determining the species of tree from which carbonized wood has come, the investigation of the object is done microscopically without previous treatment. Even in that state the wood retains its characteristic structure, although it may be changed to some extent. The ash picture (anthracogram) visible under the microscope is therefore characteristic for different species of tree. Owing to the fragility of the carbonized wood, sections must be made on the surface of the particles themselves. Even with herbaceous plants the carbon picture is characteristic. It should be emphasized here that *clues in the form of wholly or partially burned portions of vegetation (including wood)* should not be regarded as valueless and therefore neglected. Modern refined methods of botanical analysis make it possible to operate even with material of this kind with a good prospect of success. This holds especially for the identification of burned residues. Thus, for example, with the aid of the above-mentioned ashing method it is possible to identify with certainty many wholly or partially burned parts of plants.

*Plant Material*

A wide variety of materials of plant origin are sometimes sources of useful physical evidence. Besides wood, pieces of plants, leaves, seeds, bark, twigs, and pollen are sometimes collected as evidence. They may be attached to clothing, found in a vehicle, or be present on a weapon (Fig. 7.16).

Fragments of plant material generally require a high level of expertise to identify. Botanists employed at natural history museums or at a local arboretum may be willing to lend their expertise in the identification of such material.

*Pollen* is a useful material for determining whether a subject was present in an area where flowering plants are located. Vacuum sweepings of a suspect's clothing may yield microscopic pollen grains whose species can be identified microscopically.

## Glass

Glass may be useful evidence in a wide variety of cases. Hit-and-run cases often have headlamp glass or windshield glass present, burglaries frequently involve window glass, and bottle glass is sometimes found in assault cases. Broken glass may yield information about the direction and speed of a projectile and, in the case of multiple projectiles, the sequence of events.

### Broken Panes of Glass

The police investigator often has to decide whether a pane of glass was broken from the outside or the inside, or whether it was struck by a bullet or rock. Pieces from the broken pane or the hole often show marks that are characteristic of the type of injury and the direction of the force, and if correctly interpreted these indications give useful information.

Anyone who examines the edge of a piece of broken glass will note a series of curved lines that form right angles with one side of the pane and curve tangentially with the other side. These fracture lines are a result of force applied to the glass pane and are referred to as *conchoidal (shell-like) fractures*. Conchoidal fractures can be used to determine the direction from which a force came and caused the glass to break.

When an object has been thrown through a glass pane, two types of fractures will be seen that form a pattern that looks somewhat like a spider web. These fractures are called *radical* and *concentric* fractures (Figs. 7.17 to 7.19). Radial fractures are cracks that start at the center at the point where the object struck the glass and run radially outward or in a somewhat star-shaped pattern from the point at which the break starts. Concentric fractures form concentric circular cracks in the glass around the point of impact.

*Determining the direction of force* becomes a simple matter of examining conchoidal fractures along the edges of radial or concentric fractures. Before drawing any conclusions about the direction of force, the examiner must be certain as to whether a radial or a concentric fracture is being examined. It is also worthwhile to mark the pane of glass to clearly show the inside and the outside (Fig. 7.20).

The determination of the direction of force is accomplished as follows: Carefully remove a piece of broken glass. Locate an edge that corresponds to a radial fracture and examine it edgewise. Note the presence and configuration of the conchoidal fractures. Observe with

A

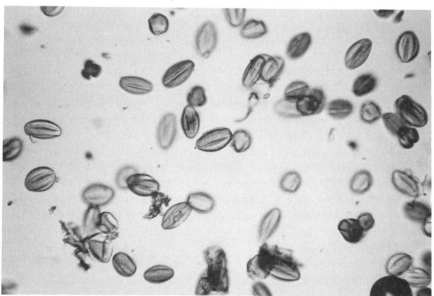

B

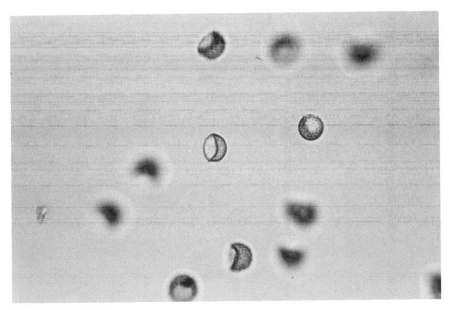

C

FIGURE 7.16. A small, fresh fragment of *Adenostoma fasciculata* containing growths on its leaves, which were found to be galls (A) of Eriophyid mites, was recovered from a suspect's vehicle. This unusual plant specimen was also present at the location where the victim's body was dumped. This particular plant exists only at certain elevations, on east-facing slopes, and only near disturbed environments such as a road. Other plant materials, e.g., pollens (B and C) are sometimes encountered as trace evidence. (*Los Angeles County Sheriff's Department.*)

which surface of the glass the conchoidal fractures make a right angle. That side of the glass is *not* the side from which the force came. The force came from the opposite side.

The results of concentric fractures are opposite to those of radial fractures. In examining the edge of a concentric fracture, keep in mind that the side of the glass forming the right angle with the conchoidal fracture *is* the side that the force came from. Because of this obvious chance of confusion it is very important to be able to distinguish between radial and concentric fractures.

In dealing with small pieces of glass, it is very important not to get the sides mixed up. It is advisable to collect all the pieces of glass and to fit them together to obtain a complete picture of the broken pane where the force acted. In the case of windowpanes a useful indication can be obtained from the layer of dirt often present on the outside of the glass.

Definite conclusions should be drawn from the curved lines of the edge surfaces *only* in the case of the fractures that lie nearest to the point of attack. Only with these closest fractures can one be sure that

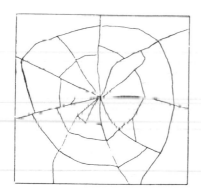

FIGURE 7.17
Sketch illustrating the radial and concentric fractures in a sheet of glass.

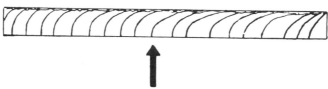

FIGURE 7.18. Diagram showing the curved lines in the edge of the glass in a concentric fracture. They are almost perpendicular to the side from which force was applied. In radial fractures, the direction is reversed.

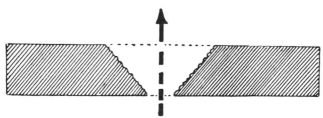

FIGURE 7.19. Diagram showing formation of a bullet hole in a pane of glass. Note the crater form of the hole. The arrow shows the direction of the shot.

the conchoidal fractures resulted from the break in question. Fractures at a greater distance from the point of attack may have been produced, for example, when the object used for breaking the glass was brought back, or by projecting and interfering points of glass being broken off by hand.

When transporting glass to the laboratory for examination, glass pieces should be carefully marked and individually wrapped in paper. The wrapped evidence may then be placed together into a box for easier transportation. Packaging should be done in such a way as to minimize breakage.

FIGURE 7.20. A case example of radial and concentric fractures in glass. (*Connecticut State Police.*)

## Glass Perforated by a Bullet

If a pane of glass has been perforated by a bullet, the hole is expanded in a crater on the side where the bullet went out. Thus the location where the cone-shaped crater is narrower indicates the direction from which the bullet was fired.

The appearance of the hole can indicate the velocity of the projectile. High-velocity bullets leave an almost circular hole in a pane of glass without noticeable cracking or with cracks merely starting. Lower velocity ammunition leaves an almost regular polygon with radial cracks running outward.

A shot at very close range more or less completely shatters the glass from the pressure of the muzzle gases, the extent depending on the power of the cartridge and the thickness of the glass. In such cases it is impossible to obtain a clear idea of the appearance of the shot hole unless the shattered splinters of glass can be pieced together. In most cases this is not possible because the splinters from the parts nearest the actual hole are too small. In a very favorable case, indications of the metal of the bullet on the edges around the hole may be detected spectrographically. A reliable indication that the glass was shattered by a shot at close range is the presence of gunshot residue particles on the glass.

It is sometimes difficult to determine whether a hole in a pane of glass was caused by *a bullet or by a stone* that was thrown. A small stone thrown at relatively high speed (such as one flung by the action of a tire of a passing car) can produce a hole very similar to that caused by a bullet. The crater-like expansion of a hole caused by a small stone may not actually show the same uniform, conchoidal fracture in the glass as in the case of a bullet hole. Further, holes caused by small stones generally do not show the same geometrical regularity in the radial and concentric cracks in the glass around the hole as usually shown by a bullet hole. On the other hand, a large stone can shatter a pane of glass in a manner that nearly resembles the results of a close-range shot. Thus a careful search for the projectile is necessary to determine the cause of the break.

If there are a number of breaks in a pane of glass, it is sometimes possible to determine *the order of events* that produced the holes. Radial cracks produced by the first incident stop either by themselves or run to the edges of the glass. On the other hand, cracks from subsequent incidents stop when they meet a crack already present in the glass that is the result of earlier fractures. Even when the damage is extensive and large portions of glass have fallen away, the order of the damage can often be established by fitting the pieces together.

## Cracked or Burst Panes of Glass

If a pane of glass has been cracked by the action of heat, it shows characteristic long, wavy fractures. Pieces that have fallen out are generally found in the same direction as the source of heat. If a limited area of glass has been exposed to a direct flame, a piece of glass corresponding to that area often breaks off.

Automobile safety glass breaks completely or partially into pieces or small rods of regular form when subjected to a violent blow or shock. Use of tempered glass is intentional by the automobile manufacturer to lessen the chance of a person's being cut by flying glass.

A pane of tempered glass shattered by a bullet may still remain hanging in position in the vehicle. In a typical crackle pattern the crack formation extends over the whole of the pane, but close around the point of fracture a large number of small pieces of glass usually come loose and fall away, so that a study of the crater formation in the glass is possible only in rare cases. If pieces that have fallen out are found, however, they can, in favorable cases, be pieced together in their places near the point of impact, and the appearance of the fracture can be reconstructed.

If a few small pieces believed to be tempered glass are found at the scene of an accident, a simple test can be used to determine whether the glass is in fact tempered. Interference patterns caused by strain in the glass are easily observed by examining the glass with polarized light. A specimen of glass is placed over a light source with a polarizing filter. The glass is viewed with a second polarizing filter and a characteristic pattern is observed indicating tempered glass.

## *Glass Splinters*

At the scene of a crime where the criminal has obtained entry by breaking a window, glazed door, or the like, the investigating officer should always remember to collect pieces of glass for comparison purposes. If a suspect is found at a later time, a careful examination of the clothing may show splinters of glass. Splinters of glass may also be found in the handle of a tool used to force an entry into a building.

When such splinters of glass are found on a suspect's clothing or tools in a burglary investigation, they will usually be too small to allow a direct physical comparison against the pane of glass from which they possibly came. There are, however, a number of other comparisons that can be made to show a common source between the exemplar and questioned glass specimens (Fig. 7.21).

Glass evidence may be examined for a number of physical and chemical properties. Density, refractive index, color, thickness, and chemical composition are some of the common characteristics exam-

FIGURE 7.21. A burglar may be linked to a window he has smashed by the tiny fragments of glass that fly backward onto his person and clothing. (*Centre of Forensic Sciences, Toronto.*)

ined to differentiate glass. Such tests will not result in a definite identification since glass is a mass-produced material with wide use. Nonidentity, however, can be proved, and this may be useful information.

When collecting known samples of glass evidence to be used as
exemplars, it is suggested that several samples be collected from different parts of the same pane of glass because there may be variation in
glass properties in the same pane of glass.

## Objects Left at the Crime Scene

It is not uncommon for a criminal to leave behind an object at a crime
scene, believing it to be of no further use or believing that the police will
find it of no value. Objects are often forgotten or lost by the suspect. The
criminal may have been surprised during the act and been forced to
leave without picking up items of potential evidence.

These items left behind can be extremely valuable to the investigator. They may help prove the suspect's identity, if fingerprints are
present, or connect the suspect to the crime in other ways.

### Paper

Paper, such as newspaper, wrapping paper, paper bags, and the like are
sometimes left at a crime scene. Besides trace evidence, handwriting
and latent fingerprints may be present (Fig. 7.22).

If the paper at the scene is torn or cut, a search of the suspect's home
or car may turn up a matching piece of paper, and the two may be fitted
together. In some cases watermarks or stains on a piece of paper may be
used to show a connection to leaves of paper located at another site.

### Articles of Clothing

Manufacturer's markings on clothing are of value in rare cases. Occasionally, the presence of a foreign label in clothing may indicate the
nationality of the wearer. However, because of the large number of
clothes that are imported, this conclusion may be open to question. Size
and laundry marks may be valuable. Size gives an indication of the
physical characteristics of the subject, and laundry marks may in some
instances identify the suspect. Other marks such as initials and even
names are sometimes found and are, of course, very valuable. Hair
should always be searched for, as should other trace evidence. If secretions or dried blood are found on an article of clothing left at a crime
scene, the subject's blood type may be determined.

Pockets should be searched as a matter of course. In some cases useful
evidence will be found.

Torn pieces of clothing are valuable. If a matching piece of clothing can be found in the suspect's home or car, it can easily tie the suspect to the location.

## Product Markings

Many commercial products bear manufacturer's marks on the label, package, or container. The markings are used to designate the date, lot number, location of manufacture, and other such details as a control to assist the manufacturer in checking on distribution and sales of the product. The markings may also assist the investigator in determining the origin of products found at crime scenes. Since the markings are usually in code form, the manufacturer or distributor must be contacted to determine the meaning of the information.

## Foodstuff

Foodstuff in the form of stains or debris is sometimes found as evidence. Such evidence may be useful in determining the type of work a subject is engaged in. Thus, for example, if vacuum sweepings are examined and a quantity of wheat starch is found, it could indicate that the suspect had been baking (Figs. 7.23 and 7.24). Through careful examination it is possible to determine the nature of very small samples of foodstuff through microscopic and microchemical means.

## Cosmetics

Cosmetics such as lipstick, nail polish, and various creams may sometimes be collected as evidence in cases. If exemplars are available, a laboratory can make a chemical comparison to determine whether the known and questioned specimens share a common source.

Cosmetic firms are constantly reformulating their products. If the brand of the cosmetic can be determined it may be possible to determine the approximate time a given specimen was on the market.

## Hair

Hair evidence is generally associated with crimes involving physical contact such as murder, rape, assault, traffic accidents, and so forth. Hair may be found at the crime scene, on the victim or suspect, or attached to a weapon, tool, vehicle, or article of clothing. Because of the small size of this evidence, hair may be difficult to find. Care and patience are required to conduct a thorough search for this evidence.

Some investigators believe that hair can conclusively prove the identity of an individual, much in the same way that a fingerprint can. Unfortunately, this is not the case. The most positive statement that may presently be made in a scientific examination of hair is that it did not come from a specific individual. Hair can exclude a suspect; however, it cannot positively prove that a sample came from one and only one person. If an examination of hair strands found at a crime scene and those of a specific person show similar characteristics, the strongest statement that can be made is that the subject could not be excluded as the possible donor of the hair, or that the hairs could have come from the subject or any other individual with similar characteristics. A statement about probabilities of a given hair coming from a specific person is not appropriate at the present state of the art of hair examination in criminal cases.

Even though it is not possible to determine the person that a strand of hair came from, much worthwhile information can be determined

**FIGURE 7.22.** A young boy was kidnapped and his parents were sent a stenciled ransom note. The stencil was later found in the suspect's home. Photograph (A) is a portion of the note, (B) is a close-up of the word "Ya," and (C) is an overlay of the stencil and the word "Ya." (*Iowa Department of Public Safety.*)

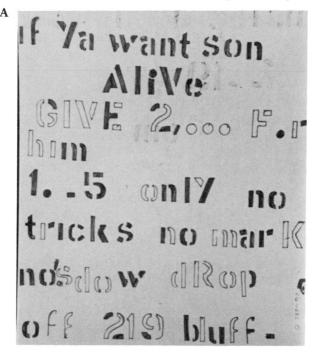

B SPECIMEN 676- 1285

C SPECIMEN 676- 1285

FIGURE 7.23. Starch has a highly characteristic appearance under polarizing light microscopy. This photomicrograph shows potato starch. (*Los Angeles County Sheriff's Department.*)

through hair examination. Species, location of growth on the body, hair treatment, and hair disease are some of the types of information that can be gained.

When conducting a hair examination, the criminalist first attempts to determine whether the hair evidence is animal or synthetic in origin. Microscopic examination of a hair quickly determines whether the evidence is animal, synthetic, or simply a plant fiber. Furthermore, it is possible to determine whether the hair is human or animal in origin and, if animal, the species of the animal. Domestic animals such as dogs, cats, cows, horses, and the like are somewhat common. Hairs from wild animals are sometimes collected at crime scenes such as the scene of skeletal remains. It is not possible to determine whether two hair specimens come from one specific animal.

Although differentiating between human and animal hair is not especially difficult, determining the species of animal requires a greater degree of expertise of a hair examiner. The ability to ascertain the species of animal is determined by the experience of the individual performing the examination.

In addition to identifying a specimen of hair as human, it is possible to determine whether the hair is from the head or from another part of the body. At one time it was possible to draw a conclusion about the sex

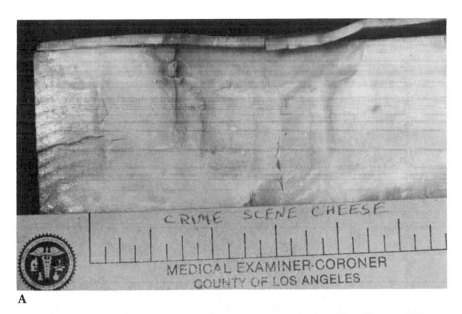

A

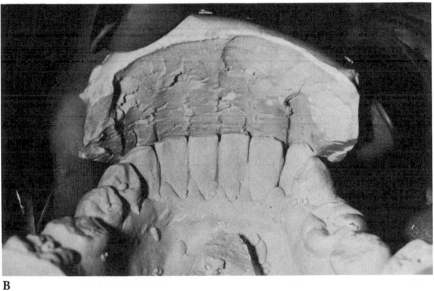

B

FIGURE 7.24. Bite mark in cheese found at a crime scene (A) is compared with a dental impression of the cheese and the suspect's teeth (B). (*Los Angeles County, Department of Chief Medical Examiner-Coroner.*)

of an individual based on the length of a hair strand. Present hairstyles do not make that deduction valid anymore.

Examination of hair may indicate that it was chemically treated. Hairs that have been bleached, dyed, straightened, or otherwise treated can be compared with specimens from a subject to determine whether the subject's hair has been treated in the same way. Sometimes hair shows the presence of lice or fleas, which can be useful as a means of comparison.

Microscopic examination of the hair root may indicate that the hair was forcibly pulled out as opposed to falling out naturally. Such information may be used to indicate a struggle.

## Case

In the prosecution of a rape case, the sole issue was consent. The law defines rape as "nonconsensual sexual intercourse." The defendant claimed that the victim voluntarily consented to sexual intercourse, whereas the victim testified that she was forced to comply. Head hairs matching the victim's were examined and found to have been forcibly pulled out. This information was used to corroborate the victim's testimony.

If hair is forcibly pulled out, an additional bit of information may be obtained. It is possible to determine the PGM (phosphoglucomutase) blood group of an individual from sheath cells found on hair roots. Sheath cells are present only when hair is pulled out, not if it falls out naturally. Another possible test using sheath cells can determine the sex of the person that the hair came from.

The search for hair at the scene of a crime can be done only by subjecting the floor, furniture, and other objects on which hair might be found to a very thorough examination. For this purpose a flashlight and pair of tweezers is suggested. Hair found on an object or in a certain location may be folded in a clean sheet of paper and placed in a properly labeled envelope. Detailed notes should be made to indicate the date, time, and location of the hair. A sketch or photograph of the area can be made. When a number of hair samples are collected from the same location at the crime scene, it is not recommended that the specimens be sorted. They should be submitted to the crime laboratory for careful and expert examination.

When collecting several hairs from different locations it is important *not* to package them together. If the hairs are different, confusion will arise if the items are all in the same package.

Hair evidence is frequently found on the body of a victim. Pulled out strands of hair may be found clutched in the hands or under the fingernails of a murder victim. A rape victim sometimes has her assailant's pubic hair present on her body or the bed or other location where she was lying.

Pubic hair combings in rape and rape-murder cases are a routine way of collecting hair evidence. It is advisable to collect hair as well as other types of evidence associated with rape cases as soon as possible. Trace evidence such as hair is quickly lost unless gathered promptly.

Clothing belonging to the victim of a murder, rape, or assault should be examined for hair evidence. Hairs may become entangled among threads of the fabric. Generally a very careful examination of the clothing is necessary to locate hairs.

In order to fully examine hair evidence collected in an investigation, it is necessary to obtain exemplars from the individuals involved. In some instances, a court order may be required to obtain hair specimens from a defendant. It is strongly recommended that if there is any doubt or question, the investigator should contact the prosecuting attorney for a ruling. It is better to make the extra effort in obtaining a court order to secure the evidence than to run the risk of having valuable physical evidence excluded from the trial because it is found to be inadmissible.

Hair specimens should be gathered from the entire body—head, face, chest, arms, pubis, legs, etc. Sufficient numbers of hairs should be taken from each location. Hair is best collected by pulling or plucking. If cutting is done, the hair should be clipped as close to the root as possible. Head hairs should be collected from several different areas of the head. Specimens should be taken from the front, back, left, right, and top areas. At least 12 hairs should be collected from the head, and, if possible, as many as two dozen. Approximately a dozen hairs from each of the areas mentioned is desirable. The reason for the large number is that hair varies greatly even on the same person. A close inspection of a person's head hair clearly shows that there are several different shades, and even colors of hair, on a given subject. Thus a large sampling is desirable.

Hair may be collected by the investigator, criminalist, or hospital personnel. The easiest method of collecting the specimens is to let the subject pull out the hair and place it into a properly marked envelope. It is important to package separately hairs collected from different parts of the body.

## Feathers

On rare instances feathers may be collected as evidence in an investigation. Most crime laboratories have very little or no expertise in analyzing this type of material. Feathers should be collected if discovered, however, because they may be identified by experts at museums and academic institutions.

**A**

**B**

FIGURE 7.25. A piece of a broken knife blade (A) was recovered from a crime scene and matched to a knife found in the suspect's possession (B and C). (*Los Angeles County Sheriff's Department.*)

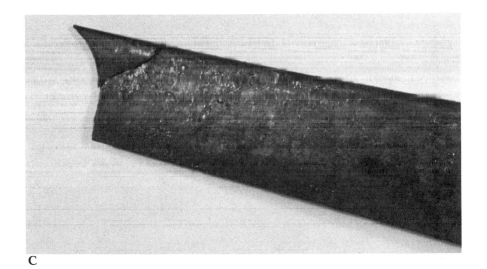

C

## Electrical Wire

Insulated electrical wire is sometimes collected as evidence. The wire may have been used to tie up a victim of a crime, or it is sometimes attached to a car stereo or tape deck stolen from a vehicle. In both cases it may be possible to show that one end of the wire was once part of another end.

Generally, electrical wire that has many strands does not lend itself to tool mark examination. Such wires are so fine that there are not sufficient markings imparted onto the wire from the tool. If the wire is of a thicker gauge, it may be possible to examine extrusion marks on both ends to determine if the pieces each have the same class characteristics.

Extrusion marks will also be present on the wire insulation. Since there will be a greater surface area on the insulation, it is easier to work with that portion of the evidence. The extrusion markings along with the cut edge, which sometimes can be made to "fit" the other piece of wire evidence, can lead to the conclusion that the wires were once from the same continuous piece.

If a positive fit cannot be made, physical characteristics such as the number of strands of wire, the gauge, the appearance of the break, and the color and markings on the insulation all may be used at least to show that the wire was of a similar manufacture. Whatever type of examination is made, it is always necessary to have an exemplar to compare with the evidence wire in order to make a conclusion.

## Broken Tools

Broken tools are frequently discovered at burglaries of safes and in cases of breaking and entering. Broken ends from screwdrivers, wrecking bars, and metal punches are all important types of physical evidence (Fig. 7.25). Their usefulness lies in the fact that if the remaining part of the tool is discovered, a positive statement can be made that the piece found at the scene and the rest of the tool were once an intact tool.

Broken *knives* are another kind of "tool" found at crime scenes. A piece of knife blade may be discovered at the scene of an assault or murder or be present in the wound of a victim. If the other part of the knife can be recovered, the two parts can be physically fitted together.

In addition to the fit, a microscopic examination of the knife and the broken piece of blade usually shows fine scratches caused by wear and use on the flat surface of the blade. These markings run continuously through the area of the break and can show conclusively that the broken piece and the blade were once a continuous piece.

## Tape

Electrical, adhesive, masking, and cellophane tape are sometimes recovered at crime scenes. The tape may have been used to bind a victim or to tape two objects together. If a roll of tape is located in the suspect's belongings, it may be possible to piece together the portion of tape from the scene and that found in the suspect's possession (Fig. 7.26). If the tear at the end of the tape is ragged enough, a conclusive statement about a common source may be made. If the cut on the tape is very sharp, such as may be made by scissors, only a statement about class characteristics can be made.

## Headlamps

Headlamps from automobiles and other motor vehicles are routinely submitted to crime laboratories in traffic accident investigations. A careful examination of the headlamp filament can help determine whether the lamp was on or off at the time of the accident. The traffic investigator should be aware of this possibility and collect any pieces of broken headlamp, tail lamp, or other debris present at the scene of the accident.

## Other Trace Evidence

The scope of trace evidence is such that anything of a small or microscopic size can potentially be trace evidence (Figs. 7.27 and 7.28). It is

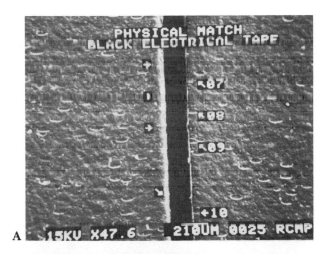

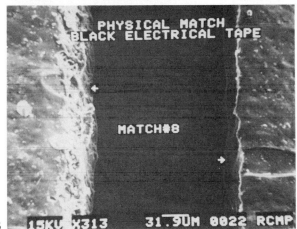

FIGURE 7.26. Photomicrographs of a physical match of cut electrical tape from a drug case. (A) Shows the cut tape edges and the markings (pits) created in the manufacturing process. The arrows illustrate pits that were cut through when the tape was cut. (B) A magnification of the previous photograph. (*Royal Canadian Mounted Police, Forensic Laboratory Services.*)

impossible to detail each and every conceivable type of trace evidence with which investigators will come in contact during their careers.

The general rules about evidence collection can be applied to trace evidence, even to such evidence not specifically delineated in this chapter:

1. Collect the evidence in a legally admissible way.
2. Package the evidence to properly preserve it.

**FIGURE 7.27.** The Scanning Electron Microscope (SEM) is an important laboratory tool in today's modern crime laboratory. (*Los Angeles Police Department, Scientific Investigations Division.*)

**FIGURE 7.28.** Photomicrograph of a physical match of postal stamps in a fraud case, showing a physical match between two stamps. (*Royal Canadian Mounted Police, Forensic Laboratory Services.*)

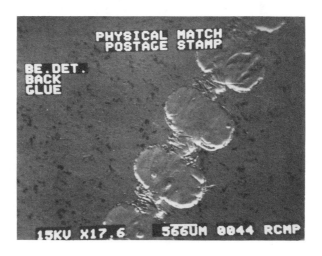

3. Package the evidence to avoid loss and contamination.
4. Use common sense!
5. When in doubt, contact your crime laboratory.

Remember, only through careful crime scene search and patience can trace evidence be effectively used in a case.

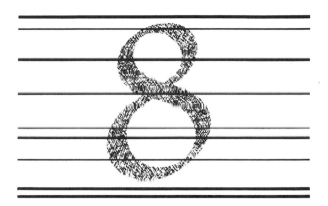

# BLOOD
# AND OTHER
# BIOLOGICAL
# EVIDENCE

**218**

E ver since Cain slew Abel, blood has been invaluable physical evidence. Indeed, it can be said that of all the significant advances in forensic science in the past decade, the greatest strides have been made in forensic serology. Blood is present at most crimes of violence. It can be used to determine the sequence of events in a crime and tie a suspect to a crime scene. Today forensic DNA typing is having a significant impact on investigations of violent crimes and may well revolutionize the ability to identify criminals in ways not thought possible a decade ago.

## A Word of Caution

Before discussing blood and other biological fluids as physical evidence, some remarks are appropriate about the potential hazards of handling these materials and the risks of *hepatitis* and *AIDS*. Persons present at crime scenes, at autopsies, and in crime laboratories where whole blood or other biological specimens are present, are advised to exercise appropriate care when handling these substances. *Surgical gloves should be worn when working with blood, saliva, semen, and other biologicals.* Smoking, eating, or drinking in these areas should not be permitted. When specific questions arise about proper handling, local public health authorities should be contacted. There is a potential risk; however, with reasonable care and caution, that risk can be minimized. Guidelines for handling these materials should be drafted and discussed with personnel who must handle them. Appropriate procedures must also be taken for disposal of biological evidence. Commercial disposal firms that specialize in biohazardous disposal may be used to destroy such materials.

## Blood Spatter Pattern Recognition

It is not uncommon to find blood evidence associated with crimes of violence. Sometimes the location of bloodstains is obvious. Other times a detailed search utilizing chemical tests is required.

### Shape and Appearance of Bloodstains

In instances where blood spatters and smears are present an attempt should be made to reconstruct the events that caused the stains.

The shape and appearance of bloodstains and smears can give useful information about the crime (Figs. 8.1 and 8.2). MacDonell has outlined several general rules regarding bloodstain evidence:

1. *Spots of blood* may be used to determine the directionality of the falling drop that produced them. Their shape frequently permits an

FIGURE **8.1.** Bloody shoe prints of the suspect's shoes found at the crime scene clearly show blood drops and splatters *on top of* the shoe prints. This evidence places the suspect at the scene during the incident rather than after, as he had contended. (*Fulton County Medical Examiner's Office, Atlanta, Georgia.*)

    estimate as to their velocity and/or impact angle and/or the distance fallen from source to final resting place.

2. *The diameter of a blood spot* is of little or no value in estimating the distance it has fallen after the first five or six feet. Beyond this distance the change is too slight to be reliable.

3. *The edge characteristics of blood spots* have absolutely no meaning or value unless the effect of the target surface is well known. This is especially true when attempts are made to estimate distance from the so-called scallops around the edge (Figs. 8.3 to 8.7).

4. *The degree of spatter* of a single drop depends far more upon the smoothness of the target surface than the distance the drop falls. The coarser the surface the more likely the drop will be ruptured and spatter. A blotter, for example, will cause a drop to spatter to a considerable extent at a distance of eighteen inches, whereas a drop falling over one hundred feet will not spatter at all if it lands on glass or other smooth surfaces.

FIGURE 8.2. A murder scene with a bloodstain pattern shows that the victim was dealt a blow at the top of the stairs and was struck an additional, fatal blow at the foot of the stairs. (*Royal Canadian Mounted Police, Forensic Laboratory Services.*)

5. No conclusion as to the cause of a very small bloodstain should ever be drawn from a limited number of stains. Very fine specks of blood may result from an "overcast" or cast off satellite from a larger drop or droplet. In the absence of the larger drop, however, and when hundreds of smaller than 1/8-in. drops are present (often down to one thousandths of an inch in diameter), it may be concluded that they were produced by an impact. The smaller the diameter of the drops, the higher the velocity of the impact. The difference between medium velocity impact, such as an ax or hammer blow, and high velocity impact, such as a gunshot, is sufficient for differentiating

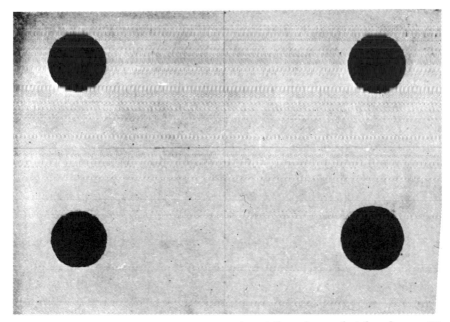

**FIGURE 8.3.** Drops of blood on a plain surface falling from a height of up to 20 inches.

the two provided an adequate sample is observed by someone thoroughly familiar with evidence of this type.

6. *Directionality of a small bloodstain* is easily determined provided the investigator recognizes the difference between an independent spatter and a cast off or satellite thrown from a larger drop. Small independent stains have a uniform taper resembling a teardrop and always point toward their direction of travel. Cast off droplets produce a tadpole-like, long narrow stain with a well-defined "head." The sharper end of these stains always points back toward their

**FIGURE 8.4.** Drops from a height of 20 to 40 inches. The scallops are large and sparse.

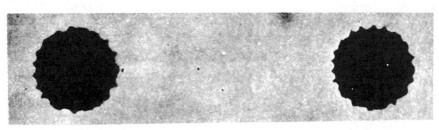

**FIGURE 8.5.** Drops from a height of 40 to 60 inches. The scallops are fine and close.

origin. Since these satellite spatters travel only a very short distance, the larger drop can almost always be traced.

7. *The character of a bloodstain*, either made by drops or smaller droplets, or by larger quantities of blood up to several ounces, may reveal movement both at the moment of initial staining or later if a body or other stained surface is moved from its original position.

**FIGURE 8.6.** Drops from 60 to 80 inches. The scallops are fine and close and spatter out in a sun ray design.

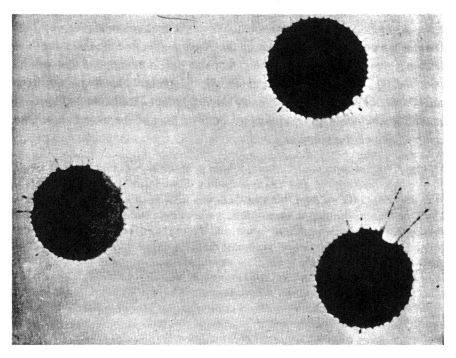

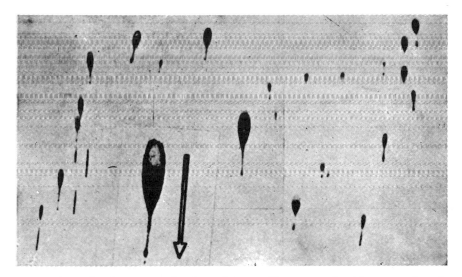

FIGURE 8.7. Blood spatters that have hit a wall at an angle. The pointed ends indicate the direction of movement (see arrow).

8. Depending upon the target and impact angle, considerable back spatter may result from a gunshot wound. The range of back spatter is considerably less than that occurring in the same direction of the projectile, however. This is especially true with exit wounds when expanding type slugs are used.

9. Blood is a very uniform material from the standpoint of its aerodynamics. Its ability to reproduce specific patterns is not affected to any significant degree by age or sex. Likewise, since blood is shed from a body at constant temperature and is normally exposed to an external environment for such a very short time, atmospheric temperature, pressure, and humidity have no measurable effect on its behavior.[1]

In summary, blood spatter evidence requires much experience and testing of the surface characteristics of the target to determine how blood falling on that surface will behave. Blood spatter interpretation courses are available, and it is highly recommended that such a course of study be taken prior to attempting this technique on actual casework. Training and experience will allow for the greatest amount of useful information to be derived from this technique. Crime scene

[1] Herbert L. MacDonell, *Flight Characteristics and Stain Patterns of Human Blood,* U.S. Department of Justice, Law Enforcement Assistant Administration, National Institute of Law Enforcement and Criminal Justice, PR 71-4, pp. 27–28, November 1971.

reconstruction through the use of blood spatter pattern interpretation is a useful technique, but it must be used only by those who have the necessary amount of training. The directionality of a bloodstain is a much easier area for interpretation. With these teardrop-shaped stains, *the pointed end will always point toward the direction of travel.*

### Presumptive Tests for Blood

At crime scenes where minute amounts of blood are present, chemical tests may be used. Chemical testing is also quite useful at scenes where the suspect cleaned up or washed the area.

Several tests are in common usage. The *luminol, orthotolidine* (a chemical similar to benzidine), *leuco malachite, green,* and *phenolphthalin* tests are among those commonly used. All are considered presumptive, that is, they are screening tests.

Each of these presumptive tests is extremely sensitive. They can easily detect exceedingly small quantities of blood. The test results are relatively unambiguous and hence lend themselves to use by crime scene technicians. Chemicals can be purchased from law enforcement supply companies or at considerable savings from chemical supply houses.

*A word of warning!* These chemicals can be extremely hazardous if used improperly. Orthotolidine, for example, is a derivative of benzidine. Benzidine is no longer used as a test for blood because it is highly carcinogenic. Although orthotolidine is less carcinogenic, care in its use should be exercised. If the chemical comes in contact with the skin, it should be thoroughly washed with soap and water. Wearing rubber gloves is advised when using these chemicals.

Of the foregoing tests, the orthotolidine test remains widely used; however, like benzidine it must be used with care. The chemicals are relatively stable and the test is quite sensitive. The test may be conducted on filter paper, cotton-tipped applicators, or the evidence itself (the latter is not recommended). A positive test is indicated by a blue-green color.

The luminol test,[2] like the orthotolidine test, can readily be used in the field. It is a very useful test for searching large areas for blood, particularly if the area has been cleaned up. The major drawback of this test is that the room must be dark. Blood reacts with luminol reagent by luminescing. The reagent is sprayed with an aerosol sprayer. The glow given off is very faint; therefore the area must be almost completely

---

[2] Potential health hazards of luminol have not been well documented. As the procedure calls for using luminol in an aerosol, it is prudent practice to wear a face mask to minimize breathing in the material and gloves to lessen skin contact.

dark in order to visualize the luminescence. The test works best on older stains. In some instances, outlines of shoes and even marks caused by mopping or wiping up an area can be clearly visualized by means of this test.

Experience in interpreting this test is required. At times pinpoint glowing is observed. This is not the result of bloodstains. Whole areas are seen glowing with a positive test.

## Searching for Bloodstains

A dried but relatively fresh bloodstain generally has a reddish brown color and is glossy in contrast to, for example, rust stains. In a very thin layer the color may be grayish green. The gloss disappears slowly under the action of sunlight and heat, wind and weather, or as the result of an attempt to wash it away; the color finally becomes gray. Bloodstains can, however, assume other colors from red to brown or black, or they may appear green, blue, or grayish white. The color, as well as the time required for the change, depends on the underlying material: the change is quicker on metal surfaces and slower on textiles. With some types of cloth the blood soaks into the threads; with others it lies on the pile. The surface gloss is often less marked on fabric. Bloodstains on wallpaper may show surprising colors because of the blood's taking up color from the paper. Certain other stains, composed of pigment, rust, tobacco, snuff, urine, feces, coffee, and the like, can easily be confused with bloodstains. In searching for bloodstains, marks should not be classified according to color and character, since a stain that appears to deviate from the normal character of a bloodstain may be composed of blood, whereas one that resembles blood may be composed of some other substance.

When searching for stains it is convenient to allow the light from a flashlight to fall obliquely against the surface under examination. Sometimes a stain shows up better against a surface when it is illuminated with colored light. Red, green, and ordinary white light are used successively.

Occasionally the assailant will clean up the premises. Furniture is straightened, damage is concealed, and blood is washed off—all for the purpose of concealing the crime, delaying its discovery, and/or destroying evidence. The search of the scene should therefore also be extended to places that are not in direct view. A criminal with bloody fingers may, for example, have opened a drawer, fingered through papers, grasped a doorknob, and so on. Wash basins, garbage pails, and the like should be given close attention. Drain traps should also be examined since there may be blood in the trap if the criminal's hands were washed there. Towels, draperies, and other fabrics that may have served to wipe off blood should also be examined. If a floor has been washed in order to remove bloodstains, blood may possibly be found in the cracks of the floor, in joints between tiles, under the edges of linoleum, and in similar places.

The search for blood on clothes must be carried out carefully and systematically. Even if blood has been washed off the more conspicuous parts, stains may still be found on the seams, on the lining, inside the sleeves, in pockets, and so forth. Stains that have been diffused by washing may be concentrated in the laboratory, and in some cases typing has been successful. Suspects may also have bloodstains not merely on their clothes, but also on their body.

In the open air, the search for bloodstains is often more difficult. Rain, snow, sun, and wind may have obliterated the marks more or less completely. The blood mark may have changed its color in a very short time because of the character of the ground. If the ground gives the impression of dampness in certain parts, these parts should be given special attention, as should blades of grass, leaves, branches of trees, and the like.

Objects on which the presence of bloodstains is suspected should be examined very carefully in cracks, joints, and seams, since bloodstains can sometimes be found in such places even after the object has been washed or cleaned. It should also be remembered that it does not follow that blood must be found on a knife or similar object that has been used in a murder or assault. The edges of the wound may wipe the blood off the blade as it is drawn out.

If blood has run through bedclothes on a bed it is necessary to consider whether it has run through all the bedclothes or has remained in, for example, the mattress. This is of the greatest importance in estimating the total quantity of blood and sometimes in enabling the pathologist to decide on the time that has elapsed since death.

## Description and Recording of Bloodstains

In the case of bloodstains, a description should be made of their form, color, size, position, direction of splash, estimated height of fall, and the like. The best way to preserve the appearance of bloodstains is through photography. Photographs depicting overall, medium-range, and close-up views should be taken. A scale should be included in close-up photographs.

Besides photography, a rough sketch is useful to show the general appearance of the stains as well as their relative position to other areas of the crime scene. The sketch should contain the location and direction of the stains, for example, a drop of blood located 25 inches from the floor and 16 inches east of the doorway on the north kitchen wall indicating a downward direction.

*Collection and Preservation of Bloodstains*

Of all the common types of evidence found at crime scenes, blood is perhaps the most fragile. The value of bloodstains for typing begins to diminish almost immediately. The stability and utility of bloodstains varies from several days to months, depending on the blood grouping system sought. Naturally, proper preservation procedures improve the chances of determining blood types. *It is a certainty that wet or damp bloodstains packaged in airtight containers, such as plastic bags, will be useless as evidence in a matter of days.* Any type of preservation technique that hastens putrefaction should be avoided. Thus storing bloodstains that are still damp in airtight containers or in warm environments will accelerate deterioration of the specimen. Conversely, an air-dried sample stored in a paper bag at room temperature, or better, under refrigeration, will retain its evidentiary usefulness for a significantly longer period of time.

Once blood evidence has been found it must be collected and preserved in such a manner to achieve maximum benefit. All too often improper collection and preservation of this type of evidence make the crime laboratory's work difficult and sometimes impossible.

Preservation of blood and other biological evidence may require special handling in those jurisdictions having case law dealing with preservation of such evidence. Biological evidence, i.e., blood, semen, saliva, and so forth, does deteriorate with time. Some of the genetic markers present in these samples, which can be typed to determine their source, last for a short time. Drying and freezing the specimens slows down this deterioration. Some courts have held that the police have an affirmative duty to preserve evidence for defendants which can prove their innocence. In those jurisdictions, it is essential that biological evidence be stored frozen. Failure to do this may result in the evidence being excluded and, in some instances, the entire case thrown out of court.

Even for those locales that do not have the legal requirement to store blood, semen, and other biological evidence in a frozen state, such a practice is recommended simply because it extends the useful life of the material. Many laboratories operate with a high case load and often it is not possible to examine the evidence immediately. Storing this evidence in a dry, frozen state will maintain its usefulness for many months and perhaps provide valuable information for the investigator.

## Removal of Bloodstains

Blood may be present in a liquid, damp, or completely dry state. Depending on the circumstance, different procedures may be used. Blood still in the *liquid* state is easiest for the laboratory to work with; it is, however, the most difficult state in which to preserve adequately the easily degraded blood grouping substances.

A specimen from a pool of blood is best preserved in *saline* solution. Saline is a dilute solution of sodium chloride (salt) and distilled water, usually about 0.85%. Collect approximately 2 ml of blood with a clean disposable pipette and place in a test tube containing a like quantity of saline. Stopper the test tube and gently invert two or three times to mix the blood with the saline. The saline solution is a suitable medium to keep red blood cells from lysing, that is, breaking, as a result of a change in the blood's salt concentration caused by water evaporation. This is helpful in some blood grouping procedures.

There are several drawbacks to this procedure. First, it requires crime scene investigators to carry saline with them. Second, and the greater problem, is that blood collected in this manner is highly susceptible to deterioration. If this evidence cannot be taken to a crime laboratory within 24 hours, collecting blood in saline solution is *not* the method of choice.

An alternative method of collection is to place an *absorbent piece of material* into the still liquid pool of blood. Materials such as filter paper, cotton-tipped applicators, and cotton gauze have been used in the past. The best procedure, in the author's opinion, is to use clean, white cotton fabric similar to that used in men's 100% cotton handkerchiefs. This material can be cut up into 1/4-inch square pieces and used in the collection of wet and dried bloodstains.

The cotton fabric square is placed in the liquid blood and allowed to become saturated. The fabric is removed from the blood by means of forceps and placed in an unstoppered test tube. The tube is purposely left unstoppered to allow the fabric to air dry. The test tube *must* be marked in such a way to clearly indicate which specimen it is and by whom it was collected. This is especially important when several blood samples are collected.

Still another method of collecting blood from a pool is to use the *gauze pad* from an adhesive bandage such as a Band-Aid®. In choosing an adhesive bandage, make certain to use only those with a cotton gauze pad. Some brands use a perforated film on top of the gauze, which is not acceptable for this particular use.

The gauze pad of the bandage is placed into contact with the pool to become saturated with blood. The bandage is then attached by means of the adhesive tape to a clean 3-by-5 index card. The card is appropriately marked with the necessary identifying information. Liquid blood collected in this manner will be able to air dry on the cotton bandage and remain useful as evidence for some time.

Most blood found at crime scenes is already dried. Collection of *dried blood* specimens may be accomplished by a variety of different methods.

If the blood is particularly crusty or flaky it can be removed by a razor blade, scalpel, or clean pocket knife and *scraped* onto a clean piece of paper. The paper is then folded in such a way to minimize loss of the blood. The folded paper is marked and placed in an envelope and sealed. The envelope is used to protect against the loss of the blood should the paper unfold.

Blood present as dried smears or dried droplets does not lend itself to the scraping technique. It should be collected on *moist pieces* of cotton cloth approximately 1/4-inch square. The cotton is *slightly* wetted with distilled water and held in forceps. The damp cloth is swabbed over the area of interest in an attempt to concentrate the dried blood as much as possible onto the moistened cotton fabric. Generally, a dark, rust-colored stain imparted to the cotton fabric indicates a sufficient sample has been collected. After the sample is collected, it is placed in a clean, dry unstoppered test tube that has been properly marked. The unstoppered tube allows the stain to air dry.

## Bloodstained Objects

Generally, it is best to submit the entire bloodstained item to the crime laboratory rather than remove the blood. The location of the object must be carefully noted and photographed. If blood on the object appears loose and likely to flake off, it should be collected and packaged separately before packaging the item of interest.

Packaging bloodstained items must be done in a way so as not to destroy the evidence. Packaging in airtight containers must be avoided. Bloodstained articles placed in sealed plastic bags or even tightly wrapped in paper will readily putrefy and render the blood evidence useless.

Items such as damp bloodstained clothing should, if possible, be allowed to air dry. The drying should be done at room temperature away from direct sunlight. Items should then be packaged separately and loosely in wrapping paper or paper bags.

If wet or damp bloodstained items cannot be air dried, they should be packaged separately in wrapping paper or paper bags. They should not be tightly rolled or bundled up since this accelerates putrefaction of the stains. Whether such items are wet or dry, newspaper should not be used.

When collecting items of *clothing*, a useful habit to develop is to immediately initial the items as soon as the evidence is received. Develop a routine of always marking the item in the same location, such as on the inside collar of a shirt or the back inside waistband of trousers.

Often it is not feasible to submit an entire *large item* of bloodstained evidence to the laboratory, for example, bloodstained carpet or mattress. There are two ways to collect blood in such instances. The first is to follow the already outlined procedure of using the 1/4-inch moistened cotton cloth. The second is simply to cut out a portion of the item containing the bloodstain. The *cutting* is then placed in an appropriate package and marked.

When cutting out a specimen of carpet or mattress for blood typing, an unstained area next to the stain should be collected as well. This is a *control sample* and is necessary to determine whether there is anything normally in the material that may cause a false positive test.

*Control samples* must also be taken when swabbing dried stains with the moistened 1/4-inch-square cotton fabric. This is accomplished by swabbing an unstained area adjacent to the stained area with a clean piece of cotton cloth.

## Blood Typing

Blood typing evidence is capable of eliminating suspects as well as incriminating them. However, to give meaning to blood collected at a crime scene, blood samples from victims and suspects must be routinely submitted to the crime laboratory along with the evidence.

### Collection of Known Specimens

It is important to collect known, whole blood specimens in an appropriate way. Only a physician, nurse, or medical technologist may draw blood. It is especially important to use the proper collection container. Most hospitals are accustomed to collecting blood for toxicology examinations such as blood alcohol and may not be aware of the best type of tube to be used for blood typing. Don't use just any tube. The best thing to do is to contact the crime laboratory. Find out which preservative/anticoagulant, if any, is most preferred for a known sample.

Beyond determining that a dried sample of material is in fact blood, there are several other useful pieces of information that a crime laboratory can determine. Species origin and blood type are the most important.

*Species origin* is simply a test to determine the species of animal from which a blood sample came. The amount of blood required for this test is very small; however, it is important to have a control specimen to rule out the possibility of false positive tests.

Approximately two dozen different animal antisera are commercially available for use in the species origin test. For criminal cases the most often used antisera are human and domestic animal antisera such as dog, cat, cow, horse, deer, and so on. Differentiating closely related species of animals may sometimes be difficult. Species determination is also useful in animal poaching cases.

## Forensic DNA Typing

For anyone attending a sporting event or being in a large crowd of people, one observation is obvious—people look different. Differences are manifested by sex, race, stature, hair color, eye color, and shape of facial features, to name but a few of the more obvious. The fact is that people can easily recognize others through some subjective mental process: "There's Steve and Barbara; they work in my office!"

We can also recognize family traits among brothers and sisters, parents and children, and sometimes even more distant familial relationships. How often have people commented that a son looks "just like" his father or mother or said, "I can see Grandmother's eyes in yours." These family characteristics can be seen over and over again in family lineage.

People's appearance and family traits are a manifestation of the biochemical blueprint and building blocks that make people unique and who they are. The notion of differences and similarities in individuals has its scientific basis in the study of genetics. Genetics' roots go back to the mid nineteenth century when Gregor Mendel suggested that genes control factors influencing heredity. Over the next hundred years and into the end of the twentieth century, major strides have been made in the study of genetics, genes, and the more fundamental units, chromosomes and the basic unit of the chromosome, DNA.

DNA, or deoxyribonucleic acid, is the biochemical key to differentiating uniqueness between individuals[3] (with the exception of identical twins). It has been called the chemical messenger, in that it conveys genetic information that is the basis of the way individual living things take shape, grow, and reproduce. Pictorially, the DNA molecule resem-

---

[3] An important issue in DNA study today is the question of the appropriate population data bases to use when determining the statistical numerical value of a subject's DNA type occurring in the population. Different ethnic groups have different frequencies of occurrence. A question yet to be resolved is which is the correct population (an average population or that of a specific ethnic group) that numerical results should be derived from.

Assume an oriental person's blood is collected at a crime scene. If the crime scene area is populated by Hispanics, which data bases should be used: Hispanic, oriental, or an average? Perhaps an alternative way to report results might be to use a range and give a high and low figure for a court to consider.

bles a twisted ladder, or double helix. The "steps" within the ladder consist of four chemical subunits or bases: guanine (G), adenine (A), thymine (T), and cytosine (A). The bases pair in predictable ways—A always with T, and G always with C—and form the steps or rungs of the double-stranded DNA helix. The combination of the A-T and G-C are referred to as base pairs. There are over 3 billion base pairs in human DNA; however, only a small portion of these base pairs determine the unique traits in persons that are of forensic interest.

DNA is folded into microscopic bundles called chromosomes and exists in all cells containing nuclei. DNA is not present in red blood cells, as these cells do not have nuclei; other cells present in blood do contain DNA, however. DNA is present in blood, seminal fluid, tissues, bone marrow, hair roots, saliva, urine, and tooth pulp. Each of these samples has the potential to yield DNA typing results.

Recent advances in biology have permitted scientists to unravel the DNA code and examine pieces of DNA to look for similarities and differences between individuals. For forensic DNA purposes, there are two procedures in current use: RFLP and PCR. Restriction fragment length polymorthism (RFLP), as of this writing, is used more often in forensic casework than polymerase chain reaction (PCR). Forensic DNA technology is evolving very rapidly, and methods are in development that will incorporate certain parts of the two present technologies.

RFLP requires a somewhat larger sample than PCR and is time-consuming, taking several weeks to complete an assay. It is a very labor-intensive technique requiring much hands-on laboratory work. An additional technical difficulty is that radioactive labeled reagents are used in the test, necessitating special laboratory practices. The benefit of RFLP testing is that it is able to individualize a sample to a very small segment of the population—sometimes as small as one person in several billion.

PCR, on the other hand, is relatively easy to use and works on very small samples. Results can be obtained much more quickly than with RFLP techniques. The major difference, however, is in the nature of the laboratory test result. PCR population results are more closely related to traditional forensic serology test results and may be on the order of one person in thousands, compared with the very small numbers generated by RFLP.

## Legal Issues in DNA Typing

As DNA typing in general is still a relatively new technology, there are still legal issues to consider. As with any new scientific techniques that must be introduced into court, legal challenges are expected. Defense challenges are more likely with DNA testing, because probability results are so great that juries may be unduly influenced by the evidence and not consider other information.

There are two legal tests that can be used to determine whether scientific tests are admissible in court. Depending on the jurisdiction in which a case is heard, the Frye test or a more liberal relevancy test may be used.

The Frye[4] rule comes from a 1923 federal case wherein the court stated:

> Just when a scientific principle or discovery crosses the line between experimental and demonstrable is difficult to define. Somewhere in this twilight zone the evidential force of the principle must be recognized, and while courts will go a long way in admitting expert testimony deduced from well-recognized scientific principle or discovery, the thing from which the deduction is made must be sufficiently established to have gained general acceptance in the particular field in which it belongs.

The Frye standard is sometimes referred to as the general acceptance test. For evidence to be considered by a jury, the court requires: (1) that the scientific field from which the underlying theory of the test is identified and (2) that the scientific principles on which the testing is based have been accepted by most of the relevant scientific community.

A different criteria base of relevancy was established in the Federal Rules of Evidence in 1975 and has been adopted by a number of states. The relevancy test departs from the requirement of general acceptance by the relevant scientific community and gives the court wide discretionary latitude. Rule 702 states:

> If scientific, technical, or other specialized knowledge will assist the trier of fact to understand the evidence or to determine the fact at issue, a witness qualified as an expert by knowledge, skill, experience, training, or education, may testify thereto in the form of an opinion or otherwise.

Whichever standard is required in a given jurisdiction, new scientific evidence, such as forensic DNA evidence, may require extensive court admissibility hearings.

As with other forensic serology testing, DNA provides the ability to determine that a subject was not involved in a case as well as to include a subject. The major usefulness of forensic DNA typing is the ability to include the subject to the exclusion of all others.

Forensic DNA data-basing is feasible. DNA typing results can be

---

[4] *Frye v. United States*, 293 F. 1013 (D.C. Cir 1923).

stored in a centralized data base and searched to help identify criminals, as well as victims in mass disasters. Consider, for example, serial sexual assault cases. Forensic science laboratories would be able to determine whether an individual rape case was associated with serial crimes and identify the suspect, provided his DNA typing data were on file.

There are a host of other methods of typing blood and other biological evidence that have come to be known as traditional forensic serology procedures. As DNA typing gains greater use, these alternative methods will be used less frequently.

## DNA and Nonsuspect Rape Cases

The use of DNA typing in crime laboratories will result in a change in the way forensic science laboratories decide which cases are worked. Prior to the availability of DNA typing, most laboratories did not conduct blood typing tests on vaginal swabs collected in sexual assault cases when the case was a nonsuspect rape case. The reasoning was simple. Typing results could not be compared with a suspect's sample, and since resources are limited such cases were not typed.

Forensic DNA capability changes this policy. DNA data banking has the potential to identify suspects based on their DNA type in much the same way that we presently use fingerprints. Local, state, and federal authorities are initiating plans to establish such data bases. Serial crimes, such as serial rapes and murders, will have a better likelihood of being solved because DNA typing results can be compared with DNA typing records collected from convicted violent felons.

## ABO Typing

DNA typing may one day make blood typing and other systems unnecessary. However, at present many laboratories continue to conduct testing in older blood typing methodologies. Of the many blood grouping systems used in forensic science, most police investigators are familiar with the ABO blood grouping system. This is because this is the same blood grouping system used in blood banking. The four major *phenotypes* in this system are the A, B, AB, and O types. ABO blood typing has been used in criminal cases for decades, yet it has drawbacks. The procedure is labor-intensive and, when used alone, the statistical breakdown of the four principal types is not particularly good. If the victim and suspect have different blood types, it is a rather simple matter to differentiate the source of the blood. If, however, the types are the same, there is little the serologist can say, other than the subject was not excluded as a source of the blood. Because the A and O groups are the most common and make up approximately 39% and 43% of the population respectively, it is likely that a significant number of people will have the same ABO type.

Blood grouping systems are derived from biochemical substances such as enzymes and proteins found in blood and other body fluids. Like the ABO system, many are polymorphic, i.e., they have small but detectable structural differences even though they perform the same function. These differences are genetically determined from one's parents and can be thought of in terms of eye or hair color. Eye color or hair color may vary between individuals, but their functions are the same. This concept is the same with blood groups. Blood types are constant, i.e., an individual will always have the same type.

To be useful in a forensic setting, enzymes and proteins must have different phenotypes. If all people in the ABO system had the same type, that system would have no value in differentiating one person from another. A blood grouping system must be relatively stable. Some biochemicals in blood are changed or even destroyed in heat or on drying. Other are light sensitive. Since evidence may be present in a variety of harsh environmental conditions, some proteins and enzymes do not lend themselves to forensic applications.

## Electrophoresis

The technique used in crime laboratories to determine which phenotype is present in a given blood grouping system (other than ABO) is known as *electrophoresis*. As its name implies, electrical current is used to separate the different types in a given system. In brief, a cotton thread is saturated with the questioned blood. The blood-soaked fiber is inserted into a thin gel which has been poured over a pane of glass (Fig. 8.8). A 1/4-inch thread is used and several cases can be run at once. Direct electric current is applied across the gel, which causes the molecules making up the enzyme or protein to migrate through the gel. After a set period of time the separated constituents are made visible by application of a biologically reactive chemical that stains the protein or enzyme. The stain can then be photographed for record-keeping purposes.

Results show up as a series of patterns or bands on the gel. Interpretation of these bands requires considerable training and, sometimes, especially in the cases of older specimens, some of the bands making up a pattern may appear weak or diffuse and difficult to see. Because interpretation of results is sometimes difficult, some laboratories may have two or more analysts review the results.

Another form of electrophoresis that is currently used in many crime laboratories is a technique known as *isoelectric focusing* (IEF). IEF is capable of further differentiating phenotypes in a given blood grouping

FIGURE 8.8. In the electrophoresis technique, cotton threads saturated with blood are embedded in a gel-like material through which an electrical current is passed that separates specific phenotypes in a blood grouping system. The photograph shows the equipment used in this technique. (*Los Angeles County Sheriff's Department.*)

system. This is important to the investigator in that it enables the laboratory to better differentiate between blood groups from two or more subjects.

Nonscientific personnel may feel somewhat intimidated by the terms used in forensic serology. Most of the blood groups refer to enzymes or proteins that perform a particular biological activity in the body. For example, a common type is known as phosphoglucomutase (PGM). This enzyme plays a role in the metabolism of glucose. In order to make the names of these types easier to use, nearly all have acronyms. Some of the more common blood grouping systems are:

| | |
|---|---|
| Phosphoglucomutase | PGM |
| Esterase D | EsD |
| Erthrocyte acid phosphatase | EAP |
| Glyoxalase I | GLO I |
| Adenosine deaminase | ADA |
| Adenylate kinase | AK |
| Haptoglobin | Hp |

| Group-specific component | Gc |
|---|---|
| Transferrin | Tf |
| Hemoglobin | Hb |

## Frequencies of Occurrence

Just as the familiar ABO blood grouping system has a statistical breakdown, so do other blood grouping systems. Each of these systems is statistically independent and hence the individual frequencies of occurrence can be combined (see Table 8.1).

Assume a subject has the following determined blood groups: ABO type A, haptoglobin type 2, and PGM type 2. ABO type A occurs in about 39.2% of the general population, haptoglobin type 2 in 36.1%, and PGM type 2 in about 5.4%. To determine the probability of a person's having these three blood grouping systems, multiply the individual probabilities together:

$$0.392 \times 0.361 \times 0.054 = 0.0076$$

or about 8 people in 1000. This means that in a random population of 1000, we could exclude 992 persons of those having contributed the questioned blood specimen.

**TABLE 8.1.** Approximate Frequencies of Occurrence of Some Blood Grouping Systems

| Blood Grouping System | Blood Group Phenotype Frequency of Occurrence[a] | | | | | |
|---|---|---|---|---|---|---|
| ABO | A | B | O | AB | | |
| | 39.2% | 12.7% | 43.5% | 4.5% | | |
| Phosphoglucomutase (PGM) | 1 | 2–1 | 2 | other | | |
| | 58.9% | 35.6% | 5.4% | 0.1% | | |
| Esterase D (EsD) | 1 | 2–1 | 2 | | | |
| | 79.5% | 19.3% | 1.2% | | | |
| Erythrocyte Acid Phosphatase | A | B | BA | CB | CA | C |
| (EAP) | 10.8% | 39.3% | 42.1% | 4.3% | 3.3% | 0.2% |
| Glyoxalase I (GLO I) | 1 | 2–1 | 2 | | | |
| | 22.4% | 49.8% | 27.8% | | | |
| Adenosine Deaminase | 1 | 2–1 | 2 | | | |
| (ADA) | 90.0% | 9.8% | 0.2% | | | |
| Adenylate Kinase (AK) | 1 | 2–1 | 2 | other | | |
| | 92.7% | 7.1% | 0.1% | 0.1% | | |
| Haptoglobin (Hp) | 1 | 2–1 | 2 | | | |
| | 14.6% | 49.3% | 36.1% | | | |
| Group Specific Component | 1 | 2–1 | 2 | | | |
| (Gc) | 50.7% | 40.9% | 8.3% | | | |

[a] In Caucasian populations.

As we continue to add more and more blood grouping systems (many crime laboratories can determine as many as a dozen unique systems), our ability to discriminate between individuals, that is, to prove that there is only a very small likelihood that any other person contributed to a suspicious stain, increases tremendously. This is the object of forensic serology.

Unfortunately, it is not always possible to determine all the forensically useful blood grouping systems. Many are unstable; they deteriorate after several days to a few weeks. Factors such as heat, direct sunlight, humidity, improper evidence packaging, and the like decrease in one way or another the chances of detecting these fragile systems. As discussed earlier, preserving blood and other biological evidence in a dry, frozen state will enable the laboratory to obtain the maximum amount of information from the evidence.

Other blood grouping systems are more stable. In the ABO system, for example, reports have been published that archaeologists have been able to determine blood groups of mummified remains thousands of years old. In any event, it is always worthwhile to try to determine as many types as possible, regardless of the age of the stain.

## Typing Other Body Fluids

Other body fluids besides blood can be typed. About four out of five persons in the population are secretors. A *secretor* is an individual who has present in certain body fluids ABO blood grouping substances. If a person is a secretor, it is possible to determine the ABO blood group from the saliva, semen (or vaginal secretions), and perspiration. It is therefore possible to determine the ABO blood group from a cigarette butt, a bite mark, and, in a sexual assault case, from seminal fluid.

To determine the ABO blood type from these substances it is necessary to obtain whole bloodstains and saliva specimens from all the involved parties. Blood can be collected in an EDTA vacuum collection tube (lavender top). Saliva should be collected in the manner specified by the crime laboratory. Some laboratories have the subject chew on a piece of cotton gauze or other clean material and submit an air-dried specimen. Other crime laboratories require a fresh, liquid specimen. The purpose of the saliva is to determine the secretor status of the test subject. The whole blood is required to determine the ABO blood group.

Secretion typing is most often used in sexual assault cases. A specimen from the vaginal smear or aspirate is typed. The results are then evaluated with the blood type and secretor status of the victim and suspect. The most definitive conclusion that can be drawn is that the suspect's blood type is not consistent with the blood type determined from the vaginal specimen. It is never possible to state that the suspect was definitely responsible for depositing the semen. All that can be stated is that the suspect cannot be excluded on the basis of a comparison of the blood groups determined from the vaginal specimen and the suspect's blood type.

## Case

Two hours before being raped, the victim had consensual sexual intercourse with her husband. A vaginal smear was tested and seminal fluid was found. The ABO blood group found on the smear was type B. Both the victim and her husband were type O and nonsecretors. The suspect was a secretor and type B.

In that case, the finding of type B is important circumstantial evidence. Although it does not conclusively show by the blood group alone that the suspect was involved, he is not exonerated by this evidence.

The PGM system also can be typed in seminal fluid. The PGM blood group is not dependent on the secretor status of the subject. It is present regardless of whether he is a secretor or nonsecretor.

## Other Examinations

Besides blood and body fluid typing, forensic serology is concerned with several other areas of potential interest to investigators.

Occasionally, the issue is raised in sexual assault cases whether a blood specimen is *menstrual* in origin. It is possible to determine the difference between menstrual and venous blood (Fig. 8.9).

Sodomy and other sex-related offenses may have *feces* present. It is possible to differentiate between human and animal feces. Further, a microscopic examination of the material might show similarities in undigested foods from two specimens and, hence, permit the inference the feces came from the same individual.

*Urine* is another material sometimes related to sexual assault cases. In some instances suspects have been known to urinate on rape victims. Tests showing the presence of urine and blood type can corroborate a victim's testimony.

*Hair* shows some limited ability to be blood typed. Attempts have been made to determine a subject's ABO type from hair, but the tests do not seem particularly reliable. The procedure for determining PGM and EAP types from the sheath cells present on the hair root of forcibly pulled hair is promising and should be attempted. Chromosome-staining procedures on hair root sheath cells have been used to determine the sex of the subject. Studies have shown that this procedure can be used with hairs maintained for at least 100 days.

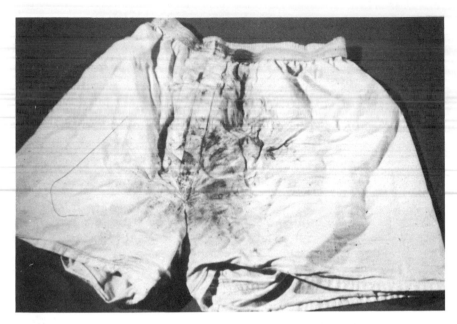

FIGURE **8.9.** The suspect's undershorts were submitted to the laboratory as evidence in a rape case. He claimed that the blood was his own; however, tests showed that it was menstrual blood from the victim. (*Los Angeles County Sheriff's Department.*)

There are sophisticated microscopic methods available whereby a bloodstain can be sexed. *Sexing* means to determine whether the stain is of male or female origin.

In some instances it is possible to determine a donor's race from a blood type. If, for example, a blood sample were found to be hemoglobin type Hb AS, this would indicate that the subject was of Negroid ancestry. Other groups seem to be ethnic-specific and suggest the racial origin of the subject.

Hemoglobin F is found in infants up to age 6 months. In a case of infanticide, typing hemoglobin might be useful.

Forensic serology is a rapidly evolving field. Each year advancements are made which improve the chances to individualize a blood specimen as having come from a specific person. The potential usefulness of serological evidence to reconstruct the crime scene and incriminate suspects makes this evidence extremely valuable in police investigations. Police investigators and prosecutors should have a comprehensive working knowledge in this field of forensic science in order to use it to the fullest.

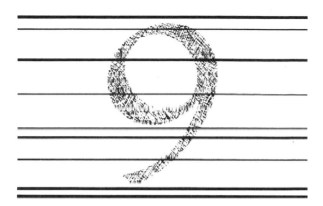

# IMPRESSION
# EVIDENCE

**M**inute imperfections on a large variety of objects such as tools, footwear, tires, and so on produce markings in their normal (and sometimes unusual) usage. These markings are often characteristic of the type of tool or object used. In many instances very small and sometimes microscopically unique markings are left that can be traced directly to the object or instrument in question.

Such marks caused by a tool are of two general types: compression marks and scraping marks. *Compression marks* are those left when an instrument is in some way pushed or forced into a material capable of picking up an impression of the tool. Examples of such marks include shoe impressions, tire impressions, bite mark impressions, fabric impressions, the mark left by a hammer hitting a piece of wood, the mark of a screwdriver used to jimmy a window, breech mark impressions on shell casings, typewriter marks, and the like (Fig. 9.1). *Scraping or striated marks* are produced by a combination of pressure and sliding contact by the tool and result in microscopic striations imparted to the surface onto which the tool was worked. Examples of scraping marks are those found on fired bullets, marks left by a cutting tool such as a bolt cutter, marks from a wrench used on a doorknob, marks from an ax used to cut wood, marks from a screwdriver blade dragged over a surface, teeth marks used to bite through a soft material capable of picking up an impression, and so on. For compression or scraping marks to be

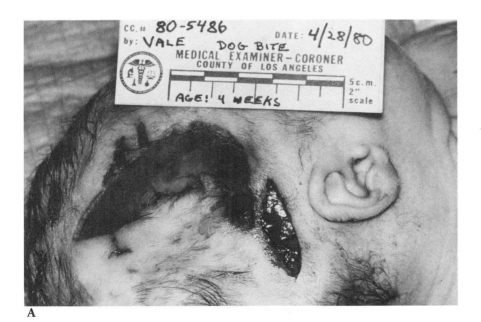

A

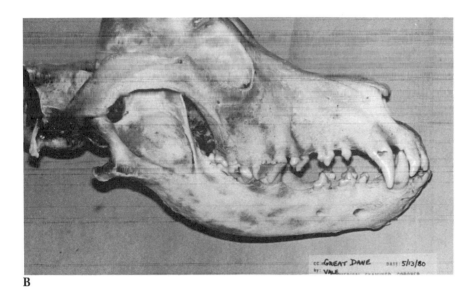

B

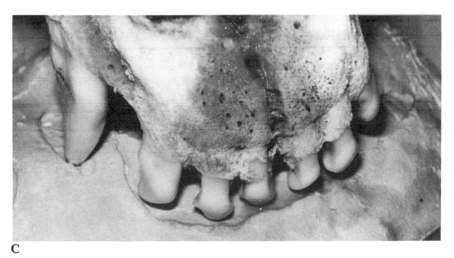

C

**FIGURE 9.1.** A 4-week-old infant was bitten by the family pet (A). The Great Dane's teeth (B) were compared with a cast of the wound (C). (*Los Angeles County, Department of Chief Medical Examiner-Coroner.*)

observed, the tool must be made of a harder material than the object on which it is used.

The random nature and microscopic imperfections found on tools are a result of their manufacture and usage. Casting, grinding, and polishing of metal instruments, as well as use, result in small but observable differences from one tool to the next. Such differences have even been demonstrated in consecutively manufactured items.

Comparative examination is the method by which impression-type evidence is studied. The marks left at the crime scene (or castings of the mark) are compared with test markings made by the tool or object in question. Through careful and often tedious examination of the known and questioned evidence, a determination can be made of whether a particular item was responsible for a specific mark.

## Footprints

Footprints[1] are a common type of impression evidence found at or near crime scenes. In favorable situations, such evidence may conclusively demonstrate that the suspect was at the scene of the crime. A detailed examination of footprints is tedious and time-consuming work, and because of this may be overlooked by the investigator. Although this discussion concerns footwear impressions, the investigator should not overlook soil evidence that might later be discovered on the suspect's shoes. (This topic is discussed in the part of Chapter 7 dealing with soil evidence.)

When a cast is made of a footprint left in soft ground, one expects to obtain a faithful reproduction of the heel and sole of the shoe that made the print. As a rule, however, the result of casting is actually quite different—the cast has an arched form. The back of the heel and the point of the toe are considerably lower than the other parts of the cast. This is due to the fact that, in normal walking, the back of the heel is placed on the ground first, after which each part of the heel and sole is pressed down on the ground in succession until the foot is lifted with a final strong pressure of the point of the toe against the earth. The pressure that regulates the depth of the impression is the greatest at the back of the heel and at the point of the toe. When a subject is running, the footprints left are less distinct, partly owing to slipping of the foot and partly to sand and earth being thrown into the print. The form of the print depends on the individual's style of running; many people run on their toes, some set both heel and toe hard in the ground, and others set

---

[1] The reader is referred to an excellent book on the subject, *Footware Impression Evidence*, by William J. Bodziak (New York: Elsevier Science Publishing, Inc., 1990).

the whole foot down in the earth at once. In deciding whether an individual walked or ran there is only one certain guide—that is the length of the step.

## The Value of Footprints

Individual footprints are generally preserved only if they contain details of value for identification. The most valuable details are signs of wear, characteristic fittings or marks of fittings that have come off, injuries, marks of nails and pegs (especially when these are irregularly placed), and repair marks. If they are particularly characteristic or occur in sufficient numbers, such details may form decisive evidence. In the interest of thoroughness, footprints should be preserved even if they do not show any details.

Although the size and shape of the shoe or a pattern in the heel or sole is of lesser evidential value, a representative print should nonetheless be preserved for its value as an investigative lead.

If footprints are found in snow that has a frozen crust, it is a waste of time to attempt to take a cast of them. When the foot breaks through the hard surface of the snow, the surface snow goes with it and forms a hard bottom to the mark. The coarse grains of ice in the surface layer do not reproduce any details of the shoe, not even such large defects as a hole through the sole. It is not possible to obtain any useful information of the size by measuring the footprint since the hard snow is broken and pressed down at points a considerable distance outside the outer contour of the shoe.

A footwear print may be a foot *impression* or a *footprint (dust print)*.

*Foot impressions* occur when the foot treads in some moldable material such as earth, sand, clay, snow, and so on.

*Footprints* are formed on a hard base when the foot or the sole and heel of a shoe are contaminated with some foreign matter such as road dirt, dust, flour, blood, moisture, or the like. Footprints may also be latent when they have been formed by naked or stocking-covered feet on a smooth surface.

Footwear impression evidence and information from the gait pattern may indicate that the subject was walking or running, had sustained an injury or walked with a limp, was possibly intoxicated, had a tendency to walk toed in or toed out, was carrying a heavy object, that the area had been "cased," and the like.

## Preservation of Foot and Tire Impressions

Although the focus here is on footprints, much of what follows concerning preservation and collecting this type of evidence applies equally well to tire impression evidence. Foot impressions are generally found outdoors, and the first precautionary measure is therefore to protect the impression from alteration or destruction, preferably by covering it with a box or cordoning off the area.

Impressions in snow are especially troublesome when it is thawing, so that they should be protected by a box covered with snow to prevent further thawing. If a foot impression is in such a position that there is a risk that it will gradually be filled up or damaged by running water, it must be surrounded by a wall of earth, sand, or snow. Alternatively, a hole may be dug close to the impression and the water led away to the hole, the latter being emptied when necessary. However, these protective measures are only stopgaps, and the actual preservation should be undertaken as soon as possible.

Interior locations often have footprints present, especially on surfaces such as tiled floors, glass, desk tops, countertops, chair seats, and the like. A simple procedure to locate these indoor prints is to turn off all interior lights and, with a high-intensity flashlight, search the surfaces by shining the light at a low angle. Often these impressions are dust prints and very easily destroyed. Once detected, care must be taken to make certain they are preserved until they can be properly preserved.

Preservation should be accomplished by both *photographing* and *casting* or, in the case of dust prints, by *lifting*. Photographing foot impressions[2] is done with the camera placed *vertically* above the impression on a tripod with a scale placed next to the impression. The film plane should be parallel to the impression so as not to cause distortion in the photograph. It is good practice to place two scales in the photograph at right angles to each other. One rule can be placed adjacent to the long axis of the foot impression, and a second perpendicular to the first in the region adjacent to the heel.

Although large-format cameras, e.g., 4-by-5-inch or 2¼-inch formats, allow for larger negatives, 35-mm cameras have become more widely used for crime scene work and produce acceptable results. The quality of today's photographic films is very good. Footware and tire impressions require film that can capture fine details, therefore fine-grained films are best for this purpose. Both black and white and color photographs should be taken of the prints.

If the bottom of the impression is appreciably deeper than the surface of the ground or snow, the scale should be brought down to the same level. Before photographing, any material that may have fallen into the impression after it was formed should be cleaned away. For this purpose

---

[2] The most common errors in crime scene photography occur in taking photographs of shoe and tire impressions, and many examples of poor quality photographs have been observed. These include not using a tripod to support the camera and not shooting perpendicular to the impression, failing to use a scale or ruler in the photograph, and not using oblique lighting. Overall, taking quality photographs is relatively simple, but it requires practice.

it is convenient to use tweezers, or a piece of paper onto which are rolled lumps of earth or other such objects that cannot be picked up by the tweezers. If it is not possible to do this cleaning without injuring details of the impression, it should be omitted. Materials trampled into the impression, such as leaves, grass, and the like, should not be removed, as they actually form part of the impression and no details will be found under them. Careless removal of a trampled blade of grass can destroy large parts of an impression. Any water that may be present should be carefully removed by a hypodermic syringe or small pump. If a foot impression has been made in snow, there may be difficulty in getting a clear picture of it. Hard snow may be dusted with aluminum powder, which gives a clearer picture; with loose snow aluminum powder can be dusted into the mark by tapping the brush.

Because details in foot impressions are three-dimensional in nature, the photograph should be made under illumination that will bring out those details to the best advantage. Direct sunlight enhances the details by creating highlights and shadows. When the sky is cloudy and the daylight diffuse and practically shadowless, artificial light must be used; either photo flood or flash illumination is suitable. These considerations, of course, also apply to situations when it is imperative that the pictures be taken at night. The important point to remember about the illumination is that the light must not be held at too low an angle, since too much shadow will obscure details rather than emphasize them.

Casting of foot impressions is generally done with *dental stone.* Other materials include paraffin, sulfur, and silicone rubber,[3] which are less frequently used.

## Casting with Dental Stone

Dental stone is a form of gypsum or calcium sulfate that can be used to cast shoe and tire impressions. At one time plaster of Paris was more widely used for this purpose; however, dental stone is superior and readily available from dental supply companies. Dental stone can be used for casting most impressions, even in snow.

*Foot impressions in loose, dry sand and earth* can be taken without any special preparation. Some literature suggests removing loose twigs and leaves. This practice can damage the print and is discouraged. Also the use of fixatives such as spray lacquers or talc is not necessary. These practices were generally recommended to be used in conjunction with plaster of Paris. They are not needed with dental stone.

---

[3] Casting impressions takes practice. It is recommended that one develops skills by working on nonevidentiary footmarks with the material, whether using dental stone or any other technique.

Dental stone lends itself quite well to casting water-filled impressions. If an *impression is very muddy or is filled with water*, no attempt should be made to remove the water as this may damage the impression.

A retaining wall or frame should be placed around the impression. The retainer should allow for a cast of at least 2 inches in thickness. Dental stone is lightly sprinkled or sifted directly into the water-filled impression to about an inch thickness, followed by normally prepared dental stone which has been made with a little less water and is slightly thicker. The cast should be poured to about a 2-inch thickness and allowed to set in place for an hour.

To cast a footprint, about 2 lbs of dental stone in about 12 oz of water is used. A clean rubber bowl can be used for mixing. Water should first be added to the bowl, followed by sifting in the dental stone. The mixture should be stirred to remove any lumps or air bubbles. The final mix should be the consistency of pancake batter. An alternative method is to use a self-sealing bag large enough to hold about 2 pounds of dental stone and to mix the material right in the bag. This procedure is reported to be very convenient. (*Note:* when dental stone is mixed with water the solution heats up. This heating causes difficulties when casting impressions in snow. For this reason, a small amount of snow or ice should be added to the mixture to keep the temperature down, and the mixture should be made slightly more viscous than the pancake batter consistency.)

After the material is mixed, it should be gently poured onto an area adjacent to the impression and allowed to flow onto the impression. If it is necessary to pour the material into the impression, a baffle such as a flat stick or spoon can be used to lessen the impact of the material. Great care must be taken that the dental stone does not destroy any of the fine material in the print. Before the cast hardens it should be marked by means of a twig, scribe, or other sharp instrument. The information that should be included on the cast is the date, investigator's name or initials, case number, and location of the impression (Fig. 9.2).

The material will harden sufficiently in about 30 minutes for removal. Clumps of soil and rocks clinging to the cast should not be disturbed, and the cast should be allowed to thoroughly air dry for about 48 hours. If the impression is deep and firmly seated, it should be carefully excavated so that it finally lies on a pillar that may then be cut off.

When casting impressions in snow, the impression is prepared first by spraying a thin layer of *Snow Print Wax*. (Snow Print Wax is available from a number of law enforcement supply companies.) The print should be photographed a second time after the application of the Snow

**FIGURE 9.2.** This dental stone tire casting was taken in a case involving the theft of several airplane propellers and investigated by the Anchorage Airport Police. The tire impression was the first cast that the officer had ever poured in snow and enabled an easy identification as the tire had several bent studs. The technique used in Alaska in snow casting is to first spray the impression with gray automobile primer. This gives good contrast for photography and acts as a shell for the dental stone. The dental stone and water need to be ice cold prior to mixing. In extreme cold, potassium sulfate is added as an accelerator to the water and has been successfully used to cast impressions in conditions well below zero. (*Alaska Department of Public Safety, Scientific Crime Detection Laboratory.*)

Print Wax spray. After the applications of spray have been applied to completely cover the print and allowed to dry, the dental stone is carefully poured into the print. The stone is prepared with cold water and snow and should be made slightly thicker than normal. The material should be allowed to set up for at least an hour before removal and to dry for about 48 hours.

Sulfur casting is another procedure used by some for snow prints. About 5 lbs of powdered sulfur is needed for a print. The sulfur is melted in a 1-quart aluminum pot and poured into the print, using a channel to direct the flow of the molten sulfur. The trick to using sulfur is not to allow the material to get too hot. Sulfur melts at 115°C, but if heated to 170°C it changes characteristics and cannot be used. For best results, it should be heated slowly and stirred continuously. The molten sulfur must be poured quickly, as it will solidify as soon as it comes into contact with the snow. The cast should remain in place for about a half hour; the cast will be very fragile and extreme care must be taken when handling it (Fig. 9.3).

### Preservation of Footprints (Dust Prints)

Footprints are *always* preserved by photographing. After this is done, one of the following methods should be applied:

1. *Recovering the object on which the footprint is made.* Footprints are often found on objects stepped on by the criminal who, for example, entered in the dark through a window. If the window is broken, all fragments of glass should be examined. This type of print is usually best detected by low-angle illumination from one side. Rubber heels and soles leave exceptionally good prints on glass. Detailed prints are often also found on paper or cardboard that may be strewn about

FIGURE 9.3. A plaster cast from a shoe impression in snow showing good detail of the shoe sole pattern. The cast surface has been "colored" with silver spray to enhance the detail for photography. (*Zurich Cantonal Police, Forensic Science Department.*)

the room during a safe burglary. All such loose objects bearing prints should be carefully preserved for transport to the laboratory. When the seriousness of the crime warrants, and when the print consists of a dried liquid such as blood or ink, it may be advisable to remove a portion of linoleum or floor tile that bears a clear impression.

2. *Lifting by a special lifter* is preferred whenever the print is made by dust or a dust-like substance from the shoe. The lifter is a sheet of black rubber with a slightly sticky surface that is pressed against the print, picking up a faithful replica of the whole print. Oblique light photography under laboratory conditions brings out this dust print to a contrast that is often better than that observed in the original print.

   If a sufficiently large *fingerprint lifter* is available, it may be used instead of the special lifter. Care must be taken not to stretch the rubber lifter whereby the dust image may become distorted.

3. *Lifting by photographic paper* may be employed when special lifters are not available. Photographic paper, either black (exposed, developed, fixed, and washed) or white (fixed and washed) is used, as determined by the color of the material in the print. The paper is dampened with water or dilute ammonia, laid emulsion-side down over the print, and beaten against the print with a stiff brush or clapped with the palm. When the whole surface has been thoroughly beaten, the paper is removed and laid out to dry.

4. *Lifting by static electricity* is a new technique. The Kinderprint Company markets a field kit called an "electrostatic dust print lifter," which picks up dust prints onto mylar-coated foil by means of static electricity (Fig. 9.4). This is a relatively new procedure that may have application in certain situations.

## Taking Comparison Footprints from a Suspect

When the original prints are from covered feet (shoes, sneakers), these should be worn by the examiner when making comparison shoe prints. When taking *comparison footprints* the soles are to be coated with water-based ink using a large ink pad. The inked shoes are then carefully stepped onto a sheet of tracing paper or acetate sheet.

In taking prints of naked feet, the feet are blackened by being pressed against a thin layer of printing ink. To get a true picture of the formation of the sole of the foot in different positions, four different prints are taken: in normal standing position, in the standing position with pressure against the outside of the foot and with pressure against the inside, and, finally, when walking. This also applies to stockinged feet.

Yet another method for obtaining known footwear exemplars involves the use of talcum powder and black carbon paper. A thin coating

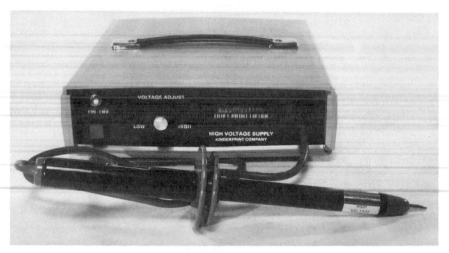

A

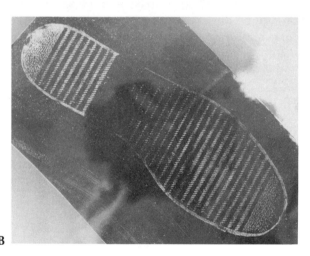

B

FIGURE 9.4. An electrostatic dust print lifter (A) and a dust print (B) lifted by the technique. (*Kinderprint Company, Martinez, California.*)

of talc is spread on a sheet of newspaper, which is placed talc-side up on top of about 10 sheets of newspaper that act as a cushion. The shoe is placed on the foot and walked onto the talc-covered newspaper. The talc-covered shoe is then impressed onto the carbon paper, carbon-side up. The carbon paper is similarly cushioned with about 10 sheets of newspaper. The resulting print is photographed 1:1, using Koda-lith™ high-contrast copy film. The developed negative will show a positive reproduction of the impression that can be superimposed over a negative from the crime scene.

## Comparison of Footprints

Comparison between footprints found at the scene of a crime and those of a suspect should be made by an expert, but this does not prevent a police investigator from undertaking a preliminary examination.

Prints or impressions of shoe-covered feet are seldom of the same size as the shoes themselves; even when they are being made, slipping and the movement of walking can damage the prints. The mark of a naked foot in movement can be as much as 1 inch longer than the mark of the same foot in the standing position. A foot impression in wet earth can become appreciably smaller when the earth dries; in clay the length can decrease by up to 3/4 inch. Thus, in establishing identity too much significance should not be attached to the dimensions. When examining the mark of a shoe-covered foot, a check of the circumference characteristics should be made. If the marks from the scene of the crime and from the suspect are similar in form, it is less important that they may differ somewhat in size.

Identification is based mainly on characteristic marks on the sole or heel (Fig. 9.5). The examination is best done by direct comparison of the preserved foot mark from the scene of the crime with the foot covering of the suspect. These are photographed side by side, and characteristic points are marked. With footprints, however, it is generally convenient to take a print of the foot covering of the suspect and to make a comparison between the prints. When it is a question of prints of naked feet, an examination is made first to see if there are any identifiable friction skin patterns and, if this is the case, then the investigation is carried out as for finger and palm prints.

In examining the foot covering of a suspect, dust, dirt, earth, and the like should be kept and, if necessary, compared with similar materials at the scene of the crime.

If the perpetrator has left overshoes at the scene, they may be compared with a suspect's shoes. Characteristic marks on the shoes, particularly on the soles, may be reproduced inside the overshoes. For this examination the overshoes must be cut open. If a shoe is found at the crime scene, it may contain characteristic marks of wear from the owner's foot. Such marks can then be compared with the markings inside shoes that can be proven to have been worn by the suspect.

## Marks of Clothes and of Parts of the Body

If clothing is pressed against a smooth surface, a latent print may be produced. Such a print is developed in the same way as a fingerprint or glove print. Clothing contaminated with a foreign body, such as blood, can also form a print. When clothing comes into contact with a plastic

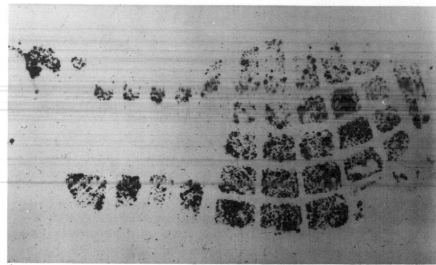

A

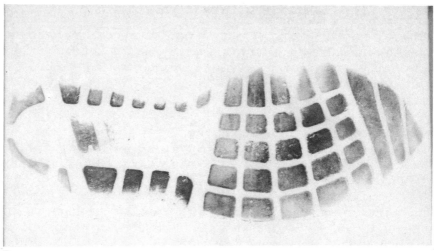

B

FIGURE 9.5. This footwear impression (A) is a photograph of a luminol reaction in a double homicide in Nome, Alaska. The impression was completely invisible prior to the application of luminol and matches the test shoe impressions of the suspect (B). (*Alaska Department of Public Safety, Scientific Crime Detection Laboratory.*)

substance (for example, clay), an identifiable plastic impression may be formed in it.

When a mark from clothing is to be recorded, it must be photographed with the camera placed vertically above or centrally in front of the mark, and a scale placed at the side of the mark in a direction corresponding with the structure of the fabric. If the mark is sufficiently large, the scale may be placed in the center of it. In such cases a number of pictures should be exposed and the scale should be moved to either side for each exposure so that details are not concealed (Fig. 9.6).

Marks of clothes are identified with the aid of the structure of the fabric, faults in the latter, seams, patches and other repairs, damage, and the like.

It sometimes happens that a whole section of the body forms a print or impression. In one case a burglar fell from a water spout onto the

FIGURE **9.6.** A suspect "picked up" a prostitute and, while in her room, produced an Australian Federal Police badge (A), hoping to get free "service." The prostitute retaliated and was assaulted. The badge was a facsimile and was in a clear plastic wallet. The suspect discarded the badge, which was subsequently located by police. The plastic wallet was found in the possession of the suspect. An examination of the plastic wallet revealed the outlines of a badge (B) of similar size and shape to the one found at the scene. (*State Forensic Science Laboratory, Melbourne, Australia.*)

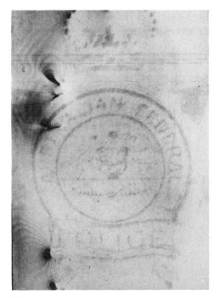

A

B

damp earth below, making an impression that showed clearly the face (with a characteristic nose) and both hands, one holding a crowbar and the other a pistol. When a hand has made a print or impression on a plastic medium, one should look for identifiable friction skin patterns. Other marks may also be found, such as those of rings, injuries, characteristic skin wrinkles, hand coverings, and so on. The preservation of marks of parts of the body is done in the same way as for footprints.

## Tooth Marks

Tooth marks may leave compression or scraping marks and occur in the form of bite marks in butter, cheese, fruit, chocolate, and the like. Bite marks may also occur on the skin of victims of rape or sexual murder, or on a criminal (Fig. 9.7). Cases have occurred in which the criminal has become involved in a hand-to-hand fight with another person; a tooth may have been knocked out, or a dental plate broken, and parts of the tooth or the dental plate may be found.

Bite marks can at times be so characteristic that they make possible the definite identification of a suspect. The relative positions of the teeth, their width, and the distance between them, together with ridges on the edges of the teeth and grooves on the back or front, vary in different individuals and may show in the bite mark. Deformations resulting from caries or illness, injury in the form of portions broken away, characteristic wear of the teeth, fillings and other dental work, the loss of certain teeth, and the like, are all noted in the bite.

Generally, tooth marks come from front teeth in the upper and lower jaws. With children and young people the edges of the front teeth usually have three ridges (sometimes more) that are distinguished by shallow incisions, sometimes in the form of furrows continued on the front and back sides of the teeth. With increasing age, these ridges and furrows generally disappear so that by the age of 30, the front teeth are generally smooth.

Bite marks should be carefully preserved by photographing and casting. They are generally formed in material that cannot be sent away or kept for a long time without the bite mark's changing in appearance because of drying or decomposition of the material. Marks made in fruit can be preserved in 0.5% formalin solution, which prevents changes resulting from drying, decay, and so forth. It is, however, not advisable to leave the fruit in the solution for sending to an expert by mail, as the fruit may be broken up and mixed with the solution as the result of shaking. An apple showing a bite mark, which is to be sent for examination, should instead be fixed by soaking in the solution for several

A

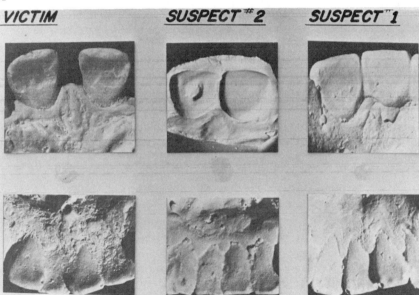

B

**FIGURE 9.7.** In a homicide case involving two suspects, a wad of used chewing gum was discovered at the crime scene (A). Dental impressions of the victim and suspects were made (B) and compared with the gum. An unusual feature of the gum's impression was a defect corresponding to an opening drilled in the back of one suspect's upper incisor during root canal therapy. In a further comparison, ABO blood grouping revealed a blood type that was the same as that suspect's. The case resulted in a guilty plea to second-degree murder. (*Norman D. Sperber, D.D.S., Forensic Odontologist, San Diego, California.*)

hours, then wrapped in tissue paper that has been moistened with formalin solution. The whole is then packed in a carton or box.

*For photography*, oblique lighting is used so that details appear most clearly. It should be noted that there is a risk that, a substance such as butter or soft cheese, for example, might melt under the heat from a photographic lamp. All bite marks should be photographed before casting, since the casting may go wrong and bite marks generally alter during casting in such a way that a fresh cast cannot be taken.

*The casting material* must be chosen with regard to the properties of the material in which the bite has been made. If the material contains water-soluble substances, e.g., chocolate and certain types of cheese, then the bite mark should be isolated from the casting mass by spraying with a thin layer of collodion or the like. Suitable casting media for different materials are described below.

*Human Skin*

Bite marks should first be photographed with a scale and traced using clear cellulose acetate and a felt-tip marker. The quality of the cast impression will depend on the depth of the bite. Silicone or rubber-based dental impression creams may be used to cast the impression. It is important to remember that saliva may be present as part of the mark. A swab of the area should be made for possible blood group determination. (Blood typing of saliva is discussed in Chapter 8.)

*Foods*

Bite mark impressions may be left in cheese, butter, sandwich meats, fruit, chocolate, chewing gum, and other such substances. If the food is water-soluble, dental impression cream such as polysulfide rubber-based impression materials may be used. Other materials such as plaster, molten sulfur (for materials not heat-sensitive), and the like have applicability. If plaster is used, the surface should first be lightly sprayed with lacquer or similar material should the item to be cast contain water.

**Tool Marks**

Marks of tools or of objects that have been used as tools are often found at the scene of a crime, especially in cases of burglary. Marks may be left in wood, metal, putty, and paint, for example. Among the tools that leave identifiable marks are axes, knives, screwdrivers, chisels, crowbars, pliers, cutters, and drill bits. Some of these tools may be homemade (Fig. 9.8).

FIGURE **9.8.** A stolen outboard motor was identified by comparison of the tool marks made when the rubber gas lines between the portable tank and motor were cut. (*Centre of Forensic Sciences, Toronto.*)

These marks are essentially of two types, those in which only the general form and size of the tool are apparent, and those in which injuries, irregularities, and other peculiar characteristics of the tool are reproduced in the form of striations or indentations.

Marks of the first type may not make a definite identification of the tool possible, but do serve as a guide when it is necessary to decide whether the tool of a suspect *could* have produced the marks or not.

Tool marks that show striations, indentations, or similar details resulting from damage or other irregularities in the tool are the most valuable as evidence (Fig. 9.9).

Tool marks should, whenever possible, be kept in the originals. This may be done by recovering the whole object or the part of the object on which the marks appear. Sometimes it can be arranged that the marks remain untouched at the scene of the crime to be recovered later if this is required. This is permissible, however, only when the marks are in such a position that they are completely protected, for example, a small mark on the inside of a door or window frame. If a mark in metal is not immediately recovered, it should be covered with a thin film of oil to prevent oxidation.

In recovering the mark it is important that it be protected against dirt, moisture, and scratching during transport. Tissue or other soft paper should be placed over the tool mark in packaging.

*Casting or other methods of taking impressions of a tool mark should be used only as a last resort.* However good a cast, it can never be equal to the original. This applies especially to tool marks made in soft materials such as wood, putty, paint, and the like, since many of the casting media best suited for these materials are unable to reproduce all

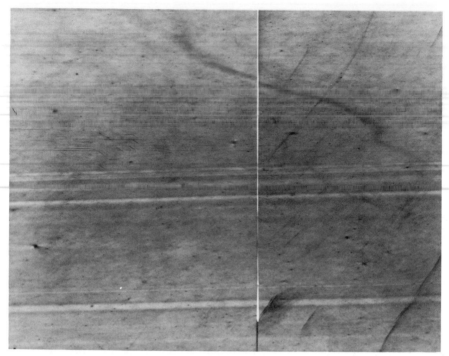

FIGURE **9.9.** Consecutive manufacture comparison of plastic trash bags in a murder case proved to be important evidence. The photograph depicts a single layer of two plastic bags placed edge to edge. Characteristic "die lines" and homogeneous mixing in the original plastic sheet are continuous between individual bags. These bags were used to link a box of trash bags from a residence and bags from the alleged crime vehicle to two bags found at the murder scene. (*Oklahoma State Bureau of Investigation.*)

the finer details that are important for identification. Experiments have shown, for example, that scratches in paint caused by extremely small irregularities in the edge of a tool cannot be reproduced by an impression or a cast. Consequently, a microscopic comparison of the cast with a mark made with the suspected tool may not lead to any positive results. If, however, the original mark is compared with one made directly by the tool, then a positive identification may be made.

In the casting of tool marks very satisfactory results may, however, be obtained with dental impression materials or silicone rubber, and the completed cast will show fine detail.

Difficulties and some expense may be involved in taking possession of the original tool mark, and it should therefore always be subjected to a close examination with the aid of a magnifier to make sure that it shows typical details from the tool, before any further steps are taken.

In each particular case, consideration must also be given to the type of crime, value of the object, whether a tool from a suspect is available or the probability that such a tool may be found, and so on.

Whether the actual mark is recovered or a cast is made, the tool mark should be photographed whenever practical. The picture should show clearly the location of the mark in relation to the rest of the object. Close-up photographs are generally taken in cases where there is risk of the mark's being destroyed in the casting process or during removal. The photographs must be made carefully, with the film plane parallel to the mark, and should include a scale. Oblique lighting is used to show up details in the mark. Close-up photographs should, if possible, be in actual size, or in the case of smaller marks, enlarged. It is generally not possible to identify the tool used from photographs.

In connection with all tool marks and suspected tools, it should be remembered that the tool may also have deposited traces in the form of paint, oil, or other contamination, and clues in the form of wood fragments, paint, or the like from the object may, in turn, be found on the tool. These traces are sometimes just as valuable as the tool mark itself. Samples of paint, wood, and so on should therefore always be taken from the area of the tool mark whenever the actual mark is not recovered. It should also be remembered that valuable tool marks are sometimes found on splinters of wood, loosened flakes of paint, chunks of safe insulation, and the like.

During the examination of the crime scene, the possibility should always be kept in mind that any tool mark found may be compared with marks from previous crimes. It happens frequently that identity is established among tool marks from different burglaries long before the criminal is apprehended or the actual tool is found.

The investigating officer should always endeavor to imagine being in the position of the criminal when the tool marks were made and to consider how the criminal held the tool, stood, or was supported when breaking in or prying open. A burglary may be faked with the object of concealing an embezzlement or of defrauding an insurance company. The investigator should, therefore, always remember to examine the opposite part of a mark (e.g., in a door frame). The faker often overlooks the fact that this other part of the mark must be present. It is, moreover, essential for the expert who is to carry out the comparative examination of the tool and the tool marks to understand how the criminal held the tool when making the marks. In most cases, if the examination is to have any prospect of leading to the identification of the tool, the expert has to make a comparison mark in exactly the same way as the criminal has done. This applies especially to those tool marks that show scratches resulting from damage or other irregularities in the tool. The distance between the scratches varies according to whether a knife, for example, is held at right angles to its direction of movement or is held askew, and the appearance of the scratches depends on the angle taken by the knife in relation to the plane of the cut. It is best if the position of a "fixed" mark and the conditions at the place are shown to the expert in a sketch or a comprehensive photograph; a statement that the suspect is right- or left-handed should be added. It is also essential that the comparison mark be made in the same material (with the same paint or surface treatment, of the same degree of moisture, etc.) as the mark at the scene of the crime, because the clarity of definition of the microscopic scratches varies with different materials. A quantity of material for use in producing comparison marks should therefore be sent with the tool and tool mark—it may be necessary to make 10 or more such marks with the suspected tool.

The police officer should not attempt to fit the tool into the mark or make a comparison mark with a suspected tool. In most cases the officer does not have access to an instrument that is suitable for the closer examination of the character of a tool mark, and this may be necessary in order to decide how the comparison mark is to be made. There is also the risk that traces of paint or foreign metal on the tool, observable only with a microscope or powerful magnifying glass, may be lost, or that the tool may be damaged.

Casts or impressions of tool marks should be packed in such a way that there is no risk of their being altered or destroyed during transport. *Positive casts should never be made,* since this may cause fine details to become obscured. If there is any risk of the negative cast of the mark's being destroyed in transmission, it is best to make two and to keep one in reserve.

Regarding *boring marks,* identifiable marks are generally left only by *wood bits* and *certain spiral bits.* Both the bottom of the boring, if there is one, and boring chips are important. Regarding *other types of bits,* identification is possible only in the most favorable cases and then, as a rule, only when the bottom of the boring is present.

At times the police officer comes up against the problem of deciding from which side, for example, of a window frame (outside or inside) a hole has been bored. In most cases this can be seen from the more or less loose wood fibers around the entrance and exit holes of the bit, but with some bits it may actually be difficult to decide the direction of boring. Reliable information is obtained by cutting through the surrounding wood in the longitudinal direction of the hole—by first sawing through the wood around the hole from each side up to about half an inch from the hole, and then breaking the wood apart. It will then be found that the wood fibers are directed upward from the hole in one edge of each half, and downward in the other edges. The wood fibers around the boring are displaced in the direction of rotation of the drill, so that on cutting the boring into two parts in this manner, they reveal clearly the direction of boring. The degree of orientation of the wood fibers varies for different types of bits, and it is possible to obtain an idea of the type of bit used by carrying out test borings with different bits.

*Saw marks* do not offer any possibility of definite identification of the saw used. In a favorable case, however, a certain degree of guidance may be obtained by noting the degree of set and possibly the number of teeth per inch of the saw used, but this can be done only if the sawing was stopped before the piece of wood had been sawn right through. Under favorable conditions it is possible to find, in the base of the saw cut, impressions of the teeth of the saw made when the saw was at rest for an instant before it was withdrawn. It is also possible to obtain, from the base of the saw cut, a measure of the width of cut and therefore of the approximate amount of set.

In the case of marks from *hacksaws* there is no possibility of identification. However, the blades are made with different numbers of teeth per inch, and if the saw blade has not gone right through the piece of metal, so that there is a possibility of examining the bottom of the cut, it may be possible to observe the impression of the teeth and thereby to obtain an idea of the number of teeth per inch. This may also be observed at places, at the sides of the actual cut, where the saw, especially when first started, jumped and left shallow marks of the teeth in the surface of the metal.

Once the tool has been found, care should be taken to preserve its evidentiary value (Fig. 9.10). It should be carefully marked or tagged. If markings are made on the tool itself, they should not be placed in the area of the working surface of the tool. Similarly, minute items of trace evidence, wood, paint, and the like, should be carefully preserved. The tool should be packaged with care for transportation to the laboratory (Figs. 9.11 and 9.12).

Tool marks made by cutting tools generally present little difficulty when the object cut, such as the shackle of a padlock, is large enough to collect sufficient characteristics. Smaller items such as wire cable, multistrand wire, and the like show identifiable markings only in exceptional cases (Fig. 9.13).

In cases where wire has plastic insulation as a covering, a physical match may be made by an examination of the extrusion markings on the cable as well as the microscopic jagged cut on the ends of the insulation. Generally, there will be insufficient striations on the fine wire itself.

Manufacturing marks such as casting, extruding, grinding, and so on are important when attempting to physically match items together. These markings and random breaks that occur when tools or other materials break or tear are important means of identification.

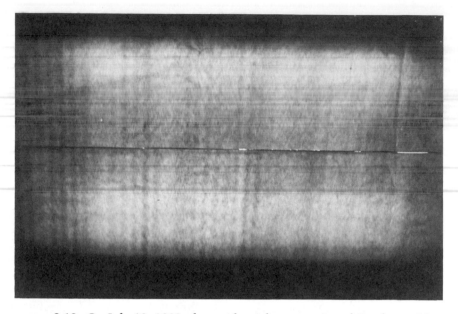

FIGURE **9.10.** On July 19, 1989, the residential community of Castleton, New York, was shocked by the brutal stabbing and bludgeoning of Carolyn J. Finkle, a 42-year-old resident of Rensselaer County. Her two teenage daughters were extremely distraught and claimed they had found their mother slain with multiple stab wounds. Troop "G" detectives mounted an intensive investigation. Plastic garbage bags used to wrap the murder weapon found in a dumpster matched bags found in the victim's house. The photograph shows back lighting of the plastic bags, revealing sequential striations caused by the manufacturing process. The daughters subsequently confessed to the crime. (*New York State Police Crime Laboratory.*)

Impression or casting media must be chosen for each particular case, taking into consideration the type of material in which the mark is formed and its orientation, i.e., on the horizontal or vertical. Some impression materials such as plaster and plasticine have a tendency to shrink or expand after setting; they should not be used for casting.

Dental impression creams have been found useful as casting materials. They generally come packaged in individual tubes, one being the catalyst and the other the setting agent. They are simply mixed and easy to apply. Other materials such as moulage, polysulfide rubber-based material, and silicone rubber are also useful.

A retaining wall should be built around the impression. Modeling clay or putty may be used for this purpose. The casting material should be thoroughly mixed according to the manufacturer's instructions and applied to the impression by means of a spatula. A tag with string

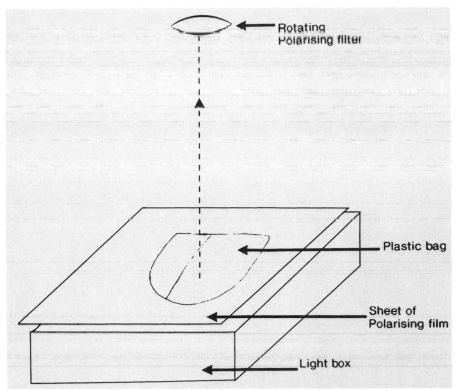

**FIGURE 9.11.** The Home Office Forensic Science Service uses a slightly different technique to that used by the New York State Police Laboratory shown in Figure 9.10. A sheet of polarizing film is placed on a light box and under a plastic bag. A polarizing filter is rotated so as to view interference patterns on the plastic. (*Central Research Establishment, Home Office Forensic Science Service, U.K.*)

attached may be used for identification purposes. The string may be inserted just below the surface of the casting material.

## Fragments of Tools

At crime scenes where doors, windows, or locked drawers show signs of forcible entry, the investigating officer must remember to examine carefully the floor immediately adjacent to the point of entry before examining the actual tool marks. It is not uncommon for burglary tools to break during forced entry. Large or small fragments of the tool may therefore be found on the scene and may prove to be very valuable as

266

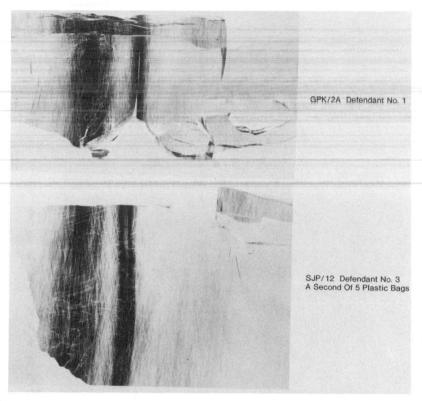

GPK/2A Defendant No. 1

SJP/12 Defendant No. 3
A Second Of 5 Plastic Bags

A

FIGURE 9.12. Following a long-term drug squad operation (A and B), three defendants were arrested and charged with conspiracy to supply and import heroin. Part of a plastic bag (GPK/2A) with brown powder was recovered from a female defendant, No. 1. A plastic bag (WB/1) with brown powder was recovered from a male defendant, No. 2. Five plastic bags (SJP/12) and some condoms with brown powder were recovered from a male defendant, No. 3. The brown powder was analyzed and found to be heroin; the condoms were found to have vaginal epithelial cells present. It was believed that the female smuggled the heroin secreted in her vagina and handed it over to defendant No. 3 for the purpose of supply. The plastic bags were examined by transmitted polarizing light and observed through a rotating polarizing filter. A pattern of interference bands were observed. This property originates in the manufacturing process. In some makes of bags the interference pattern is continuous through several bags, while in other makes the pattern tapers out within the length of one bag. Of the five bags in SJP/12 (Defendant No. 3), different patterns showed on at least two. One was found to be the same as the bag in WB/1 (Defendant No. 2), and another was found to be the same as bag GPK/2A (Defendant No. 1). The evidence was able to link all three defendants. (*Central Research Establishment, Home Office Forensic Science Service, U.K.*)

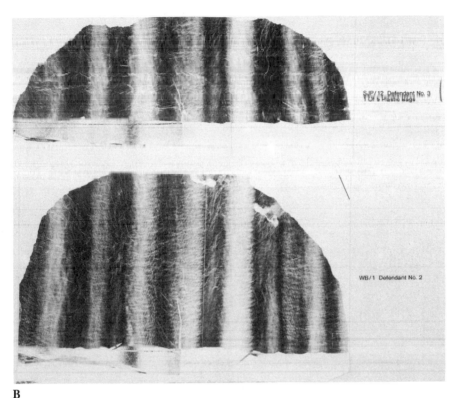

B

FIGURE **9.12.** (*Continued*)

evidence. Broken pieces of a tool might also be found inside a lock on which picking or prying has been attempted.

In many cases it is possible to establish that such broken fragments were originally parts of tools found in the possession of a suspect. The physical matching of two or more pieces that originally were one—a so-called "fracture match"—is a most convincing and easily demonstrable type of proof against an offender (Fig. 9.14).

The converse situation should also be kept in mind. A broken tool left by the burglar at the crime scene can be matched with fragments of that tool that may be found in the suspect's clothing, home, or place of business. Pieces may also have been left at the scene of another burglary.

The search for such tool fragments is best done with a flashlight, the beam of which is directed over the search area at a very low angle. When the light strikes a metallic fragment, it will give off bright reflections that make the particles easy to find. Any suspected fragment should be recovered and placed in a vial, envelope, or pillbox that can be labeled as to the time and place of recovery.

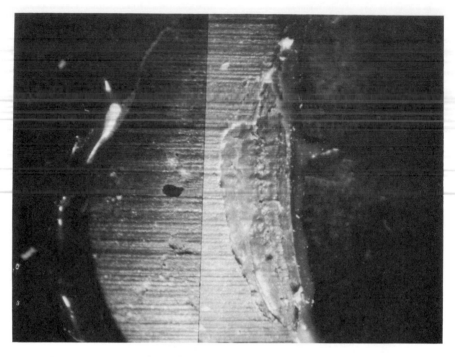

**FIGURE 9.13.** A young girl was found stabbed to death on her bed. A search of the crime scene uncovered a broken fingernail in the vicinity of the bed. Fingernail clippings were collected, and a comparison was made on silicone rubber castings of the underside of each nail, using reflected, oblique lighting. The examination established that the broken nail came from the victim. (*New York State Police.*)

**FIGURE 9.14.** Physical match can be made on a wide variety of objects. In this case, pieces of a broken automobile antenna are shown pieced together. (*Los Angeles County Sheriff's Department.*)

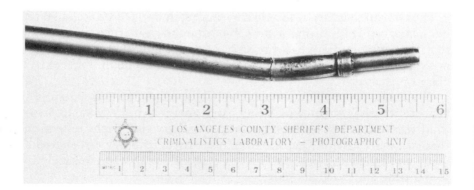

A magnet can also be used in searching for tool fragments. If a deliberate effort to look for such pieces of broken tools is not made, there is the risk of trampling them into the ground, embedding them in the officer's own shoe, or kicking them aside while engaging in other routines of crime scene search.

## Typed Documents

Marks from typewriters and check protectors are a special class of tool marks. As with other tool markings, these impressions may show specific and unique characteristics that may aid in the identification of a class or specific model of the instrument used.

Frequently, documents found at a crime scene may be typed or have some typing present. The investigator would like to determine the make, model, and specific typewriter or instrument used. In some instances this is possible; however, with the widespread use of electric typewriters and interchangeable type balls, this may be difficult.

The best results are obtained in instances where the suspect typewriter has a functional defect or a damaged typeface. With electric typewriters, factors such as key stroke pressure may not be a factor in identification.

It is preferable to bring the suspect typewriter to the questioned document examiner for comparison with the typewritten material in question. If this is not possible, the investigator should obtain ample specimens at the scene. These specimens should include several exemplars of all typefaces, both upper and lower case, and several prepared portions of the text copied from the document. These exemplars must be properly identified by the investigator's initials, date, make, model, serial number, and location of the machine. If the location is in an office, it should be thoroughly searched (including wastepaper baskets) for discarded typewriter ribbons and interchangeable type balls. Care must be taken when handling typewriters not to inflict additional damage on a machine.

*Check protectors* are widely used by financial institutions and many businesses. They are frequently used to imprint the amount in stolen or forged checks and money orders. Often checks are taken in burglaries and imprinted on machines located in the offices of the victim prior to the suspect's leaving the scene.

Generally, the make of the machine can be determined without too much difficulty by an experienced document examiner. However, the machine should be taken to the examiner for inspection and comparison with impressions on the questioned document. If the machine cannot be moved, extensive exemplars must be made in the field. Several exemplars of the questioned amounts should be prepared, preferably on specimen checks or money orders similar to the questioned documents. Additionally, specimens of all numerals and characters on the check protector should also be prepared on plain sheets of paper. All of these exemplars must contain proper identification, including the investigator's initials, the date, and the machine's make, model, and serial number.

Impression evidence is often encountered at crime scenes. A properly preserved impression submitted to the laboratory with the suspected item that caused the impression is important for obtaining the maximum usefulness of this evidence.

# FIREARMS
# EXAMINATION

C rimes involving the use of firearms represent a significant area of police investigation. Firearms evidence may be present in crimes such as murder, attempted murder, suicide, assault, and rape. A number of questions may be answered by means of the proper utilization of firearms evidence: What kind of weapon was used? Was the weapon in proper working order? How far away was the weapon fired? In what direction was the weapon fired? Did a specific weapon fire a bullet? Did a particular person fire the weapon?

Because of the importance of reconstructing the circumstances of a crime and corroborating accounts of the crime by witnesses, suspects, and victims, firearms evidence is particularly valuable. This chapter deals with the major areas of firearms examination as they relate to crimes of violence.

The field of firearms identification is sometimes improperly referred to as forensic ballistics or, simply, ballistics. This is an improper use of terminology. Ballistics generally refers to the trajectory taken by a projectile and assumes an understanding of physics. Firearms identification, on the other hand, refers to the study of firearms and includes the operation of firearms, cartridges, gunshot residue analysis, bullet and cartridge case comparisons, powder pattern determination, and the like.

## Characteristics of Firearms

There exist today literally thousands of types of firearms. They can be classed broadly into two groups: *shoulder firearms*, such as rifles and shotguns, and *handguns* such as revolvers and pistols or automatic and semiautomatic pistols (bipod, tripod, and other "exotic" weapons are also sometime encountered). Of interest to law enforcement, handguns represent the firearms most often used in crimes; shoulder arms are used less frequently. Obsolete weapons such as muskets, unusual firearms such as those disguised to appear as something other than a handgun, and homemade weapons such as "zip guns" are used with even less frequency.

Firearms may also be characterized by smoothbore and rifled weapons, the former manufacture used in shotguns and the latter in most other firearms. Rifling in a gun barrel is a system of spiral grooves cut into the barrel that impart a twisting motion on the bullet as it leaves the barrel, resulting in a more stable trajectory. Muskets are another type of smoothbore (and sometimes partially rifled) firearm (Fig. 10.1).

Firearms may be single shot, revolver, automatic, or semiautomatic. The single shot firearm is loaded manually, fired, and unloaded manually. The revolver differs from the single shot pistol in that it has a

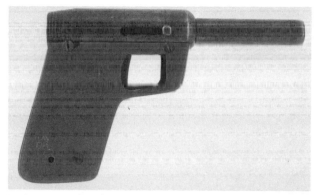

FIGURE **10.1.** An example of a homemade firearm. (*Los Angeles County Sheriff's Department.*)

rotating cylinder holding from 4 to 24 cartridges. Each time a cartridge is fired, the cylinder revolves by means of cocking the hammer or pulling the trigger, placing the cartridge into position to be fired. The automatic firearm, generally found in military weapons, is a repeating type. Cartridges are fired in succession as long as the trigger is pressed. The semiautomatic pistol (often referred to improperly as an "automatic") functions similarly to the automatic but fires only one shot each time the trigger is pulled.

In single shot and revolver-type firearms, the cartridge casing generally remains in the weapon after firing, although there have been single shot weapons that eject cases automatically. In automatic and semiautomatic firearms, the cartridge case is ejected from the weapon automatically.

There are two major differences between shotguns and other firearms. First, shotgun barrels are not rifled, but smoothbore. Second, shotguns fire a different type of ammunition consisting of many lead pellets, rifled slugs, or shot. Shotguns are of the single- and double-barreled break action for reloading, pump action, semiautomatic, or bolt action types (Fig. 10.2).

The caliber designation of a firearm is a somewhat complicated topic. Caliber is a measure of the bore of the barrel and is measured either in one hundredths or one thousandths of an inch or in millimeters (Fig. 10.3). The caliber designation is only an *approximation* of the bore diameter and usually somewhat closer to the groove diameter. Thus, for example, a .45-caliber semiautomatic has a bore diameter of approximately .45 inches (the actual bore diameter is .444 inches, whereas the groove diameter is .451 inches).

Shotgun bores are measured in gauges; the smaller the number, the larger the diameter. Thus, a 12-gauge shotgun has a larger diameter bore

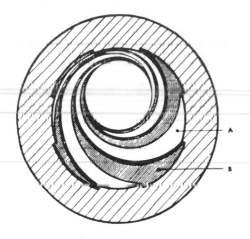

**FIGURE 10.2**
The appearance of the barrel of a weapon with a righthand twist: (A) land, (B) groove.

than a 20-gauge shotgun. The term *gauge* was originally the number of lead balls of that size weighing one pound. This system does not hold for the .400 "gauge," which in actuality indicates a caliber.

## Ammunition

Small arms cartridges or rounds are of two general types: *rimfire* and *centerfire*. Rimfire ammunition is almost exclusively .22 caliber, whereas larger calibers are centerfire. Some older firearms, other than .22 caliber, did use rimfire ammunition. The terms *rim* and *center* refer to the position of the primer located in the base of the cartridge. In rimfire rounds, the primer is in the rim in an area around the circumference of the base, but centerfired rounds have the primer in the center. The primer is a small shock-sensitive explosive charge in the base of

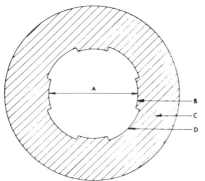

**FIGURE 10.3**
The caliber of a rifled weapon is generally determined from the diameter of the bore, measured between two opposite lands. There are, however, exceptions to this rule. (A) caliber, (B) land, (C) barrel, (D) groove.

the round used to set off the propellant powder when struck by the firing pin.

The bullet is the projectile that is fired from the weapon. Bullets are generally a lead alloy and either jacketed with a harder metal, such as copper or brass, or nonjacketed. The purpose of the jacket is to keep the bullet intact (so that it does not break up when it strikes a target), to prevent damage while in the weapon, and to control expansion.

Gunpowder or smokeless powder consists of tiny cylinders, balls, or discs of nitrocellulose or nitrocellulose and nitroglycerine in so-called double-based powder. When confined and ignited, the powder rapidly burns, giving off a large quantity of gas. The expanding gas propels the bullet through the barrel and out of the weapon. Black powder is also used in certain ammunition.

## Firearms Evidence

When a weapon is fired, the firing pin strikes the base of the bullet, detonating the primer, which in turn ignites the gunpowder (Fig. 10.4). Expansion of gases forces the casing against the breech, which resists the rearward movement, and propels the bullet down the barrel. As the bullet passes through, it picks up the tiny imperfections of the bore. Scratches, or striations, are caused by the imperfections in the lands and grooves placed in the barrel at the time of manufacture and caused by use of the weapon.

Characteristic markings caused by the mechanical action of loading,

FIGURE **10.4.** Determination of the make of pistol: cartridge case fired in the Austrian Glock 9 mm pistol; the rectangular firing pin hole is distinctive. (*Los Angeles County Sheriff's Department.*)

chambering, and firing the round, as well as by extracting and ejecting the casing, will be present on the bullet, cartridge casing, and cartridge base. These marks, if compared with rounds fired from the same weapon, will show similarities. The firearms identification expert can use these to determine that certain rounds were fired from the same gun (Figs. 10.5 and 10.6).

Beyond the determination that two rounds were fired from the same weapon, a great deal of other information can be developed from evidence associated with firearms. The presence of cartridge cases may be indicative of an automatic, semiautomatic, bolt action or slide action firearm, or of a single shot firearm when more than one round was fired. The relative location of the cases to the shooter may sometimes suggest the type of weapon fired, or indicate that a revolver was emptied at the scene.

Bullets and even fragments of bullets may be used to determine the type of weapon used, from both the size and weight of the projectile and an examination of the striations on the outside surface. Thus, for example, the number, direction of twist, and measurements of land and groove markings can be useful in determining the type, make, model, and caliber of a firearm. Examination of the area into which the bullet struck will yield information about its path and distance from which

FIGURE **10.5.** The firearms identification expert makes use of a comparison microscope to compare bullets and cartridge cases. (*Los Angeles County Sheriff's Department.*)

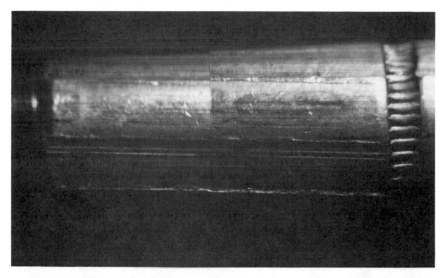

FIGURE **10.6.** Two bullets shown end to end under a bullet comparison microscope. The bullets show characteristic markings imparted by the barrel onto the bullet's surface. These markings are used by the firearms examiner to determine whether two bullets were fired from the same weapon. The horizontal band around the circumference is the cannelure. (*Los Angeles County Sheriff's Department.*)

the weapon was fired. This is also possible with shot fired from a shotgun.

Tests can be made on the shooter's hands to determine whether he or she has recently fired a weapon. Finally, if the firearm itself is recovered, it can be tested to determine whether it is in proper working order and whether it could have been accidentally discharged. The owner of a firearm can possibly be determined by serial number examination.

## Gunshot Residue Analysis

When the primer is detonated, microscopic particles of gunshot residue (GSR) are deposited on the hands of the shooter. These particles adhere to the hands but are removed by washing, wringing the hands, placing the hands in pockets, and even handcuffing behind the back (Fig. 10.7). Studies have shown that GSR material will remain on a shooter's hands for up to about 6 hours. The particles are in the highest concentration immediately after shooting and are eventually all lost over time, depending on the actions of the shooter. Because of this time factor, it is particularly important that GSR evidence be collected as quickly as possible.

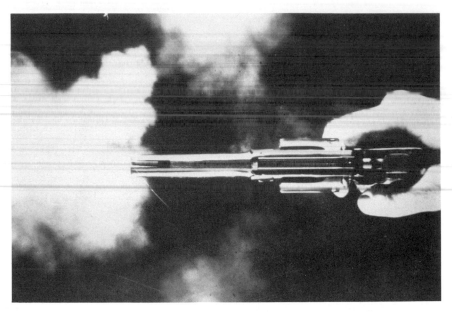

FIGURE **10.7.** When a firearm is discharged, gases from the detonation of the primer and burning of gunpowder escape from the barrel and cylinder. These gases, along with burned and unburned particles of gunpowder and primer, can be used to test whether a person recently fired a weapon or to estimate the distance to a target. (*Los Angeles County Sheriff's Department.*)

There are today three methods used for testing GSR evidence: neutron activation analysis (NAA), atomic absorption spectrophotometry (AA), and scanning electron microscopy/energy dispersive X-ray analysis (SEM/EDX). The procedure used by the crime laboratory to analyze the evidence determines the way in which the evidence is to be collected.

GSR evidence is collected in one of two ways: by means of cotton-tipped applicators or other substrates and dilute nitric acid solution for collecting the residue in the case of NAA and AA, or by aluminum stubs with double-sided cellophane tape attached to the surface of SEM. The "dermal nitrate" or "paraffin test" is no longer in use and is generally considered unreliable in GSR testing because of its nonspecificity.

The chemical components of the primer are the substances tested for in the GSR procedure. They are present on the shooter's hands, the greatest concentration being in the web area. The elements barium and antimony are characteristic of most ammunition, with the exception of .22-caliber ammunition manufactured by other than the Federal Cartridge Company.

GSR evidence collection kits are available both commercially and through local crime laboratories. In all cases, the person collecting the evidence should be certain to wear plastic gloves to prevent possible contamination of the evidence. Information concerning the subject's occupation and hobbies should be noted. This is important for interpretation of test results.

Evidence collection kits for use with the NAA and AA procedures consist of cotton-tipped applicators. The applicators best suited for the procedure are Johnson & Johnson Swabs™, made with cotton placed on the ends of plastic rods. One of the two cotton ends is cut away for use in the kit. Wooden applicators are not used because they contain materials that interfere with the test. The applicators should be placed into plastic, not glass test tubes. Glass also contains materials that may interfere with the test results.

A total of six tubes containing applicators are used. Each plastic tube is labeled: left back, right back, left palm, right palm, control, and cartridge, and contains two swabs each, except the tube for the cartridge, which contains only one. The swabs are used in succession to collect GSR evidence from the shooter's hands.

There are two commonly used methods to collect the evidence: either a solution of 5% nitric acid is used to moisten the applicators that are then used to swab the hands, or the acid is sprayed onto the hands of the subject and then swabbed with the dry applicators. Tests have shown that the second procedure results in a somewhat better collection.

The SEM procedure utilizes 1/2- to 1-inch aluminum discs, on the surface of which are placed double-sided cellophane tape. Two discs are required for an evidence collection kit, one for each of the top webbed portions of the two hands. The person collecting the GSR evidence dabs the disc over the area of interest by firmly pressing it down onto the skin. This procedure is continued until all the adhesive is used.

A word on the interpretation of test results is called for. A negative result may mean that a subject either did *not* fire a weapon or took some action that resulted in removal of any particles that had been present; a positive test result means that the subject fired a weapon sometime during the past 6 hours (approximately), or handled a weapon during that time period. The location of the particles, of course, may be important. If the palms, but not the backs, of a subject's hands contain GSR, this might indicate that the person held but did not fire a weapon, or that the weapon was relatively "clean," i.e., gave off a small amount of GSR particles when fired.

The shooter's hands should be protected as well as possible until the test is given. They may be bagged loosely with paper bags but should not be protected with plastic bags, which cause perspiration and, hence, a cleansing effect. In the case of a deceased subject, the 6-hour time limit is flexible, but the hands should be protected until such time as the evidence can be collected.

## Collecting Firearms Evidence

The crime scene in which a firearm was involved should be processed in much the same way as discussed earlier in the text. In addition, a number of other considerations must be taken into account in a case of this type.

When sketching and measuring the crime scene, it is particularly important to note and measure carefully the location of all shell casings, bullet holes, bullets and bullet fragments, and shotgun shot patterns that are found. This information is vital to the reconstruction of the crime and can be used to verify statements by witnesses and suspects. Special care must be taken when walking through the location so that casings or bullets are not stepped on or inadvertently kicked (Figs. 10.8 and 10.9).

If a weapon is found at the scene it should not be moved until its location is noted through measurement, sketches, and photographs. The investigator should remember that fingerprints may be present so that when the weapon is moved, it must be handled in such a way that will not destroy any fingerprints. The floor below the weapon should be examined for a depression or other marks that would indicate that it was dropped from some height or fell from the shooter's hands. The weapon should be examined for traces of wood, fibers, paint, building material, blood, and hair, which, if found, should be carefully preserved.

If a dead person is holding the weapon it is important to note the exact grip and the position of the weapon in the hand. It may have been placed there by the murderer. In such a case, the way in which a weapon is held in relation to the injuries on the body are decisive in deciding whether the dead person could have personally produced the injuries. In the case of an automatic pistol, the recoil of the slide may have caused a surface graze in the region of the thumb or the web of the hand, and the presence of such an injury is suggestive of the possibility that the dead person fired a shot with an automatic pistol. A closer examination of the hand of the dead person may show marks of powder, especially if a revolver has been used. From these marks, the investigator may deduce that both hands were in the vicinity of the muzzle blast or the gap of the revolver. One hand may have been used as a guide while the other pressed the trigger, or both hands may have been held up in defense (Fig. 10.10).

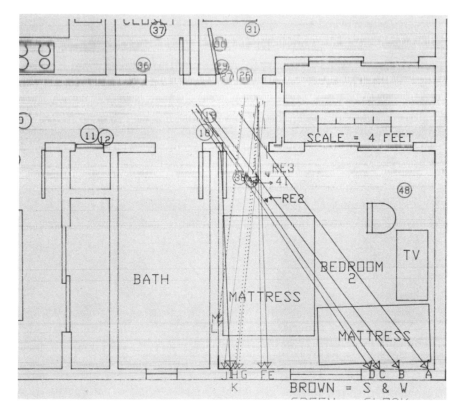

**FIGURE 10.8.** An example of a CAD (computer-aided design) program used to sketch a crime scene and depict the approximate trajectories in a shooting. (*California Department of Justice, Bureau of Forensic Services.*)

In the case of long-barreled guns, rifles, and shotguns, special attention should be given to the possibility of the dead person's having fired a suicide shot with the weapon. Special arrangements such as string, belts, sticks, and the like may have been used, and these in turn may have left marks in the form of fibers, dirt, soot, or the like on the trigger or trigger guard. One shoe may have been removed in order to press the trigger with a toe.

The positions of cartridges, cartridge cases, and bullets are just as important as those of weapons. From their positions, it may be possible to deduce the position of firing, direction of the shot, and, in certain cases, the path of the bullet. If a bullet has penetrated a tree, a piece of furniture, or a wall, the shot track gives information regarding the direction of the shot and, often, the path of the bullet. There is a much better opportunity of determining the exact course of a bullet when it

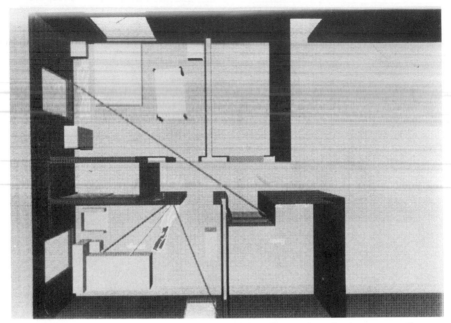

FIGURE 10.9. A computer depiction of a three-dimensional crime scene from a two-dimensional CAD drawing. (*California Department of Justice, Bureau of Forensic Services.*)

has passed through a fixed object, such as a windowpane, and then struck a wall. With the aid of the path of the bullet and of shot wounds on the dead person it is possible to determine the deceased's attitude and position when shot. In calculating the distance of the shot, the depth to which a bullet has penetrated, e.g., a wall, may be significant. The penetrating power is dependent on the distance of the shot, but allowance must also be made for the loss of energy in its passing through an object, such as a body. A more accurate determination of distance can be made with the aid of gunshot injuries on the clothes and body of the dead person (Fig. 10.11).

The position of a bullet found at the scene of a crime should be recorded in the same way as are weapons, and bullets should be collected separately and packed so that there can be no confusion. If two or more weapons have been used, it is important that the bullets should not get mixed up, so that at a later date the place where each one was found can be fixed exactly. Great care should also be taken in collecting and packing them, so that the microscopic marks from the barrel of the weapon are not injured or destroyed. For this reason, a bullet that has penetrated or lodged in a wall should *not* be probed for and dug out by means of a knife, ice pick, or chisel. Instead, a portion of the wall surrounding the bullet should be carefully removed in one piece and the

**FIGURE 10.10.**  The subject entered the Casino Bar in the early morning hours, then robbed and shot the cashier, who was the sole occupant of the bar at the time and was working in the cashier's cage. The victim was shot in the back. A large portion of the lead slug was removed from his body during an autopsy. Two ricochet marks were found at the crime scene. When the suspect was apprehended, a 20-gauge Ithaca shotgun along with several 20-gauge "Slugger" shotgun shells of Remington-Peters manufacture were found in his possession. To reconstruct the crime scene, a portable laser was placed outside the cashier's cage and the beam was directed at the area of the bullet's first deflection on the cage. A mirror was placed in this area. A beam deflecting from the mirror traveled to the steel door of the vault and hit a ricochet mark on the door. Another small mirror was placed in this area on the vault door, and the laser beam deflected onto the right shoulder of a model standing in the doorway, the same area where the lethal wound was located on the victim's body. (*South Dakota Attorney General's Office, State Forensic Laboratory.*)

bullet recovered by breaking away the supporting material. Since it may become important to ascertain other objects that came in contact with the projectile, it must not be handled by persons who have touched blood, nor should adhering dirt be removed until a microscopic study is possible. Care should be exercised that the investigator's marking of the bullet does not destroy this trace evidence.

FIGURE **10.11.**  An evidence bullet carelessly marked in the region of the rifling impression. Valuable evidence was thereby destroyed. Bullets should be marked for identification on the base, and cartridge cases on the inside, near the mouth. However, a preferable procedure is to place the bullet in a container and label the package instead of the bullet. (*Los Angeles County Sheriff's Department.*)

The same considerations with respect to fixing the position and taking possession of weapons and bullets apply to cartridges and cartridge cases found at the scene of a crime. The position of a cartridge that has misfired or of a cartridge case that has been ejected from an automatic pistol may give an indication of the type of automatic pistol used and form a valuable supplement to the determination of the make of pistol from the marks left by the weapon on the bullet and case. Many automatic pistols differ in respect to the ejection of the cases; some throw them out to the left, some to the right, and some straight up. The case is thrown out with a force that varies among different types of pistols but is generally considerable, so that it may rebound against furniture, walls, wall coverings, and so on and change direction. The position may give some indication of the type of weapon; however, there is often variation from weapon to weapon. If a cartridge case has not bounced off any object and has, moreover, fallen onto an underlayer that prevents it from rolling (carpet, lawn, etc.), then its position gives a direct indication of the type of weapon and place or direction of firing. If three of these factors (position of cartridge case, type of automatic pistol, place of firing, direction of shooting) are known, then the fourth can be determined. Outdoors, however, it is necessary to take into account the direction and strength of the wind, and in all cases the inclination of the weapon must be considered.

The positions of wads and overshot wads (the latter are no longer used in shotshells), which often remain relatively undamaged, from shotgun cartridges and muzzle-loading weapons also give information regarding the direction of shooting. These can generally be found about 5 to 8 yards or more from the place of firing in the approximate direction of fire, but it is necessary to take into consideration the direction and strength of the wind. The overshot card placed in front of the charge of shot shows, if found, a manufacturing mark and also the size of shot given by a number or letters.

As mentioned previously, weapons, as well as cartridge cases, bullets, shot, and wads, may carry marks from the victim or the criminal, with the aid of which the crime can be solved.

It should always be remembered that both latent fingerprints and fingerprints in blood, grease, or the like may be found on weapons and that these must be protected (Fig. 10.12).

On a weapon that has been used in a case of murder, suicide, or assault, marks from the victim may be found in the form of blood, hair, fragments of textiles, cloth fibers, and so on. Such clues may appear to be of little value, but it must not be forgotten that it may be necessary to prove that the weapon was actually used in the particular case, and these clues are then of the greatest value. Loose hairs, dried blood,

FIGURE **10.12.** Investigators should keep in mind the possibility of latent fingerprints on bullets. (*Alaska Department of Public Safety, Scientific Crime Detection Laboratory.*)

fibers, and the like should be placed in a test tube, and the weapon taken and packed in such a way that fingerprints or other clues are not destroyed but are kept for investigation. A container that suspends the weapon with the minimum of bearing surfaces is preferred. Such a container can be constructed from pegboard, heavy cardboard, or similar material. Wrapping an object in cotton, gauze, or tissue will more than likely dislodge trace evidence.

If both fingerprints and bloodstains are found on a weapon, it should be remembered that the latter may be destroyed if the whole of the weapon is dusted with fingerprint powder. It is therefore convenient, first, to make sure that there are such traces of blood, hair, and the like that are not on or near the fingerprints. The presence of latent fingerprints on metal surfaces can be observed easily under proper lighting.

Contamination in the form of oil, cement, paint, or similar material may also be significant in elucidating the way in which a criminal acquired a weapon, or it may give an indication of where it was kept previously. It may possibly have been taken from the criminal's place of work or taken in an earlier burglary where the criminal was less careful and left fingerprints or other clues that can be used as incriminating evidence.

If the weapon has been concealed either at the scene of the crime or in the vicinity, or taken away by the criminal, it is of the greatest importance to know the type of weapon for which one is searching. The only means of determining this is from a study of the injuries on the victim or by removal of the bullet at autopsy. In practice it is often difficult to draw the correct conclusions from the appearance of the wounds, since it is affected by the elasticity of the skin, the underlying bones and muscles, the angle of application, and other such factors. In such cases, however, the pathologist can give valuable assistance.

## Handling of Firearms

In lifting firearms, great care must be taken not to destroy evidence. When lifting a pistol or revolver, the best way is to hold it with two fingers on the checkered part of the butt or possibly by the ring on the butt. Shotguns may conveniently be held around the checkered part of the neck of the butt, or, if necessary, the weapon can be lifted by a steady grip with the fingers on the trigger guard. It is undesirable to lift a weapon by placing a stick or similar object in the trigger guard, even with a light weapon such as a revolver or pistol, as the weapon may be cocked and a shot might be fired if the trigger happens to be touched. It should be taken as a general rule never to lift a weapon found at the scene or a crime before first making sure that no one is in the direction in which the muzzle is pointing, and, of course, one should not expose oneself to the risk of being hit when lifting the weapon should it happen to go off. The weapon may actually have gotten caught in some way so that even the slightest movement would cause a shot to be fired.

It is *absolutely wrong* to lift a weapon by putting a pencil, stick, or the like into the barrel. This may destroy valuable clues in the barrel that might possibly have been of use in elucidating the case. In a contact shot, i.e., when the muzzle is in contact with a body, which is common in cases of suicide, it often happens that blood, grease, fragments of fabric, and textile fibers are blown into the barrel of the gun by the violence of gas pressure and the splash of tissue and blood in all directions. In a contact shot it has sometimes happened that such particles have been recovered in the magazine of an automatic pistol.

There may also be found in the bore a layer of dust, spider webs, or loose rust particles, showing that no shot has been fired from the weapon for some time. The absence of a powder deposit or the presence of grease in the bore may also indicate that the weapon has not been used, and an examination of the powder layer in the bore may show that the fired cartridge was loaded with black powder or with smokeless powder. It is difficult to decide, from the appearance of the powder deposit, how much time has elapsed since the last shot was fired from the weapon. Therefore, it can be appreciated that if the bore of a weapon is to be examined for any such clues, the introduction of any object into the bore will interfere with its examination or make it impossible. For the same reason, cotton or the like must not be put into the muzzle during transport of the weapon or when it is sent to the expert. To protect any deposit in the bore, a twist of paper, rubber cap, or muzzle protector can be placed over the muzzle. The layer of dust in the bore is always thickest near the muzzle and decreases in thickness progressively toward the breech, assuming that it has resulted from a long period of storage. The confirmation of such a distribution of the deposit nearest the muzzle is therefore of great importance. Under no circumstances should an investigating officer put the weapon into his or her own pocket for safekeeping. After only brief contact with pocket dust, the gun will appear to have been unfired for some time.

## *Homicide*

A man was found in his house, dead, with two shot wounds in his head. A little to the right of the body lay a revolver, which belonged to him. The revolver was not loaded and did not contain any empty cartridge cases. An investigation of the barrel showed that it was contaminated with dust to such an extent that it could hardly have accumulated during the 2 days that were supposed to have elapsed from the time of the shooting. Further investigation revealed that the man had been shot with a revolver of the same caliber and type as his own, and that the murderer had placed the latter near the body to give the appearance of suicide.

After a weapon has been picked up, any loose objects or particles such as hair, fibers, dried blood, brain substance, and the like that might fall off in transport are removed and kept. In the case of a near shot against a hair-covered part of the body, strands of hair can sometimes be found, held fast between the slide and barrel of an automatic pistol. Any traces on the weapon in the form of fibers of wood, paint, cement, or the like, which might indicate that the weapon had fallen on the floor, should also be collected while at the scene of the crime.

When taking possession of a weapon, it should be subjected to a preliminary examination for fingerprints. Fingerprint impressions in grease or blood can easily be seen. Latent fingerprints on metal surfaces can, as previously mentioned, be made evident by breathing lightly on the object. If both fingerprints and bloodstains, fibers, and so on are found on the weapon, and all have to be preserved, it is convenient first to make sure of the marks that are not in the immediate neighborhood of the fingerprints, as otherwise they could easily be destroyed by the fingerprint powder. Here a warning is necessary: if the weapon is found outdoors or in an unheated room in cold weather, and there are fingerprint impressions in grease on it, then the weapon should not be brought into a warm room, since the grease would be softened or melted and the prints would be lost. If latent fingerprints are to be developed by powder, care must be taken to keep the powder from entering the barrel. Likewise, when a revolver is processed by powder dusting, the front of the cylinder must be protected so that the mouth of each chamber can be examined for flares.

Everything found in the first examination of the weapon should be written down accurately, and any objects or particles removed from it should be placed in a test tube or envelope labeled accurately as to the exact place of finding. For the sake of identification, any maker's or type markings should also be indicated, as well as the caliber marking and serial number. The investigator's initials should be inscribed on some major part of the weapon, such as the barrel or frame, or the weapon may be tagged.

It is most important to write down whether the weapon is at safety or not, which can be seen from the position of the safety catch (on revolvers there is generally no visible safety device), and whether the weapon is cocked and loaded. In some automatic pistols the latter cannot be observed by a superficial glance, but where it is shown by, for example, an indicating pin, it should be noted. In the most common types of weapon this condition can easily be confirmed from the position of the rear part of the bolt. It should also be noted whether the bolt (breechblock or slide) is closed, partly open, or fully open. If a cartridge case is jammed in the ejection port, this should be noted, together with a statement of the exact position of the cartridge, whether the base or neck of the case is turned outward, and so on, and also whether the magazine is firm or loose (not pushed right home).

After the exterior of the weapon has been processed for fingerprints, the gun may be unloaded and rendered safe before shipping to a laboratory. In an automatic pistol, the magazine is loosened, after which the slide is moved to remove any cartridge in the chamber. In doing this it should be remembered that fingerprints may be found in grease on the cartridge in the chamber and on the sides of the magazine, which should therefore be examined first before any further handling. The weapon should not be considered unloaded until an inspection is made by looking into the chamber through the port of the gun. A broken extractor, jammed cartridge, or other factor may cause a cartridge to remain in the chamber. It is poor practice to assume that a weapon is unloaded simply because a cartridge was not ejected. The cartridge is placed in an envelope or container with a label attached, and a label can also be tied on by a thread around the groove of the cartridge. Any cartridges in the magazine should not be "stripped" if the weapon is to be sent to an expert for examination. Cartridges may carry fingerprints, as well as marks from the guiding surfaces of the magazine, and it may be of significance to confirm them (e.g., as to whether the cartridges have been charged into the magazine several times). Further, the order of the cartridges in a magazine may be of importance in certain cases and should always be noted.

In the case of a revolver, nothing should be done with the cartridges in the cylinder if the weapon is to be examined further. The exact position of the cylinder at the moment when the weapon is found is significant from many points of view and should be noted; e.g., note the position of the fired cartridge in relation to the hammer. The position of the cylinder can be marked, if so desired, with a pencil or chalk mark, provided that this does not destroy other clues. The cylinder should not be "rolled," since in that case irrelevant marks from the recoil plate or firing pin could then be formed on the base of the fired cases and the cartridges.

In the case of weapons of single shot or repeating types, nothing should be done with the bolt unless the weapon is cocked, nor with the empty case in the chamber. If, however, the hammer is cocked, there is reason to suspect that an unfired cartridge is in the chamber, and this should be removed to prevent any accident. The cartridge is taken out and labeled as described above. Semiautomatic or fully automatic weapons generally have a cartridge in the chamber unless the bolt is in the backward position, so that the slide should be moved while making sure that no fresh cartridge is introduced into the chamber. To prevent this, a detachable magazine is removed from the weapon; in the case of a fixed magazine the uppermost cartridges are held back with a piece of wood or some other object that will not injure the cartridges or deposit any fresh marks on them.

All precautions that are taken with a firearm must be put down accurately in the report. Later, possibly, the investigating police officer may be required to describe the precautions taken, in connection with legal proceedings. What may appear to be of subordinate importance during the investigation of the crime may later be found to be especially significant.

In connection with all firearms, when a weapon is to be sent to an expert for examination the only clues that need to be preserved are those that might be destroyed in transit, and the only measures taken are those that cannot be omitted without risk of accident, or which are essential in assisting the search for the criminal. Many traces on the weapon or significant facts in connection with the mechanism can be of such a character that special instruments or specially trained personnel are necessary to deal with them properly.

On the breech face or recoil plate there may perhaps be marks of colored lacquer from the sealing around the primer, and a chemical examination may be required to confirm whether this could have come from a specific fired cartridge. Even in the bore there may be found lacquer pigments from the sealing between the bullet and case, or metallic particles from the jacket of the bullet. In grease and dirt on the breech face there may also be an impression of the markings on the base of the cartridge case, and special arrangements will be required for photographing this impression (Fig. 10.13).

FIGURE 10.13.   This figure illustrates a headstamp impression in the grease on a breechblock. (*Contra Costa County Sheriff's Department, Criminalistics Laboratory, Martinez, California.*)

As mentioned earlier, from the point of view of identification, any marks indicating the maker, type, or caliber should be recorded, together with the serial number. In many weapons, in particular in certain pistols and revolvers, such markings are often lacking. The butt plates are, however, usually marked with the maker's or seller's initials, which can be a good guide.

Many weapons also carry *proof marks*. A number of European countries strictly regulate the manufacture of firearms and require a special mark to be stamped on the weapon's barrel to indicate that it has been tested and found safe. Proof marks are also found on some American-made weapons sold in foreign countries. In cases of inexpensive firearms, the proof mark may be the only clue to the manufacturer of the weapon.

Occasionally, firearms are recovered in which serial numbers have been ground off for the purpose of concealing the ownership of the weapon. When numbers are stamped into the frame of the weapon, changes in the metal structure deep below the surface result (Fig. 10.14). If the process that removed the stamp was not sufficiently deep, the *serial numbers or markings can be restored*. Depending on the nature of the metal, a number of techniques are possible: chemical etching, electrochemical etching, and heating.

## Cartridge Cases

If no cartridge cases are found at the scene of a shooting, it may be suspected that a revolver, single shot pistol, automatic pistol with cartridge case collector, rifle, or shotgun was used. Theoretically, one might expect that criminals would attempt to guard themselves by picking up the cartridge cases thrown out by an autoloading weapon, but in practice it is hardly ever done, since it would often waste time and the criminal would run the greater risk of being discovered, especially if the shooting was heard by persons in the vicinity.

In taking possession of cartridge cases, one should not forget the possibility that significant clues may be found on them in the form of loose particles or fingerprints. They may be picked up by means of a clean matchstick or the like, introduced into the case, and then placed in an envelope marked with the place of finding. The internal diameter of a cartridge case corresponds at the neck with the diameter of the bullet. From the size, form, and appearance of a cartridge case, it is possible to obtain an indication of the type of weapon used.

Revolver cartridge cases are almost always fully cylindrical, with a rim but no extractor groove (a groove for the extractor running around the case with the rim). They may be made for rimfire (smooth base) or centerfire (with primer cap). Many manufacturers make revolvers to take automatic pistol cartridges. Thus both Colt and Smith & Wesson

FIGURE **10.14.** This is an actual case in which two revolvers were factory-stamped with the same serial number. When one of the guns was submitted to the laboratory as part of a criminal investigation, a record check showed that the weapon belonged to an individual residing in northern California. He was contacted and advised that his revolver had been recovered. To the investigator's surprise, the owner reported that he had the gun in his possession. The firearms investigator obtained the second gun to record photographically this unusual occurrence. (*Los Angeles County Sheriff's Department.*)

make revolvers of .45 caliber so that automatic pistol cartridges of .45 caliber can be used in them. Similarly, automatic pistol cartridges of 7.65 mm can be fired in .32-caliber revolvers, and automatic pistol cartridges of 6.35 mm can be fired in .25-caliber revolvers. Automatic pistol cartridges (with the exception of .45 rimless cartridges, 9-mm Parabellum cartridges, and bottle-neck cartridges) have a rim that, although not much larger than the cylindrical surface of the cartridge, is quite sufficient to hold the cartridge fast in the chamber of a revolver cylinder when the internal diameter of the latter corresponds with the diameter of the cartridge. In many revolvers provided with one common extractor for all the cartridges, this also functions quite satisfactorily when pistol cartridges are used (Fig. 10.15).

Revolver cartridges of .320 caliber can also be fired in certain automatic pistols of 7.65-mm caliber, and there are also cases in which such

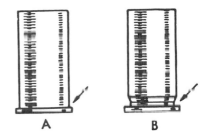

FIGURE 10.15
The difference between a revolver
cartridge case (A) and a cartridge case
intended for an automatic pistol (B). The
former has no extractor groove.

pistols have also repeated normally and even ejected revolver cartridge
cases, but these ejected cases are often ruptured and sometimes jam the
pistol.

Smaller caliber projectiles can be fired in larger bore weapons with
serious effect. An example of this is the ability of a .38 Special revolver
to fire a .32–20 cartridge (Fig. 10.16). Desperate persons, in need of
ammunition, wrap cartridges in paper to accommodate a larger chamber, reduce the diameter by filing, or even perform the dangerous act of
driving a cartridge into a chamber with a hammer. Only an expert can

FIGURE **10.16.** Identification of a cartridge case of 7.65-mm caliber (.32 Auto)
(A) with a suspect cartridge case (B). The microscopic details in the marks of the
firing pin on the primer agree completely in the two cartridge cases. (*Los
Angeles County Sheriff's Department.*)

A                                              B

determine with reasonable certainty the type of gun that might have been used in a shooting by an examination of the fired bullets or cartridges. An investigator must be careful not to pass up a weapon because it does not *seem* to correspond to the ammunition at hand.

On the base of the cartridge case there are generally both caliber and manufacturer's marks, and sometimes the year of manufacture as well. Sometimes the maker's marks are in code, consisting of letters and figures or of only letters or figures.

Fired cartridge cases are especially valuable from the point of view of identification, since they show marks from the weapon that in most cases make it possible to decide with certainty whether they were fired from a particular weapon or not. It is therefore of special importance in the case of an outdoor shooting that all possible efforts be made to determine the location of the shooting so that one can look for any cartridge cases left behind. The most valuable marks on cartridge cases are those made by the firing pin on the primer and by the breech face on the primer and base of the case, but the marks produced by the extractor, ejector, and the edge of the breech may also be important. Flaws or damage in the chamber may also show on the metal case and make identification of the weapon possible.

If the criminal, when found, has already thrown away the weapon where it cannot be recovered (e.g., in water), it is important to attempt to find out whether the criminal or some other person (e.g., the previous or legal owner) ever fired a test shot and, if so, where. It is possible that both the cartridge case and bullet may be found there. In regard to cartridge cases, it is not of great importance whether or not the test shot was fired a long time before. The part of the weapon that leaves marks on the case may not have altered even though there was a long interval of time between the test shot and the crime. It is different in the case of bullets, since sometimes the bore of a weapon may undergo such changes in a comparatively short time that comparison of a bullet with a test shot fired previously is useless. The nature of the place where the weapon has been kept and the number of shots that have been fired with it are important factors.

From the marks made by the extractor, ejector, and edge of the breech of an automatic pistol on a cartridge case, it is also possible to determine the make of automatic pistol from which the case was fired (Fig. 10.17). Automatic pistols of different types and makes are often constructed differently with respect to the position of the extractor and ejector, and this in turn affects the formation of the breech. The combination of these factors forms what is known as a system, that is, the characters mentioned give classification of the type of construction of the pistol.

If both cartridge case and bullet are available for the determination of the make, the possibilities are, of course, increased, since the number of

**FIGURE 10.17.** Firing pin drag showing movement of barrel during unlocking; breech face marks caused by file. (*Los Angeles County Sheriff's Department.*)

land marks on the bullet, their width, and the angle of twist can also be characteristic of a type of weapon and, in any case, form a valuable contribution to the investigation.

Under no condition should a cartridge case that is to be examined be tried in the chamber of a weapon, since any marks made by the weapon on the case may be destroyed and other marks may be formed.

It happens sometimes that at the scene of a crime where a firearm has been used, a cartridge is found that has misfired and has been thrown out by movement of the slide or bolt, or that has jammed between the breechblock and the edge of the breech and has been removed by hand. Even such an unfired cartridge may carry valuable marks that can make possible an identification or determination of the make of the weapon used.

## Bullets

Bullets that penetrate hard objects are often severely mutilated, sometimes to the degree that the weapons from which they were fired cannot be identified. Therefore, every effort must be made to preserve what little remains of the rifling impression when a bullet is lodged in a wall, a tree, or a bone. In the latter case, the method of removal, if at all, will depend on whether the shooting victim is dead. If the victim is dead, the principles for bone, tree, or wall are alike. *No projectile should be pried from its position.* Instead, the supporting material and the bullet should be cut out as one piece. Then the surrounding bone, plaster, or wood can be broken away carefully, leaving the projectile in the best possible condition, considering all circumstances. If the investigator wishes, the bullet embedded in supporting material may be sent to the laboratory. Bullets removed by probing show ample evidence of the destructive effect of improper technique.

Prior to removal, some careful testing will indicate the direction of the bullet's track.

After removal, the bullet should be initialed on the base. No mark should be placed on the rifling impression or on areas of ricochet. If in doubt as to the proper area to mark, the investigator should place the bullet in an envelope, a plastic vial, or a small box, then seal and mark the container.

Bullets may be of different sizes and shapes and made in different ways. The commonest types are either entirely of lead or semi- or fully jacketed; but there are also bullets with a hole in the point (hollow point), bullets with the point covered with softer metal, lead bullets with a copper cone pressed into the point, and the like.

In fully jacketed (solid nose) bullets, the jacket encloses entirely the point of the bullet but is open at the rear end of the bullet, exposing the lead core. With a semijacketed (soft nose) bullet, on the other hand, the jacket encloses the whole of the rear end of the bullet, and the core is free at the point to a larger or smaller extent. The semijacketed bullet breaks up when it meets a bone or other hard part of the body, but if it passes merely through soft parts it may remain relatively undamaged. If it strikes against the branch of a tree in its flight, it may actually be split or deformed before reaching its objective. On the other hand, a fully jacketed bullet often remains undamaged or only slightly deformed on striking, for example, a body. Less scrupulous shooters sometimes file the point of a fully jacketed bullet in order to produce the same effect as that of a semijacketed one. This result is obtained if the bullet leaves the barrel whole, but because of the jacket's being open at both ends there is a risk of the lead core only being driven out and the jacket remaining behind in the barrel. If this is not noticed, then when the next shot is fired the result will be that the weapon bursts or a bulge is produced in the barrel.

Lead bullets may be of different degrees of hardness. Bullets of soft lead are often greatly deformed and sometimes break up when they strike a body, whereas those of hard lead may retain their regular shape to the same extent as a fully jacketed bullet.

Ammunition intended for automatic pistols usually has fully jacketed bullets, whereas revolver ammunition usually has lead bullets. There are, however, also automatic pistol cartridges with lead or semijacketed bullets and revolver cartridges with fully jacketed bullets (Figs. 10.18 and 10.19). An intermediate position is taken by the previously mentioned cartridges of .22 caliber with lead bullets, which can be fired in certain automatic pistols, in single shot pistols, in revolvers, and in rifles. Also, as mentioned previously, revolver cartridges of .320 caliber, which are provided with lead bullets, can be fired in pistols of 7.65-mm caliber.

The type of jacket, if any, and the contour, weight, and composition of the bullet and the number, size, and design of cannelures may give an indication of the maker of the cartridge. In American cartridges, for example, lead bullets are sometimes copper-plated. On a fired bullet the bore of the weapon will have left marks from the lands and sometimes also from the bottom of the grooves. A microscopic examination of these land and groove marks sometimes shows characteristic details that make possible an identification of the weapon used (Fig. 10.20).

FIGURE **10.18.** Automatic pistol cartridges (19-mm Luger) that have been damaged by malfunctioning. The cases were jammed in the ejection port. (*Los Angeles County Sheriff's Department.*)

298

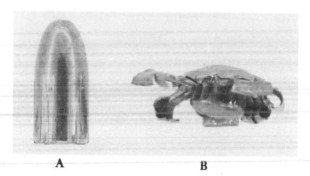

A                          B

FIGURE **10.19.** A fully jacketed bullet (A) is usually not deformed to any extent on striking (e.g., a body), but a semijacketed bullet breaks up (B). (*Los Angeles County Sheriff's Department.*)

FIGURE **10.20.** Identification in the comparison microscope of two jacketed rifle bullets of 9.3-mm caliber from the microscopic marks in the engravings of the lands: (A) bullet from the scene of the crime, (B) comparison bullet from weapon of suspect. Note the well-defined score in the mark of the land (see arrow) caused by one serious injury to the actual land in the bore of the weapon. (*Los Angeles County Sheriff's Department.*)

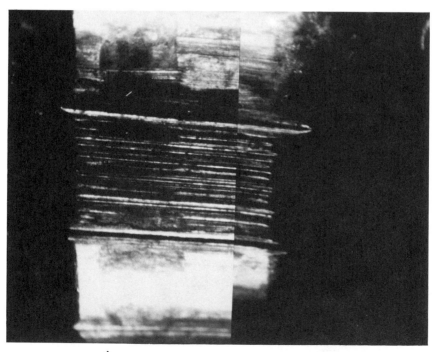

A                          B

Further, the number, width, and direction of twist of the lands and grooves make possible a determination of the make or makes of weapons from which the bullet may have been fired. The angle or rate of twist can be determined, but this is difficult and inaccurate when the projectile is mutilated.

The number and width of the land marks together with the direction and angle of the twist vary among different manufacturers and types of weapons. Under no condition should a bullet be tested in the bore of a weapon by pushing it into the muzzle, if the bullet and weapon are to be subjected to further investigation with the object of identification. The microscopic marks on the bullet might be completely destroyed in this way. If it is necessary to *search for a weapon* in connection with a bullet that has been found, the police officer can obtain a useful guide from a study of the land marks on the bullet. The number of marks, their width, and the direction of the twist can be compared with a suspected weapon. If it is such a long time after the actual shooting that any deposit of dust or powder in the barrel would no longer be significant, or if the barrel has evidently been cleaned or oiled, then a suitable piece of plasticine, which has been molded to a point, can be introduced into the muzzle of the weapon to obtain an impression of the lands so that their number and width can be compared with the marks on the bullet. Otherwise this information must be obtained from inspection of the muzzle of the weapon, possibly with the aid of a flashlight.

Generally, the number of "suspect" guns in any investigation is not large. Therefore, it is better to let the laboratory sort these weapons by firing test shots. A number of factors affect the width of land impressions so that an exact comparison between a cast of the barrel and the bullet cannot be made. Anything within a reasonable range of tolerance should be submitted for laboratory tests.

If there is reason to suspect that a bullet that has been found has *ricocheted*, and it is important to confirm this, it must be remembered that small grains of sand or other foreign matter may have stuck in flaws in the bullet, which should therefore be treated with care so that such particles do not fall off. Damage resulting from a ricochet can often be identified microscopically.

If a *muzzle-loading weapon* has been used, it is possible that the bullet may show marks from the ramrod used, so that these should be looked for. Homemade bullets can possibly be identified with the mold used. In the case of muzzle-loaders, it is also necessary to search at the scene of the crime for any paper wads or the like that might have been used in loading the gun (Figs. 10.21 and 10.22). These often remain uninjured, and the paper can perhaps be identified as torn from a newspaper or from a piece of paper in the possession of a suspect.

The *rifled slugs and single balls* of lead sometimes used in shotguns

FIGURE **10.21.** Fabric impression on the nose of a lead bullet, denoting its passage through fabric. (*Los Angeles County Sheriff's Department.*)

FIGURE **10.22.** A bullet with wrist watch parts embedded in the nose, and a damaged watch recovered at the scene. (*Los Angeles County Sheriff's Department.*)

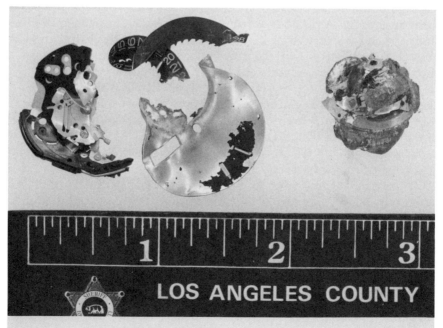

may give an opportunity for identification of the weapon used. They can give information only as to the caliber. Homemade balls can possibly be identified with the molds in which they were made.

## Small Shot

At close range, the charge of shot that has not yet dispersed, makes a large wound in a body, but at longer range the shot spreads out, more or less depending on the degree of choking of the gun, barrel length, size, and amount of shot. The amount of spread gives an opportunity of estimating the distance of the shot. If scaled photographs of the wound or shot pattern are available, comparison shots can be fired using the suspect weapon and ammunition of the same make and vintage. These are usually fired at heavy poster board or blotting paper. Without scaled photographs or comparison tests, only very broad estimates are possible, since the patterns produced by various combinations of guns and ammunition vary over a considerable range.

Table 10.1 gives an example of the influence of the degree of choke on shot patterns. These figures will not apply to all shotguns and all ammunition.

At a distance of 5 to 8 yards or more from the place of firing in the approximate direction of fire, one can sometimes find wads. The size of shot is sometimes given by a number, and sometimes shown by letters. There is no internationally uniform method of designation of shot. The procedure varies in different countries.

By measuring the diameter of any shot found it is possible to find the size of shot that would be marked on the cartridge. In this connection, it should be noted that there may be certain minor variations in size of shot in one and the same cartridge. It is therefore important to collect as many pellets as possible, so that the determination is more reliable. Often the shot is deformed to such an extent that it is impossible to measure its diameter with the desired accuracy. In this case it is convenient to weigh as large a number of pellets as possible and calculate the

TABLE **10.1.** Diameter in Inches of the Spread at Various Ranges of a Shotgun Charge

| Boring of Gun | Range in Yards | | | | | | |
|---|---|---|---|---|---|---|---|
| | 10 | 15 | 20 | 25 | 30 | 35 | 40 |
| True cylinder | 19 | 26 | 32 | 38 | 44 | 51 | 57 |
| Improved cylinder | 15 | 20 | 26 | 32 | 38 | 44 | 51 |
| Half choke | 12 | 16 | 20 | 26 | 32 | 38 | 46 |
| Full choke | 9 | 12 | 16 | 21 | 26 | 32 | 40 |

mean weight, and then to weigh the same number of pellets from cartridges with the different sizes of shot that may be supposed to come into question and to calculate their mean weight for comparison.

If a weapon is sent to an expert to determine whether a bullet or a cartridge case has been fired from it, a sufficient number of cartridges (five, six, or more) of the same type as that used in the actual incident should be sent with it. This is particularly necessary if powder or shot patterns are to be fired. All ammunition in the weapon and any partial boxes of unfired ammunition associated with a victim or a suspect should be submitted with the weapon. There may be sufficient differences between ammunition found in the gun and other ammunition available to the expert so that comparison tests are difficult, inconclusive, or impossible.

If a number of tests must be fired for transmission to various laboratories for comparison, inquiries should be made as to the nature and make of test ammunition desired in each investigation. For best results, these test specimens should be obtained by a laboratory and not by the field investigator.

## Test Firing

Test firings of a weapon must be done in such a way that the bullet can be recovered undamaged. For all jacketed bullets and most types of lead bullets, a cotton wad box or water trap is used to stop the bullet. In a cotton wad box, as a consequence of its rotation the bullet twists itself up in the waste, which finally forms a ball around the bullet, and the velocity progressively decreases until the bullet is finally held in the cotton waste. Occasionally, long staple surgical cotton is placed in front of the cotton waste. This forms a ball around the bullet, further protecting the surface. Because of the mild damage to the bullet's surface resulting from the abrasive action of the cotton, water is frequently used as a collecting medium. Five to six feet of water is ample for the collection of projectiles fired from handguns. Generally, it is undesirable for the police officer personally to carry out test shots with the weapon, since the microscopic imperfections in the bore of the weapon may be destroyed in the process. It is particularly important that the expert have an opportunity to examine the weapon before any tests are fired.

## Powder Pattern Examination

When a weapon is fired at close range, up to several feet, burned and sometimes unburned particles of gunpowder are discharged onto the target. This effect is referred to as *powder pattern deposits*. The appearance of the powder pattern is sometimes helpful in establishing the distance from where the weapon was fired to the target.

If the weapon was fired perpendicular to the target, the resulting powder pattern distribution will be located in an approximately circular area around the bullet entry hole. The diameter of the circle and the distribution of particles can be used to establish the distance.

The type of firearm, barrel length, and type of ammunition are all factors that affect the size and density of the powder pattern. If the muzzle of the weapon is in contact with the skin or within approximately 1/2 inch, the powder pattern is generally absent. This is due to the lack of space available for expansion of the powder that at close range will penetrate the body through the entrance wound.

To make a distance determination, it is important to use both the same firearm and same ammunition used in the crime. A series of test firings are made into paper or cardboard at different distances, and the test patterns are compared with the evidence. In most instances it is also useful to make the tests on material that is the same as or similar to the evidence.

In certain instances the powder pattern is not easily visible. Bloodstained clothing or dark-colored clothing cause these difficulties in visualization. Infrared photography is helpful in cases of bloodstained clothing. Chemical tests for nitrates present in the gunpowder, such as the *Walker Test* or the *Griess Test*, or for lead and barium in the primer, such as the *sodium rhodizonate test*, are useful to develop the powder pattern.

Firearms evidence occurs in many crimes such as assault, murder, and the like and is particularly important because of the large amount of useful information it can provide. Because this type of evidence is encountered so frequently, investigators must be familiar with the proper methods of handling it and its value to the case.

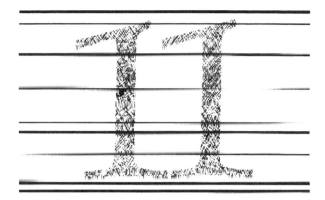

# ARSON AND
# EXPLOSIVES
# EVIDENCE

A rson may be defined as the willful and malicious burning of another's property or the burning of one's own property for some improper purpose such as defrauding an insurer. As a crime, arson ranks only behind traffic-related incidents in the highest losses of life and property. In dollars, property losses resulting from arson are estimated to cost billions of dollars annually.

## Arson Investigation

Arson investigation requires a considerable amount of care, attention to detail, and skill on the part of the investigator. Arson scenes present a host of problems that are uncommon to most other crime scene investigations. In most criminal investigations, once the crime has been committed and the police notified, the scene may be secured in relatively the same condition in which it was found. This is rarely the case in fire investigation. By the time the arson investigator arrives on the scene, it will have been well traveled by numerous individuals including fire fighters, supervisory personnel, onlookers, possibly the owner of the property, and so on. The careful preservation of the crime scene is frequently one of the last things to be considered when "knocking down" a fire (Fig. 11.1).

The issue of criminal intent is another major difference in arson investigations as compared with others. In most other crimes, the investigator frequently knows upon arrival or shortly thereafter that a crime has been committed. In arson cases, determining whether a fire was caused accidentally or was intentionally set may require a considerably more extensive investigation.

Arson and explosion crime scenes are also unique in the amount of destruction and devastation present. Items that under normal circumstances are readily identifiable as important evidence in an investigation may be totally or partially destroyed by the fire or by fire fighters. In spite of these as well as other difficulties inherent in arson investigation, a careful and thorough search of the scene of a fire can produce much information useful to the investigation (Figs. 11.2 and 11.3).

A number of motives are frequently associated with the crime of arson. Probably the most common motives for arson are concealment of other crimes and defrauding an insurance company. Fire investigation often uncovers other crimes such as murder, burglary, embezzlement, or fraud, which the fire was set to cover up. The attempt in these cases is to destroy records, destroy evidence of the crime that could identify the suspect, and/or make the identification of the victim of a murder impossible. In insurance fraud cases the suspect may have suffered a business reversal or be heavily in debt. A fire is set so as to appear to be

A

B

**FIGURE 11.1.** The scene of an arson fire at Universal Studios in Los Angeles (A) showing the clock tower from the movie *Back to the Future,* and an aerial view (B) of the whole scene showing the extent of the devastation. (*Los Angeles County Sheriff's Department.*)

**FIGURE 11.2.** A burned-out electrical timer device located at a fire scene can give the approximate time at which the power went out as a result of the fire. (*Los Angeles County Sheriff's Department.*)

**FIGURE 11.3.** A melted aluminum awning indicates the approximate temperature of the fire. Aluminum melts at approximately 660.2°C. (*Los Angeles County Sheriff's Department.*)

accidental, with the intent of filing a false insurance claim. Other motives, such as malicious mischief caused by juveniles, revenge, extortion, sabotage, terrorist acts, and pyromania, all represent potential reasons for setting fires.

The arson investigator should focus the investigation to answer several questions:

1. Where did the fire originate? Information can be obtained by questioning fire fighters about the location of hot spots, which direction the fire was moving, how fast, etc. The greatest amount of information will be gained by going through the scene and noting which areas suffered the most fire damage and exposure to heat. The origin is evidenced by the depth of char on burned items, degree of destruction, spalling, metal or glass bent or melted by exposure to heat for a longer time than other areas, and burning or heat fading of paint (Fig. 11.4). The investigator should be alert to the possibility of multiple sources or the entire structure as the origin.
2. How was the fire started? The investigator should look for faulty electrical wiring, the presence of ignitors, matches, flammable material, kindling, and other means of starting a fire. Flammable fluids will run into cracks and under objects on the floor and cause burning in locations that would not normally burn. Such fluids will also char deeper in areas where they were located, sometimes burning through the floor.
3. Was the cause of the fire an accident or was it intentionally set? This is the key issue in determining whether the fire was the result of arson. Evidence such as indications of breaking and entering, the presence of flammable liquids, and the location of multiple points of origin may indicate a maliciously set fire (Fig. 11.5).

*Physical Evidence*

The most commonly sought physical evidence in arson investigation is the presence of flammable fluids. Even in those cases where fire damage was particularly extensive or where the scene was completely wetted down, there is still a good probability of detecting flammable fluids. The search for flammable fluids should be concentrated at the point where the fire started. If charred rags or carpeting is noted, these should be collected and sent to the laboratory. Wood flooring, furniture, and carpet padding into which gasoline or kerosene may have been absorbed should also be collected, as well as empty containers or broken glass jars found at the scene.

Flammable fluids are highly volatile and evaporate easily. For this reason, appropriate packaging must be used to preserve these items for

**FIGURE 11.4.** (A) Chipping or splintering, commonly known as spalling, on a brick wall caused by a hot spot at the scene. (B) Another example of spalling on a cinder block wall. (*Los Angeles County Sheriff's Department.*)

laboratory analysis. Packaging this kind of evidence in paper or plastic bags or containers will not preserve it. Such packages allow volatile liquids to dissipate completely. The best packaging for these items is clean metal cans, such as those used for paint. The items should be placed in the cans, and the cans tightly sealed with metal lids. An alternative method of preserving evidence is to use glass jars with metal screw cap lids. Metal and glass containers retain small amounts of liquids and vapors that can be analyzed by the crime laboratory. The quantity of material needed for a chemical analysis of a flammable substance is extremely small. Instruments are presently available that can readily identify a flammable liquid whose quantity is less than one drop (Fig. 11.6).

Laboratory analysis can differentiate between the many types of accelerants used in arson. The common types of accelerants are gasoline, kerosene, charcoal lighter fluid, paint thinner, and turpentine. It is generally not possible to determine the brand of gasoline used; however, in some cases it is possible to determine whether it is leaded or unleaded. In some cases the dyes contained in gasoline can be used as a means of comparison with known samples. Highly sophisticated scientific instrumentation located at some laboratories may be able to differentiate brands of gasoline.

A careful search of all entrances and windows should be made to determine whether the building had been forcefully entered. If tool marks are observed, the area should be cut out or an impression made and submitted to the laboratory. In addition, samples of building materials such as glass, paint, plaster, stucco, wallboard, and cement, which may have been deposited on a suspect's clothing, should be collected for purposes of control or known samples. All evidence must be properly marked for identification and properly packaged. In some instances, it should be considered that an apparent forced entry may have been used to cover up an act of arson, so that such things as the side from which a window was broken, screen cut, etc., should be checked.

The investigation should include a search for igniting materials; burned matches and matchbooks should be collected. Burned matches, in some cases, can be physically fitted into a matchbook found on a suspect, and matchbooks can be chemically processed for fingerprints. Occasionally, pieces of a timing device used to delay the ignition of a fire may be discovered. Other types of ignitors such as candles, black powder, smokeless powder, sodium and water, electrical devices, and the like should all be noted and collected if found (Figs. 11.7 and 11.8). It is important to establish the manner in which the fire started. This determines the M.O. (*modus operandi*) of the arsonist.

If the scene of the arson is a business establishment, the investigator may notice that file cabinets have been pulled open and papers strewn about. Burned papers should be carefully collected and placed in cardboard boxes, handling them as little as possible. Burned papers may be examined at the laboratory and often yield useful information. For example, it may be very beneficial to know what files were burned or are missing.

If a fire was started outdoors, the area of the fire's origin should be examined. Soil from that area should be collected to be tested for the presence of flammable materials. To accomplish this, a gallon paint can

FIGURE 11.5. (A) Melted safety glass may indicate exposure to heat for a period of time, thereby suggesting a point of origin of the fire. (B) Deformed pipe as a result of the heat of the fire. (C) Typical appearance of burned lumber, referred to as "alligatoring," indicating the surface texture of the burned wood. (*Los Angeles County Sheriff's Department.*)

should be filled with soil, sealed, and submitted to the laboratory along with a control sample.

Any items left at the scene by the arsonist should be preserved. Traces such as pieces of clothing, hair, blood, tools, broken tools, and so forth all may prove important as a means of establishing the identity of the suspect.

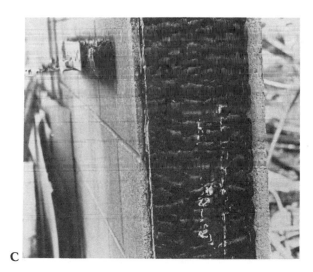

C

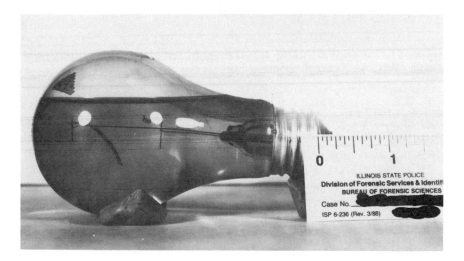

**FIGURE 11.6.** This incendiary device, a light bulb with a small hole drilled into the base, filled with medium petroleum distillate, and sealed with a putty-like material, was found in a light socket connected to a timer in a house under construction. The device probably would not have worked because there was too much liquid in the bulb, which covered the filament. (*Illinois State Police, Bureau of Forensic Sciences.*)

When a suspect is apprehended, a careful search of the suspect's property should be made to determine whether anything can be tied to the crime or the crime scene. Any accelerants such as gasoline or kerosene should be packaged and submitted to the laboratory for comparison with solvents detected at the scene of the arson. Similarly,

FIGURE 11.7.  A portion of a "Molotov cocktail" with a shot shell. (*Illinois State Police, Bureau of Forensic Sciences.*)

objects such as tools, matches, matchbooks, incendiary devices, and the like should be collected. The suspect's clothing and shoes should be collected, packaged, and sent to the laboratory for examination for the presence of various materials.

The suspect's vehicle should be inspected for the presence of material either removed from or transported to the scene of the arson. Any search of the suspect's vehicle or residence may require a search warrant. The local prosecutor should be contacted if there is any question as to its necessity.

In those cases in which a dead body is discovered in the investigation, a determination of the cause of death is necessary to ascertain whether the victim died as a result of the fire or the fire was set in order to conceal the killing. The pathologist will be able to determine at the time of the autopsy whether the person died of smoke inhalation or was dead prior to the fire.

## Explosives

Explosives are useful tools by which people have accomplished some remarkable engineering feats. However, like many other things, explosives are used for criminal ends as well. Murder, burglary, extortion, terrorist activities, and so on involving explosives require the attention

**FIGURE 11.8.** An improvised incendiary device consisting of a cigarette and matches can produce sufficient heat to cause the contents of the bag to burn. (*Los Angeles County Sheriff's Department.*)

of the investigator (Fig. 11.9). Bomb scene investigation is frequently treated as a specialty within some police agencies and is often associated with arson investigation. Although certain aspects of investigation in a bombing differ from the "usual" crime scene investigation, the basics remain the same.

In broad terms, an explosive is a material capable of rapid conversion from either a solid or a liquid to a gas with resultant heat, pressure, and loud noise. Many chemicals, alone or in mixtures, possess the necessary properties of an explosive. Except for chemical compounds classed as explosives, the rest usually come to the investigator's attention only as the result of an accident. In such cases, consultation with a forensic chemist or criminalist will provide a satisfactory explanation for the explosion.

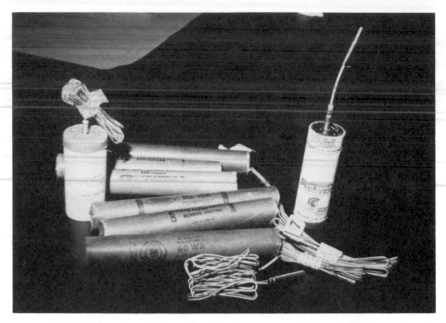

**FIGURE 11.9.** Examples of boosters, blasting caps, and dynamite. (*Los Angeles County Sheriff's Department.*)

Explosives can be classed into two broad groups: low explosives and high explosives. High explosives consist of primary and secondary explosives. Low explosives burn rather than explode. Damage by low explosives is caused by the force exerted by the rapid expansion of gases formed by burning. Low explosives must be confined to explode. High explosives, in general, are detonated by shock, have much higher detonation velocities, and need not be confined to explode.

## Low Explosives

*Black powder* is the most common type of low explosive. It is a mixture of potassium or sodium nitrate, sulfur, and charcoal. There has been wide variation in the formulation of this mixture over the years. Black powder is sensitive to heat, impact, friction, and sparks. When put into a confined area, such as a pipe bomb, black powder can be a destructive explosive. Detonation can easily be accomplished by means of a safety fuse. If an unexploded pipe bomb is encountered, it is very important to exercise extreme care in opening the device, since it can be set off by friction. One of the most common uses of black powder is in the manufacture of safety fuse. Safety fuse is used to initiate explosives nonelectrically. Safety fuse is generally composed of black powder with a protective covering of cotton yarn or jute, and an asphalt layer for water resistance. The asphalt layer is then covered with an insulating material such as a polyethylene plastic or a wax-impregnated yarn jacket. The color of the fuse is generally white, black, or orange.

Safety fuse should normally burn at a definite rate of speed but may burn faster or slower, depending on several factors such as age, handling, altitude, and humidity. Usually, safety fuse burns at about 30 to 40 seconds per foot; however, the actual rate should be determined by testing a given length (Figs. 11.10 and 11.11).

*Smokeless powder* is another low explosive encountered in bomb investigations. It is mainly used for small arms ammunition, but is frequently used in pipe bombs. Two types of smokeless powder are marketed, single and double base. Single base smokeless powder consists of nitrocellulose, and double base smokeless powder is composed of nitrocellulose and nitroglycerine. Although smokeless powder is not as sensitive to friction as black powder, it should be handled with the same care used when handling black powder.

## High Explosives

*Primary explosives* detonate when subjected to heat or shock. They are typically used as initiators of high explosives, to detonate main charges, in blasting caps, and in firearm primers. The major interest in this type of explosive in bomb investigation is in blasting caps.

FIGURE **11.10.** Debris from a pipe bomb packed with a low-order explosive. (*Los Angeles County Sheriff's Department.*)

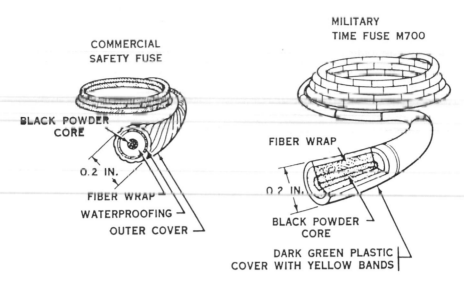

COMMERCIAL
SAFETY FUSE

MILITARY
TIME FUSE M700

BLACK POWDER
CORE

0.2 IN.

FIBER WRAP

WATERPROOFING

OUTER COVER

FIBER WRAP

0.2 IN.

BLACK POWDER
CORE

DARK GREEN PLASTIC
COVER WITH YELLOW BANDS

FIGURE 11.11. Safety fuses. (*U.S. Department of Justice.*)

*Blasting caps* are of two types: electric and nonelectric. They are small explosive devices, about 1/4 inch in diameter and from 1 to 3 inches in length. The case may be made of aluminum, copper, or bronze. The electric blasting caps have colored wires extending from them.

*Secondary explosives* detonate by shock from a suitable primary explosive. Their detonation velocities range from 3300 feet per second in the case of ammonium nitrate, to 29,900 feet per second in the case of *HMX*. Typically, high explosives are used to shatter or destroy objects.

*Detonating* cord is a cord-like explosive, similar in appearance to safety fuse. It contains a central core of RDX or PETN covered with cotton or other textile, followed by a waterproof material or plastic covering. The cord detonates at velocities from 18,000 to 23,000 feet per second. It is very insensitive to shock and heat and presents no special problems in handling (Fig. 11.12).

Detonating cord is used to set off charges of high explosives in much the same way as safety fuse is used to set off multiple pyrotechnic devices. The detonating cord may be inserted, tied, or knotted inside the high explosive to initiate detonation (Fig. 11.13). Detonating cord is used to set off simultaneous charges and is itself detonated by means of a blasting cap.

*Boosters or primer explosives* are used to detonate very insensitive high explosives. The booster itself consists of a secondary explosive such as RDX, PETN, tetryl, or pentolite and is detonated by means of a

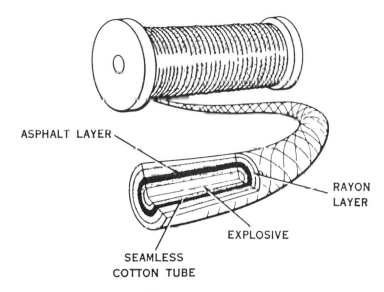

ASPHALT LAYER

RAYON
LAYER

EXPLOSIVE

SEAMLESS
COTTON TUBE

FIGURE **11.12.**  Detonating cord. (*U.S. Department of Justice.*)

blasting cap. Boosters are usually cylindrical in shape with a small opening to permit insertion of a blasting cap.

There are a large number of high explosives used commercially and by the military. The following are some of the more common ones encountered in law enforcement work. The list is not intended to cover all of the many types.

*Nitroglycerine* was first developed in 1847. It was not until 1867 that Nobel developed a method to desensitize this explosive sufficiently so it could be used commercially. Nobel's invention, *dynamite,* was a mixture of nitroglycerine and diatomaceous earth. Today, dynamite contains EGDN (ethyleneglycloldinitrate) in addition to other materials used to desensitize the nitroglycerine. Inert materials such as wood pulp or sawdust, cornmeal, sodium nitrate, and many other materials are found in dynamite.

Dynamite is usually packaged in cylindrical sticks and wrapped in waxed paper. The sticks come in a variety of sizes, most commonly 1⅛ to 1½ inches in diameter and 8 inches in length. Other sizes may be as large as 12 inches in diameter and 4 to 36 inches long.

There are four basic types of dynamite used today: straight dynamite, ammonia dynamite, gelatin dynamite, and ammonia-gelatin dynamite.

*Straight dynamite* is manufactured in strengths of 15 to 60% of nitroglycerine by weight. The nitroglycerine is generally absorbed onto a material such as wood pulp or ground meal (cornmeal, cornstarch, or the like).

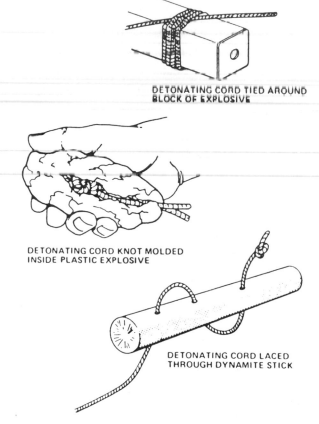

DETONATING CORD TIED AROUND
BLOCK OF EXPLOSIVE

DETONATING CORD KNOT MOLDED
INSIDE PLASTIC EXPLOSIVE

DETONATING CORD LACED
THROUGH DYNAMITE STICK

FIGURE 11.13. Examples of use of detonating cord to prime explosives charges. (*U.S. Department of Justice.*)

Dynamite has a sweet, pungent odor and may frequently cause headaches. Straight dynamite has an oily, slightly moist appearance and resembles a mixture of oil, sawdust, and clay. In older sticks of dynamite, the outer wrapper may often look oil-stained because of the nitroglycerine seeping out of the mixture. Police should treat such dynamite with extreme caution since it is in a highly unstable form.

In *ammonia dynamite*, some of the nitroglycerine is replaced with ammonium nitrate. Ammonia dynamite is less sensitive to shock than straight dynamite and has a less shattering effect, but is more suitable for "pushing." The color of ammonia dynamite is light brown, as compared with the slight reddish tint of straight dynamite.

*Gelatin dynamite* is a water-resistant form of dynamite manufactured by combining nitroglycerine with nitrocellulose. The resulting "gel" forms a thick, viscous liquid useful under wet conditions.

*Ammonia-gelatin dynamite* is a combination of the last two formulations. The addition of ammonium nitrate is a cost-saving factor, and the gelatin allows the explosive to be used in wet conditions.

Ammonium nitrate is a readily available material used both as an explosive and in a less pure form as a fertilizer. In its pure form it is a white crystalline material but may be a light tan color in a less pure form. As an explosive it is relatively insensitive and requires a booster charge to be detonated.

Because of its easy availability as a fertilizer, although less pure than explosive grade ammonium nitrate, it is readily available for use in homemade bombs. A modification of ammonium nitrate sometimes used is a mixtures of ammonium nitrate and fuel oil, also known as ANFO.

*Water gels or slurries* are classified as either blasting agents or explosives, depending on what they contain and whether or not they are cap sensitive. Water gels typically have an ammonium nitrate base, a sensitizer, a thickener, and 5 to 40% water. The sensitizer may be an explosive such as TNT, nitrostarch, or smokeless powder, or it may be a nonexplosive such as sugar, fuel oil, carbon, or a powdered metal. These explosives are rapidly gaining in popularity as substitutes for dynamite. Most slurries require a primer or booster for detonation; however, some manufacturers make cap-sensitive gels.

## Blasting Agents

Blasting agents, also known as nitrocarbonitrate (NCN), are insensitive chemicals and chemical mixtures that are detonated by a high explosive primer or booster. To be considered a blasting agent, the material must be unable to be detonated by a No. 8 blasting cap and contain no high explosives such as TNT or nitroglycerine. Blasting agents consist largely of ammonium nitrate. ANFO is considered a blasting agent and consists of 94% ammonium nitrate and 6% fuel oil. The advantage of blasting agents is that safety regulations governing shipping and storage are considerably less severe than those applicable to high explosives.

*Binary explosives* are two inert, nonexplosive chemicals that, when mixed, form a cap-sensitive high explosive. The materials contain either both liquids or a powder and a liquid and, in their unmixed states, are very insensitive to shock or friction. One component is usually ammonium nitrate, and the other is a nonexplosive sensitizer.

## Military Explosives

*Sheet explosives* are flexible, rubber-like sheets approximately 1/4-inch thick that can be cut with a knife. These explosives are used both in commercial and military applications. The high explosive used is either RDX or PETN. Sheet explosives are known as Flex-X, Detasheet, or M118 Demolition Block (the latter being military sheet explosives).

The most common type of military explosive is *trinitrotoluene (TNT)*. Military explosives differ somewhat from commercial explosives in that they must be used in combat conditions. Typically they must be relatively insensitive to heat, shock, friction, and bullet impact, have high destruction power (brisance), be lightweight and convenient to use, be usable underwater, and so on.

TNT is generally encountered in military explosives in 1/4-, 1/2-, and 1-lb blocks. The blocks have metal ends with a threaded well for a blasting cap at one end. The container is cardboard, and the TNT is a light yellow to brown color, although some TNT may be gray as the result of the addition of graphite in newer formulations.

RDX is used in the so-called *plastic explosives.* Plastic explosives contain plasticizers in addition to RDX and are easy to mold in warm temperatures.

Composition C-3, containing 77% RDX, is a yellow, putty-like material that has a distinctive heavy, sweet odor. When molded, it will stain the hands and clothing. The M3 block weighs 2 1/4 lb and is enclosed in glazed paper that is perforated around the middle for ease in breaking open. The block does not have a cap well.

Composition C-4 is replacing C-3 in military use. C-4 contains 91% RDX, is white to light brown in color, has no odor, and does not stain the hands. The M5A1 block demolition charge contains C-4 in a clear white plastic container with a threaded cap recess at each end. It weighs 2 1/2 lb. Composition C-4 also comes in the M112 block demolition, which is an improvement of the M5A1 and replaces it as a standard issue. The M112 contains 1 1/4 lb of composition C-4 with a pressure-sensitive adhesive tape on one surface, protected by a peelable paper cover. The C-4 in some blocks is colored dull gray and packed in a clear mylar-film bag. In blocks of more recent manufacture, the C-4 is white and packed in an olive drab mylar bag.

*Military dynamite,* not actually dynamite, is a mixture of 75% RDX, 15% TNT, 5% SAE 10 motor oil, and 5% guar flour. It is packaged in waxed manila paper and marked M1, M2, or M3. Military dynamite is buff-colored granular material that crumbles easily and is slightly oily to the touch. It does not have the characteristic odor usually associated with dynamite since it contains no nitroglycerine.

The explosives discussed to this point are those available through commercial and military sources and are some of the more commonly encountered types. The explosives industry, however, is a rapidly changing one, and the reader should understand this when studying its products. It is suggested that the investigator consult explosives manufacturers, law enforcement agencies who routinely deal with explosives cases, and forensic science laboratories for the latest information on the subject

## Homemade Explosives

If commercial or military explosives are not available, it is not particularly difficult for an individual to improvise from a large number of chemicals that, when mixed together, can produce highly destructive explosive devices. The investigator should recognize at least some of the more common materials that often find their way into homemade explosive devices.

Materials such as starch, flour, sugar, cellulose, and the like can be treated to become effective explosives. Powder from small arms ammunition, powder from firecrackers, matchheads, and ammonium nitrate from fertilizers can all be used in explosive devices. To detonate an improvised explosive device several methods are available:

*Blasting caps.* Caps, especially electrical blasting caps, lend themselves to homemade bombs. Such devices may be set off by a timing mechanism, by movement, by wiring into an automobile ignition system, or the like.

*Percussion primers.* Primers from shotgun, rifle, or pistol ammunition are sometimes used to detonate explosives that are heat sensitive.

*Flashbulbs.* Flashbulbs may be used to ignite heat-sensitive explosives such as black powder. If the bulb is placed in contact with the explosive, the resulting heat from the flashbulb will ignite materials such as black powder, smokeless powder, incendiary mixtures, etc.

As mentioned earlier, black powder, because of its relative ease of manufacture, is frequently used in homemade bombs. Other materials that are found regularly are listed:

*Matchheads.* Matchheads are frequently found confined inside pipe bombs. Matchheads are sensitive to heat, friction, and shock. When confined in this type of device, they can produce an effective explosion.

*Smokeless powder.* Powder from ammunition or for reloading purposes is frequently used as the main charge in pipe bombs.

*Ammonium nitrate fertilizer.* Ammonium nitrate mixed with fuel oil and an appropriate booster makes an extremely effective homemade explosive device.

*Potassium or sodium chlorate.* These compounds and sugar are used as incendiary and explosives materials.

The list of possible chemicals for improvised explosives is endless. An officer who comes upon a location with large amounts of chemicals such as nitrates, chlorates, perchlorates, nitric acid, aluminum powder, magnesium, sodium, sulfur, charcoal, sugar, and sulfuric acid, to name just a few, should be aware that this is where homemade explosives are being made.

## Bomb Scene Investigation

Physical evidence in bombing cases is useful in answering many questions. Some of the questions that the investigator will be interested in answering are as follows:

1. What were the materials used to make the explosive device?
2. What was the level of skill or expertise of the suspect?
3. What was the target of the bomb?
4. Was the explosion accidental, or was there criminal intent?
5. Where was the bomb made?
6. Where was the bomb placed?
7. Where did the suspect obtain the materials to construct the device?
8. Who was the victim or intended victim?
9. Who made the bomb and who placed it?
10. How was the bomb detonated?

The nature of the target, whether or not the bomb exploded, the extent of damage, the location of the incident, and weather conditions are some of the factors that influence the action to be taken by the investigator. If an unexploded bomb is found, it is necessary to call in a bomb technician to render the device safe (Fig. 11.14). The first priority of the technician is the safe disarming of the bomb. If possible, the investigator should photograph the bomb prior to moving it and have the bomb technician note any changes made in the device when dismantling it. If the bomb must be exploded to be disarmed, it should be done in such a way as to avoid total destruction of the device.

The scene itself should be thoroughly searched for evidence that may have been left by the suspect. Collection of evidence should include a search for a forced entry and accompanying tool marks, fingerprints, footprints, and any other traces that may help link a suspect to the crime scene.

In cases where the explosive device has been detonated, the work of the investigator is considerably more complicated. The duties of the crime scene investigator are basically the same as those outlined in Chapter 3; however, the investigator will have an additional consider-

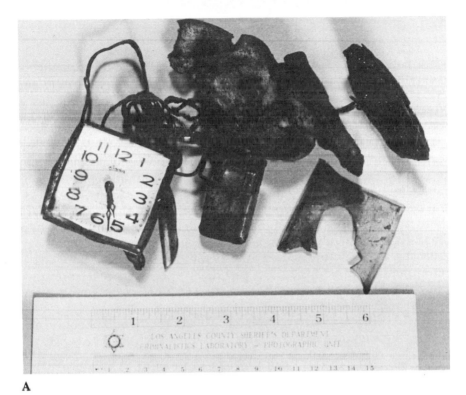

A

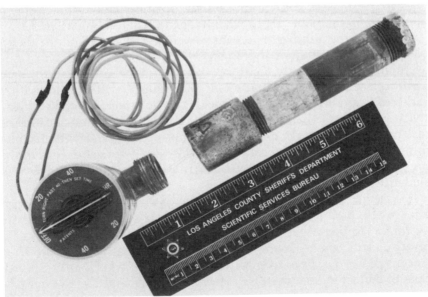

B

**FIGURE 11.14.** (A) Debris from a homemade explosives device with a timing mechanism. (B) An example of an unexploded homemade device with a timer. (*Los Angeles County Sheriff's Department.*)

ation. Safety will be a major area of concern. The scene of a bombing is generally very unsafe. The structure of a building where a bomb has exploded may be seriously weakened and can collapse. Other unexploded devices may still be in the area, and there may be additional hazards, such as broken gas mains and downed electrical lines.

Securing the crime scene is another problem. Unlike most crime scenes, bomb scenes frequently attract a large number of people such as police, fire department personnel, medical and ambulance personnel, paramedics, utility companies personnel, property owners, the press, and sightseers. One of the first orders of business must be to coordinate the activities of the large number of people likely to be present and to remove those individuals who are not needed.

Because of the nature of the crime, bomb scenes frequently include a certain amount of confusion. It is particularly necessary to restore order and control quickly, so that the investigator is able to accomplish the task of processing the scene.

The first officers to arrive at the scene of a bombing will be concerned with emergency and safety-related activities such as rescue, evacuation, and assisting fire department personnel, if required. Once the emergency phase is complete, efforts should be made to secure the crime scene and begin developing information on the circumstances of the case. Witnesses and victims should be interviewed, and as much information as possible about what happened should be gathered.

Because of the number of persons present at the scene and the likelihood of several different investigative agencies being involved, it is useful to set up a team to coordinate and control the investigation. Such a unit can act as a clearinghouse of information so that all information gathered from the investigative process can be integrated and studied.

Investigation of the actual scene of a bombing is a time-consuming task requiring a considerable amount of physical work and attention to minute pieces of physical evidence. It is also dirty work and requires the investigator to sift through large quantities of debris to locate items of evidence.

It is useful to have proper equipment to go through the scene. Coveralls, gloves, hard hats, goggles, work shoes, and other such items are useful for the investigator. Hand tools such as shovels, rakes, brooms, a heavy-duty magnet, cutting tools, and so on are also helpful. Sifting screens of various sizes to go through the debris, wheelbarrows, trash cans to collect debris, portable lighting, ladders, and the like may be required.

A leader should immediately be identified who is responsible for processing and directing the bomb scene investigation. The leader also serves as a link between those coordinating the overall investigation and the crime scene investigators.

The extent of the crime scene must be identified. The seat of the explosion can be a focal point, and the location furthest from the seat where fragments from the explosion were located can define the outer perimeter of the scene. A buffer area equal to approximately half the distance from the seat to the furthest point should be added. This represents the total area that should be secured and searched.

The bomb scene should be recorded. This may be accomplished by the standard means of photography and sketches. If the capability exists, the scene may be videotaped. If needed, aerial photographs should be taken. Photographing, measuring, and sketching the crime scene may be done while the scene is searched (Fig. 11.15).

Collecting physical evidence at the scene consists of the search for and recovery of items that may lead to information about the nature and type of explosive and the identity of the suspect. The area should be searched for the fusing mechanism of the bomb. Items such as timing mechanisms, batteries, pieces of wire, safety fuse, blasting cap debris, and the like may yield information about the way in which the bomb was set to detonate.

The scene should be searched for evidence to determine the type of explosive used. The seat of the explosion should be carefully examined for unexploded material and packaging material that may indicate the type of explosive used. If a portion of the container that held the device is found, laboratory tests may indicate the type of explosive. Similarly, the extent of damage to the container (for example, a pipe bomb) can

FIGURE 11.15. If the explosion takes place in an open space, the area in which the fragments are found and a surrounding buffer zone should be secured. (*U.S. Department of Justice.*)

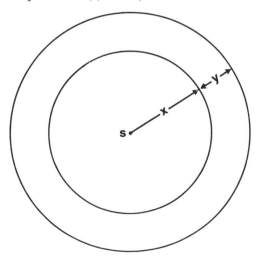

s – Seat of explosion.

x – Farthest distance from seat at which fragments are found.

y – One-half distance x;

**Area To Be Secured = x + y.**

indicate whether the explosive was a low-order or high explosive. In general, large fragments of a pipe bomb indicate a low explosive such as black powder, whereas small fragments indicate a high explosive.

The package that contained the explosive device may contain evidence to lead the investigator to a suspect. Fingerprints, names, addresses, and postmarks may be important information in the investigation.

The investigator should not forget to search for other evidence besides the bomb debris. Items such as fingerprints, tire tracks, tool marks, and the like are valuable and must not be overlooked.

If a suspect is apprehended shortly after the explosion, his or her clothing should be collected and submitted to the laboratory for examination for the presence of trace evidence and explosives debris. The suspect's hands should be swabbed with cotton applicators moistened with acetone, which can be tested for the presence of certain explosives. If the suspect's vehicle is located, it too should be carefully searched for tools, trace evidence, explosives residue, and materials that may have been used by the suspect in the crime.

All evidence discovered should be photographed in the place where it is found, measured, and located on a crime scene sketch prior to being moved. The investigator should remember to search also high areas such as trees, roofs, ledges of buildings, and other such places that may contain pieces of the exploded device.

Because of the large number of persons involved with the bomb scene search and the amount of evidence collected, it is helpful to keep an evidence log to detail each item collected, including the date, time, and name of the person collecting the material. The use of a log facilitates establishing a chain of evidence and makes the inventory of all of the evidence somewhat easier.

The crime laboratory plays an important role in bomb scene investigation. Often, the nature of the explosive used and information about the type of mechanism used to detonate it cannot be determined in the field. The laboratory will carefully and systematically examine all the items of evidence and attempt to answer some of the questions submitted by the investigator to assist in the solution of the case.

Both bomb and arson scene investigations require much time, patience, and extremely close attention to detail on the part of the crime scene investigating officer. The officer's willingness to go through large amounts of debris and rubble, carefully and painstakingly, in the attempt to locate pertinent physical evidence may result in a successful conclusion to the case.

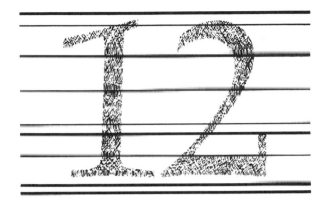

# ILLICIT DRUGS
# AND TOXICOLOGY

**D**rugs in bulk form and in blood and/or urine specimens are often involved as physical evidence in a wide variety of criminal cases. These substances are encountered in cases such as traffic accidents, traffic fatalities, driving while under the influence of alcohol or other drugs, public intoxication, possession or sale of controlled substances, and illicit manufacture of controlled substances. The purpose of this chapter is to describe the various types of drugs commonly encountered by police and examine some of the issues of crime scene investigation with regard to drugs and toxicology.

To simplify the topic, a distinction is made between bulk drugs (that is, drugs in their usual solid or liquid form) and toxicological specimens (that is, blood or urine samples that are to be tested to determine whether a drug is present).

## Psychoactive Drugs

Drugs that find their way into police investigations are typically called psychoactive drugs. These drugs affect the user's psychological processes and change his or her mood, thinking, perception, and behavior. Psychoactive drugs may be illicit (e.g., LSD) or ethical (e.g., barbiturates). They may be controlled (i.e., requiring a prescription) or uncontrolled (not requiring a prescription; e.g., alcohol or certain over-the-counter preparations).

Drugs can be divided into several types based on their effect on the user. The seven major categories discussed in this chapter are central nervous system depressants, central nervous system stimulants, hallucinogens, cannabis, designer drugs, steroids, nonprescription drugs, and inhalants.

### Central Nervous System Depressants

*Narcotics* are an important class of central nervous system depressants. They are used medically for their analgesic (pain-killing) properties and have a high potential for abuse. There are two categories of narcotics: opiate alkaloids, and synthetics and semisynthetics. Opiate alkaloids are derived from the opium poppy, *Papaver somniferum.* The most frequently encountered opiates are raw opium, morphine, and codeine. Common synthetics and semisynthetic narcotics are Demerol, methadone, heroin, dialudid, and Percodan (Fig. 12.1).

The second category of central nervous system depressants consists of the *sedative-hypnotics.* These are generally prescribed for treatment of insomnia and tension and have a high potential for abuse and addiction. Drugs in this category include barbituric acid derivatives such as

FIGURE **12.1.** "Tar heroin," a form of heroin with a tar-like consistency. (*Los Angeles County Sheriff's Department.*)

secobarbital, amobarbital, phenobarbital, and the like, and the nonbarbiturates such as glutethimide (Doriden), methaqualone (Quaalude), and chloral hydrate. Another drug classified as a sedative-hypnotic is the illicit drug phencyclidine (PCP or "angel dust"). Persons taking PCP report hallucinations and feelings of weightlessness and unreality.

The third category of central nervous system depressants comprises *tranquilizers and energizers.* Tranquilizers are grouped in major and minor tranquilizer groups. Major tranquilizers such as chlorpromazine, prochlorperazine, trifluoperazine, etc., are prescribed for treatment of neurosis, psychosis, and other psychological disorders and are considered addictive.

With prolonged use, minor tranquilizers can produce psychological dependence. Drugs in this category include meprobamate (trade name Equanil or Miltown), chlordiazepoxide (Librium), diazepam (Valium), oxazepam (Serax), and chlorazepate dipotassium (Tranxene). These drugs are generally prescribed for treatment of tension and anxiety.

Energizers or antidepressants are used for the treatment of moderate to severe depression. Drugs in this group include imipramine (Tofranil) and amitriptyline (Elavil).

Perhaps the most widely used and best known central nervous system depressant used today is ethyl alcohol, or ethanol. Its usual short-term effects are sedation, euphoria, impaired judgment, slowed reaction time, decrease of coordination, and decreased emotional control.

## Central Nervous System Stimulants

One of the few types of psychoactive drugs that has not become a law enforcement problem is the *xanthine alkaloids*, which contain such drugs as theophylline, theobromine, and caffeine.

*Cocaine* is the second of the central nervous system stimulants. It is derived from the leaves of the erythroxylon coca tree native to South America. The drug in its pure state is a white crystalline substance and is not generally used medicinally except as a local anesthetic in certain eye, nose, and throat surgical procedures (Figs. 12.2 to 12.4). In recent years, the illicit use of cocaine in the United States has been on the rise.

The third class of stimulants is the *amphetamines*. Drugs in this group are amphetamine (Benzedrine), dextroamphetamine (Dexedrine), methamphetamine (Desoxyn), mixtures of Dexedrine and amobarbital (Dexamyl), and nonamphetamine stimulants such as Ritalin and Preludin. These drugs are often prescribed for fatigue, narcolepsy, hyperkinesis in children, and in combination with barbiturates for obesity.

## Hallucinogens

Hallucinogens are a group of drugs that currently have no accepted medical use. The drugs produce perceptual alterations, intense and varying emotional changes, ego distortions, and thought disruption. Drugs in this group include mescaline, which is derived from the *Lophophora* cactus, psilocybin, which occurs in several species of mushrooms (e.g., *Psilocybe mexicana*), lysergic acid diethylamide (LSD), dimethyltryptamine (DMT), diethyltryptamine (DET), phencyclidine (PCP), which is actually a central nervous system depressant), and methyldimethoxymethyl-phenethylamine (STP) (Fig. 12.5).

## Cannabis

Marijuana is defined legally as derivatives from the plant *Cannabis sativa L.* Marijuana is most often consumed by smoking the dried crushed tops and leaves or resinous material known as hashish. Pharmacologically, marijuana is not classed in any of the preceding drug categories. Its usual short-term effects include relaxation, increased appetite, some alteration of time perception, and impairment of judgment and coordination.

A

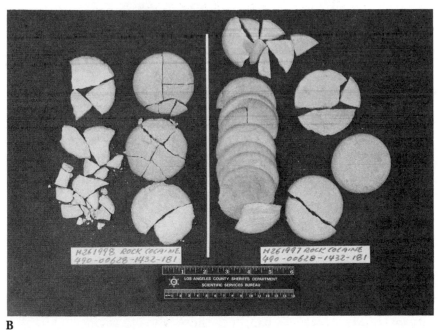

B

**FIGURE 12.2.** (A) "Crack" or "rock" cocaine, the free-base form of cocaine hydrochloride. (B) Part of the manufacturing process of rock or crack cocaine the round pieces, called "cookies," are in the shape of the glass beakers used in the final processing. The cookies are broken into "rocks" for sale. (*Los Angeles County Sheriff's Department.*)

**FIGURE 12.3.** Kilogram packages of cocaine are often wrapped in fiberglass. This may be an attempt to minimize the odor that drug dogs can detect or to keep the packaging from breaking apart when dropped from aircraft. (*Los Angeles County Sheriff's Department.*)

## Designer Drugs

Every few years a new type of drugs become popular. The latest are the so called "designer drugs" which, at this writing, have only gained popularity in California. Designer drugs are a class of synthetic drugs, synthesized by skillful chemists working in clandestine drug laboratories. The motive is profit. Clandestine drugs present a serious problem for law enforcement and a danger to those who use them.

Illicit chemists do what pharmaceutical researchers do to develop new active drugs. They synthesize drugs having similar structural features to known psychoactive substances. But with designer drugs there is no quality control or testing of the substances to determine if there are any harmful side effects.

FIGURE **12.4.** A large cocaine seizure.' (*Los Angeles County Sheriff's Department.*)

FIGURE **12.5.** A form of LSD packaging with the "Peanuts" cartoon character Woodstock. Other examples have used other cartoon characters, a concern to educators and police because a youngster might mistake them for skin decals. (*Los Angeles County Sheriff's Department.*)

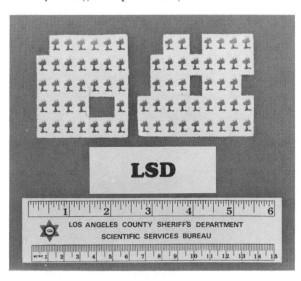

At present there are three classes of designer drugs: fentanyl analogs, meperidine analogs and MDMA (3,4-methy-lenedioxymethamphetamine). MDMA is known on the street by several names, e.g., MDM, Adam, Ecstasy and XTC. The three classes have a high likelihood for abuse, are very profitable to manufacture and may well cause a significant law enforcement problem in the future.

## Steroids

Steroid abuse has long been a factor in professional sports, amateur athletic competition, and body building. Anabolic steroids build muscle mass and thereby enhance performance. Negative side effects, however, have been experienced. Steroids are reported to cause liver and adrenal gland damage, infertility and impotency in men, and virilization (development of masculine characteristics) in women (Fig. 12.6).

Steroids are scheduled, controlled substances. Their use has become a law enforcement problem as illicit sales of anabolic steroids have been noted. Many of the steroids sold to athletes through illicit channels are not manufactured for use in human beings, but are instead veterinary drugs. Steroids are often manufactured outside the United States, and the packaging and labeling claiming a drug to be a specific steroid is usually not correct. These drugs come in a wide variety of forms and may be injectable solutions, capsules, or pills.

## Nonprescription Drugs

Nonprescription drugs rarely present law enforcement with major difficulties. They are included here as a reminder to officers investigating traffic accidents, fatalities, and cases of driving while under the influence. Over-the-counter drugs, particularly sleep aids, sedatives, and antihistamines, contain materials that make the user drowsy. If an

**FIGURE 12.6.** Steroids are now controlled drugs. (*Los Angeles County Sheriff's Department.*)

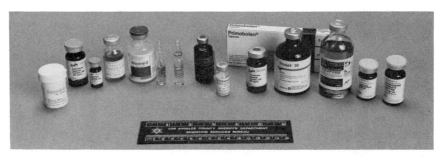

investigator finds a subject who has taken these drugs alone or in combination with alcohol and is exhibiting unusual behavior, he or she can reasonably assume that the individual is likely to be under the influence of such drugs.

## Inhalants

The last group of psychoactive substances are chemicals that are inhaled. Such materials include glue, gasoline, paint, solvents, and the like. These chemicals are frequently used by juveniles. The most common method of use involves placing the material into a plastic bag or onto a piece of cloth (such as a sock) and sniffing the material to obtain the intended result, intoxication.

Another class of inhalants contain amyl nitrite, a vasodilator, used to relieve symptoms associated with angina pectoris. Amyl nitrite is also sometimes used recreationally by homosexuals and is sold under various trade names.

## Crime Scene Search

Searching a crime scene for contraband drugs is somewhat different from investigating other types of cases. In a contraband drug investigation, the officer is looking for evidence that has been hidden on a person, in a dwelling, or in a vehicle. The various rules of evidence (including search and seizure and requirements for establishing a chain of evidence) hold in these cases as in others, and the investigator must be aware of current laws regulating search activities.

### Searching a Suspect

Concerning personal search, the officer must be aware of unusual places where contraband may be hidden. Clothing and personal property should be carefully examined. Evidence may be concealed in cigarette packages, small cases, film cans, hollowed-out compartments in canes or umbrellas, the lining of clothing, luggage, shoes, wallets, and other such items (Fig. 12.7). Suspects have been known to swallow contraband or hide it in a body cavity such as the mouth, nose, rectum, or vagina. Thoroughness and experience will aid the officer in the search.

### Searching a Dwelling

When searching a dwelling, the investigation should be done in a thorough, systematic manner. In addition to contraband, investigators should be alert for intelligence information such as telephone and

A

B

FIGURE 12.7. A dollar bill (A and B) used to try to smuggle a small quantity of heroin into a jail. (*Los Angeles County Sheriff's Department.*)

address books, names and telephone numbers on loose pieces of paper, and so on. Sums of money and possibly stolen property should be documented and collected. Additionally, any damage to personal property or to the residence should be carefully noted and, if possible photographed. Notification should be given to the owner.

One officer should be assigned to record the location and the name of the finder of each item of evidence. To assist in the recording, a crime scene sketch should be made so that each piece of evidence can be charted. The officer should also make certain that each item of evidence is correctly marked for identification and properly preserved.

If possible, two investigators should be assigned to a room. The search should begin at one wall, and everything hanging on that wall or resting against it should be carefully examined. Light switches and outlet boxes should be examined to determine whether paint on the screws or around the plate is chipped. The plates should be removed and searched. Molding around door frames should be examined for signs of stress to determine whether they conceal a hollow area. The tops of doors and door frames should be examined for indentations. A plug on top of a door or hinges may conceal a hiding place. Walls should be checked to determine whether they were replastered.

Pictures on walls and the backs of television sets and radios should be examined. Curtain rods, the tops and bottoms of window blinds, and shades should be searched.

After the walls have been searched, furniture should be inspected. Items should be turned upside down and their bottoms examined. Throw pillows and cushions should be unzipped and the contents searched. Rugs should be rolled up. When searching the bathroom, an officer should look for waterproof containers inside flush tanks, containers under sinks or laundry baskets. Each prescription medicine bottle should be examined to determine whether it contains the drug listed on the container and for whom the prescription was intended.

When evidence is located, it should be brought to the officer maintaining the evidence log, and the search should be continued. It is good practice to search each room a second time. Occasionally, evidence overlooked the first time will be noticed in a subsequent search.

## Searching a Vehicle

Automobiles are often used to hide contraband drugs. Searches involving motor vehicles should be conducted in a systematic and thorough manner. The vehicle can be divided into three areas for the search: the front end, interior, and rear.

The front end of a vehicle offers many areas in which to hide contraband. A careful search should include the grill, bumper, radiator, inside surface of the fender, air filter, and body frame. Use of a hydraulic lift helps in the examination of the undercarriage of the vehicle.

The interior of the vehicle is frequently used in concealing drugs. The seats should be removed from the car and carefully searched. The area behind the dashboard, the door side panels, head liner, and floor are all possible areas where drugs may be hidden.

Finally, the trunk and rear of the vehicle should be examined. Areas such as the spare tire wall, spare tire, rear fender, bumper area, and undercarriage of the vehicle are all potential hiding places.

## Clandestine Drug Laboratories

An important source of illicit drugs today is the clandestine laboratory. Illicit drugs, such as LSD, PCP, and some ethical pharmaceuticals, are manufactured in illicit laboratories. Police become involved in crime scene investigations involving illicit laboratories through intelligence gathering means, complaints from neighbors, fires and explosions, and often from detection of chemical odors while on routine patrol. Whatever the means of detection, the investigator must have an understanding of how such crime scenes are processed.

The trained forensic chemist or criminalist should be an integral part of any such investigation. Training and experience in dealing with chemicals is extremely important both from the standpoint of identifying drugs as finished products or intermediate products and as a safety consideration.

In larger police agencies, specialized hazardous chemical response teams have been developed who handle chemical spills and disposal of toxic substances. These teams are especially helpful and should most certainly be included in any clandestine laboratory investigation.

The clandestine laboratory scene is a potentially dangerous and hazardous one. The chemicals present are often flammable, explosive, toxic, and corrosive. Proper precautions must be taken to ensure the safety of personnel at the scene. Such locations should be approached with extreme caution (Figs. 12.8 and 12.9). It is not uncommon for chemicals to be unlabeled, and there are even reports of laboratories being booby-trapped.

As soon as the area has been secured, all windows and doors should be opened to ensure adequate ventilation and minimize the risk of fire. Light switches should not be turned on until the area is adequately ventilated; sparks can easily ignite highly flammable chemicals. Under no circumstances should anyone be allowed to smoke. The fire department should be notified and asked to stand by.

Certain chemicals are especially dangerous if mixed with others. Chemicals such as lithium aluminum hydride when combined with

FIGURE **12.8.**   The fire department is often the first agency to arrive at the scene. In this clandestine PCP laboratory, ether, a highly flammable solvent, was ignited by the pilot light of a hot water heater. (*Los Angeles County Sheriff's Department.*)

water are extremely explosive, as is sodium and water. Cyanide salts will liberate hydrogen cyanide gas when in contact with acid. Most chemical solvents such as ether, benzene, and the like are highly flammable. Acids and alkaline materials are dangerous and can cause severe burns.

Others such as piperidine may cause headaches. Prolonged exposure to many volatile organic chemicals may likewise be injurious. *Extreme caution must be exercised* in clandestine laboratory investigations!

Before collecting any evidence, the laboratory should be photographed. Photographs should be taken of individual pieces of equipment, chemicals, laboratory glassware, finished product, and intermediates.

The location should be searched for fingerprints and for laboratory notes, recipes, records, sales receipts from chemical supply companies, and other related items. Samples of chemicals from the final product, chemical precursors or intermediate products, and basic raw materials should be collected for crime laboratory analysis. A complete inventory should be made of all chemicals, equipment, packaging material, and the like. Such evidence will be very important should no final product be found. Laboratory notes, recipes, chemical precursors, and glassware

FIGURE **12.9.** Clandestine laboratories frequently have large quantities of chemicals present, as well as final and intermediate products. This seizure of chemicals in a PCP laboratory uncovered in a single-family dwelling is typical. (*Los Angeles County Sheriff's Department.*)

will be important evidence at trial to prove conspiracy to manufacture controlled substances.

## Collection and Preservation of Evidence

As with all physical evidence, the ultimate aim of collecting drug evidence is its legal admissibility in court. To assure this end, the investigating officer must be concerned with maintaining the integrity of the evidence from the time of seizure until its presentation to the court.

In addition to the usual requirements to maintain a chain of possession of the evidence, some other procedures are important. All drugs should be accurately weighed. The gross weight of the package, including the drug and packaging material, should be made and recorded. Individual pills, tablets, packets, balloons, and so on should be counted and the number written on the outer package and in the report. (In cases involving a large number of units, 100 capsules can be weighed and the total number of units can be estimated by determining the total weight and dividing that weight by the unit weight.) Liquids should be measured in metric units such as liters or milliliters.

The packing material seized with the contraband should be kept with the evidence and properly marked for identification. All items should be placed in appropriate evidence envelopes, sealed, and marked. Liquids should be placed in clean stoppered containers to minimize evaporation, sealed, and labeled. If its original container can be tightly sealed, it may be used to preserve a liquid.

## Toxicology

Toxicology is the study of poisons. The term is used in this section to describe the detection of drugs and alcohol in blood and urine samples collected from suspects in certain types of criminal investigations. The presence or absence of drugs or alcohol in a person's body and the issue of whether the subject was under the influence of a drug is important in traffic investigations, in cases of driving under the influence, in the legal defense of diminished capacity, and in public intoxication cases.

The most common substance tested for in most police laboratories is alcohol in blood and urine specimens submitted in so-called drunk driving cases. Cases of driving under the influence of alcohol represent a large percentage of all traffic fatalities and traffic accidents.

Implied consent laws require a driver suspected of being under the influence of alcohol to submit to one of three tests—blood, breath, or urine—to determine the blood alcohol level. The majority of states in the United States set a blood alcohol level at 0.10% (i.e., 0.1 gram of ethyl alcohol per 100 ml of blood) as the level at which a person is presumed to be under the influence of alcohol such that a driver is unable to operate a motor vehicle in a safe and prudent manner. The 0.10% level represents approximately 4 ounces of 100-proof alcoholic beverage in the body of a 150-lb individual.

Blood, breath, and urine testing are routine procedures available in all jurisdictions to measure the blood alcohol level. If blood is taken, it should be collected in a medically approved manner. The syringe used should *not* have been cleaned with alcohol, and nonalcoholic cleansing agents (e.g., aqueous zephiran) should be used to cleanse the area of skin from which the blood is to be taken. Approximately 10 to 20 ml of blood should be collected in a container with an appropriate preservative and anticoagulant.

If urine is collected, the subject should first be requested to void the bladder, wait approximately 20 minutes, and then urinate into a container in which has been placed an appropriate preservative. Approximately 25 ml of sample should be collected.

An officer should be present in each case to observe the collection procedure and to mark the evidence properly. The specimen should then be submitted to the laboratory for analysis.

Officers will find that some subjects, although exhibiting alcohol-like intoxication symptoms, have no or only a small amount of alcohol in their blood. The reason for this is often that the suspect had taken some other central nervous system depressants with similar physiological effects. When questioning the suspect, the officer should try to determine whether the suspect had taken any other medication, or when searching the individual during the booking process, it should be noted whether any solid dose drugs were found. This information is helpful to the forensic toxicologist when running tests on blood and urine specimens.

A large number of depressant-type drugs are routinely encountered in traffic-related incidents today. Barbituric acid derivatives, valium, Quaalude, PCP, cocaine, and marijuana are among the more common substances encountered. The type and quantity of sample required for analysis may vary from one jurisdiction to another, and the local crime laboratory should be contacted to determine the best sample for the specific drug analysis requested.

In homicide cases in which a suspect is arrested shortly after the killing, it is sometimes a useful practice to obtain blood and urine specimens from the suspect to be screened for the presence of drugs and alcohol. This strategy is particularly useful in those cases in which the suspect may raise the issue of diminished capacity at the time of trial.

Illicit drugs in bulk or in toxicological specimens are encountered in criminal investigation in a large number of cases. Investigators must be familiar with the hazards of various chemicals and the pharmacological effects of psychoactive substances, as well as the usual considerations involved in the collection and preservation of physical evidence.

# SEXUAL ASSAULT
# INVESTIGATIONS

F ew crimes rely so heavily on physical evidence as does the crime of rape. There are not many other instances in which the testimony of the victim is viewed with as much mistrust by juries, courts, and sometimes even prosecutors and police. It is for this very reason that physical evidence is so important to the investigation and prosecution of this crime.

## Rape Investigation

Rape investigation is different from that in many other major crimes. Unlike homicide, robbery, or assault, the first officer at the crime scene is required to play a much greater part in the collection and preservation of physical evidence.

In a murder investigation, it is the first officer's responsibility to secure the crime scene until the investigators arrive. This is not the case in a rape investigation. The first officer is required to make certain that fragile physical evidence that may be lost during the medical examination or by the victim herself be collected and preserved.

### Preliminary Interview

The first officer must be knowledgeable about the types of evidence generally found at the rape crime scene. The officer must also be a skilled interviewer in order to elicit from the victim the painful details of the assault and able to determine from these details what evidence may be available.

The first officer at a rape scene may find training in crisis counseling helpful in assisting the victim to deal with her trauma. *Outmoded attitudes that women provoke rape or deserve it, because of situations in which they placed themselves, have no place in modern police theory.* The victim should be treated nonjudgmentally and with sensitivity.

Observations about the victim noted in the crime report will be important at a later time. The psychological state of the victim may be significant. The officer should realize, however, that people in serious emotional crises may not immediately exhibit the states of anguish and grief that might be expected. The victim may appear perfectly calm and in control of herself when being interviewed by the police. This behavior is not uncommon. The officer should not assume that the victim is being untruthful because she is not exhibiting extreme emotion. Statements in police reports such as, ". . . the victim appeared unusually calm, considering her complaint of rape . . ." do nothing but confuse the investigation and raise doubt at the trial.

The investigator should be aware that many rape victims do not volunteer particularly sensitive details of the assault. Questions about oral and anal intercourse should be asked. The officer should ascertain whether the victim is sexually experienced and, hence, able to testify whether penetration and/or ejaculation took place.

After a rape, the victim may feel psychologically "dirty." She may have a compulsion to wash, bathe, douche, throw away her clothing, and clean up the scene of the rape. During the interview the officer should determine which, if any, of these actions has occurred. If any did, an attempt to collect evidence should still be made. A piece of tissue or washcloth used by the victim to clean herself might still have semen present. Underwear and clothing worn at the time of the crime, even if thrown away or cleaned, should be collected for examination.

The crime scene should be processed as outlined earlier in this book, but several other aspects require attention. What was the M.O. of the suspect? Did he practice any unusual acts such as urination or defecation? Did he do or say anything unusual? Is there any physical evidence to substantiate these acts? Did he bite the victim? Was the victim or suspect scratched or bruised? All of these details together with any physical evidence will greatly assist the investigation of the case.

## Medical Examination

Following the preliminary interview, the victim should be taken to a hospital emergency room or clinic for a thorough examination. Since much of the evidence associated with rape is of a very fragile nature, time is of the essence. The victim should be taken to the emergency room as rapidly as possible. A change of clothes should be obtained so that the clothing worn during the rape may be collected.

Many hospital emergency rooms have established protocols to deal with rape victims. Rape victims are ranked in medical priority immediately after life-threating cases. Hospitals are responsible for the victim's medical and psychological well-being as well as the collection of physical evidence.

Once the victim has been transported to the hospital, the officer should briefly go over the case with the attending physician or nurse. Pertinent information gleaned from the interview should be given to the doctor. This may facilitate the doctor's examination for physical evidence.

The doctor first takes a *medical history* from the victim and again goes over the details of the assault. Doctors should be encouraged to take detailed notes and later couple the notes with medical findings during the examination phase. Details such as the date of the last menstruation, the time of the last consensual intercourse, the presence of bruises not related to the assault, the presence of bruises from the assault, and other related factors are pertinent information.

After obtaining the medical history, the doctor should *conduct a thorough examination*. Some hospitals examine only the genital area and miss a great deal of useful evidence. The location of any cuts, bruises, lacerations, or contusions should be noted in the medical report. A helpful practice is the use of an anatomical diagram, on which the location of cuts, bruises, and the like can be charted. If the victim is wearing clothes worn during the assault, they should be collected and packaged in a paper bag. A chain of custody for any evidence collected during the medical examination should be started.

Many hospitals, police departments, and commercial hospital and/or law enforcement supply firms have sexual assault evidence kits (Fig. 13.1). These kits greatly facilitate the collection and preservation of rape evidence. They also direct the physician to look for certain of the more common types of evidence found in rape cases.

After the medical history is taken, the thorough examination can be begun with a cursory examination of the victim. *Photographs of bruises or wounds may then be taken.* If the hospital does not have this capability, the police officer may take the victim to the police station for this purpose. In some instances the officer may wish to wait a day or so until the bruises become black-and-blue and better show the location and extent of the assault.

FIGURE 13.1. Example of a sexual assault evidence collection kit. (*Los Angeles County Sheriff's Department.*)

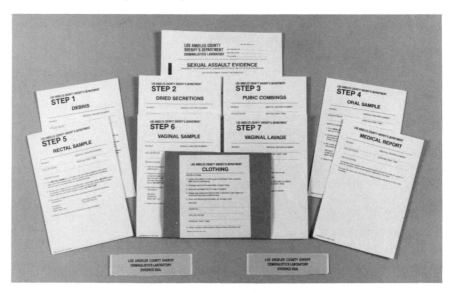

The victim should next be carefully examined for *trace evidence* adhering to her body. The location of any debris, grass, soil, vegetation, dried semen, dried blood, loose hair, fibers, and so on should be noted and collected. The presence of dried seminal fluid, dried blood, and dried saliva (from bite marks) is especially useful since such evidence may be typed for blood group substances. They are easily preserved by using a slightly moistened cotton-tipped applicator.

After examination of the extremities and torso, the *genitalia are examined.* Some facilities use a Wood's Lamp (UV lamp) to examine for semen. Semen is fluorescent under ultraviolet light.

Next, *pubic hair combings* are taken in an attempt to find foreign hairs and fibers or other debris. The hairs, any debris, and comb are all submitted for examination. As with all other evidence, these items should be appropriately documented in the medical report and labeled to maintain a chain of custody.

A *vaginal specimen* is collected with two cotton-tipped applicators, and a portion is smeared on two microscope slides. The slides should be air dried, but *not* stained. The slides should be placed in a slide protector, *not* in alcohol (Fig. 13.2).

Finally, a *vaginal aspirate* is taken. Three to 5 cc of sterile saline are used.

FIGURE **13.2.** Microscopic examination of a vaginal smear may disclose the presence of spermatozoa, which is helpful in establishing an element of the crime of rape, vaginal penetration. (*Los Angeles County Sheriff's Department.*)

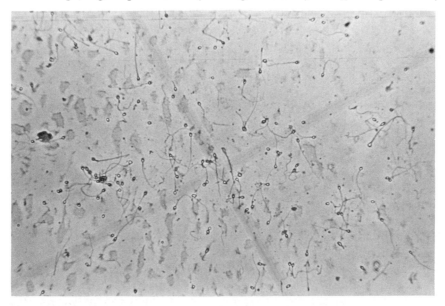

## Collection of Physical Evidence

Other evidence should be collected if indicated. If anal or oral intercourse occurred, appropriate rectal and mouth swabs should be collected. Fingernails may be examined and, if sufficient debris is present, nail scrapings can be collected. Toxicology samples should be collected if the victim appears to be under the influence of alchohol or another drug.

Physical evidence collected in rape cases is used for three major purposes:

1. *To establish that penetration occurred.* The presence of seminal fluid and spermatozoa in the vaginal pool is suggestive of vaginal penetration. The presence or absence of this evidence can be explained in any number of ways.

The absence of seminal fluid in a case where it was expected could be caused by the following factors: the time period between the rape and medical examination was too long; the suspect wore a condom; the suspect penetrated but did not ejaculate in the vagina; or the doctor did not take an adequate sample.

Similarly, seminal fluid and spermatozoa may be present from a consensual intercourse and not from an alleged rape. In this instance, seminal fluid typing is indicated.

2. *To establish nonconsensual intercourse.* Physical evidence may prove that the victim did not consent to the intercourse. Evidence such as torn or soiled clothing, bruises, pulled out hair, cuts, and other indications assist in proving that a struggle occurred during the time of the intercourse, hence rape.

3. *To establish identity.* The suspect's identity may be established by usual means: eyewitness testimony, fingerprints, hair, fibers, or bloodstains left at the scene. Additionally, there is the possibility of determining the assailant's blood type through seminal fluid typing or typing of cellular material at the hair root (especially prevalent in freshly pulled hairs).

The suspect may have left an article of clothing at the crime scene or unknowingly picked up some trace material such as fibers from a rug or clothing (Fig. 13.3). A cigarette butt, beer can, or piece of paper may yield fingerprint evidence. These are all possible types of evidence that can be obtained from a carefully and thoroughly conducted crime scene investigation.

Rape evidence should be refrigerated and submitted to the crime laboratory quickly. Much of the biological evidence deteriorates rapidly, particularly evidence that is to be blood typed.

Crime laboratory tests involving comparative analysis, such as hair examination and blood and semen typing, require known specimens. Semen and saliva specimens require known blood and saliva samples from the parties involved in the incident.

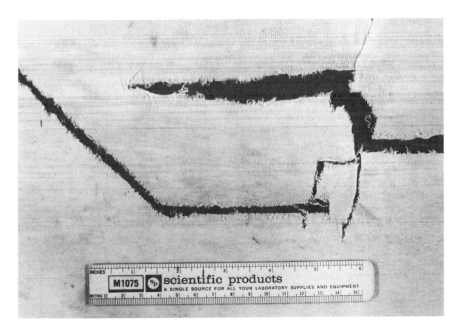

FIGURE 13.3. In this rape case, the victim's hands were cut while reaching for a knife. The suspect tore off the bottom of his undershirt and gave it to the victim to bandage her hands. A physical match of the torn pieces conclusively shows that the shirt was once whole. (*Santa Ana, California, Police Department.*)

Rape investigation presents unusual challenges to the investigator. Issues such as myths about rape, psychological trauma of the victim, and, in some cases, the investigator's feelings of uncomfortableness must be addressed when investigating this crime of violence.

## Other Sexual Assaults

### Child Molestation and Incest

Child molestation and incest investigations have two related problem areas: difficulty in interviewing the victim and possible problems regarding the child's competency to testify in court. These difficulties, coupled with the family's reluctance to pursue or cooperate in the matter, make these cases a challenge.

The key person in the sexual assault case involving a child is the physician. The physician's ability to examine the victim and document findings of sexual assault are of major import in this type of case. Because of the usual inability of the victim to testify, the physical evidence and medical testimony are particularly important.

Child psychologists are also playing an increasing role in child abuse and child molestation cases. They can be of help to investigators in pointing out specific child behavior patterns generally associated with this type of crime. However, investigators should be aware that a child psychologist may inadvertently cause a young victim to color his or her story so as to tell the psychologist what he or she wants to hear.

Physical evidence is often scant in child molestation cases. In cases where the molestation occurrs out of the home, the child's parents are often incredulous about the crime. Telltale signs such as nightmares, bed wetting, urinary tract infections, strange stories, and so on eventually point to their cause. If molestation is suspected, the police are brought into the investigation. If clothing is available, which was worn at the time of a recent assault and was not laundered, it should be collected. Beyond this, the police will need to rely heavily on medical findings.

Child abuse cases also rely on the findings of the pediatrician. Here, unexplained bruises, X-rays showing broken bones, and so forth will be important in the investigation. In addition to physical abuse, there may also be instances of malnutrition and poor hygienic conditions.

These types of cases are almost always emotionally charged and are difficult to prosecute and take to trial. To be sure, such crimes certainly do occur; however, investigators must be especially careful in these cases. Innocent people's names can be tarnished irrevocably if a careful investigation is not made.

## Homosexual Sexual Assault

Assaults involving anal intercourse or sodomy are not limited to female victims. Male homosexual sexual assaults occur with some frequency in jail and prison environments as well as elsewhere.

Of particular importance in these cases is the physician's examination of the rectum, as well as swab evidence taken for the examination of semen. Medical examination conclusively indicates whether anal penetration occurred and whether the person was accustomed to anal intercourse.

Beyond the medical examination and search for semen, other evidence is sometimes uncovered in such cases. Feces may be found on clothing or other articles. Sometimes a lubricant such as petroleum jelly or the like may be used and should be looked for.

Crimes referred to as "sexual assault" are improperly named. In reality, they have little to do with sex except that the genitals may be involved. They are, in fact, *crimes of violence* frequently involving suspects exhibiting "nonnormal" psychological behavior. The investigator who understands the psychological as well as the physical evidence aspects of these crimes will likely be more effective in their investigation.

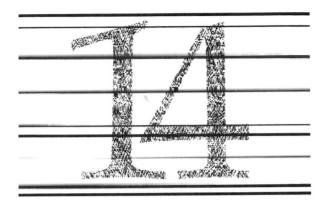

# BURGLARY
# INVESTIGATION

**B**urglary is one of the most commonly encountered crimes investigated by police. Because the nature of the crime is so varied, it is difficult to set down specific guidelines for its investigation. Many of the techniques and procedures outlined in earlier chapters of this text are pertinent to the burglary investigation. This chapter discusses some of the aspects of crime scene investigation that deal more specifically with the crime of burglary.

The first officer to arrive at the burglary scene must be concerned with the suspect's location. In cases of a burglary in progress, in which an officer has been called by someone reporting the presence of a prowler, by a silent alarm, or by a ringing burglar alarm, the first consideration must be to apprehend the suspect.

Once the suspect has been located or a determination has been made that the suspect is not at the scene, the location must be secured. Witnesses should next be located and separated for interviewing at a later time. The crime scene search should then commence.

The officer conducting the crime scene investigation of a burglary should understand that most experienced burglars take care to leave behind only the minimum amount of evidence at the location. The officer should also remember that it is impossible for the suspect not to change the crime scene in some small way by leaving traces or by picking up small items of evidence when leaving the scene (Fig. 14.1). The officer must therefore collect any evidence left by the suspect (e.g., fingerprints, shoe prints, tool marks, etc.) as well as evidence from the suspect that may have been removed from the scene (e.g., glass fragments, paint chips, wooden splinters, etc.).

The investigator should also be aware of the M.O. (*modus operandi*) of the burglar. Frequently, a suspect may be responsible for a large number of burglaries in a particular area, and similarities in the case may enable the investigator to concentrate on one rather than a number of suspects. Thus, in some instances it may be useful to examine tool marks left at different crime scenes in order to determine whether the same tool was used (Fig. 14.2).

## Points of Entry

The point of entry is an important location of physical evidence in burglary investigations. The experienced burglar attempts to gain entry by the easiest and safest available entrance.

### Entry Through Windows

Entry through windows is usually accomplished by breaking a hole through a pane and removing the broken glass so that the latch can be reached. To minimize the noise from falling glass, the burglar may press

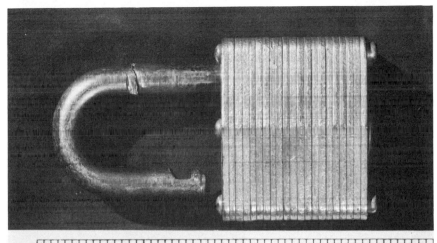

LOS ANGELES COUNTY SHE
CRIMINALISTICS LABORATORY

A

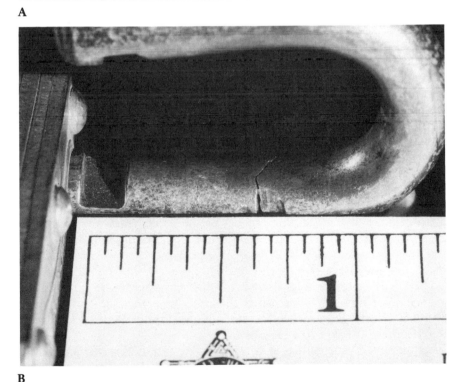

B

**FIGURE 14.1.** Evidence in a burglary case: (A) a cut lock hasp and (B) close-up of hasp shown pieced together. (*Los Angeles County Sheriff's Department.*)

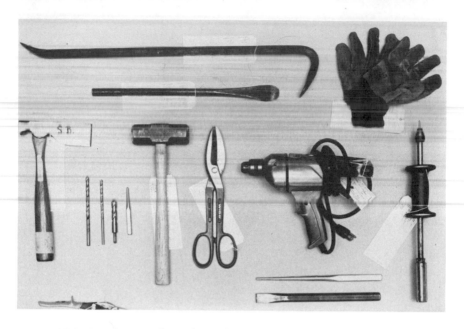

**FIGURE 14.2.** Burglary tools such as these may be a source of many types of physical evidence such as paint, glass, other building materials, tool marks, and the like. (*Los Angeles County Sheriff's Department.*)

a rag against the window; sometimes adhesive tape may be used. In some cases, the burglar may remove the entire windowpane by removing the putty holding the glass in place. It has even happened that the burglar has replaced the glass intact and put in new putty.

Where a window is covered by a screen, a careful examination of the edges for any cuts may show fibers from a sleeve where the suspect's arm was inserted to open or break the window (Fig. 14.3).

Glass is one type of evidence often found on the suspect when a window was broken to gain entrance. When a window is broken, it is almost unavoidable that some pieces of the flying glass will adhere to the suspect's clothing. Specimens of the broken windows should therefore be collected by the investigator for possible comparison with any glass found on the suspect's clothes.

The investigator should also search for any fingerprints present on the windowpane as well as prints that may be present in the window putty. Similarly, fingerprints should be looked for in the dust that may be present on the window or ledge.

Entry may also be gained by forcing in a tool to push back a window latch. In such cases, tool marks should be looked for and samples of wood and paint taken for comparison in case a tool is found later.

A pry bar, screwdriver, or other tool is also sometimes used in forcing

FIGURE **14.3.** A window is often a point of entry in a case of breaking and entering or burglary. This screen shows prying marks in the lower left corner. (*Los Angeles County Sheriff's Department.*)

a window. In these cases, tool marks and specimens of building debris should be collected. Sometimes the burglar may try to force several different windows in order to enter the building. The investigator should therefore examine all windows to determine whether there are any jimmy marks present and collect appropriate tool mark evidence.

Paint chips are frequently dislodged during the course of breaking in, and the investigator should always collect samples for later comparison. Subsequent examination of the suspect's clothing and tools may uncover paint that matches paint recovered at the crime scene.

## Entry Through Doors

A burglar usually opens a door by using a pry bar to attack the door and jamb around the lock until either the bolt can be pushed back or the bolt is actually freed from the striker plate. A door jamb may sometimes be so weak that it may be spread apart far enough to free the bolt. This can be done by mere pressure from the body or by inserting a jack horizontally across the door frame. The lock might also be made accessible through a hole that is drilled, sawed, or broken in a door panel. Far too many doors are fitted with glass that is simply broken so that the lock may be reached (Fig. 14.4).

Other weak points that may be attacked are mail slots, the frames of which may be removed, and transoms, which may have been left open.

FIGURE **14.4.** Exterior doors are another favorite point of entry. (*Los Angeles County Sheriff's Department.*)

A common method of entry is to push back spring-loaded bolts by means of a knife. The knife is inserted between the door and the jamb and the bolt is gradually worked back. The bolt is kept from springing back by outward pressure on the door. This method is easily detected by the series of scratches that run lengthwise along the bolt (Fig. 14.5). Burglary by this method is prevented by safety catches and deadlocks.

Snap-lock bolts can also be opened by inserting a knife, spatula, or piece of celluloid that is pressed against the beveled face of the bolt, pushing it back. The instrument can be inserted either between the door and the jamb or behind the molding on the jamb. This method of entry is generally difficult to detect because a piece of celluloid can be used without leaving any marks. It is, however, possible that pieces of celluloid are broken off and may be found in or near the lock. On locks where the beveled face of the bolt faces inward, the bolt may be pushed back by a suitable tool or a piece of wire that forces the bolt back by a pulling movement. It is usually discovered through the scratch marks on the face of the bolt.

Special attention should be given to the opening for the bolt in the striker plate because of the possibility that it may contain wadded paper

**FIGURE 14.5.** Scratches are easily visible on this spring-loaded bolt. (*Los Angeles County Sheriff's Department.*)

or other material. It has happened that a burglar surreptitiously stuffed something in the opening in the door jamb during an earlier visit to the premises. The effect of the wadding is to prevent the bolt from locking, so that the burglar may later return and push the bolt back.

If there is reason to suspect that the lock has been picked, the lock should be disassembled with great care. The investigator should avoid making new scratch marks inside the lock. If a pick has been used, it may have left marks in the coating of dust and oil usually found inside locks. Broken knife points, metal fragments from lock picks, and the like may also be found inside the lock.

Cases have been recorded wherein the mechanic who installed a lock made certain alterations in order to facilitate a later burglary.

Entry can also be gained by cutting off the hinge pins by means of a bolt cutter. More commonly, however, the pins are simply knocked out with hammer and chisel or screwdriver. With the pins out, the door can be lifted off the hinges. The door may then be replaced and the pins reinserted. This method of entry is readily revealed by the damage to the hinges and the chips of paint or metal on the floor below the hinges.

Cylinder (pin-tumbler) locks may be picked by special picks, but usually the whole door is forced or the cylinder is removed. The cylinder may be pulled out by means of a special puller shaped from a pair of large nippers. To prevent detection of the removal, the lock cylinder is sometimes replaced or a similar cylinder put in its place. Sometimes the retaining screw is removed surreptitiously during an earlier visit to the premises, which facilitates the removal of the cylinder.

Still another means of gaining access through a door is by means of a wrench placed on the doorknob (Fig. 14.6). The twisting motion exerted on the doorknob is sufficient to defeat the locking mechanism of inexpensive locking devices. Examination of the doorknob shows characteristic markings caused by the tool. The doorknob should be removed and submitted to the laboratory for comparison with tool marks made by the wrench and with any metal shavings found in the teeth of the tool.

In instances where a padlock was used on a hinged hasp to lock a door, the padlock and cut shackle should be collected and sent to the laboratory. If a pair of bolt cutters or a similar cutting device is found, test cuts can be made and compared with tool marks left on the lock shackle.

### Entry Through Basement Windows and Skylights

Basement windows and skylights are forced in the same manner as ordinary windows, but the investigator should pay special attention to the possibility that the burglar's clothes may have become torn and cloth fragments or fibers may have been left behind. The officer should also take samples of the dust and dirt usually found in such places.

### Entry Through Roofs

The presence of convenient utility poles, ladders, and other aids, plus the concealment of the edge parapet, makes entry through flat roofs a favorite *modus operandi*. Many otherwise well-protected stores have "tissue paper" roofs.

Building material may contaminate the clothing of any burglar using this technique. A careful search will also show signs of ropes for entry and exit.

Most stores are equipped with roof ventilators and exhaust fans. Entry through the ventilating system may result in tool marks, fingerprints, and dust contamination of clothing.

**A**

**B**

FIGURE **14.6.** An exterior doorknob showing tool marks (A) and a pair of adjustable grips on a doorknob (B). *Investigators should never attempt to match a tool to an object in this fashion!* (*Los Angeles County Sheriff's Department.*)

## Entry Through Walls

Walls are broken either by tools or by explosives. A brick wall is easily broken by a hammer and chisel or a sledge hammer. Since the burglar can be expected to become covered with dust during such an operation, samples of mortar and brick should always be collected in these cases. In blasting, a hole is usually chiseled between two bricks and the charge inserted. Several small charges are normally used in order to avoid severe detonations and the possibility of the whole wall's collapsing.

Small hydraulic jacks may be used to force holes into a wall. In this operation, a narrow passageway is usually chosen where the base force can be distributed over a wide area by padding. After the initial hole is made, repeated thrusts are used to enlarge the hole sufficiently to gain an entry.

Where an empty or infrequently occupied store is adjacent to the target, plaster walls may be cut to a thin supporting layer and the entire section removed at once.

Entry into a vault is usually accomplished through the walls, which are easier to force than the door. The walls are often constructed of reinforced concrete that can be broken by repeated blasting or by hammer and chisel and oxyacetylene torch.

## Entry Through Floors

Entry through floors is often preferred in the case of a warehouse or another building that has a crawl space underneath. The burglar usually drills or saws a hole in the floorboards large enough to crawl through. Entry through a wall or floor is also made when the criminal suspects or knows that the premises are protected by burglar alarms on doors and windows.

## Simulated Burglaries

Simulated burglaries are most often attempts at insurance fraud. To create a successful imitation of a burglary that will deceive police officers, the simulator must strive to carry it out as naturally as possible. Otherwise there will be gaps in the sequence of events.

When windows are entered, the officer should always check whether the windowpanes were in fact broken from the outside, whether there are footprints outside the window, whether broken glass has been trampled in these prints, whether the burglar really could have reached the window, whether there are traces of actual entry (sand, dirt, etc.), whether objects inside the window are so placed that the window could be opened to permit entry, and so on. If the outside of the window glass is very dirty, there should be marks from the object used to break it. If the glass is relatively clean, the side on which the force was applied might be revealed by dusting with aluminum powder.

In cases of forced doors, the damage should be examined to see whether it is only on the outside portions. Marks of prying should be present on the door as well as on the door jamb. If the tool marks are located so high up that the burglar must have stood on a box or a ladder, the support should be examined.

Whenever a burglary is suspected of being simulated, all tools belonging to the victim should be compared with the tool marks present and, if necessary, recovered for further examination.

Holes in floors, walls, and ceilings should be examined to determine the side from which the attack was started. The holes should also be examined to determine whether there is evidence of a person's having crawled through.

The officer should further make an estimate of the length of time the burglar spent on the premises. The officer should follow the burglar's actions in searching for valuables—whether doors were opened and drawers emptied first, or whether the burglar went directly to the right place and made the theft.

## Detailed Examination of the Scene

Generally, the detailed examination of the crime scene proper should begin only after the surrounding areas have been searched. Failure to search the surrounding areas initially may result in the inadvertent destruction of evidence by sightseers as well as officers present at the location (Fig. 14.7).

Approaches leading to and away from the scene should be examined for the presence of footprints, tire impressions, drag marks (such as those caused by a heavy object, e.g., a safe), and abandoned items such as tools, clothing, opened cash boxes, and so on. Obstacles leading to the building such as fences, gates, and the like should be examined for traces of blood, fabric and fibers, and tool marks. The number of suspects involved should be estimated from footprints when possible. Areas where a suspect had to crawl or climb should be examined for traces of clothing. Samples of building material and soil should be collected for comparative purposes. The location from which the burglar "staked out" the location or where a "lookout" was standing should be examined for footprints, cigarette butts, cigarette package wrappers, matches, and other such items.

The point of entry should be examined for broken tools, tool marks, broken window glass, fibers, hair, blood, fingerprints, footprints, paint chips, wood, and other building material (Fig. 14.8). Known samples

FIGURE **14.7.** A footprint showing little definition. Investigators should consider the possibility of comparing soil at the scene with any noted on a suspect's shoes. (*Los Angeles County Sheriff's Department.*)

of materials should be collected. Photographs, measurements, and sketches should, as always, be made before any items are moved or collected.

The examination of the interior of the burglarized premises must sometimes be carried out while taking into account the wishes of the owner of the premises. Business activities of a store or office cannot be completely stopped. The investigator may allow the owner or manager to specify which area of the premises is available for searching first.

The investigator should carry out the inside crime scene investigation in the normal detailed and systematic way. Attention should be given to evidence such as fingerprints, footprints, broken tools, tool marks, blood, and any other evidence that will aid in the solution of the case. As the examination of various areas of the location is completed, the proprietor should be notified. If evidence is found that requires time-consuming recovery, the owner and other personnel should be asked to stay out of the area until the examination is complete.

A complete inventory of all items missing should be obtained from the owner. A complete description of the items, including brand names, labels, markings, serial numbers, size, shape, color, and value, should

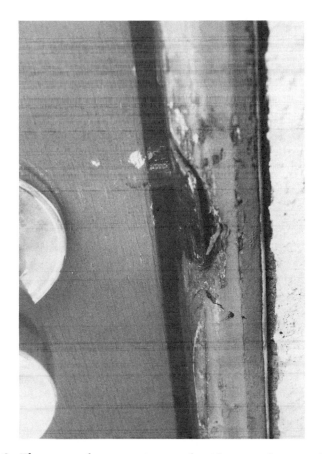

FIGURE **14.8.** There may be many items of evidence to be considered in a burglary: tool marks on the bolt and doorknob, paint, wood, building material, glass, etc. Investigators need to be aware of these when searching for physical evidence in such cases. (*Los Angeles County Sheriff's Department.*)

be obtained from the owner. This facilitates identification of the stolen property in the event the items are recovered.

An apprehended suspect should be thoroughly searched. Cuts and scratches should be noted. The clothing should be collected for examination for tears and building material that can place the suspect in contact with the crime scene.

The suspect's vehicle should be searched for stolen property, burglary tools, and any other items of physical evidence. The investigator should remember that in some instances a search warrant may be necessary before the vehicle may be completely searched.

The investigator should attempt to form a picture of the whole crime scene in order to estimate whether or not the burglar was familiar with the premises. If the burglar removed valuables from a rather unlikely location without disturbing the rest of the scene, or if keys were used that were hidden, the officer might infer that the suspect was familiar with the location.

The investigator should try to make a determination about the type of person being sought. Was the burglary the work of a professional burglar? Was the crime simply a case of vandalism involving juveniles? Was anything unusual left at the scene such as feces, which might point to a suspect who might have a history of sex-related crimes? Answers to these questions, information obtained from interviews, and physical evidence examination will prove useful in the overall investigation.

## Safe Burglaries

Safes may be classified in two basic types: fire-resistant safes and burglar-resistant safes. Fire-resistant safes, although providing a minimum resistance to attack by a professional burglar, are designed to withstand, resist, and retard the penetration of heat and to protect documents from destruction by fire. Such safes are constructed of metal and insulation consisting of a variety of materials such as vermiculite, cement, diatomaceous earth, sawdust, and the like.

Burglar-resistant safes are specifically designed to resist the efforts of safe burglars. They are constructed of steel that is resistant to forced entry by tools or torch. Burglar-resistant safes are not burglar-proof, but are designed to resist attack for a certain period of time.

Safes can be opened by a number of methods such as manipulation, punching, peeling, prying, ripping, chopping, drilling, burning, or by means of explosives.

*Manipulation* is essentially a lost art that involves opening a safe by means of listening to and feeling the combination lock mechanism. Most safes today employ manipulation-proof locks. Therefore, if a safe is found with the lock opened, the investigator should assume that the suspect had knowledge of the combination.

The *punching* method involves knocking off the dial and punching the dial spindle into the safe. Newer safes have punch-proof spindles and relocking devices that automatically relock the safe when an attempt at a "punch job" is made.

Peeling involves *prying or peeling* the face plate from the safe door in such a way as to expose the locking mechanism. This is sometimes accomplished by first pounding the door with a sledge hammer until the door buckles and then inserting a pry bar.

Entry by *ripping or chopping* is achieved by tearing a hole through a part of the safe other than the door, such as the top, side, or bottom.

*Drilling* is usually effective, but it is a time-consuming method and is therefore only rarely used in safe burglaries. It is commonly done by perforating the door plate around the keyhole with a series of holes close together. A large portion of the lock mechanism is thereby bared so that the bolts can be manipulated. The front plate of some safes can also be peeled back if some of the screws or rivets in the edge are first removed. The paint covering the rivets is first scraped off so that the rivets are bared. The rivets are then drilled deeply enough for the plate to be separated. After a few rivets have been removed, the front plate is then forced up sufficiently to insert a chisel that is used to break the remaining rivets without drilling. On some safes, the locking bolts can be reached by drilling through the side of the safe, directly against the face of the bolt. The bolt can then be driven back with a punch. The exact location of the bolts can be determined by the marks in the door frame that occur in daily use when the safe door is shut while the bolts are protruding.

In cases of drilling, the burglar can be expected to have used some kind of lubricating oil for the bit. Samples of such oil and samples of metal shavings should be collected because the burglar's body or clothing may contain these materials.

Simpler types of safes with combination locks may be opened by means of a thick, square steel plate provided with an opening at the center to be slipped over the dial knob. The corners of the plate are equipped with threaded bolts, the points of which touch the safe door. By tightening the bolts with a wrench, the knob and spindle are torn out.

It also happens that safes are opened by a special bridge device screwed to the safe with bolts. The portion of the bridge over the door frame contains a threaded hole. A strong bolt is fitted into this hole and tightened far enough to force the door open.

Another method employs a circular cutter. Such devices are made in several different forms. Some are affixed to one or more holes that have been drilled into the safe, whereas others are strapped to the safe by long bolts and nuts or steel cable. Common to all types, however, is one or more hardened steel cutters held against the safe under tension and turned by means of a handle. The result is a round hole in the safe wall. These devices are normally not used on the safe door since the locking bars would interfere, but rather on the side or back of the safe.

Cutting by oxyacetylene torch is a very effective method against which only specially designed steel chests are completely resistant. A considerable disadvantage of this method lies in the fact that the apparatus required is heavy and difficult to transport. For this reason the burning method is usually used only where complete welding equipment is available on the premises. Some burglars have used compact equipment that is large enough to do the job but light enough to be carried easily.

*Burning* is another method utilized by safe burglars using the so-called "burning bar." The bar, a metal pipe, is packed with a mixture of powdered aluminum and iron oxide. The mixture is known as *thermite* and, when ignited, gives off a very intense heat that can be directed to the safe.

Burning is usually started around the dial hole. A sufficiently large hole is cut in the front plate of the door so that the lock mechanism is accessible. The operator may cut this hole in the form of a tongue that is folded back. Where the cutting is done on the sides or back of the safe, the inside plate must also be cut through. This method often ignites the contents of the safe, whereupon the burglar may use a soda pop bottle as a fire extinguisher. Sometimes the burglar cuts off the safe door hinges, which reveals an ignorance of the construction of the safe.

The manner of opening the safe by burning reveals the skill of the burglar. When the investigator is unable to estimate this skill, a specialist should be consulted. Samples to be collected at the scene are molten particles of metal (beads), slag, molten safe insulation, and the like. Such particles may be found in the clothing of a suspect. The investigator should also keep in mind the possibility that there might be minor burns in the burglar's clothes from flying particles. When the contents of the safe have caught fire, the burglar may have been able to recover paper currency, some of which may be charred.

Safe burglaries are often carried out by transporting the safe to an isolated location where it is opened with tools or explosives. In such cases the burglars are usually less careful in their movements at the place of opening. Valuable footprints or tire tracks may be found at such locations. The investigation should be carried out as soon as possible since inclement weather conditions may destroy the most valuable evidence.

## Safe Burglary

A safe was hauled out during a burglary and transported in a car to a wooded area, where it was opened with explosives. During the examination of the outdoor scene, a door handle from an automobile was recovered. The car of a suspect was found to have a broken handle. The handle from the scene matched the remains of the handle on the car. It had apparently been broken off while the safe was taken out of the car. The suspect was arrested and, subsequently, confessed.

## Safe Burglaries with Explosives

It is sometimes very difficult to gather physical evidence that will convict a safe burglar specializing in explosives. As a rule, such a burglar is skilled at this method and takes pride in sweeping the crime scene clean of all traces that may be used as incriminating evidence. When examining such burglary scenes, the investigator should, therefore, proceed very thoroughly and take advantage of the mistakes that are sometimes made even by the skilled perpetrator. Experience has shown that this burglar usually makes mistakes when disturbed or when having to flee the premises. The burglar may then leave behind or drop objects that have potential value as evidence.

One weakness of the specialist of this type is that the individual usually sticks to one method in all burglaries. The investigator thereby gets an opportunity to tie certain burglaries to a given criminal or to others whom this burglar has trained. This fact may be valuable even when the burglars are not known.

Explosives operators usually do not pick locks or make their way into the premises by other light fingered methods. Since their work is carried out with a great deal of noise, this is also characteristic of their method of entry. They generally use great force on doors and windows and may even use a charge on a door that could much more easily have been opened the usual way. On the other hand, they are very careful to protect themselves from surprise. They very rarely work alone and may have several helpers whose only duty is to act as lookouts.

Regarding the placing of the safe for the "blowing," three methods are normally found: the safe is left in place; it is pulled out from the wall; or it is laid on the floor. The first method is the most common. The second method is used by burglars who do not want to have the safe blown against the wall and create vibrations in the building that may be more noticeable than the detonation. It has happened that a safe was thrown so violently against the wall that it broke the wall and started cracks that ran into an apartment above. The third method is more seldom used. Its advantage is that it facilitates the placing of the charge.

In examining safes that have been moved or laid down, the investigator should be very careful in searching for latent finger and palm prints. Although explosives specialists will be sure to use gloves or other covering, it is still possible that they may leave identifiable fragments of palm prints on a safe that they have moved. A glove may slip during the heavy work, exposing a small piece of the palm—enough to produce a valuable print. In developing prints that have been deposited under such conditions, great care must be exercised because the prints easily become smeared or even completely filled in because of the great pressure.

The charge is usually placed in the dial spindle hole after the dial is knocked off. The charge may be dynamite in powder or paste or other explosives. The hazard and the refined technique associated with the use of nitroglycerine usually limit its use to only the elite of safe burglars. Round door safes, however, have discouraged the use of explosives.

Wrappers from explosives should be searched for and recovered, even though latent fingerprints are usually not found on waxed wrappers. In a favorable case, the wrapper may still be valuable as evidence.

In general, the adhesive material used to affix the detonator that is found on the scene (such as clay, putty, plasticine, or soap) is brought in by the burglar. These substances must be soft and well kneaded in order to serve the purpose. As the burglar may have kneaded these materials without wearing gloves before going to the scene, there is a possibility that plastic fingerprints are present. Such prints should be searched for not only on the surface, but also on inside layers of the kneaded material. Plastic prints may also be found on strips of tape, but these are usually hard to detect.

Pieces of safety fuse—when it is used—may vary in length. Explosives specialists usually cut these lengths before going to the scene, and the fact that they have widely varying ideas of the proper length may be of some value. Those using the longer fuses usually prefer to light the fuse and then retire to a safe place from which they can observe the effect of the explosion and whether it was noticed.

Safe burglars vary as to whether they use a dam or sound-absorbing blanket to contain the explosion. Those who use a dam probably do so to muffle the detonation and to keep windows from bursting. Since the charge is mostly inside the door, the effect of the explosion is not enhanced by the use of a dam. When the burglar intends to demolish the door completely, a dam does have some effect, but it is usually an effect that the burglar wants to avoid. The burglar runs the risk of having the inside door plate blown into the safe with such force that new charges have to be placed to dislodge it. Many explosives specialists make a habit of not using a dam at all. Instead, they open windows in the room where the safe is located so that the shock wave will dissipate without breaking windows or attracting unwanted attention. Some burglars soak the dam with water, partly to make it denser and heavier, and partly to prevent the possibility of fire.

The materials used in dams are either brought to the scene or collected at the scene. The damage to the material gives an indication of how many separate charges were used. Material that has been brought to the scene may sometimes give good leads for the investigation and the search for the criminal.

The ideal explosion occurs when the charge is so well balanced that the locking bolts are pulled back and the door flies open. In such cases the external damage to the safe may be limited to a slight bulge in the front plate around the dial hole. It does happen, however, that the locking bolts remain more or less closed, so that new charges must be set off. To avoid this snag, some burglars put weight on the door handle in the direction of opening of the handle. A heavy cord is commonly tied to the handle and a heavy object, such as an adding machine or a typewriter, is attached to the other end. Another method is to tie a heavy metal bar to the handle to act as a lever. At the detonation, the handle is turned by the weight of the heavy object so that the locking bolts are turned back.

Locked drawers and compartments inside a safe are either forced open or blown. The investigator should keep in mind the possibility of finding parts of broken tools as well as tool marks at these places. Fragments of tools should be searched for with a magnet since they are very difficult to find in the powdered insulation that usually pours from the broken safe.

The search for fingerprints at scenes of safe blowing is usually complicated by the layer of finely divided safe insulation that settles on everything in the room. This dust should be removed before developing with powder. It is preferably done by careful blowing. To brush off the dust is wrong, because the dust usually consists of gritty particles that can destroy fingerprints. Visible prints that have been deposited by a dusty finger must be treated very carefully.

Whenever an unexploded charge is found in a safe it should be neutralized with great care.

An apprehended suspect's clothes should be thoroughly searched for the presence of safe insulation or paint. Anyone who has been present in a room where a safe has been blown can hardly avoid getting dust and safe insulation on clothing. The dust may also adhere to the burglar's skin, in the hair, ears, and nostrils, or under the fingernails. Such dust may be found on any part of the clothing, but particularly in the pants cuffs and on the shoes, mainly in seams and lace holes and on the soles. Paint chips are usually loosened in an explosion, and burglars run the risk of picking up such chips on their clothing when examining the safe after the detonation.

In searching the scene, the investigator should, therefore, collect samples of the safe insulation and paint on the outside and inside of the safe for use in possible comparisons. The investigator should also evaluate the possibility that wall paint, loosened by the explosion, has fallen on the burglar. The investigator should note the manufacturer of the safe, so that it may later be contacted for information on the composition of insulation and paint.

If safe insulation or paint is not found on a suspect's clothes, the investigator should remember that the suspect may have done everything possible to eliminate such traces. The suspect's hands and clothing should also be examined for the presence of traces of explosives. If the hands are not immediately washed, there may be traces of explosives under the fingernails. In the clothing, such traces should primarily be searched for in the pockets. Even gloves may contain traces. If the burglar carried safety fuses in the pockets, there may be characteristic stains on the pocket lining.

When a safe is blown, it sometimes happens that the burglar is injured by sharp metal edges. It may also happen that the nose starts bleeding from the shock of the detonation. This is more common when electric detonators are used since the burglar is forced to stay rather close to the safe. If blood is found on the scene, it should be recovered for later examination. It may even happen that the burglar is so severely injured that immediate aid must be sought.

Burglary is such a common crime that frequently a less than thorough investigation is conducted. However, a careful and detailed examination of the crime scene may result in developing evidence useful in an ultimate solution of the case.

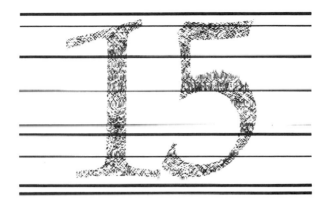

# MOTOR VEHICLE
# INVESTIGATION

**374**

*Case*

D. Cotton, a 23-year-old male, residing on Vincent Street, Hendon (a suburb of Adelaide) South Australia,[1] died as a result of a motor vehicle accident on Saturday evening, September 3, 1988. He was the sole occupant of a Gemini sedan, which had overshot an intersection in the Adelaide Hills and slammed into a solid stone wall (Fig. 15.1).

The Gemini was, in fact, registered to a Mr. Caffrey living on the same street as Cotton. When the police went to question Caffrey at his home as to why Cotton had been driving his car, they found that Caffrey had been murdered. His body had numerous knife wounds (Fig. 15.2).

The crime scene investigation suggested a sole assailant. The Gemini was examined, and a bloodstained knife was found in a plastic bag in the rear compartment. The very tip of the knife had been snapped off (Fig. 15.3).

Postmortem examination showed stabbing wounds to the head. The possibility of the knife's having left a piece of blade in the skull was confirmed when an X-ray revealed a small metal fragment lodged in the skull behind the left ear (Fig. 15.4). A physical match between the piece of metal and the knife confirmed it as being the murder weapon.

Because the blood evidence (on the knife and on a glove worn by Cotton) was similar to Caffrey's, and the bloodied shoe sole impressions at the scene were similar in size and pattern to Cotton's shoes, the state coroner was satisfied that Cotton had in fact been responsible for the death of Caffrey and had stolen his car.

The widespread use of motor vehicles in today's society has resulted in their being associated with many different types of police investigations. Motor vehicles may be the instrumentality of a crime such as in hit-and-run cases or traffic fatalities. A vehicle may also be the crime scene itself, such as in cases where a crime was committed in an automobile or in cases of auto theft. This chapter discusses evidence commonly associated with crimes in which a motor vehicle is involved.

## Vehicle Theft

A vehicle may be stolen by juveniles for "joyriding," in connection with another crime as a means of fleeing, or for the purpose of stripping the vehicle of parts that are to be sold for profit (Fig. 15.5). Unfortunately, vehicle theft is a crime of rather high frequency, and some police agencies do not have the personnel resources with which to conduct a

[1] This case was submitted by Sergeant Ted Van Dijk, Police Forensic Science Section, South Australian Police Department, Adelaide, South Australia.

**FIGURE 15.1.** An apparent automobile accident led to an unexpected turn of events. (*South Australia Police Department, Adelaide, South Australia.*)

thorough investigation. This fact often results in the search for physical evidence consisting of only dusting the vehicle for latent fingerprints.

Stolen vehicles may be located in a variety of circumstances. Often they are observed by uniformed officers while on patrol. An officer may make use of a "hot sheet" listing licenses of stolen vehicles, use a description from a police bulletin or broadcast, or notice some furtive movement on the part of a driver that results in a routine traffic stop and subsequent check for a stolen vehicle. Once a vehicle has been identified as stolen, the examination for physical evidence begins.

A short preliminary investigation will determine whether a full search for physical evidence is needed. In those instances where the driver of the stolen vehicle turns out to be the thief, the need for identity determination by means of physical evidence is removed. A careful check of the vehicle and inventory of the property is still necessary. It is a good idea to look for evidence of other crimes. There have been instances in which an automobile was recovered and, at the officer's request, towed to an impound yard. Some days later, much to the officer's chagrin, a dead body was discovered in the trunk. Remember, theft may be only one of other more serious crimes involved; with this possibility in mind, the first officer to locate the stolen vehicle should take appropriate precautions (Fig. 15.6).

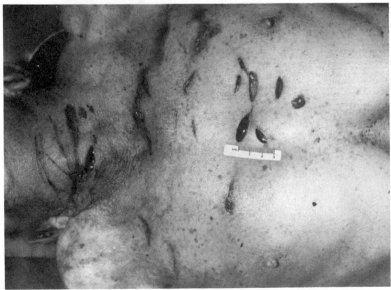

**A**

**B**

**FIGURE 15.2.** (A) The police found the owner of the vehicle murdered. (B) The autopsy revealed numerous stabbings. (*South Australia Police Department, Adelaide, South Australia.*)

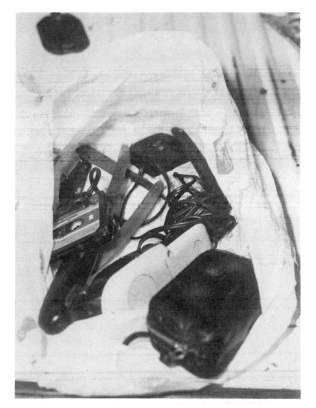

A

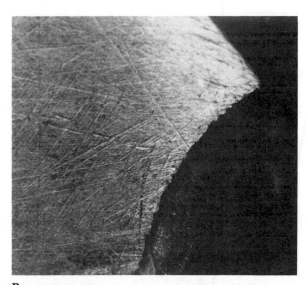

B

FIGURE 15.3. (A) Burglary tools, including a bloody knife, were found in the vehicle. (B) The tip of the knife was broken off. (*South Australia Police Department, Adelaide, South Australia.*)

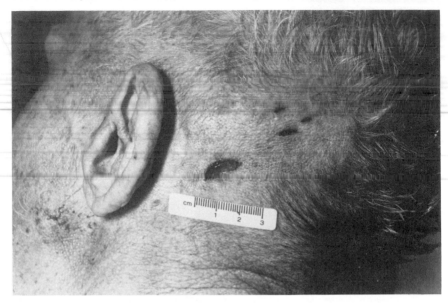

A

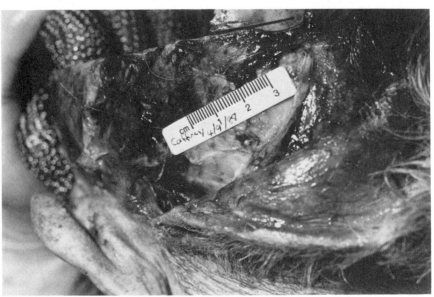

B

FIGURE 15.4. (A) At autopsy, several head wounds were noted. (B) A small metal fragment was found in the skull. (C) A close-up of the fragment. (D) A physical match of the knife blade and the metal fragment leaves little doubt that they were once one. (*South Australia Police Department, Adelaide, South Australia.*)

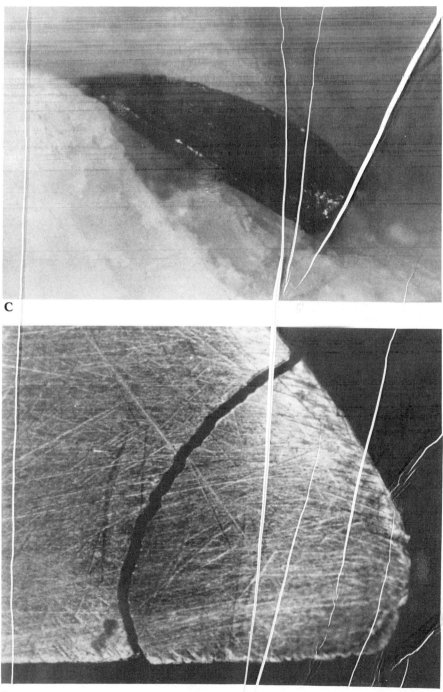

C

D

380

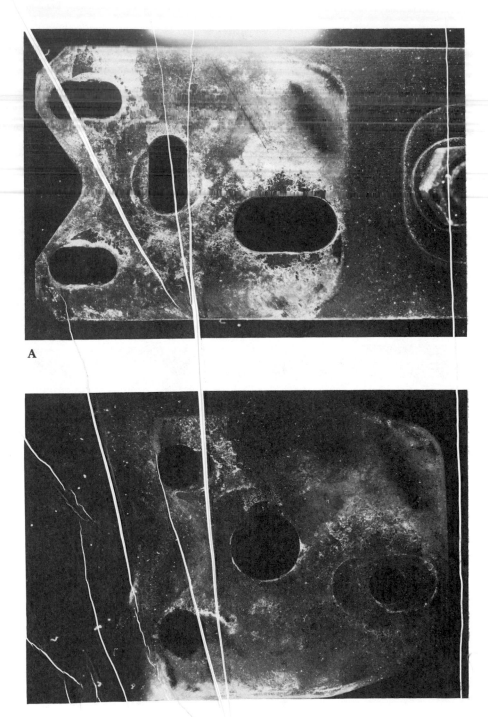

A

B

FIGURE **15.5.** A Porsche 924 Turbo was stolen and subsequently recovered, but it was missing numerous parts. Automotive parts suspected of being removed from the stolen Porsche were found in a suspect's possession. Examination indicated that the rear axle link mounting brackets exhibited sufficient detail for comparison purposes. The right mounting bracket from the vehicle (A) and the right axle link mounting bracket (B) (reversed) are shown. To enhance the detail of the pattern present on the bracket, ultraviolet photography was used. (*Michigan State Police.*)

As in other crime scenes, the most fragile evidence should be collected first. This usually means fingerprints. It is recommended that the vehicle be moved to a special location such as a tow yard or police garage for the purpose of taking prints and looking for other physical evidence. Further, before any extensive search is undertaken, the need for a search warrant should be considered (Fig. 15.7).

When the vehicle is moved, care should be taken not to destroy fingerprints or other evidence. If possible, the vehicle should be towed to the impound yard. Driving it might accidentally destroy certain

A

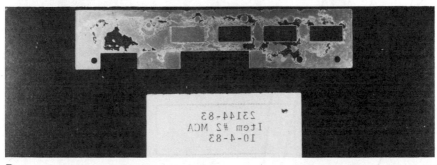

B

FIGURE **15.6.** A radio stolen from a vehicle (A) and the faceplate (B) (shown reversed), which was left at the scene, are compared and indicate a common source. (*Michigan State Police.*)

**A**

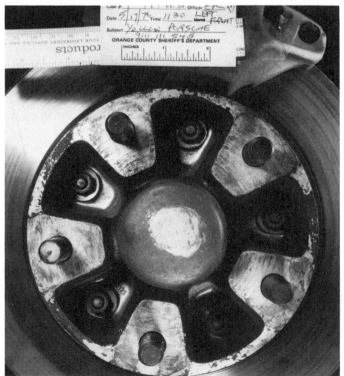

**B**

C

D

FIGURE **15.7.** Comparison of wheels from a Porsche (A) with a corresponding mount from the victim's vehicle (B). Note that the negative has been reversed in (A). Photographs (C) and (D) show comparisons of the markings on each. (*Orange County Sheriff-Coroner, Santa Ana, California.*)

evidence. Personnel at the tow yard should be reminded not to touch the vehicle until it has been processed for evidence.

If the vehicle is wet from dew, it should first be allowed to dry. In cold weather, the vehicle should be placed indoors and allowed to warm up to room temperature before fingerprints are taken. The examination for fingerprints should be conducted in a systematic manner. Areas that are most likely to have been handled by the suspect should be carefully fingerprinted. These include the rear view mirror, steering wheel, shift lever, door handle, glove compartment, and windows. After prints have been lifted, the location, date, time, and other identifying information should be noted on the fingerprint card.

Signs of forced entry should be noted. Known specimens of broken glass, chipped paint, and the like should be collected for future comparison. If the radio, tape deck, CD player, cellular phone, or CB radio is missing, the electrical wires should be removed for possible comparison against recovered property (Fig. 15.8). The wires should be marked in such a way to show clearly which ends were originally connected to the unit.

## Abandoned Vehicles

Any officer who finds or investigates an ownerless vehicle that has not been reported as stolen should *not* drive it away or subject it to more detailed examination until having been informed by the driver or owner of the reason the vehicle was standing at that place. If it is known that a serious crime has been committed, it must be remembered that the investigation of the vehicle has to be done with the utmost care and thoroughness.

The investigation must be planned carefully. The basic search for evidence in and on the vehicle should be carried out in a well-sheltered place, preferably in a garage or other suitable building, because rain or snow or even strong sunlight can destroy certain evidence. The vehicle should, therefore, be driven or towed from the place of finding as soon as possible, but only after certain preliminary investigations have been carried out.

The place where the vehicle is found should be photographed and sketched in the usual way. Photography is done while the vehicle is still on the spot, but sketching can wait until later. In sketches, the distance to the nearest occupied dwelling and to the nearest town or city should be given. If necessary, a sketch plan may be made of the immediate surroundings, and another of neighboring districts; however, the latter may be replaced by suitable maps. The recording of the odometer or taximeter should be noted; it is best to inquire of an expert whether there is anything of special significance to be observed. The supply of

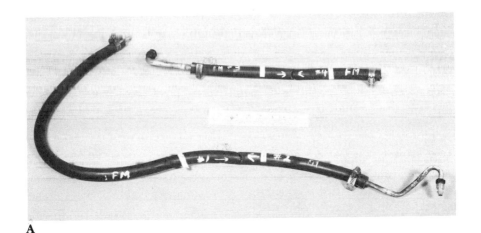

A

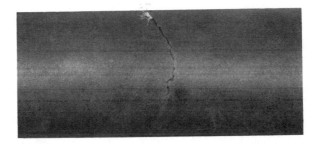

B

**FIGURE 15.8.** Cut hoses (A) in a vehicle theft and a close-up physical match (B). (*Los Angeles County Sheriff's Department.*)

gasoline is checked. An attempt is made to determine whether the vehicle stopped at that point for some reason unforeseen by the driver (for example, engine trouble, depleted gasoline supply, inability to drive it farther, and so on). The floor in front of the driving seat is examined carefully. Preferably, all dust and dirt at this place should be kept. The exterior is examined for the presence of any evidence that might fall off when the vehicle is driven or towed away. Further, a preliminary examination of the whole of the vehicle should be made for evidence that is easy to collect or that for any reason might be damaged or destroyed when the vehicle is driven away.

The detailed investigation of a vehicle should *not* be carried out at the place where it is found, but the site chosen should be as near to the place of finding as possible. A long drive or tow can cause a deposit of dust or dirt that may completely destroy any possibility of finding evidence in the form of fingerprints. Only the person who is to drive the vehicle away should sit in it, remembering not to touch any object in the vehicle other than what is necessary for driving. Gloves should be worn, but if any fingerprinted object is touched with a gloved hand, the print may be destroyed.

After removing the vehicle to a sheltered place, a thorough investigation is made of the location where the vehicle was found and of the surrounding area. It is possible that the criminal, after committing the crime, unconsciously dropped or threw away objects that show the route taken or supply incriminating evidence. The investigation must be done quickly, especially if snow is anticipated. If larger areas or stretches of road have to be searched, it may be advisable to call for the assistance of a search team. All helpers, before they begin to search, must first be instructed in how they are to act if they find any evidence.

The detailed investigation of a vehicle is done only when it is completely dry. In general, the floor of the vehicle and seats are examined first, and only after this is done are any fingerprints developed. It may be convenient first to examine the outside of the vehicle in order to avoid the risk of anyone unthinkingly destroying evidence or leaving prints. The contents of ashtrays are examined and kept, the various objects being noted in *the order in which they occur from the top.* The contents of the glove compartment and any other storage spaces are examined and noted in a similar way. Objects that the criminal has dropped are often found in and under the seats. Any bloodstains in or on the vehicle are examined for direction of fall, height of fall, direction of movement, and so on, after which they are preserved. Marks of the swinging of a weapon, damage from gunshot, and the like are preserved. The engine and baggage space are examined. In the investigation of a vehicle in which a crime of violence has been committed, it is advisable, after collecting the evidence, to take measurements of the amount of room in the vehicle. There may arise a question of the possibility of a criminal swinging an instrument, handling a firearm, and other such acts. Any evidence of the vehicle's being used in any crime should be noted; safe paint and insulation in the trunk, outlines of boxes or tools, and even bullet holes should be sought.

All normal serial numbers should be checked in order to detect alterations in the identity of the vehicle.

Any damage to the vehicle may indicate that its abandonment and reported "theft" were intended to hide an accident. The exact condition of damage should be carefully noted and photographed. In suspicious circumstances, the temperature of the water in the radiator and the surrounding air temperature should be recorded. From these data, it may be possible to establish the duration of time since abandonment.

A careful search of the trunk is indicated in those cases where a dead body was transported in it. If the victim was killed in one location, transported in the vehicle, and dropped at another site, there may be only a very small amount of evidence in the trunk. In some cases, the interior may have been cleaned to remove traces of blood. In such cases it may be worthwhile to remove the liner to search for blood that has seeped through and was not noticed by the suspect.

Removal of the seats should also be considered for a thorough search. Weapons, tools, and sometimes trace evidence that can link the victim to the vehicle may be uncovered. In cases of rape, the seat covers or the entire seat should be submitted to the laboratory for testing for the presence of seminal fluid.

## Homicide in a Vehicle

Taxicab drivers are sometimes the victims of robberies, often in combination with assault that may be fatal. For a criminal who is desperate enough, it is a relatively simple matter to order the driver to a desolate area, assault the driver from behind without great risk of personal danger, and then rob the driver. Since it would be dangerous to attack the driver while the cab is moving, the driver is asked to stop under some pretext or other. After the robbery is completed, it is not uncommon for the attacker to hide the victim and then drive the car as far as possible away from the scene.

In those cases in which the robbery victim dies, one can expect to find the vehicle and the victim in different locations; sometimes the vehicle is found first. There is a great risk, therefore, that the examination of the vehicle is made difficult or impossible because an overzealous officer has the vehicle removed, thinking that the case is only one of "joyriding." For this reason, every office who finds an abandoned vehicle should suspect the worst and exercise extreme care. After a license check has revealed that the vehicle may have been the scene of a crime, the procedure suggested in "Abandoned Vehicles" should be followed, as well as the procedure for the specific type of crime.

The search of a vehicle in which a homicide was committed must be conducted with the same degree of care as would be used in conducting the search of an indoor or outdoor crime scene involving a murder. Because of the cramped working area, it is especially important to exercise care so as not to destroy any physical evidence in the vehicle. The procedures discussed elsewhere in the text for processing the crime scene are generally the same for a vehicle.

Cases involving sabotage or acts of terrorism in which a vehicle was blown up by means of an explosive charge require a thorough investigation to recover as many parts of the device as possible. The debris from the explosion may cover a wide area, and a careful and systematic search is necessary to locate, chart, and recover as many pieces of the damaged vehicle and bomb as possible. Pieces of a timing mechanism, electrical devices, wires and batteries, as well as explosives residue may prove to be valuable evidence in the investigation.

## Hit-and-Run Investigation

Hit-and-run cases are of two types: damage to other vehicles or property, and death or injury to individuals. In both cases, physical evidence can assist in identifying the hit-and-run vehicle, establishing a connection between the vehicle and the victim or crime scene, and reconstructing the scene in general to determine the events surrounding the crime (Fig. 15.9).

Cases involving damage to other vehicles are often the result of a person's driving under the influence or in a careless or reckless manner. The usual types of physical evidence found at the scene are paint chips or scrapings, glass, pieces of headlamps or plastic reflectors, and pieces from the grillwork of the vehicle. Most of these items are of a very small size and are, therefore, easily overlooked when searching the crime scene. In addition, the impact of the crash may throw certain items some distance from the vehicle, and loose or broken parts still attached to the hit-and-run vehicle may subsequently fall off at considerable distance from the scene. These considerations make a search of a greater area important in such cases.

The hit-and-run crime scene often has a factor not present at other scenes: traffic. If the fatality occurred in a busy intersection or well-traveled street, the officer may feel pressured to complete the investigation more quickly. Although time may be a consideration, it should not deter the investigator from doing a thorough and complete job of processing the scene.

The scene should be photographed. Overall crime scene photos should be taken in addition to photographs from different views. Close-up photographs of the victim, as well as of items of physical evidence, must be taken. If the crime occurred at night, portable lighting should be brought in so that the area is adequately lighted.

The area should be examined for tire impressions and, particularly, for skid marks. Skid marks can be used to determine the direction and speed of the suspect vehicle and are therefore important in the case.

Trace items of evidence present on the victim's body are also important. Care must be taken when moving the deceased so as not to lose valuable trace evidence. When the deceased is brought to the morgue, clothing should be carefully searched for paint, glass, and other parts from the suspect's vehicle. These items should be packaged, tagged, and submitted to the crime laboratory for examination.

A

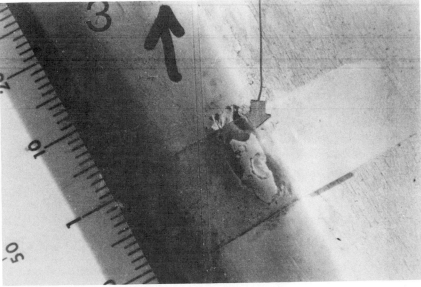

B

FIGURE 15.9. A small fragment broken from a vehicle next to the damaged area on a car fender (A) and the piece fitted into the damaged area (B) from a hit-and-run case. (*Israel National Police.*)

If the victim was on a bicycle or motorcycle, the vehicle should be carefully examined. Various types of trace evidence such as paint may be present that can be used to tie the suspect vehicle to the crime. Lights from the victim's vehicle should be recovered and submitted to the laboratory to determine whether they were operational and whether they were on or off.

Clumps of soil or dirt found at the scene should be documented and collected. These can be compared with dirt found on the undercarriage of the suspect's vehicle and may demonstrate a connection.

The scene should be examined for specific damage to the unknown vehicle. Broken parts of the vehicle should be collected for possible physical matching. In certain cases, the vehicle's make and sometimes the model can be determined by these parts. This information may be helpful if the investigator contacts automobile repair body shops or parts stores to determine whether anyone recently came in to have a vehicle repaired.

Occasionally, the force of impact is so great that impressions from the vehicle are made on the victim's body or clothing. Such evidence should be photographed and preserved for later comparison.

Paint chips are especially important items of physical evidence. If they are sufficiently large chips, it is possible to fit them physically into the vehicle in jigsaw-puzzle fashion. Paint will at a minimum be useful to determine the color of the hit-and-run vehicle, and in some instances the make of the vehicle can be determined through laboratory examination. Further, physical and chemical comparisons of paint recovered at the scene can sometimes be matched with that from the suspect's vehicle.

As part of the autopsy procedure, specimens of the victim's blood and hair should be collected for later testing. A toxicological sample of blood should be taken to determine whether the victim was under the influence of alcohol or other drugs and to identify blood type. Clothing, as mentioned before, should be retained for fabric and fiber exemplars, as well as examined for patterns and other traces present.

Once the suspected vehicle is found, it should be taken off the road to a nearby place for examination. When the vehicle is first found, if any evidence or obviously damaged areas are noted that might be lost in moving the vehicle to a garage, then those items should first be collected. If the owner of the vehicle claims that the car had been stolen, fingerprint examination is especially important to prove or disprove this contention.

The exterior of the vehicle should be thoroughly searched, including the undercarriage. The vehicle should be placed on a hydraulic lift to facilitate this examination. Evidence such as hair, blood, skin, and fabric and fiber evidence may be located there. Specimens of grease and dirt should be collected for comparison with debris found on the victim.

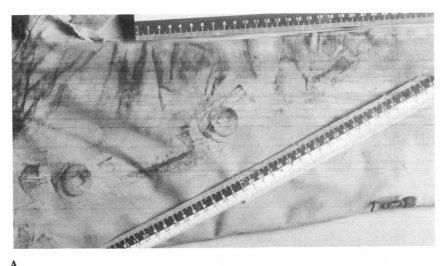

A

B

FIGURE **15.10.** Various imprints and impressions, including round and hexagonal marks found on a victim's coat from a traffic accident (A). The suspected bus driver denied hitting the victim; however, examination of the bus's underside (B) determined that part of the oil sump could have made the marks. Since several buses had passed the location, they were brought into a garage and the sumps of each were examined and photographed. A random sample of additional buses was also examined. Because the bolt orientations were shown to be unique, the conclusion was made that the suspect bus caused the imprints. (*Israel National Police.*)

The front area of the vehicle and the hood should be thoroughly examined. Occasionally, fabric impressions from the impact appear in the dust on the bumper. These should be carefully photographed with a scale, and, if possible, the bumper or fender removed and submitted to the laboratory (Fig. 15.10).

392

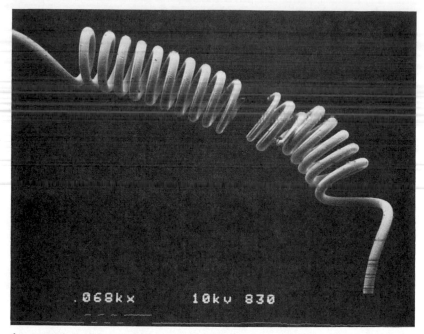

A

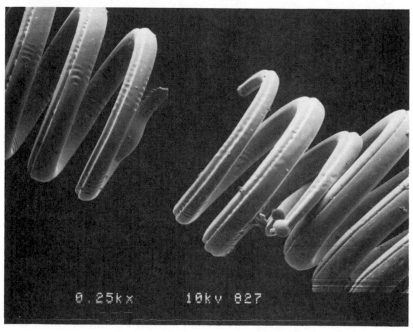

B

FIGURE 15.11. Although this case is not about motor vehicle investigations per se, it illustrates the examination of lamp filaments. (A) A scanning electron microscope photomicrograph of a lamp filament showing that there had been a break that reconnected and then a second break. (B) A close-up of the same filament. (Centre of Forensic Sciences, Toronto, Ontario.)

All broken parts and damage to the vehicle are important items of evidence. Damage to the front end, such as a broken grill or headlight, scratched paint, other scratches, and the like, are to be carefully noted and, if possible, removed and submitted to the laboratory. In some instances, evidence from a motorcycle or bicycle that the vehicle hit may be present, and these items should be preserved.

Known specimens from the hit-and-run vehicle should be collected, especially paint, which should be collected in the area of any damage to the vehicle. If scrapes containing other paint material are noted, these too should be collected to be compared with the victim's vehicle.

In some cases, the victim may have been hit and thrown onto the vehicle's hood or windshield. Keeping this possibility in mind, the investigator should search for fingerprints belonging to the victim, as well as hairs, fibers, and blood. If the windshield is broken, glass should be collected and a search made for hairs and blood.

Headlamps and tail lights should be examined to determine whether they work and, if possible, sent to the laboratory. Examination of the filament can determine if lights were on or off at the time of impact. Broken headlamp lenses and signal light reflectors should be removed for comparison with evidence collected at the scene. Sometimes it is possible to make a physical match with these items.

---

*Case*

During a sailing race[2] on Lake Ontario in the summer of 1990, one boat was struck by lightning. The crew radioed to the race organizer that they were dropping out of the race and heading for Rochester, New York; this was the last contact anyone had with the crew. No SOS was received, and no search for the boat was undertaken.

Three days later, an American fisherman found two bodies (tied together) floating with a beacon light attached to one of them. The beacon was lit at the time of the discovery. When the beacon later came into the possession of Canadian authorities, the bulb was burned out.

At the inquest in January 1991, there was apparently conflicting evidence:

The type of light bulb (no. 13) used can last for approximately only ½ to 2 hours with a set of new batteries. Thus, if the fisherman found the beacon lit, the boat must have capsized only hours before the bodies were found.

---

[2] The case was submitted by Ray Prime, Centre of Forensic Sciences, Toronto, Ontario, Canada.

A

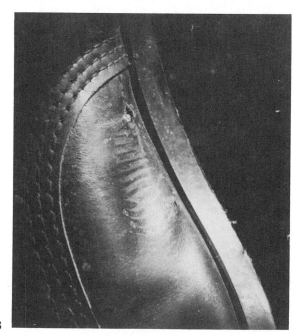

B

The examining pathologist from the United States found the bodies "to be dead" approximately 70 hours.

Scanning electron microscopic (SEM) examination of the filament discovered two breaks, both while the bulb was hot (ON). This is an indication that the bulb had a "second life." The conflicting evidence can be explained with the bulb's "two lives" (although it is not proof) (Fig. 15.11).

In the case of the very fine filament in the lamp, the SEM had a considerable advantage over conventional microscopes in demonstrating the breaks and the reestablished contact by providing a clear photograph with good depth of focus and a reflection-free image.

---

If tire impressions were made at a scene, photographs containing a scale should be made of each tire. Inked tire impressions on paper can be made for comparison with tire impressions located at the crime scene.

If the suspect driver is apprehended soon after the hit-and-run, a blood sample should be obtained. The sample should be submitted to the laboratory for testing for alcohol and other drugs to determine whether the suspect was under the influence.

## Marks from Vehicles

Vehicle marks are composed of tracks of wheels or of runners. In a specific case there may also be an indication of a particular type of load, for example, slipping branches in a load of wood, ends of logs in a load of lumber, the smell of fuel oil or lubricating oil, and so on (Fig. 15.12).   ·

### Wheel Marks

With the aid of wheel marks, direction of movement can be determined. When the ground is damp, the underlayer on which the wheel rolls forward is compressed, and the bottom of the mark is formed as a series of steps. The compressed clods of earth in the mark are lifted in the

---

FIGURE **15.12.** A car left the road, striking a bridge abutment and throwing a woman from the vehicle to her death. The officer arriving on the scene found a man unconscious in the back seat. The subject refused to identify the driver of the vehicle. The investigating officer submitted both of the man's shoes, as well as the brake and gas pedals, hoping the laboratory could find a pedal impression on the bottom of the shoes. The man's right shoe (B) had a series of 18 striations on the left side and a puncture mark in the leather. These striations matched the 18 rubber ribs on the brake pedal (A), and the puncture matched the location and size of the bottom banding wire from the bottom of the pedal, which was bent outward. The subject was subsequently convicted of vehicular homicide. (*Ohio State Highway Patrol.*)

FIGURE 15.13. An investigator submitted a speedometer head to determine the speed of a vehicle at the time of impact. The speedometer dial was examined under ultraviolet light, and a "speed mark" was detected in the area of 25 mph. This speed mark is an imprint of the speedometer pointer (needle) on the dial caused by the force of inertia at the time of impact. (*Forensic Laboratory, Office of Attorney General, Pierre, South Dakota.*)

same direction as the wheel is rolling. This rule about wheel marks is easy to remember: For the mark to become level again, the wheel must roll in the opposite direction.

A vehicle that travels in a straight line actually leaves only the track of the rear wheels; to observe marks of the front wheels it is necessary to find some place where the vehicle has turned sharply or has reversed.

In examining wheel marks it is necessary to look for places showing defects or repairs in the tires. With the aid of successive marks of this type, the circumference of the tire can be determined. The track is measured between the center points of the two wheel marks.

Preservation is achieved by photography and casting, selecting points that show characteristic marks or wear. When photographing, a scale is placed across the track and another along one side of it. Casting is done in the same way as for foot impressions (discussed in Chapter 9).

A

B

FIGURE **15.14.** An altered registration document viewed under (A) visible light and (B) infrared light, showing the obvious fabrication. (*Victoria State Police Forensic Science Laboratory, Melbourne, Australia.*)

In examining vehicle marks, it should be noted whether wheels that follow one another go in the same track or whether there is any deviation. If dual wheels are found, both tread marks should be recorded simultaneously, since the relationship of one tread pattern to the other provides additional characteristics for the identification of the vehicle (Fig. 15.13).

## Skid Marks

The speed of the suspect vehicle at the time of impact is sometimes at issue. If skid marks are present at the scene, a traffic officer with training in skid mark interpretation should be contacted and requested at the scene. Based on factors such as the length of the mark and the coefficient of friction of the road surface, an approximation of the speed at which the suspect vehicle was traveling may be calculated.

Investigations involving motor vehicles occur in many cases such as vehicle thefts, abandoned vehicles, homicides, hit-and-run investigations, and so on (Fig. 15.14). Physical evidence consisting of fingerprints, tool marks, glass, paint, fabric impressions, tire marks, physiological fluid, hairs, fibers, and the like should be carefully searched for, collected, and documented as in all crime scene investigations.

# HOMICIDE
# INVESTIGATION

Of all major crimes, homicide investigation requires the greatest effort on the part of the police. The investigator is responsible for collecting a vast amount of evidence and coordinating information from a variety of sources such as witnesses, the suspect, the officers involved with the crime scene, the forensic pathologist, and the criminalist. Death investigation requires a team effort, and only through cooperation of persons from many disciplines, coordination of efforts, and extreme attention to detail can a successful conclusion of an investigation be realized. This chapter brings together many of the concepts discussed elsewhere in the text and examines areas unique to the investigation of death.

The finding of a dead body is the starting point and initial focus of the death investigation. The rules for the first officer to arrive at the crime scene are the same as those outlined in earlier chapters. The first officer to arrive is required to determine whether the victim is dead and, if so, to notify the homicide investigators. Determination of suspicious death at this point is critical. There have been many cases in which the first officer to arrive at the scene has erred and pronounced the death to be of natural causes, only to learn at a later time that the actual cause of death was an unnoticed bullet wound. The point is that care and attention to detail are critical in this type of case.

Once the investigation has begun, the investigator should attempt to find and collect all evidence that may be used in the case. Even items that may seem unimportant and of no value should be considered as potential evidence. In a murder investigation, there is usually an abundance of evidence even in those cases in which the perpetrator attempted to clean up after the crime. Even in the so-called "perfect murder," there will be much evidence to aid in the crime's solution. There is, in fact, no perfect murder—only cases in which there is a failure to prove a deliberate killing.

In the majority of cases, it is not difficult to determine that the suspicious death was the result of a murder rather than a suicide or accident. The more difficult cases are those that at first appearance seem to be an accident or suicide. In those cases, the first officer and investigator must be thoroughly familiar with all aspects of homicide investigation. The initial analysis of the situation and the evaluation of the case require at least as much knowledge as the subsequent investigation of the crime scene.

The officer should keep in mind that if a supposed suicide is later judged to be a murder, a serious error has not been committed, even though the investigation may become more extensive than is necessary. If, on the other hand, a murder is judged as a suicide, the officer has not only failed in the investigation, but may also have made the solution of the crime and the apprehension of the killer more difficult, if not impossible.

## Murder, Suicide, or Accident?

When evaluating whether a death is the result of an accident or suicide, or whether death was caused by another person, it is generally best to suspect the worst—murder. Even if circumstances give the over-whelming appearance of suicide or accident, the investigation should be conducted in as much detail as possible (Fig. 16.1). Murderers have been known to purposely make the death appear to be an accident or suicide. The investigating officer must be aware of this possibility. Only through systematic and accurate investigation can such a decep-tion be uncovered and homicidal intent revealed.

When investigating cases of sudden death, the officer should as quickly as possible attempt to evaluate the circumstances revealed at

FIGURE **16.1.**  A body was dumped in a wooded area. By the time it was discov-ered about 24 hours after the killing, it had already been attacked by animals and a significant amount of the body had been eaten. (*Los Angeles County Sheriff's Department.*)

the crime scene. The following questions should be answered immediately:

1. What was the cause of death?
2. Could the deceased have produced the injuries or brought about the effect that caused death?
3. Are there any signs of a struggle?
4. Where is the weapon, instrument, or object that caused the injuries, or traces of the medium that caused death?

These are but four questions that can be asked out of the many that will arise in death investigation. They are probably the most important questions for guiding the continued investigation.

## Cause of Death

The first question the officer is required to answer is, What was the cause of death? It should be noted here that the determination of the cause of death at this time is the apparent cause of death and not the actual cause of death, which will be determined by the medical examiner through an autopsy. Determining the cause of death, whether it be by stabbing, shooting, strangulation, or other means, represents a starting point for the investigator and helps to begin to put into focus the facts and circumstances surrounding the death (Fig. 16.2).

In evaluating the cause of death, it is very useful for the investigating officer to have a good knowledge of the appearance of different types of injuries and wounds. The investigator is not expected to have the same expertise in this area as the forensic pathologist, but must have at least a working knowledge of the subject in order to take the initial steps of the death investigation. An erroneous estimate of the cause of death may lead the investigation into a wrong channel and may even jeopardize the ultimate solution of the crime. Thus, for example, if an inexperienced officer mistakes a gunshot injury for a stab wound, the whole investigation may be sidetracked.

The officer should not confuse experience with expertise, for it is the pathologist's province to determine the cause of death, no matter how much experience the investigator has. On the other hand, the officer's primary duty should be to keep in mind that success is usually the result of cooperation and teamwork between the medical examiner and the homicide investigator.

### Suicide

Could the deceased have produced the injuries or brought about the effect that caused death? A determination of whether death was the result of suicide or murder is extremely important in the initial phase of

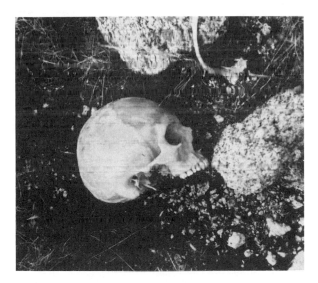

FIGURE 16.2. Body parts may be discovered in uninhabited areas, sometimes as a result of wild animal activity. A forensic anthropologist may be of assistance in developing information concerning identity from a skull. (*Los Angeles County Sheriff's Department.*)

the investigation. Usually, the decision is based on an evaluation of the injuries that resulted in the death and other factors about the deceased's mental and emotional state prior to death.

The common modes of death by suicide are drowning, hanging, shooting, poisoning, jumping from heights, cutting of arteries, stabbing, and strangulation. These factors must be considered along with the ability of the deceased to accomplish the act, from both a physical and a psychological standpoint.

A detailed examination of the crime scene should be undertaken to determine whether the facts are consistent with the theory of suicide. Thus, for example, it is reasonable to expect the means of death, such as a weapon or poison, to be close at hand and in proximity to the body. Failure to discover a weapon in the case of a suspected suicide makes that possibility unrealistic.

The nature and position of the injuries are useful considerations in drawing a conclusion. Hesitation marks are quite common in suicide cases involving slashing of the wrists. Similarly, gunpowder tattooing located around a gunshot wound is consistent with the firing of a weapon at close range. Such facts could be consistent with suicide. Defense wounds, however, would not be expected on the hands or arms of a suspected suicide victim (Fig. 16.3).

Wound location should be considered. The wound location should be within reach of the deceased—generally, in the case of stabbing or

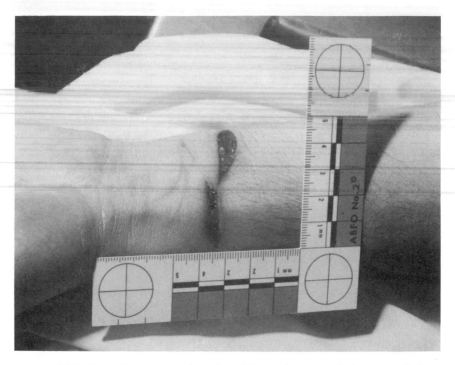

**FIGURE 16.3.** Investigators need to be able to distinguish between defense wounds and hesitation marks in a case of suicide. This is an example of the latter. (*Los Angeles County Coroner's Department.*)

cutting—on the wrists, neck, abdomen, or chest. A wound to the back of the head would, therefore, raise suspicion. Wounds are also generally grouped in one area, as in the case of hesitation marks on the wrist.

In suicides involving handguns, the victim usually drops the weapon or throws it—up to several feet away—when the arms are flung outward. In such cases the floor or ground should be examined for dents or scratches resulting from the impact. Occasionally, the weapon is found in the victim's hand, but this is usually due to the gun or hand's having been supported in some way at the moment of discharge.

If there is no blood on the insides of the hands or on the corresponding parts of the grip of the gun—when the rest of the hand is bloodsoaked—it is usually a good indication that the victim fired the shot personally. The same condition applies to knife handles when the slashes are caused by the victim. When the palm of the hand and the grip of the gun are both bloodstained, murder is not necessarily indicated. However, there is reason to be suspicious if the blood marks on the hand and grip do not match. There have been cases in which a murderer placed a gun in the victim's hand after rigidity had set in.

When someone is found dead in a room where the door is locked from the inside, it is usually considered to be a case of suicide or natural death. The crime scene investigator should not, however, be satisfied with this simple conclusion. There are methods by which doors, windows, or other openings can be "locked" from the outside. The investigator should, therefore, pay particular attention to unusual traces and marks on doors, locks, latches, windows, and the like.

Suicide by jumping from a building is not uncommon in large cities. The body may then land at some considerable distance from the perpendicular. For example, in a jump from an 80-foot vertical cliff, a body was found 42 feet from the base. This circumstance may seem suspicious, but it is explained by the fact that the force of an outward jump continues to act on the falling body.

A determination of suicide should also be based on the results of interviews with the deceased's relatives and friends and on information from the physician or psychologist who may have had the victim under care. An individual's history of suicide threats or suicidal tendencies is, of course, significant to the investigation. A careful and thorough search for a suicide note at the crime scene, the victim's residence, and place of work is particularly important. When such notes are found, they are frequently in plain view and near the body. However, the note may have been written earlier and left in another location. In some instances, several notes have been written and placed around the house or even mailed to friends or relatives. The note should be examined by a questioned documents examiner to verify its authenticity. The investigator should collect known handwriting exemplars for this purpose and should search for the writing instrument and paper used. Latent fingerprints should also be searched for on the document (Fig. 16.4 to 16.6).

Motives for suicide should be considered. Terminal illness is sometimes a reason to take one's life, and the investigator should gather information from the deceased's physician, prescriptions, medical records, and the like. A poor financial situation may also be a cause, and an investigation of the person's finances and debts should be undertaken. Other motives, such as marital or family problems and psychological problems, must also be investigated.

In cases of mental disorder, it is not uncommon that the suicide is preceded by the killing of other family members. These cases must be investigated as thoroughly as other homicides. If the killer in such an instance survives an attempted suicide, it will be necessary to produce evidence about his or her mental state. Psychiatric evaluation of a defendant may be considerably influenced by the findings at the crime scene. Even if the suicide victim does not survive, the investigation must be conducted with care. Inheritance and insurance matters will be influenced by the order in which the victims died.

Cases of suicide do happen where none of the commonly accepted

**A**

**B**

motivations are apparent even after some investigation. The investigator should not be unduly influenced by the opinions of relatives or friends of the deceased who are reluctant to accept the fact of suicide. In many cases, the motivations for suicide are so deeply hidden that they may remain a mystery forever.

## Signs of Struggle

If, at the scene of a death, there are found distinct signs of a struggle having taken place, the case may be decided from the start as one of death by violence by the action of another person. In a room, the signs of a struggle generally consist of bloodstains, pulled out hair, overturned or displaced articles of furniture, rumpled rugs, marks of weapons, and injuries caused by the deceased in self-defense.

Signs of a struggle show most clearly when an injured victim has retreated, or when an attempt was made to avoid the attack of the criminal. From the visible signs, the course of events can usually be reconstructed accurately. Bloodstains can be considered the best clues for the reconstruction of the course of events in a case of murder. Generally no bloodstains are produced during the first stage of the attack, before bleeding has commenced. If victims do not immediately become unconscious at the first blow, stab, cut, or shot, it can nearly always be assumed that their hands will become covered with blood from touching the injured parts of their body. If victims try to escape or to put up a resistance, their blood-covered hands leave marks that often indicate their position in certain situations. After a struggle in a furnished room, a surprisingly large number of marks of bloodstained hands may be found on the legs of tables and chairs. A frequently occurring bloodstain is the typical one that comes from bloody hair. Such hair imprints in blood are often found on the underside of tables and chairs. Those who examine the scene of a crime should look very carefully for bloody imprints on doors (and especially on keys, door handles, and knobs), telephones, hung-up clothes, draperies, curtains, and the like. If blood has spattered on a door, it is not sufficient to state on which side it is; it is also necessary to consider what the position of the door was when the blood was spattered against it, and from what direction it came.

---

FIGURE 16.4. (A) A team of hazardous material specialists, crime scene investigators, and detectives responded to an apartment complex to investigate a murder-suicide. Levels of hydrogen cyanide gas in the apartment were such that crime scene personnel wore protective clothing and self-contained breathing apparatuses. (B) The principle crime scene was the bathroom of the apartment. Two persons were found dead. A male (who worked as a fumigator) was located by the toilet and a female was face-down in the bathtub in black-colored water. (*El Cajon Police Department, El Cajon, California.*)

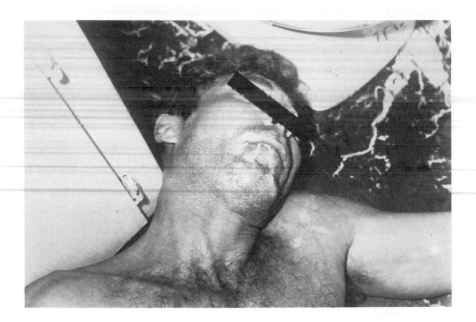

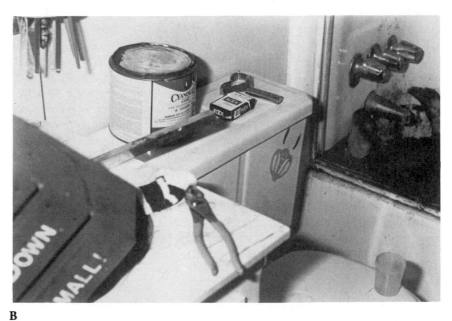

B

FIGURE 16.5. (A) There were stains on the male victim's mouth and chin and (B) a can of Cyanogas on the toilet tank. (C) The black color of the water in the tub was caused by cyanogas. (*El Cajon Police Department, El Cajon, California.*)

C

FIGURE 16.5. (*Continued*)

Drops of spattered blood can indicate how far the drawer of a piece of furniture was pulled out, or whether the door of a closet, kitchen cupboard, or other piece of furniture was open during a struggle. An especially important clue is a footprint in blood. Usually, such a print is blurred and hardly suitable for identification, but it may be possible to decide whether it was made by the victim or by the criminal. One should not forget to pull down any window shades and to look for marks on them. The parts of the legs of tables and chairs that touch the floor should also be examined.

Pulled out hair found in a case of death by violence is a certain indication that a struggle has occurred. When found, it should be recovered immediately, as it can easily disappear or have its position altered (e.g., from a draft).

Overturned and displaced furniture gives a good idea of the direction in which a struggle proceeded, or the route by which the victim attempted to escape. Chairs, pedestals, and other light pieces of furniture fall in the direction in which struggling persons are moving. If there is reason to suspect that a criminal has righted overturned furniture, the articles should be examined for possible fingerprints. Murderers are usually in such a state of mind after the deed is done that they do not consider the risk of leaving fingerprints. When a print is found on a light piece of furniture, its position should be examined carefully; a firm grip on a chair may give rise to the suspicion that the chair was used as a

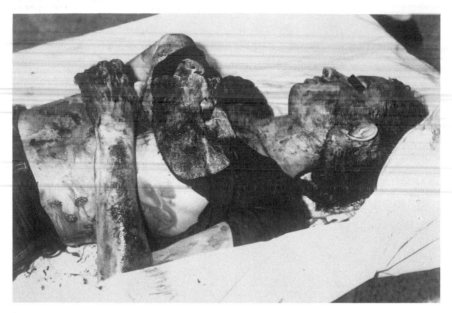

A

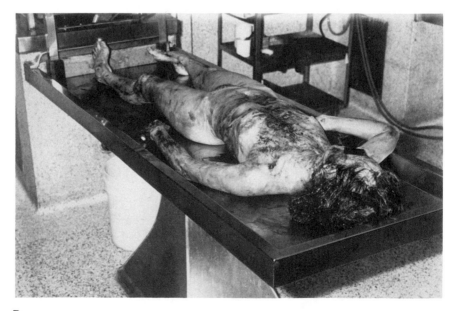

B

FIGURE 16.6. The female was stabbed multiple times in the abdomen, side, and neck. (*El Cajon Police Department, El Cajon, California.*)

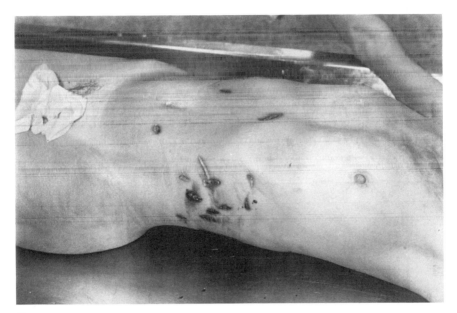

C

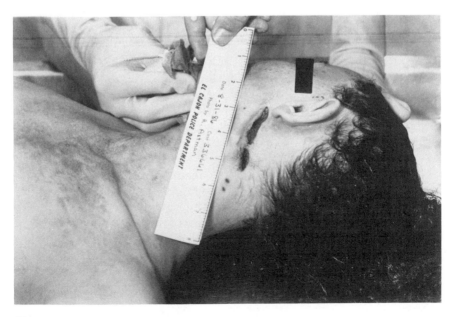

D

weapon. When heavy furniture has been displaced, the amount of force required to move it and the way in which this force must act should be determined. Furniture placed irregularly often gives the impression that it has been displaced from its original position. Marks of scraping indicate displacement, and the floor generally shows clearly whether furniture has previously stood in a different place.

Rumpled rugs often provide signs of a struggle, and marks of sliding on the floor sometimes form a useful guide. A murder victim in self-defense in a lying position may kick against a wall, the floor, or furniture, and the shoes then leave marks of shoe polish, dirt, and rubber scraping. The investigator should also look for such marks on the undersides of the furniture.

Marks of weapons may occur, e.g., when an ax is swung and scrapes a ceiling or slips along a piece of furniture, or when the victim avoids the blow and the weapon hits the wall, floor, or furniture instead. In the case of a murder with an ax or similar weapon, a frequently occurring mark is one formed on walls when the criminal swung the weapon back and up before striking. A bloodstained weapon may leave a bloodstain at a place where it was laid down or dropped. If it is wiped, for example, on a handkerchief, the edge or head may leave a print in blood. Among the indications of weapons are also included the presence of cartridges, cartridge cases, bullets, and bullet holes.

Defense injuries are a fairly certain indication that there has been a fight. In cases of suicide and accidental death, marks are often found that at first sight appear to be marks of a struggle. A person weary of life may have taken a number of measures at various places to shorten his or her life. In a state of confusion, the individual may overturn or move furniture as well as leave blood and other marks that at first cause suspicion. A careful investigation of the scene, however, can give a clear picture of the true course of events.

In cases of death by violence outdoors, signs of a struggle are in general not so distinct as indoors. If a fight preceded the murder, the ground will be trampled. When foot marks made with shoes of different size and appearance are found, or if the marks have the form that results from the feet being set down obliquely against the ground, these marks must be considered as evidence of a fight. At the scene of a suicide, especially in a case of hanging, the ground may be trampled, but as a rule the marks have the normal appearance of those of a person walking. Other signs of a struggle outdoors may be bloodstains, pulled out tufts of hair, marks of weapons, and resistance injuries. Broken-off twigs, trampled leaves, torn-up moss and grass, footprints at places that a person would normally avoid, and other such indications can also be considered signs of a struggle.

## Location of Weapon

In cases of death by violence, the cause of death must be decided as
as possible, so that one may search for the weapon, tool, instrument, or
other lethal object. The absence of a weapon or instrument at the scene
indicates murder. If the weapon or instrument has been found, then the
analysis of the situation must produce a preliminary decision as to
whether the case is one of murder or suicide. In searching for a weapon,
nothing should be moved or altered at the scene of the incident, and if
there is danger that evidence may be destroyed in the search, then the
search must be postponed. If the weapon is found, it should be photographed and described in the position in which it lies. A pathologist
should always be consulted when it is necessary to determine whether
an object can be considered a dangerous weapon.

## Examination of a Dead Body at the Crime Scene

Before examining a dead body, the police officer should consider all the
precautions that should be taken during the course of the work. A
careless move—even one so slight as undoing a button or lifting a flap of
a garment—may subsequently prove to be a great mistake. An example
is on record of a police officer, in misdirected zeal, proceeding so far
with the examination of a dead body that an attempt was made to
determine the track of a bullet and the depth to which it had penetrated
in the body by probing the wound with a pencil. Such measures are
entirely misguided. When clothes are found on the body, they must be
examined at the same time as the body, but if no pathologist is present
the examination should include only the visible parts. The position and
state of any clothes should be described in the report, including, among
other matters, how they are buttoned or attached, creases and wrinkles,
injuries, stains, and so on.

The position of the clothes, for example, how far the pants are pulled
up, whether garments are twisted sideways, pulled down, or even inside
out, may be of great importance. Any displacement from the normal
position is measured. Buttoning and other fastenings, e.g., zippers,
safety pins, casings, and the like, are described. Unbuttoned or torn-off
buttons are indicated, as are buttonholes. Shirts should be checked to
determine whether they button right-to-left or left-to-right. Men sometimes wear women's clothes and vice versa.

Folds in clothes should be examined, especially on the lower parts of
the body. The report should indicate whether the folds go horizontally
or vertically, or if they have resulted from a crumpling of the garment.
When a body is dragged along, horizontal creases occur that are dirty on

the outside but clean in the folds. When a body is lifted or moved by a grip on the clothing, characteristic formations are produced. If the raised part of a fold is bloodstained but the inner part is free from blood, then the position of a part of the body when violence was exerted can be determined with certainty. If a garment is bloodstained, and on the inside of the bloodstain there are sharply delineated clean areas, then the fold formation can be reconstructed.

Damage to the clothes occurs from tearing, crushing, cutting, or penetration by edged weapons, ax blows, and the like. The damage should be measured, and the report should contain statements of the kind, position, size, and manner of occurrence of the damage. In pertinent cases the damage to the clothes should, during the autopsy, be compared with the position of corresponding wounds on the body. In this way important information can be obtained regarding a particular body position when an injury was inflicted.

Stains may consist of blood, semen, saliva, phlegm, vomit, feces, urine or other liquid; or of dust, dirt, or other contamination. They are described with reference to type, location, size, and, in pertinent cases, direction of flow. If liquid stains go through clothing material, it is necessary to determine from which side the liquid has penetrated.

In describing blood marks on a dead body, the terms generally used are bloodstain, blood smear, blood spatter, and stains from dropping blood. Bloodstain means marks containing a lot of blood, which occur either from direct bleeding or when, for example, a garment is soaked in an accumulation of blood. Blood smear means a mark with a smaller amount of blood, and can occur when a bloodstained object brushes against or touches something. A special form of blood mark is a fingerprint in blood.

From stains of blood, saliva, phlegm, vomit, urine, or other liquid on a dead body, important information can be obtained if the direction of flow is observed. Streams of blood especially can contribute to the reconstruction of events in a case of death by violence. All marks of blood flowing "in the wrong direction" are examined and photographed.

A special form of blood mark is blood froth. When a person continues to breathe after blood has penetrated the air passages, a thick froth is formed. This can become so extensive that if the face is turned upward, it comes out of the mouth and nasal passages in the form of billowing foam that can be several inches thick. Frothing can also occur on putrefied bodies when gases create foam in the decomposition fluids (Fig. 16.7).

Occasionally investigators encounter a case of murder in which the criminal wipes or washes the blood away from the victim. Such cleaning is generally easy to detect, especially when the skin is clean

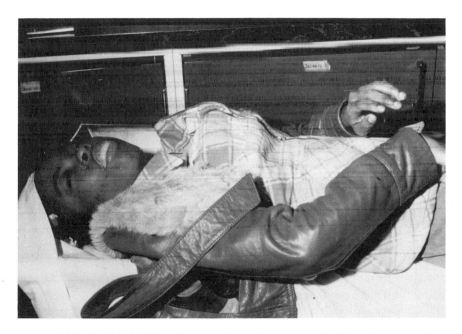

FIGURE 16.7. Frothy fluid at the mouth in this case probably indicates a drug overdose. (*Alabama Department of Forensic Sciences, Mobile, Alabama.*)

around the wound. Washing or wiping the hands generally leaves a thin rim of blood on the nails near the cuticles. When the blood has co-agulated, small rolls of blood and dirt are often formed, which penetrate cracks and hollows of the skin. If blood has been washed from the head, this fact is often easily detected by the traces of blood that remain in ears, nostrils, and hair. Moisture around the body may also indicate that it has been washed with water.

In connection with the occurrence of blood at the scene of a crime, some attempt should always be made to estimate the amount. If blood has flowed out onto an absorbing layer, the depth of penetration should be determined. Floorboards should be lifted.

## Murder

A woman was found lying dead outdoors. Her head was partly shattered by a number of ax blows, from which it could be assumed that most of the blood had been lost from the body. Under the head of the dead woman there was found actually only a small amount of blood, possibly a half pint. From this it appeared that the woman had not been murdered at the place where she lay. On further investigation, the lost blood was found at a place about a quarter of a mile from the body. It was discovered that the woman had been murdered here and that the body had then been transported to the place where it was found. If the lack of blood at the place where the body was found had not been noticed, it is possible that that place would have been considered the scene of the crime and investigated as such, while the actual scene of the crime would never have been known. Investigation of the latter produced evidence against a local suspect, who later confessed the crime.

In examining a dead body, it is generally possible to take the necessary steps in a certain order, which is a guarantee that nothing will be forgotten or neglected. The various steps in an investigation, when a pathologist is present, are described below. When the pathologist does not arrive in time, the investigation is carried out in the same way, but the investigator's moves must be reconsidered so that the clues that only a medical expert is capable of judging and investigating are protected as much as possible.

The first measure that should be taken without delay is to confirm the appearance of signs of certain death, of which the type, development, and time of their confirmation, should be noted in the report.

The body is then photographed. Preferably, all photographing should be completed before the position of the body is altered. If for some reason a change has been made after it was discovered, e.g., when relatives cover it up or the pathologist looks for signs of death, the actual position should be photographed first, and then the original position reconstructed and photographed. The camera should thereafter be held in readiness for additional pictures during the course of the examination.

A preliminary investigation of the pockets of the dead person may precede the more detailed investigation only when it is considered absolutely necessary. This is to be avoided if possible, but it may be necessary to confirm quickly whether the pockets contain any identification documents, wallet, purse, watch, or other valuable articles. This examination must be done so carefully that the original position of the clothes can easily be restored later. It should be noted whether the pockets are turned inside out—this may show that they have been examined earlier.

A preliminary sketch of the position of the body is made. In view of the fact that the position will have to be altered by degrees, marks are made at certain places on the floor (e.g., at the top point of the head, ears, elbows, hands, crotch, knees, heels, and points of the toes), and these points are measured on sketches. The whole of the outer contour of the body may be marked with a continuous chalk line. If the body lies on some loose base, its position should be marked in a similar manner. If later, when the body has been removed, it is found that the original position has to be reconstructed, it can then be done easily with the aid of the chalk outline.

The position of the body is next described briefly, without any details. The position of the body in relation to the nearest article of furniture, object, or fixed point is measured and noted. Then the visible clothing is described, without details.

The next step is the detailed examination. Only visible details are examined and described. The original position must not be changed. It is preferable to describe the head, then the trunk, arms, and finally the legs.

The head is described and examined as to its position in relation to the body, whether the eyes and mouth are open, color of the skin, injuries, presence of blood, state of the hair, presence of saliva, phlegm, vomit, or foreign bodies (soil, sand, vegetable matter, hair, etc.). The direction of flow of liquids is easily determined on the skin of the face and should therefore be noted.

In examining the trunk, note should be made of its position, any bending or twisting, the position of visible clothing and its condition, folds, injuries to the body and clothes, and the presence of any blood, saliva, semen, phlegm, vomit, or foreign bodies (especially hair).

Then the arms, and finally the legs, are examined in the same way as the trunk. The hands should be given special attention. The presence of rings, jewelry, wristwatch, or marks left by these objects should be noted. Foreign objects are examined, especially fragments of hair or skin under the nails. The dirt from the nails should be collected. If a detailed examination of the hands cannot be made on the spot, the hands should be enclosed in clean paper bags tied securely at the wrists. When examining the legs, the distance between the knees and between the heels should be measured. Special attention should be given to the soles of the feet or shoes with respect to the presence of blood or other material in which the person may have stepped.

After the examination of the visible parts of the body, the police officer should attempt to visualize the course of events as deduced from observations. The officer's own judgment should not be relied on solely; the opinions of others, especially the pathologist, should also be considered. From a number of opinions it is often possible to get a good reconstruction of events.

The underside of the body and those portions covered by clothes should not be examined at the scene unless the examination is done in the presence and at the request of the pathologist. Normally, the body will not be turned over or undressed until the time of the autopsy. However, after the body has been photographed and described in all pertinent detail and has been lifted onto a stretcher, the area under the body should be examined. A critical piece of evidence may have been hidden under the body, perhaps in a large pool of blood. Bullets, or fragments of bullets, sometimes penetrate a body completely but are stopped by clothing. The projectile may thus roll out of the clothing of the victim, and may even be overlooked, unless great care is exercised in lifting and transporting. The relationship between the location of injuries and bloodstains on the floor should also be established.

The body should be transported in the position in which it was found, if possible. If necessary, the clothing can be fixed in its original position by means of pins. In appropriate cases the body should be moved on a clean sheet of cotton or plastic or on an undertaker's impregnated paper sheet. This is partly to protect the body from contamination and partly to prevent the loss of minute evidence.

An officer should accompany the body to the hospital, morgue, or other location where the autopsy is to take place.

## Detailed Examination of the Scene of the Crime

After the preliminary investigation has shown that death was caused by the intent or agency of some other person, or by suicide or accident, the detailed investigation can begin. How thoroughly this is to be done must be decided for each particular case. In suicide or accidental death, the detailed examination can be limited simply to those matters that appear to be directly related to events. If the death has been caused by the intent or action of another person, everything should be investigated, even in cases in which the criminal has been arrested immediately after the crime and has confessed. In such cases, the investigation should decide whether the statements of the criminal are consistent. In a first statement, a criminal often makes consciously incorrect statements about personal actions in order to create extenuating circumstances. Those who investigate the scene of a crime have an opportunity to produce such an accurate reconstruction of the actual course of events that such an attempt by the criminal cannot succeed.

When the examination of the body has been concluded, the body can generally be removed for the autopsy. Photographing the scene of the crime should have been completed before this. Before the body is taken away, the places at the scene where ambulance personnel have to walk should be examined for evidence that might be destroyed, including the presence of blood. Even if the body is well wrapped up, drops of blood may fall from it as the result of unforeseen circumstances. Such marks can cause much unnecessary work for investigators later. Those who carry away the body should be warned not to step in any blood.

As a rule, the investigation can then be continued, with attention to such details or places where anything of significance might be expected. Then follows a methodically planned examination of the scene of the crime as a whole; this is the basis for the report of the investigation. It is started at a suitable point, and everything is inspected in such a way and in such an order that nothing is forgotten. It may be convenient first to examine and describe the entrance, doors, and lock arrangements. Then follows a description of the room as a whole, without going into detail. The length, width, height to ceiling, windows, doors, floor covering, paint of walls and ceiling, color of wallpaper, lighting conditions, and other features should be described. Following this, the room is described in detail and investigated in a certain order, commencing from the entrance or from the place of death. Everything must be examined and described as a coherent whole. If, for example, a writing desk is examined, then there follows a description of the nearby parts of the floor and walls and also of the surface of the floor under the piece of furniture. Generally, it is best for the ceiling to be described and examined last and as a whole. If for some reason a place has been examined in detail and described earlier, then a reference to it is put in the notes to facilitate the writing of the final report.

In the investigation, everything is noted—even if it appears to have no significance in the case. Such unessential details are sorted out when the report is written, as are similar details that appeared to be important at first but are later found to be immaterial. The notes made at the scene of a crime must not under any circumstances be thrown away, but should be placed in the file and kept with the records. Experience shows that such rough notes may be of great importance at some future date if the investigator is required to prove that the examination of certain details was not omitted.

It is convenient to develop and preserve finger and palm prints at the same time as the final detailed investigation. As far as possible, everything should be put back into its original position. When furniture is moved, it should be replaced with the greatest accuracy, because the scene must be in its original state in case the suspect or witnesses are returned to the scene for questioning. Before any furniture is moved, a chalk mark should be made around the legs or other suitable parts. Objects placed on furniture can be treated similarly.

A final important step prior to sketching the scene of the crime is measurement. It is desirable—but not always possible—that this be done earlier, for there is a risk that those who do the measuring may destroy evidence that has not yet been discovered, or that they may produce fresh and misleading clues. One method that can be used is to have a preliminary sketch made as early as possible. Gradually, as the investigation proceeds, and before each object is moved, measurements are made and recorded on the sketch. This method is, however, somewhat inconvenient, since the measuring cannot be done as systematically as is desirable. Under such conditions, even experienced sketchers can easily forget important measurements.

When there has been a shooting at the scene of the crime, it is necessary to look for weapons, cartridges, cartridge cases, and bullets. If a weapon is found, it is photographed at the spot where it is found, and a chalk line is drawn around it before it is moved. Fingerprints are recorded before the weapon is examined. In cases of presumed suicide, it is necessary to check whether the weapon lies in a place to which it might have either dropped or slid. The base on which the weapon lies should always be examined. A dropped or thrown weapon generally leaves a mark (e.g., a scratch or dent in the furniture or floor), and the absence of such marks should be considered suspicious.

When cartridge cases are found, their position should be noted in the report, on the sketch, and on the envelope in which they are then placed. Bullets and bullet holes are examined. The place from which the shot was fired can be determined quite accurately from the direction of the bullet penetration—a string being stretched along the calculated path of the bullet. The reconstruction is then photographed. A bullet that has buried itself in a wall is cut out, but great care must be used so that the bullet is not touched by the tool used. In cases of suicide, the shooter may fire one or more trial shots before firing the actual suicide shot.

The following is a list of certain details that should be examined where appropriate. Some of the items are of a changeable nature and should be examined immediately or as soon as possible; some are those that have been found to be easily forgotten or passed over even by an experienced investigator:

☐ *On stairs, passages, and entries to the scene, together with streets, passages, and yards in the immediate vicinity:* Are there bloodstains; fingerprints on railings; objects that the criminal has dropped or thrown away? What kind of illumination? If there is an elevator, the elevator shaft should be examined. Note evidence in trash cans.

☐ *Outer doors:* Bolted? Locked? Marks of breaking in? Does the doorbell work?

☐ *Windows:* Bolted? Position of window catch; marks of breaking in, possibility of seeing in? Position of curtains and blinds? Are there indications of marks outside the windows?

☐ *Mailbox:* Date on mail or papers; are they in the right order of time?

☐ *Other papers and mail, daily milk supplies, etc., at the scene of the crime:* Date marks. Have the letters been opened? Do the papers give the impression of having been read? What is the number of milk bottles?

☐ *Inside doors:* Bolted, locked? On which side is the key?

☐ *Hall, entrance:* Presence of clothing and objects that do not belong to the place or to residents there, especially outer garments, headgear, scarves, gloves, galoshes, umbrellas.

☐ *Lighting:* Which lamps were on when the crime was discovered? Electric meter readings.

☐ *Heating conditions:* Is there any fire or embers in fireplaces; any remaining heat? Do not forget to examine ash and burned residues; setting on thermostat.

☐ *Cooking conditions:* Is the oven or stove on? Is there any remaining heat? Was food or drink in preparation?

☐ *Odors:* Gas; gunpowder; strong tobacco fumes; alcohol, perfume.

☐ *Clocks and watches:* Are they running and showing the right time? When did they stop? Time set on alarm clock.

☐ *Signs of a party:* How many bottles? Labels on them; contents (not always same as label). Are seals or corks on or in the bottles? How many glasses or cups of different kinds? Contents, residue, or odor in them. Spilled liquor; overturned objects. Have cigarette butts and matchsticks been thrown on table or floor? How many persons were set for? What dishes? Are there any fingerprints?

☐ *Contents of ashtrays:* Remains of smoked tobacco; brand marks on cigarette butts; way in which they have been extinguished; marks of lipstick; burned matches.

☐ *Drawers and compartments in writing desks, cabinets, or other furniture:* Shut; locked? In which drawer is the key? Drawers pulled out or taken away; objects taken out. Are there signs of disorder such as might result from a hurried search? Are cash, bank books, and objects of value exposed in a conspicuous or easily detected place?

☐ *Wastepaper baskets, trash cans:* Any object thrown there by the criminal; torn letters.

☐ *Kitchen, bathroom, toilet:* Are towels, rags, and like objects damp, or do they show bloodstains? Are there bloodstains on counter, bath, sink, toilet, or buckets? Are there objects or suspicious liquids in watertrap or toilet? Are there fingerprints on any used paper?

☐ *Damage to ceiling, walls, and furniture:* Investigate how it could have occurred in connection with the crime; marks of plaster or paint soon disappear from the floor from trampling.

☐ *Garments taken off:* At what places; in what order beginning from top? Turned right side out or inside out; properly hung up or in disorder?

☐ *General disorder:* Is this typical of violent happenings or a struggle? Can it result from lack of cleaning up over a long period, or incidentally, for example, in carrying out ordinary household operations, etc.?

☐ *Shooting:* The investigating officer should either be able to account for the actual number of bullets fired together with a corresponding number of cartridge cases, or give a good explanation of why they are not found or cannot be found in the correct number (consider the possibility of a cartridge case getting caught up in the clothes of the dead person and not being found before the autopsy).

☐ *Hanging and strangling:* Quick confirmation of whether the cord used was taken from the scene or locality.

☐ *Suicide note:* Is it in the handwriting of the victim? Has the writing instrument been found; has indented writing come through onto other paper underneath? Is there more than one note; are there fingerprints of persons other than the deceased?

☐ *Hiding places for weapons or objects that the criminal wished to conceal quickly:* Some of the places that are most often forgotten by the investigating police officer are locations above appliances and high furniture, or between these and the wall, behind books in a bookcase, among bedclothes in a bed, behind heating elements, and on high shelves in wardrobe, pantry, and kitchen cupboard.

☐ *Compost heaps, manure heaps:* These are very convenient for concealing objects without leaving distinct signs of digging.

It is suggested in cases of serious crime that when the investigation has been concluded, the scene of the crime be kept intact until the final report has been written and read through by the superior officer concerned and by the prosecutor, recovered evidence has been examined, and the postmortem examination has been completed. When material recovered for examination has value as evidence, it should be preserved even after the criminal has been tried. There may be a review of the case, perhaps several years later, and the evidence may then have to be produced.

## Outdoor Scenes

The examination of a crime scene located outdoors must be planned quickly and carried out as soon as possible. Changes in weather conditions may completely jeopardize the chances of finding any existing evidence. A number of different clues that are easily detected at first may disappear in a very short time, for example, because of precipitation, drying, vegetation, flood conditions, and the like. It is even more difficult to examine such a scene at night.

Bloodstains on grass change color rapidly so that they are difficult to detect. A brief shower may completely wash away smaller stains. Other biological evidence, such as hair, seminal fluid, urine, feces, vomit, saliva, nasal secretions, skin fragments, brain substance, and so on, is quickly changed by drying or may be washed away. During the time of year when insects are particularly plentiful, biological evidence may be destroyed by their action. The path of a person through dewy grass may be discernible to the naked eye, but after even an hour or so of direct sunlight, the dew has evaporated and the grass has recovered its original shape. It may subsequently take hours before this track can be followed. Footprints and tire marks should therefore be protected and recorded as soon as possible.

When a shooting has taken place outdoors, the direction of firing must be determined quickly. A bullet's path through foliage, bushes, or hedges is usually marked by fresh twigs and leaves that have fallen to the ground. After a few hours, these traces may have already taken on the appearance of the surroundings. It may thus take hours to establish the direction of firing from these clues. Evidence of a bullet striking the ground is usually found in the form of soil or sand thrown over the surrounding vegetation. A quick shower may wash off these traces and make the location of the impact impossible to find. Cartridge cases may be trampled into the ground.

The crime scene must be effectively roped off, and the investigating officer must follow a definite plan of action. Experience has shown that most of the evidence found at outdoor crime scenes was put there by officers who carelessly and aimlessly wandered around the area.

In cases of suspicious death, the officers can anticipate that the person, or persons, who discovered the body did not enter the scene with caution—which is to be expected. One of the first duties of the crime scene investigator is, therefore, to find out where those persons walked. The records of many cases have shown that clues created by these citizens have caused a tremendous amount of unnecessary work, which could have been avoided if the person had been properly interviewed.

In making up a plan of action, the officers should decide on a path to be used in going to and from the body. Since this path will be used frequently, it may suitably be marked with stakes. The examination of the body then follows according to the outline given earlier in this chapter. Before much attention is given the body, the ground around it should be carefully examined. A second chance will hardly be available after a number of persons have looked at the body and trampled the area.

The area surrounding the central scene should then be examined. The investigators must try to remember their own tracks so that they can distinguish them from others that may be discovered. On snow-covered ground, this is easily accomplished by the investigators' dragging their feet so that their own tracts become distinctive.

Insofar as possible, examining outdoor crime scenes at night should be avoided. This rule should be followed even where suitable illumination is available. Most clues at outdoor scenes consist of minor changes in the ground cover, such as matted grass, torn moss, broken twigs, indistinct footprints, and the like. Such tracks may be visible from several yards away in daylight, but are almost impossible to detect at night even with powerful illumination. If a scene is viewed at night and an estimate made of the topography, it might be found in daylight that the picture is quite different from that seen at night. Since it is difficult to survey the scene and to interpret correctly even gross evidence, it follows that it is even more difficult to find evidence as small as bloodstains, fragments of cloth, fibers, and so on. Such evidence may be overlooked or destroyed if a thorough examination is attempted in darkness.

Prevailing weather conditions or expected weather changes play an important role in deciding whether to postpone the examination until daylight. If there is a chance of snow, the examination must be started—even though important evidence may be destroyed. Other weather conditions may, depending on the type of crime involved, also have a certain influence. If snow should fall before the examination is completed, some evidence may be covered and not retrieved until the snow has melted.

Whenever the examination must be done immediately, it is better to refrain from recovering the evidence and instead cover it with tarpaulins, boxes, or similar protective devices and then wait for daylight for the completion of the examination.

Before the arrival of daylight, certain precautions should be taken. Some flash exposures should be taken of the body. The body should then be covered with a clean sheet, over which is laid a tarpaulin to keep out dust, leaves, and other debris. If the body is suspended, the noose may break, and it is advisable to secure the body with a rope tied loosely around the chest. If the body is on the shoreline, it should be lifted far enough onto the beach so that swells will not make changes on the body.

In taking the photographs and the precautionary measures, the officers should not walk around aimlessly. As described above, a path should be selected and marked with stakes.

The investigator should, of course, make note of changes that may take place on the body, such as signs of death, moisture on the clothing and under the body, and so on.

## Discovering a Body Hidden at Another Location

When a homicide victim has been moved from the actual crime scene and hidden at another location, conditions are somewhat different. Although the examination of such places is generally carried out in the same way as in crime scenes, a reliable reconstruction of the crime is usually not possible. Such locations normally do not yield as much evidence of the criminal as the place of attack.

The question often arises as to how long the body has been lying at the place where it was found. The vegetation and other conditions surrounding the body may give some indications (Fig. 16.8).

The path over which the body was transported should be established at the outset. This detail should be attended to immediately, especially when there is risk of precipitation. If the criminal's footprints are not clear enough, the path should be estimated as that most easily traversed if someone were carrying a body. Even when there are no footprints,

FIGURE 16.8. Identification of decomposed remains requires techniques such as forensic odontology and forensic anthropology, as discussed in Chapter 6. This victim was murdered and dumped in Los Angeles County's high desert, where animals consumed facial tissue and hands. (*Los Angeles County Sheriff's Department.*)

there may be other signs, such as trampled grass, stains of dripping blood, marks from dragging, broken twigs, and the like. If the criminal left the scene by another route, this path should also be examined in due time.

The body should be examined as described earlier in this chapter under "Examination of a Dead Body at the Crime Scene." Dust, dirt, and other traces on the skin and clothing that might point to the scene of the crime should be recovered. A preliminary evaluation of such traces may suggest leads for the search for the actual scene. In removing the dead body from the location where found, it should be placed on a clean plastic sheet or bed sheet that is then wrapped around the body. Blankets and tarpaulins should not be used because one can never be sure that they are absolutely clean. Since it is almost impossible to examine properly and recover traces on the body, it should be transported intact to the place for the autopsy where the detailed examination can take place.

After the body has been removed, the area beneath it should be examined. The amount of blood and body fluids should be estimated. It should also be determined how deeply into the ground such fluids have penetrated. If the murder weapon could reasonably be expected to be found in the area, a search for it should be started. If branches, straw, and the like were used to cover the body, they should be examined for the possibility that the criminal may have dropped something while engaged in covering the body.

## Investigation of a Greatly Altered Body or Skeleton

There are often difficulties in the identification of a dead body that has undergone such a great amount of alteration that only the skeletal parts and portions of tissues and organs are left, or when the usual methods for the identification of a body can be employed only to a limited extent. Important information can be obtained from a skeleton found wholly or partly preserved after a very long time, from as body after burning or other destruction, as well as from any remains of tissues or organs. Clothing or other objects that belonged to the dead person, or can in some other way be connected with the discovery of the remains of the body, can also yield valuable information.

Such bodies or their remains are most frequently discovered outdoors; occasionally they are found indoors in a cellar, attic, heating furnace, or other place. The remains may be those of a person who was murdered, run over by a vehicle, or committed suicide, or who was lost and became the victim of exhaustion or exposure or was suddenly overcome by sickness and death.

From what has been said, it follows that the nature of the place where the discovery is made can vary considerably. Remains may be found under the ground, or under a floor or the like; or they may be lying in the open, covered with brushwood, moss, sacks, or other materials, or overgrown by vegetation. If the body was originally outdoors in the open, then the remains (both bones and clothing) are often dispersed over a large area as a result of animals' dragging them away. It is not uncommon for remains and objects having some connection with them to be found several hundred yards away from the main site. This also applies to parts of a dismembered or burned body that have been buried or left on the ground, since different parts may have been concealed or buried at different places, often a long way apart.

If there is reason to suspect that the individual from whom the remains are derived was killed at or near the place of discovery, it is possible that the murder weapon or objects thrown away by the deceased or by the murderer (shoes, fragments of clothes, ornaments, etc.) may be found within a comparatively small area around the site. In the case of an individual who was lost, it may have happened that in the course of wandering a backpack was thrown off and that making a bed of clothing, etc., was attempted. This is another reason that the investigation should not be restricted to the actual site of the discovery. Remains and fragments of clothing, and especially objects in pockets and the like, often play an important part in the identification of the dead person. The possibility of determination of sex from the clothes is especially important when the remains of the body are only fragmentary or inconclusive with regard to sex. Under certain conditions, clothing may be in a better state of preservation than the remains of the body. Near the remains there may also be found foreign objects connected with the body or with the transport of the body to the site (bags, sacks, cords, etc.), which possibly form the sole proof of a crime and may even indicate a means of tracing the criminal.

There have been a number of cases in which a correctly performed and accurate investigation of the place of discovery, combined with careful technical and pathological investigation of the remains of the body and other related objects, has led to the identification of the body.

To achieve the best result, the investigating officer needs a good knowledge of the proper method of investigation and preservation of the remains and objects, and of the factors that affect the distribution of the objects within a larger area. The officer also needs a knowledge of the special methods used for the further investigation of the discovery and of how these methods can assist in the identification and determination of sex and age of the deceased and of the time that has elapsed since the objects were first placed there. This knowledge is absolutely essential if the police officer is to pay the necessary attention to the possibly small and apparently insignificant objects that are actually of special significance in these respects. The precise determination of the characteristics necessary for establishing age, sex, body structure, and so forth must be left to the anthropologist at the museum or university. Likewise, the investigator must use the services of entomologists for regarding the life cycle of insects, the botanists for growth rates of roots, grasses, and other plants; the meteorologist for weather conditions that might suggest the time of repose of the body, and any other experts whose special knowledge will assist the investigation.

## The Scene of Discovery

The task of investigating the scene of discovery includes searching for and recovering the remains of the body and all the objects in the area that may be of value for identification. (The methods of identifying human remains are discussed in detail in Chapter 6.)

In all cases in which a body is found under such circumstances that a crime is suspected, the police officer should contact the pathologist so that right from the start the latter has an opportunity to become familiar with the case. For the purpose of identifying the body, the expertise of a dentist may be needed. The procedure for the investigation is, of course, not always the same, but depends on whether the discovery was made indoors or outdoors.

*Outdoors.* A discovery outdoors may be one of three different types according to whether the remains are found buried, lying exposed on the ground, or in water.

Remains that have been buried usually come to light when a person or persons have been digging or during other similar operations and are generally purely historical finds at old burial sites and the like.

The police officer who is called to such a scene should first photograph it in the state in which it is found, and then expose the body with great care. During this work, which should preferably be done with assistants and in the presence of a pathologist, detailed photographs should be taken as necessary in order to show the position of the body, noteworthy details or conditions, and so on.

In exposing the body, special attention should be given to the occurrence, above the body, of any filling material that differs from the surrounding earth, to any objects used as covering near the body, and to any foreign material or bodies in the ground or near the body. Quicklime has been placed on bodies to accelerate their decomposition and make identification difficult. If anything of this kind is suspected, a sample of the earth should be taken so that it can be examined. Attention should also be given to the properties of the earth (type of soil, dampness, etc.) as this is very important in determining the length of time the body has been buried.

The color of bones can vary from light grayish white to dark brownish black, depending on the age of the find, kind and properties of the soil, whether the parts are or were enclosed or covered in some way, and the measures that may have been taken with the body before burial (e.g., more or less complete burning). It is often difficult to distinguish between small bones and stones, twigs, or other objects in the earth; therefore the search should be carried out with great care, and all remains, even if very small, should be kept. Certain very small bones, as well as the teeth, are very important for the determination of the sex and age of the deceased. If the skeleton is much disintegrated, the earth should be sifted through a small mesh sieve. It is also important that any remains of hair be sought and kept.

Of great importance for investigation and identification are all remains of clothing and other objects that may be connected with the find, e.g., contents of pockets, buttons, ornaments, rings, coins, etc., and objects that may be connected directly with the crime, transport to the scene, or the like, such as ropes, cords, sacks, bullets, or objects pushed into the mouth of the victim. Such loose objects are looked for—if necessary, by sifting the earth—and kept with great care, as the risk of their falling to pieces may be great. Objects that are on or attached to the remains are not moved from their position before the discovery has been fully investigated. The position of loose objects in relation to the remains of the body should be accurately marked and sketched or, preferably, photographed.

In taking possession of bones, and especially of remains of clothing and the like, attention should be given to their association with any vegetation. Roots of trees or shrubs that have grown through them form a valuable aid in determining the length of time the object has been there. A determination of the age of a root of a tree that has grown through clothing gives a minimum value for the time the object has lain in the ground, and this can be used as a starting point for further investigations and calculations. As far as possible, such roots should be cut off and allowed to remain with the object; otherwise they must be kept and labeled with the necessary information as to their origin.

Even at the scene of the discovery, attention should be given to the occurrence of insect larvae and pupae or remains of them on the body. These are placed in a test tube for examination by an expert. If, for example, remains of fly larvae are found on a buried body, that indicates that the body was above ground for a certain period of time before being buried, and the stage of development of the insect, larvae, or pupa can give further valuable information.

If only a part of a body is found, then dismemberment may have been carried out before burial. In such a case, a large area of the surroundings must be investigated carefully, attention being directed especially to all changes in the surface of the ground that give the impression of having been produced by human agency. Should the find be of a very early date (i.e., very old), it can be assumed that any signs of disturbance of the ground will have disappeared, and the investigation becomes very difficult. The character of the ground, the possibility of burial at different places, and so forth must then be used to guide the search. In some cases police dogs can be used with advantage. A sketch should be made of the terrain, giving the place where each object is found, and both total and detail photographs are taken. In photographing, each site is marked with a number or letter visible on the photograph, and these are also shown on the sketches. The objects found at the different sites are placed in cartons or boxes marked with the number or letter given to the location of discovery in the photographs and sketches.

A search for evidence in the vicinity of such a discovery, e.g., evidence of the criminal, vehicle tracks, or the like, usually has a low payoff because of the long time that has generally elapsed since the crime was committed. Marks made by vehicles on stems, trees, or the like, or a bullet, for instance, can, however, be found after a comparatively long time, so that a routine search should be made if the find is thought to be not too old. It should be remembered that trees and bushes may have grown considerably since the crime was committed.

The discovery of a dead body found lying *free on the ground* is usually made in a forest, on a mountain slope, or at other lonely places.

If the discoveries are of dismembered body parts, the investigation of the scene must be extended to cover a large area. It can be quite normal for parts of a body to be scattered over a number of places at some distance from one another. The same applies, however, to bodies that have not been dismembered, as various animals and birds can drag the parts for a distance of up to several hundred yards from the original site.

Careful attention must be given to those cases that appear to be hiking, mountain climbing, or camping accidents. These may be the result of an attempt to cover up criminal assault or robbery. Lone hikers or naturalists can be easy prey in criminal attacks. Special attention must be paid to the absence of valuables, minor bruises from subduing blows, and evidence of soil or vegetation that is not normally found in the immediate vicinity. The investigation of a discovery of this kind is made in exactly the same way as for a body that has been buried. Special attention should be given to the relation of the vegetation to the find, as this may be decisive in determining the length of time the body has lain there. Under the remains at the original site may be found plants that have been smothered, or possibly no vegetation at all. Plants may have started to grow over the remains. If the body has lain there for several years, grass, brambles, undergrowth, moss, or other vegetation may have completely concealed part of the remains. The remains may have gradually become covered with a layer of soil or leaf mold from falling leaves and dead plants. Roots of trees and bushes may grow through parts of the find, and especially through remnants of clothing. The vegetative conditions should be described carefully, stating the type of vegetation, and supplemented with photographs on which the different remains are marked in the manner described above. Any tree or other roots that have grown through the remains are kept for a determination of their age. If there is no risk of the roots falling out of the remains when collected, then they should be removed with the remains. A sketch should be made as described above.

The place of discovery is cleared, and any remains and objects found are kept. If necessary, the earth is sifted and may be preserved for further examination or analysis. The character of the ground, i.e., type of soil, dampness, etc., is described. If there are signs of foreign matter such as lime, samples are taken. When exposing the body, attention should be given to any indications of its having been covered with stones, brushwood, sacks, or the like. When necessary, detail photographs are taken.

If remains of a body are found *in water*, it is generally impossible to investigate the place of discovery accurately, unless it is merely a small pool that can be emptied by draining. If this is not possible, the investigation must be limited to dragging and the examination of the shores. It must be remembered that currents, ice, floating timber, and other items may have carried parts of the body to places a long way from the site of discovery. The find also may be composed of a part of the body that has been carried to the place of discovery in the same manner, possibly from a considerable distance.

If the discovery has been made in a harbor or river where there are steamers and motorboats, some of the injuries on the body may have been caused by propellers. A propeller can cut off a leg or arm in such a way that it appears as if the body has been dismembered intentionally. Injuries to tissues and organs produced in this way often show clean cuts, as from an edged tool.

*Indoors.* Very rarely do remains of a body indoors undergo such extensive changes from decay or other causes as described in the previously considered cases. There have been instances when a body has been buried in a cellar or cut up and burned in the furnace of the heating system, or when remains of a dismembered and/or burned body have been placed in a suitcase in an attic or garage. The procedure in such a case is the same as that described above.

In the case of a body that has been buried, or of remains that have been found in a suitcase, sack, or the like, all objects that have been used to conceal the body or for wrapping are of special interest. With such discoveries indoors, the floor, walls, and ceiling of the place should be examined for bloodstains and the like, and objects should be looked for that might be supposed to have been used in connection with the crime, with the burial, and so on.

If, for example, a heating furnace has been used to burn a body, it should be examined very carefully. A skeleton is not destroyed by fire, and even in modern cremations the remains never consist of ashes but of cracked and distorted bones. After a cremation the volume of the bones of an adult amounts to 2 to 3½ liters (3½ to 6 pints). In a freshly burnt state, bones have a white to yellowish or grayish white shade, which quickly changes under the ground to brown or brownish black. At a certain state of the burning, the bones are soft and may then assume peculiar twisted forms that may to some extent depend on the underlayer.

The contents of both the firebox and the ash space should be sifted, and every fragment of bone must be kept. Certain very small bones have been found to be quite resistant to fire and may therefore be very valuable for the determination of the age and sex of the deceased. Teeth are, of course, especially valuable. The crowns of the teeth generally break up and split under the action of heat, but the roots often remain whole. On the other hand, teeth that have not come through (e.g., in children) rarely break up and do not change in form or shrink to any appreciable extent. After burning, these have a whitish color and chalky consistency.

In searching for and taking possession of burnt skeletal remains, great care should be observed because of their fragile nature. If remains that are especially brittle or liable to fall to pieces are found, they should be packed separately in test tubes, glass jars, or cartons—according to size—with cotton, tissue paper, or the like as underlayer and filling for the container.

## Packing and Transporting

The packing of remains of a body, along with any associated objects that are to be moved or sent to an expert, should be done in such a way as to eliminate any danger of destruction or falling apart of associated objects as the result of shaking or other movement. A skeleton, of which the long bones are still hanging together, with or without remains of soft tissues or organs, should be packed in such a way that it will remain in that state during transport. Styrofoam, rags, tissue paper, or similar materials can be used as filling in the container and for the support of parts that do not rest on the bottom. Well-burnt remains should be transported in the charge of a police officer, who keeps the package under control at all times and sees that it is not exposed to shocks or other trauma. Suitable packing materials are thin, soft paper, soft and flexible cloth, tissue paper, cotton, and the like, which is packed in the container in such a way that the object has a soft support and is also supported in a definite position.

## Determining the Number of Individuals

The question of number arises only when a discovery is composed of a collection of bones that are not connected or placed in such a way that it is possible to determine whether the remains are of one or more individuals. An investigation with this objective is based on the fact that certain parts of the skeleton occur singly or in pairs in the human body. Especially significant in this respect are the tooth processes of the second neck vertebra and the wedge bone of the inner ear. In the body there is one of the former, with a characteristic form, and two of the latter, which have an obliquely directed opening for the auditory nerve. Both of these parts of the skeleton are resistant to fire. They are of small size so that great care (sifting) is required in searching for them.

## Examining Remains of Clothing and Other Objects

The investigation of any remains of clothing or other objects has as its objective the determination of the original appearance of the garments, kind of cloth, color, and so on and the detection of any manufacturer's or laundry marks. Shoes are examined for maker's marks, size, repairs, and other such identifying marks, and any object found in the clothes or at the scene is investigated. It must be kept in mind that the item may be characteristic of a certain trade or able in some other way to give information about the deceased or conditions in connection with the death (murder weapon, suicide weapon, objects used in transporting the body to the place, objects thrown away or forgotten by the criminal, etc.). In these investigations, special attention should be given to everything that might assist in a determination of the length of time the remains have been there (e.g., alterations resulting from weather conditions, penetration of roots and other parts of plants into clothing, and the like.

Everything that arises from this investigation is combined to form, if possible, a description of the deceased and an explanation of the cause of death, time of death, and so on, which information can subsequently be used for identifying the body as a person reported to be missing, for tracing the criminal, for checking the statements of a suspect, and other such purposes.

The examination of any remains of clothing or other objects that may be found, and that can be connected with the discovery of remains of a body, is a matter for the police officer, who can call in the assistance of experts if necessary. The pathologist should always be given the opportunity to be present at or should be informed of the results of the examinations since these, like the investigation of the scene of discovery, are closely connected with the pathological investigation.

Before the examination is commenced, all objects should be laid out to dry on a table, as this considerably facilitates the work.

*Clothing.* Roots or other parts of plants that have penetrated portions of clothing should be kept and provided with a label showing type of garment and of vegetation, after which the material is given to a botanist for determination of age. From tree and shrub roots that have penetrated the remains, it is possible to determine the minimum period of time that the object has lain at the site. In the case of *unburied* remains this estimate must be increased by 1 or 2 years since the material has first to be "merged into" the soil before it can be penetrated by roots.

The type of cloth, color, type of garment, and the question of whether it is ready-made or tailor-made are determined, possibly with the assistance of an expert. An expert should preferably also be called in to decide the length of time the material has been lying at the site, based on any changes in the garments resulting from climatic effects. Manufacturer's and laundry marks are looked for, using an ultraviolet lamp in the latter case. Buttons, together with the manner in which they are sewn on (by machine or hand) may be significant, as are any repairs in the garments. The remains of clothes are examined also for damage caused by edged tools, firearms, vehicles, and the like that may possibly correspond to marks and injuries on the body. The assistance of the pathologist is required for this examination. The nature of the damage can often be determined with certainty. Damage caused by animals may also occur on clothing, but this can generally be distinguished from other damage.

The remains of underclothing and stockings or socks are also examined for color, textile material, manufacturer's marks, other marks, repairs, etc.

*Boots and shoes.* The original color of boots and shoes may be very difficult to determine because of the changes undergone by the leather under the action of earth, dampness, and so on. Inside the heel, at the back of the heel, or at other points on the inside, there may be the name of the maker, which is sometimes embossed, and stamped marks may sometimes be a guide for identification. Any rubber soles or heels, their make, size, and type are also significant. The size of shoes can be determined from the length. Sometimes a distinct impression of the sole of the foot and the toes can be observed on the inner sole of a shoe, and this may be of value for comparison with shoes that may possibly be found in the house of a missing person. Any repairs may also be a guide in identification.

*Other objects.* Of great importance for identification are all objects found in the pockets of clothing or at the scene of the discovery that may be suspected of having belonged to the deceased. These objects are examined carefully for name, initials, trademarks, other markings, and the like. The description of a missing person may mention such objects, or possibly, relatives of the deceased may be able to identify them as belonging to the deceased. It may also be important to determine the application of a particular object that may be characteristic of a particular trade. It should also be noted that a particular collection of objects may be typical of, for example, a hiker or a person interested in sports, fish, or game, and so on.

## Estimating the Time of Death

In cases of murder, suicide, or suspicious death, the determination of the time of death is very important. The most reliable estimate of the time of death is determined from a variety of sources: postmortem changes, such as body temperature, rigor mortis, lividity, and decomposition, and information developed during the investigation such as the last time the victim was seen alive. The correct estimation of the time of death is important when interviewing suspects in a homicide investigation. Such information can serve to eliminate a suspect who was elsewhere at the time of death or to establish opportunity, i.e., the suspect could have been with the victim at the time of death. The investigator should realize that the estimate of the time of death is only an *estimate*. In certain unusual cases, a more precise determination can be made with the presence of other evidence.

### Postmortem Signs of Death

A number of postmortem changes occur after death that are useful in determining, within limits, the approximate time of death. The various methods available are useful to make estimates, that is, to determine ranges of times. The precise moment of death can be determined only in rare instances, such as when a clock was stopped by a bullet. The amount of time between the death and discovery of the body also has a bearing on the time of death estimate. The shorter the time interval between death and discovery of the body, the better the estimate of the time of death.

*Changes in the eyes.* After death, changes become noticeable in the eyes. The cornea becomes dull, and a film may appear over the eye. This may appear in several minutes to a few hours, depending on whether the eyelid is open or closed, temperature, humidity, and air current. Because of these factors, clouding of the cornea is not considered a reliable indicator of the time of death.

*Temperature of the body.* Cooling of the body is another sign of death. The rate of cooling depends on several factors, including the body temperature at the time of death, the temperature of the environment, body covering and clothing, and the relationship of the surface area to body weight. Body temperature will continue to fall until it reaches ambient temperature, which usually occurs in about 18 to 20 hours.

Body temperature is generally considered one of the more reliable indicators of the time of death up to approximately 18 hours. The usual procedure for determining body temperature is to insert a thermometer into the liver. A comparison between that temperature and ambient temperature is used to determine the approximate time of death.

*Rigidity of the body.* After death, the body becomes flaccid. Biochemical changes in the body produce a stiffening known as rigor mortis, which usually appears within 2 to 6 hours after death. Rigor mortis begins in the muscles of the jaw and neck and proceeds downward in the body to the trunk and extremities and is complete within 6 to 12 hours. The rigidity remains for 2 to 3 days and disappears in the same order in which it appeared.

An examination of the body for rigor mortis can indicate the time of death. If the rigidity is broken, it will generally not reappear unless the body is in the very early stages of rigor mortis. The victim's muscular development will affect the intensity of the rigidity. The very young and very old will likely develop less rigidity than adults with well-developed musculature.

Cadaveric spasm, or instantaneous rigor, is another form of rigidity of the voluntary muscles. It is characteristic of the final act of the victim, such as firing of a weapon. A gun or knife held rigidly in the victim's hand cannot be simulated after death.

*Lividity.* After blood circulation stops, blood settles to the lowest portions of the body because of gravity. This is noted by the appearance of blue or reddish violet marks on the skin (in cases of poisoning by carbon monoxide and cyanide the marks are "cherry red"; with potassium chlorate poisoning, the marks are light brown). The first indications of lividity occur in approximately 1 hour, with full development after 3 to 4 hours. Lividity can be confused with bruising or black-and-blue marks (Fig. 16.9). The pathologist can differentiate between the two during the autopsy.

Under certain conditions lividity can move or change if the body is moved or the position of the body is changed. Postmortem lividity does not form on parts of the body exposed to pressure, e.g., those parts that lie against the floor. If the position of the body or the position of articles of clothing pressing on the body is changed within 3 to 4 hours, the original lividity discolorations may partially disappear and new ones form. After this time, the original discoloration will remain. Even 9 to 12 hours after death, and sometimes later, new but successively weaker stains are produced when the position of the body is changed, although the discoloration that was first formed is usually fixed by this time and does not change. If there was a large blood loss, livid stains will be weak. As a rule, fresh livid stains are not produced by a change in position 12 hours after death.

Lividity discoloration provides two types of information. The degree or extent of discoloration is an indication of the time of death and can demonstrate a change of position or movement of the body several hours after death.

## Decomposition of the Body

The most certain sign of death, one that cannot be misinterpreted by anyone, is the beginning of putrefaction. Decomposition, or putrefaction, is a combination of two processes: autolysis and bacterial action. Autolysis, the softening and liquification of tissue, occurs by means of chemical breakdown of the body. Bacterial action results in the conversion of soft tissues in the body to liquids and gases.

Putrefaction begins immediately upon death and first becomes noticeable within 24 hours by a discoloration of the skin in the lower abdomen and groin. The discoloration has been described as greenish-red or blue-green and is pronounced within 36 hours. Bacterial action produces gases, causing the body to swell up, and an unpleasant odor becomes quite noticeable. The swelling is particularly noticeable in the penis, scrotum, breasts, and other areas of loose skin attachment.

Blisters filled with watery fluid and gas appear on the skin, which gradually darkens in color. The contents of the stomach may be forced out through the mouth, nose, and anus. Within 3 days, the entire body shows signs of decomposition. The rate of decomposition of the body is affected by the environment. Colder temperatures tend to impede putrefaction, whereas warmer temperatures increase it. Similarly, if the body is placed in water containing a large amount of bacteria, such as that from sewage effluent, decomposition is accelerated. A body in water generally decomposes more slowly because of colder tempera-

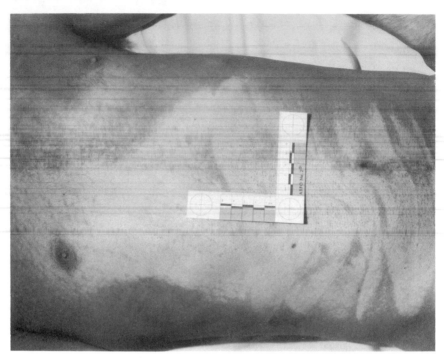

A

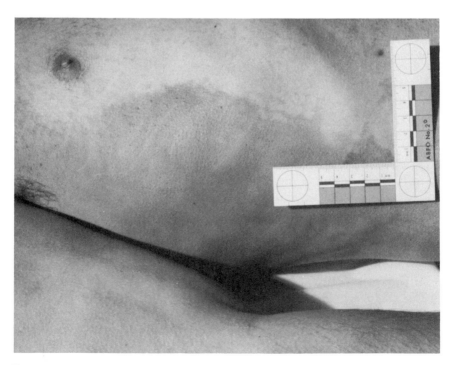

B

tures and lack of oxygen. Because the body has a greater specific gravity than water, it sinks initially. Prolonged submersion in water causes a wrinkling effect around the skin of the hands and feet. The body orients itself in a head-down position that sometimes results in scraping of the forehead when it comes into contact with the rough sea floor.

After a period of 3 to 4 days in warmer water and about a week in cold, the body will surface because of the formation of gas. Sometimes the skin and tissues burst and the body sinks again to the bottom. The process may repeat itself and the body floats to the surface again.

When a body is buried in a shallow grave with loose earth, it is destroyed fairly quickly; in 1 to 3 years all the soft tissue will disappear. The skeleton remains much longer but is generally destroyed within 10 years. These time figures will vary greatly according to the type of soil, amount of water, drainage, and other such factors. In peat bogs, for example, the body will remain relatively well preserved for many years. Bodies buried in clay soil decompose at a slower rate than in other soils.

In certain cases, bodies are relatively well preserved through mummification or the formation of adipocere, a wax-like substance caused by hydrolysis of body fat. In very dry conditions, putrefaction is retarded and mummification may begin. It can become complete in warm, dry air or when a body is buried in dry, porous earth. Formation of adipocere occurs in bodies located in damp environments such as swamps, wet soil, or even water. Adipocere is characterized by reasonably well preserved external contours of the body. Adipocere formation is noticeable in about 6 to 8 weeks and complete in 18 months to 2 years.

When a body lies in a cellar or other damp place, it may become completely covered with mold, which can leave black marks on the body. Buried bodies may also have mold present.

## Action of Insects and Other Animals on a Dead Body

When a dead body lies above ground, it is generally destroyed quickly by the action of insects and their larvae. Different kinds of insects lay their eggs in the body, and these rapidly develop into larvae (maggots) which, when weather conditions are favorable, can appear in such numbers that the dead body positively "teems with life." The body of an adult can be completely destroyed in less than 2 months, only the skeleton remaining; that of a child in less than a month. It has been found that the insects that appear on a body, either to feed on it or to lay their eggs in it, always come in a certain definite order, depending on the state of

FIGURE 16.9. Examples of postmortem lividity (A, B) showing that the body was lying face down at the time of death. (*Los Angeles County Department of Coroner.*)

decomposition of the body. This phenomenon has attained great importance in medico-legal practice, since by examining the insects found on
a body at a particular time, it is possible to obtain a good idea of how
long it has lain at a particular place.

The insects that typically first attack the body are flies. Even before
death actually occurs, flies may begin to lay their eggs in the body,
preferably in the mucous membrane (e.g., in the eyes, nose, and mouth)
but also in wounds and bloody parts of the body. The eggs are white,
about 1/16 inch long, and are laid in clumps. On a body lying indoors
they come especially from common houseflies (*Musca domestica*).
This may be a significant point in an investigation, since if eggs, larvae,
or pupae of houseflies are found in a body lying outdoors or buried, it
must be concluded that it has previously lain indoors. On bodies lying
outdoors it is chiefly common bluebottles (*Calliphora erythrocephala*),
greenbottles (*Lucilia caesar*), and sheep maggot flies (*Lucilia sericata*)
that lay their eggs. Flies can also lay their eggs in bodies buried in
shallow graves. After only 1 to 2 days, the larvae of the fly come out of
the eggs and immediately commence their work of destruction, changing into pupae after 10 to 14 days, and after a further 12 to 14 days the
flies emerge, to multiply again in their turn after a couple of weeks.

Among the beetles that live or multiply on a body, the burial beetles
and other kinds of carrion beetles should be noted first. These may
appear in enormous numbers on a dead body. Ants also attack bodies
and produce brownish withered areas and skin damage that, when
found in the face, may be mistaken for the effects of sulfuric acid
poisoning. When a body is buried immediately after death, the insects
are not able to lay their eggs in it, but the process of decomposition is
accelerated in that case by certain types of worms that bore into the
body. A certain species of fly can live and multiply for years in a buried
body.

When larvae, pupae, or insect eggs are found on a body or in its
clothing, there is a possibility of calculating the shortest time during
which it has lain at the scene. This applies also to fully developed
insects that, in their natural course, must have gone through all their
stages of development in the body. The examination should, of course,
be done by an entomologist.

If insects are to be sent for expert examination to an entomologist,
they are first killed by being placed in gasoline or a commercial insecti-
cide. They are then preserved and dispatched in 85% alcohol. Insect
eggs, larvae, and pupae are killed and preserved by placing them in 70 to
80% alcohol.

Unburied bodies are often attacked by animals. Rats attack the
projecting parts of bodies, e.g., nose, ears, and fingers. When they attack
the hands, the injuries may produce the impression of being defense

injuries. When such injuries are discovered, the pathologist should examine them immediately, since they dry comparatively quickly, making it difficult to decide on their origin. Other animals may also produce injuries on a body, and sometimes eat it. Gulls, ravens, and crows may eat the loose tissues, e.g., in the eye sockets. Bodies in water are exposed to injury from lampreys, crabs, lobsters, water beetles, and mackerel. Eels use the hollows of the body as hiding places, but do not eat it to any extent. Starfish cause injuries by attaching themselves firmly, the injury taking the same pattern as the animal itself.

## Other Indications of Time of Death

In certain cases, the pathologist can draw conclusions from the stomach contents and intestines regarding the time of the last meal, its quantity, and composition. The investigator can assist the pathologist by relaying any information found with regard to the composition of the last meal.

Watches and clocks may be valuable guides in determining the time of death. A clock may stop when it receives a blow during a struggle or is moved from its position, as may happen with an explosion or shot. When investigating a suspicious death, the police officer should therefore give careful attention to any clock found at the scene and should give indications in the report of the investigation regarding the position of the hands of the clock, noting whether it has stopped as a result of external action. If clocks or watches are running, it should be noted whether they are showing the right time, and the time at which they finally stop should be determined. In the case of alarm clocks the report should state the time for which the alarm was set and whether the ringing mechanism has run down or the alarm has been shut off. When a more detailed investigation is required, a watchmaker should be consulted.

Watches of older construction generally stop immediately if they come into contact with water, but a watch provided with a tight-fitting case and glass can run for a little while before stopping (Fig. 16.10). Watertight watches run for a long time under water. If a pocket watch or wristwatch is found on a body, the police officer should not carry out any further examination of it or do any tests, but should consult a watchmaker. Digital watches unfortunately do not lend themselves to these techniques.

In investigating cases of suspicious death, certain conditions can give a good indication of an approximate determination of the time of death. This may be obtained from papers and letters in a mailbox, dated receipts, the state of decomposition of food materials, the dampness of washing that has been hung up, dust on furniture, cobwebs, the evapo-

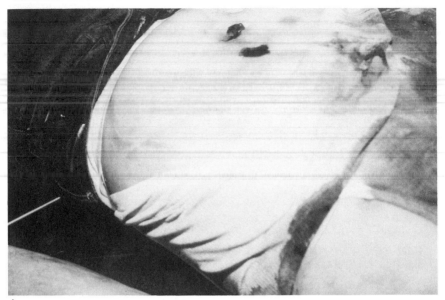

A

B

FIGURE **16.10.** A pocket watch absorbed the impact from a slug aimed at the decedent's torso. The abrasion on the decedent's abdomen (A) is from the watch, and the slug is shown in the position in which it was found. The watch (B) shows the small hand between 1:00 and 2:00 o'clock. The time that the witnesses placed the defendant at the decedent's home was approximately 1:30. (*Washoe County Coroner's Office, Reno, Nevada.*)

ration of liquid in a glass, cup, or other vessel, the withering of flowers, drying in flowerpots, date on a calendar or diary, food product dating codes, and so on.

When a dead body is found outdoors, the growth of vegetation under and around it can be a good guide in deciding the time when the body began lying there. Flowering plants may be buried and may thus indicate closely the time of burial. The coloring matter of plant leaves beneath the body undergoes certain changes; chlorophyll generally disappears after a week. A good indication can also be obtained from a comparison between the stage of growth of plants under the body and that of similar plants in the vicinity. When a body has lain in one place for a considerable time, in favorable cases, the decaying vegetation under it can indicate the time of year when the body was placed there. If the weather had changed, the amount of moisture under the body, compared with that in the surrounding area, may give some information. When a dead body is found in snow, its position in relation to the layers of snow produced by successive snowfalls should be determined accurately.

Some guidance may also be obtained from the extent of decay of clothing. Cotton fabrics decompose after 4 to 5 years; wool after 8 to 10 years; leather and silk only after 20 years or even longer.

## The Autopsy

The investigator present at the crime scene should also be present at the autopsy. The investigator's attendance is desirable so that the forensic pathologist can be briefed about pertinent finds at the crime scene as well as other information that will be of value in the examination. Additionally, information uncovered at the autopsy and communicated verbally by the pathologist to the homicide investigator will be helpful in the criminal investigation.

In addition to being photographed at the crime scene, the victim should be photographed at the morgue, both clothed and unclothed. The pathologist and investigator should be present and carefully examine the victim prior to undressing the body. Color photographs should be taken of all pertinent details: the overall appearance of the body, close-ups of the face, injuries, ligatures and marks, and the like. A scale should be included in the photographs.

Care should be taken in undressing the body. It should be undressed in the usual way; the clothing should not be cut, if possible. If cutting is required, care should be taken not to cut through bullet holes, knife cuts, tears, or stains. The garments should be packaged separately. If they are wet or blood-soaked, they should be allowed to air dry at room temperature and away from direct sunlight. The clothes should either be hung up to dry with paper draped loosely around each article of clothing to catch any trace material that might fall, or be carefully spread out on clean paper. It is important that bloodstained articles be properly preserved in order to obtain the most from serology testing (see Chapter 8 to review preservation procedures for bloody evidence).

After the clothes have been dried, they may be packaged for submission to the crime laboratory. The investigator and pathologist should be careful to establish a chain of custody of the evidence so it can be admissible in court.

Trace evidence present on the victim and the clothing should not be overlooked. If a litter is used to carry the body from the scene to the morgue, it should be carefully inspected for debris and trace material. Any trace evidence found on the body should be removed and properly packaged. Traces noted on the clothing should be removed and packaged only if there is a danger of losing that evidence in transit to the laboratory; otherwise, the traces should remain and be packaged with the clothing. Investigators at the scene may wish to leave written instructions for the forensic pathologist or assistant responsible for collecting trace evidence from the body when it arrives at the morgue. Of course, it is strongly recommended that homicide investigators make every attempt to be present at the autopsy and to discuss the case with the pathologist.

Following photography, initial examination, and undressing, the body should be fingerprinted. The surface of the body should be searched for bloody fingerprints. The techniques earlier described to obtain latent fingerprints from skin may be attempted on promising areas. Fingernail scrapings and hair samples should routinely be taken from all murder victims. A blood specimen should be collected during the actual postmortem examination.

The body should next be washed and rephotographed. Identity photographs of the victim's face should be taken at this time. The entire body, including injuries, should again be photographed. Photographs taken during the remainder of the autopsy may be of value in the subsequent investigation and should be encouraged. If the victim died as a result of a shooting, X-ray films are useful in finding the location of the bullet.

The purpose of the autopsy is to establish the cause of death as well as the circumstances immediately surrounding the time of death. The homicide investigator uses this information together with information gathered from other sources in the solution of the crime. The degree of care and skill with which the postmortem examination is conducted and the level of cooperation between the investigator and forensic pathologist have a significant bearing on the outcome of the case.

The remainder of this chapter discusses the various types of injuries by different modes encountered in death investigations.

## Injuries from External Mechanical Violence

Injuries from external mechanical violence are made by either blunt or sharp instruments.

*Injuries from blunt external violence* may consist of abrasions, contusions or bruises, crushing wounds, or bone injuries.

### Abrasions

Abrasions generally result from violence applied obliquely, but can occur from violence directed straight against the body, and may reproduce the shape of the weapon, e.g., the radiator of a car, or the details of the weapon's surface. As a rule, there is no bleeding. In a favorable case there is a possibility of deciding from which direction the body received the violence and, with some degree of certainty, what caused the injury. In general, it is very difficult to determine whether scraping of the epidermis was produced before or after death, and removal or undressing of the body must therefore be carried out with care, so that no injuries are produced.

Included in abrasions are fingernail marks that are narrow and usually somewhat curved. If the fingers slip, the nails produce scratches or tears.

### Contusions or Bruises

Contusions or bruises are injuries to the tissues and organs produced by blunt external violence and result from compression, usually against the parts of the skeleton lying underneath. The most usual type of contusion is an extravasation of blood; and when this is close to the skin it is commonly called a bruise or black-and-blue mark. In extravasation the blood comes out into the surrounding tissues and remains there without being able to get away either to the outside or to the body cavities. A bruise or black-and-blue mark initially shows a swelling and has, at first, a reddish color; it then assumes a blackish-blue to bluish-red color, changing gradually to brownish with strong shades of green and yellow. In rare cases a bruise resulting from a blow with a weapon will have the same form as the striking surface of the weapon used. If a bruise is found on a dead body, it may be concluded with certainty that the injury was produced when the person was living. At the autopsy, it is usually possible to determine whether a contusion has been produced some time before, or in direct connection with, the death. Only a pathologist can distinguish the livid stains found on a dead body from bruises.

Contusions may occur at places other than those where violence was applied. A blow against the back of the head, for example, can produce bruises around the eyes. Similarly, with an abnormal accumulation of blood in the blood vessels, as in cases of hanging or other forms of suffocation, bruises can appear in the face. Diffusion of blood may also appear in cases of poisoning and, in some diseases and infections of the blood, injury to the walls of the blood vessels.

### Crushing Wounds

Crushing wounds occur most readily, with blunt violence, at those places where the skin is near the bones. They are characterized by irregular form, gaping and swollen edges to the wound, and often con siderable bleeding into the surrounding tissues. The wound rarely takes the form of the object producing it, but an impression of the latter may be found. Sometimes a crushing wound is remarkably straight and even at the edges, this occurring when the skin breaks over the uniform edge of a bone, or where it splits along a parallel fibered tissue structure. Such a wound may give the impression of having been produced by a sharp weapon. This type of wound can, however, be detected with certainty, since in its deeper-lying parts the walls of the wound are uneven and connected together by bridges of elastic tissue.

A crushing wound resulting from a blow on the head with a hammer or the head of an ax sometimes has the same form as the round or angular edge that produced it. If a blow of this type is so powerful that the weapon penetrates the cranium, the injury to the latter may have the same form.

When blunt violence is used against the body, it is possible for vital organs such as the brain, heart, lungs, liver, spleen, and kidneys to be damaged without any visible external injury. Bite wounds are a special form of crushing wound. The form of a bite wound may reproduce the arrangement of the teeth of the person who caused it.

### Bone Injuries

Bone injuries may result from blunt external violence, for example, directed against the head. If a bone injury has occurred during life, diffusion of blood is generally found near or around it. Blunt violence against the cranium may produce a fracture. The direction of the crack often makes it possible to determine the direction from which the violence came.

*Injuries from sharp external violence* may consist of cutting wounds, stab wounds, or chopping wounds.

## Cutting Wounds

Cutting wounds have even, sharp edges. When the direction of cutting is across the direction of the fibers of elastic tissue, the wound gapes, but when the direction of cut is parallel to the fibers, the edges of the wound generally lie against one another. There is often great difficulty in deciding whether a cutting wound occurred during life or after death, since contusion injuries, which may form a guide in such cases, are not found around the wound. As a rule, a cutting wound is deepest at the place where the cutting object was first applied. The wound leaves hardly any detailed information about the instrument that caused it.

In cases of suicide the cutting force is generally directed against the throat or insides of the wrists, and sometimes against other parts of the body. The intent of the suicide is usually to produce bleeding by cutting the arteries. There may be one or several cuts, generally not of a dangerous type, that are parallel or run into one another. If it is established that such surface cuts were produced before the final fatal cut, it is quite certain that the case is one of suicide. Such surface cuts are made because the individual does not know how much force is required to produce a fatal cut, or because of fear of the anticipated pain. The police officer should not, however, draw hasty conclusions from superficial cuts that give the impression of having been made before the fatal cut. There is nothing to prevent a murderer, who has knowledge of these circumstances, from adding superficial cuts after making the fatal one in order to give the impression of suicide. Only a pathologist is competent to decide in what order the cuts were made. There have been cases of suicide in which the individual has made a number of trial cuts at places other than the one where the fatal cut was made. Such trial cuts, which as rule are superficial, may be situated on the temples, arms, or legs. In the case of an active or desperate person, the first cut may be a fatal one, but that does not prevent the victim from adding a number of others before losing consciousness.

A suicidal person generally cuts in the direction where the cutting hand is placed. When a right-handed person cuts his or her throat, the position of the cut is generally on the left side of the throat; if the victim is left-handed, the position is reversed. In regard to cuts in the throat, it should not be forgotten that a murderer may handle the weapon in exactly the same way as a suicide victim, if the murderer overcomes the victim from the rear.

In cases of suicide by cutting the throat, there may be incisions in the free hand that can easily be confused with defense injuries. Such wounds may be produced when the suicide victim stretches the skin of the neck with the free hand, so that the weapon can penetrate more easily. Wounds may also be produced from the blade itself being held in order to put more force into the cut.

In cases of death caused by cutting the throat, there is reason to suspect murder when the position of the wound does not correspond with a natural hold on the weapon, or the direction of the wound does not correspond with the right- or left-handedness of the victim. Murder may be suspected if the wound is very deep, or if it is irregular. Special attention should be given to the possible presence of fingernail marks and scratch injuries that would be produced if the murderer held the head of the victim fast, as well as to the presence of defense injuries on the hands and arms. If there are cuts on the clothing, the case may be one of murder, since suicide victims generally bare the part of the body that they intend to cut.

## Stab Wounds

Stab wounds are generally produced by a knife, dagger, or scissors, but may also result from other weapons, e.g., an ice pick, awl, pointed stick, and the like. If a stab wound has been produced by a sharp knife or dagger, it is not possible to determine the width of the blade from the size of the surface wound, since the wound channel is generally wider than the weapon, especially if it is two-edged. When the weapon is stuck into the body, the edge has a cutting action, so that the surface wound is considerably longer than the width of the blade, and when the weapon is withdrawn, it usually assumes a different position so that the wound is enlarged still further. The weapon may also be turned when being withdrawn, so that the surface wound becomes curved or angular. A knife with a thick back produces a wedge-shaped wound.

When stab wounds are produced with a weapon with a blunt point, the outer wound is smaller than the cross-sectional width of the instrument. In such cases, when the weapon is driven into the body, the elastic skin is actually pressed inward and stretched until it breaks; when the weapon is withdrawn the skin returns to its normal position and the external wound contracts. If the weapon is cone-shaped and rough, the skin around the wound may break in radial cracks.

With a stab wound in the heart, death may not occur immediately. If the heart is full of blood, death occurs instantly, but when there is only a little blood in it, it may be a while before the individual dies. There have been cases of persons surviving a wound in the heart.

When an attempt is made to commit suicide by stabbing, this is generally in the region of the heart or, in exceptional cases, in the stomach or other parts of the body. It is often found that a number of stab wounds are concentrated in a small, limited region, i.e., around the heart. In such a case, the individual has stabbed the body several times without result, in the same way as described above under "Cutting

Wounds." One fact that indicates suicide is that the clothes are unbuttoned or have been taken off. In suicide, the stab is generally directed into the body at right angles.

In cases of murder, the stab wounds are usually not concentrated in one place but scattered, especially when the victim has attempted self-defense. Knife stabs are, as a rule, directed in an oblique direction against the body, with the exception of cases when the victim was lying down. A number of deep wounds and wounds in the back indicate murder. When the victim tries self-defense, the wound channel may be curved as the result of the body's being in a certain position when it received the stab. At the autopsy it may be found that a wound channel does not go right through. This is due to the fact that the position of the body was such that the muscles were displaced from their normal position when they were penetrated (Fig. 16.11). In such a case the position of the dead person when stabbed can be reconstructed.

## Chopping Wounds

Chopping wounds are generally produced by an ax or, more rarely, by a blow with some other edged tool (e.g., a heavy knife, sword, broadax, or the like). Usually the wound is similar to a cutting wound, but is easily distinguished from the latter by a ring of contusion injury around the wound and by the crushing effect produced when the blow meets bony parts. If the edge of the weapon is deformed, tool marks may appear in these bony parts, which can, in favorable cases, lead to the identification of the weapon that was used.

When a person has been killed by a blow from an ax or other edged weapon, murder can nearly always be assumed. In cases of murder or other violent death from an ax, the wounds are generally in the head, and are in different directions. In certain cases they may have the same direction, as, for example, when a sleeping person, or one who is held, is struck. Usually the criminal first delivers a few blows with the head of the weapon before completing the job with the edge.

Suicide with an ax has occurred, but is rare. Generally, the individual directs the weapon against the forehead and crown of the head. The first blow is relatively light and produces only superficial injuries that are not in themselves fatal. The person then continues by putting more force in the blows and possibly using the weapon with greater accuracy, so that fatal injuries are produced. The wounds have a typical appearance that cannot be mistaken—they are directed from the forehead to the back of the head, approaching one another at the forehead.

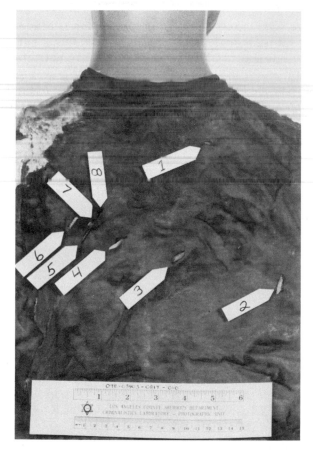

FIGURE **16.11.**  A bloodstained undershirt was placed on a mannequin to show more clearly the location of tears caused by stabbing. (*Los Angeles County Sheriff's Department.*)

## Marks or Damage on Clothing

In the reconstruction of events, marks or damage on clothing can be of great significance. An impression of the weapon causing the injury may be found on the clothing, in cases of blunt violence, and headgear may show a clear mark of a hammer or other tool. In the case of a blow against the head, the tool used may even chip out a piece or corner of the headgear, this piece having the same form as the striking surface of the weapon. An impression in the corresponding part of the outer clothing may show that a bruise on the body has resulted from a kick or from trampling. Impressions in clothing may be mixed with dust, dirt, or other contamination from the object producing the injury. Injuries to the clothes may be a good guide for the reconstruction of the course of events in a case of injury from cutting violence. In stabbing cases, the hole in the clothing may have a position different from that of the wound. A victim who has been stabbed may lift the arms in self-defense, so that the clothing moves out of its usual position on the body; in such cases the defensive position can be reconstructed. A garment perforated in several places by one and the same stab indicates that there were creases in the clothes.

## Defense Injuries

On the hands and arms of the victim of a murder are often injuries caused by the individual's attempt at self-defense. If a knife was used, the insides of the hands may be badly gashed from gripping the blade of the knife. Stab and cut wounds may be produced on the arms and hands when a victim attempts to parry an attack. When a crushing weapon is used in a murder, the hands of the victim may be badly injured from putting the hands on the head to reduce the violence of the blow. Among defense injuries are also included those injuries that occur when the victim attempts self-defense by attacking, e.g., injuries to the knuckles when using fists against the criminal, or breaking the nails when scratching.

## Firearm Injuries

Firearm injuries must be considered as a special group of injuries, since their investigation differs substantially in important respects from the investigation of other injuries. One might think that since a police officer should not touch a wound, it is not necessary to have a detailed knowledge of firearm injuries on a body. They are, however, so frequent and so important that whenever the pathologist cannot arrive in a reasonable time, the police officer should be prepared to make personal observations and to take whatever measures are necessary. As firearm injuries are frequently covered with blood, it is often impossible for a police officer to distinguish between a gunshot injury and one produced by other external mechanical violence. Under these circumstances it is necessary to wait patiently for the arrival of the pathologist; this holds even when it is of the greatest importance that the type of injury be determined at an early stage. The police officer should never probe in or around a gunshot wound, because that may destroy or reduce the chance of the expert's being able to determine the type of injury and to reconstruct the course of events.

*Bullet Injuries*

When a bullet strikes a body, the skin is first pushed in and then perforated while in the stretched state. After the bullet has passed, the skin partially returns to its original position, and the entry opening is drawn together and is thus smaller than the diameter of the bullet. The slower the speed of the bullet, the smaller the entry opening. The bullet passing through the stretched skin forms the so-called "contusion ring" around the entrance opening, as the bullet slips against the skin that is pressed inward and scrapes the external epithelial layers. The skin itself, in the contusion ring, becomes conspicuous by drying after some hours. In a favorable case, rifling marks on the bullet leave such a distinct mark in the contusion ring that the number of grooves in the rifling can be counted. The combined section of the contusion ring and entrance opening corresponds to the caliber of the bullet, or exceeds it slightly. When a bullet strikes the body squarely, the contusion ring is round; when it strikes at an angle it is oval.

Along with the contusion ring there is another black-colored ring, the smudge ring, which often entirely covers the contusion ring. This does not contain any powder residues or contamination from the bore of the firearm, but consists wholly of small particles originating from the surface of the bullet. The smudge ring may be absent in the case of clean-jacketed bullets or when the bullet has passed through clothing.

A bullet passing through the body forms a track that is usually straight, but can also be bent at an angle in an unpredictable manner if the bullet meets or passes through a bone. Thus it is not possible to determine with certainty, from observation of the entrance and exit openings, the direction of the weapon when the shot was fired. This direction must be calculated by the pathologist from the results of the autopsy. The velocity of the bullet has a great influence on the appearance of the track; straight tracks indicate a high velocity, and bent or angular ones indicate a low velocity.

In gunshot injuries in soft parts of the body, especially in the brain, the bullet can produce a considerable explosive effect, which is greatest with unjacketed or soft-nosed bullets from large caliber firearms. Such a bullet may split into several parts, each of which forms its own track, and thus there may be *several exit wounds*. When such a bullet strikes the head, large parts of the cranium can be blown away and the brain scattered around. A soft-nosed bullet that, before hitting the body, is split by striking against a tree branch, can produce a number of regular entrance holes.

A shot through the head is not always fatal. To be immediately fatal the bullet must either produce a bursting effect or injure an artery of the brain or a vital brain center. A shot through the brain that is not immediately fatal does not always produce unconsciousness. Even when the heart has been perforated by a bullet, it occasionally happens that the injured person lives for several hours, retaining some capacity for movement.

It is often difficult to distinguish the exit wound from the entrance wound, especially from a shot at long range with a metal-jacketed bullet, assuming, of course, that the bullet passes through the body intact. In a favorable case, the exit wound may have a ragged appearance with flaps directed outward. To determine the direction of the shot with certainty in such a case, an autopsy is necessary (Fig. 16.12). If the bullet has been damaged by its passage through the body, or if there has been a bursting effect, then it is generally easy to determine the exit wound, which is then considerably larger than the entrance wound and shows a star-shaped, ragged character, with flaps directed outward. Note, however, that in contact shots the entrance wound may be ragged and star-shaped. A bullet that ricochets may strike with its side or obliquely and produce a large and characteristic entrance wound.

## Close and Distant Shots

It is very important to be able to estimate the distance from which a shot was fired. In many cases this fact is the only evidence available that can distinguish between suicide, a self-defense killing, manslaughter, or murder.

In practice, a distinction is made between contact, close, and distant shots. A *contact shot* is one in which the muzzle of the weapon is pressed against the body when the shot is fired. In a *close shot*, the distance of the muzzle is less than about 18 inches from the body, whereas a *distant shot* is one fired at a distance greater than 18 inches (see Figs. 16.13 and 16.14).

In the case of a contact shot against an exposed part of the body, soot, metallic particles, and powder residues are driven into the body and can be found there during the autopsy. Blackening, caused by soot and powder, around the entry opening is often absent. A contact shot against a part of the body protected by clothing often produces a powder zone on the skin or in the clothes, and soot, powder residue, and fragments of clothing are driven into the track. In a contact discharge, the entrance wound differs considerably from an entrance wound in a close shot or distant shot. When the shot is fired, the gases of the explosion are driven into the track, but they are forced out again and produce a bursting effect on the skin and clothes. The entrance wound is often star-shaped with flaps directed outward. It is also possible, in a contact shot, for the muzzle of the weapon to mark the skin, causing an impression that reproduces the shape of the muzzle of the weapon (Fig. 16.15).

454

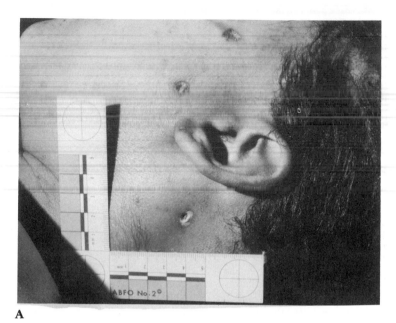

A

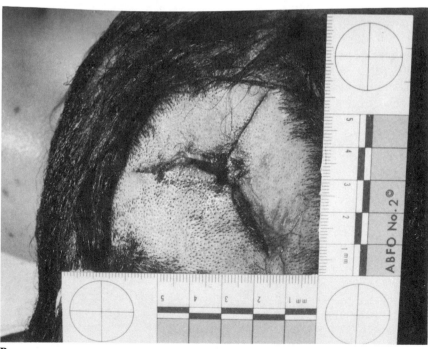

B

FIGURE **16.12.** Bullet entry (A) and exit (B) wounds to the head. (*Los Angeles County Department of Coroner.*)

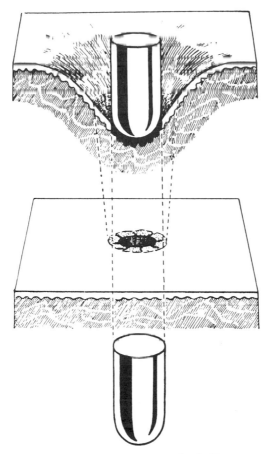

FIGURE **16.13.** Diagrammatic representation of a bullet penetrating the skin. The skin is pressed inward, stretched, and perforated in the stretched condition, after which it returns to its original position. The entry opening is smaller than the diameter of the bullet. Immediately around the opening is the contusion ring, caused by the bullet's rubbing against this part of the skin and scraping off the external layer of epithelial cells.

A close shot produces a zone of blackening around the entrance wound of the track, either on the skin or on the clothes. Sometimes the flame from the muzzle has a singeing action around this opening, hair and textile fibers being curled up. The zone of blackening is formed of substances carried along with the explosion gases. When a cartridge is fired, the bullet is forced through the barrel of the weapon by the explosion gases. Only a small amount of this gas passes in front of the bullet. The combustion of the powder is never complete even with smokeless powder and still less with black powder, and the explosion

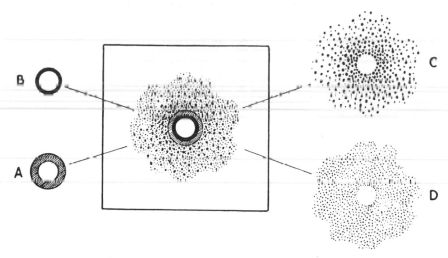

FIGURE 16.14. A diagram showing the marks that may be found around the entry opening of a bullet in a close shot: (A) contusion ring, (B) smudge ring, (C) grains of powder, and (D) deposit of powder residue.

gases therefore carry with them incompletely burned powder residues, the amount of which decreases as the distance increases. Thus, in a close shot, a considerable amount of incompletely burned powder residue is found on the target. Together with this residue, the gases also carry along impurities from the inside of the barrel, consisting of rust (iron), oil, and particles rubbed off the bullet. Metallic residues from the percussion cap and cartridge case also occur in the gases of the explosion. If the shot is fired at right angles to the body, the zone of blacken-

FIGURE 16.15. In a contact shot, the weapon is pressed against the head or the body. The gases from the explosion expand between the skin and the bone, producing a bursting effect and a ragged entrance wound.

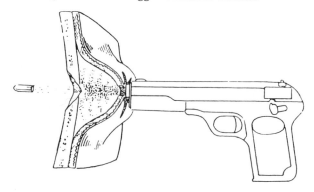

ing is practically circular; if fired obliquely, the zone is oval. The extent of the zone of blackening is often difficult to determine by direct observation, and it is often better to photograph it, using infrared-sensitive material, which intensifies the zone of blackening so that its extent is more easily determined. The zone of blackening gives valuable information for determining the distance from which a shot has been fired, which may be an important factor in deciding between murder and suicide. It is important that comparative test shots be fired with the *same weapon* and *same type of ammunition* as those used in the actual crime.

*Close shots* with black powder show marks of burning up to a distance of 4 to 6 inches, and a distinct deposit of powder smoke up to 10 to 12 inches. Dispersed grains of powder embedded in the target may be detected even at a distance of 3 feet.

A *distant shot* is one in which none of the characteristics of a close shot can be detected (distance over about 18 inches).

*Powder residues* occur on the object fired at in the form of incompletely and completely burned particles. A careful microscopic examination should precede any chemical examination, as it is often possible to establish in this way the shape and color of unburned powder particles and to distinguish many kinds of powder (Figs. 16.16 and 16.17).

Black powder, which consists of potassium nitrate, sulfur, and char-

**FIGURE 16.16.** Close shot, short distance. Both incompletely burned powder grains and smoke deposits in the zone of blackening. The powder grains are concentrated immediately around the entrance hole.

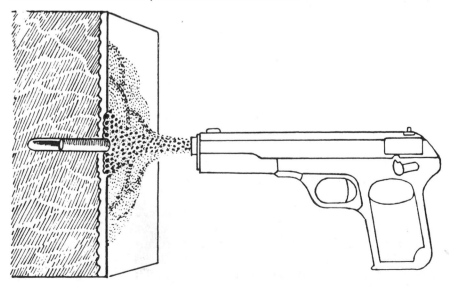

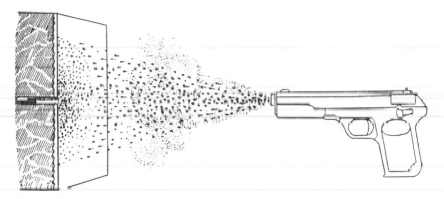

FIGURE **16.17.** Close shot, greater distance than in Figure 16.16. Unburned powder grains, but no smoke deposits, in the zone of blackening.

coal, is identified by the presence of potassium and nitrate in the entrance wound. Smokeless powder consists chiefly of nitrocellulose or of nitrocellulose with nitroglycerine and is identified by the presence of nitrite, which can be detected by various microreactions. The grains of smokeless powder are generally coated with graphite and occur in many forms (e.g., round or angular discs, pellets, and cylinders).

*Marks from primers.* At one time, a primer generally contained a percussion composition of fulminate of mercury, stibnite (antimony sulfide), and potassium chlorate with a varying amount of powdered glass. Primers now have eliminated the mercury and the rust-forming products from the potassium chlorate. This has resulted in the replacement of the mercury fulminate by lead compounds such as lead azide and lead styphnate (lead trinitroresorcinate) and in the replacement of the potassium chlorate by barium nitrate. Stibnite is still used, however, to a limited extent.

Thus, in a chemical examination of a gunshot injury, the metals that first come into question are barium, lead, and antimony. By determining, for example, the lead content of a bullet wound and comparing it with that obtained from a test discharge against a similar object with the same ammunition from different distances, it is possible, in favorable cases, to obtain quite reliable information regarding the distance from which the actual shot was fired.

*Traces from bullets.* In injuries from plain lead bullets, such as are usually used in ordinary revolver ammunition, there is always a considerable amount of lead, both in the zone of blackening and in the smudge ring; and in the latter it is even possible to detect lead from a distant shot. Lead traces from the surface of the bullet can also be found frequently in the exit hole. In some types of ammunition, the bullet is greased; residues from these substances may be carried along with the bullet and found around the entrance opening. Metal-jacketed bullets, which are used chiefly for automatic weapons, consist of an inner lead core with an outer shell of some hard metal or alloy—the so-called jacket—the usual material being copper, cupronickel, or brass. Traces of all these metals may be found in gunshot injuries.

*Traces from cartridge cases.* It is often possible to detect copper in the track and in perforated clothing, up to a range of 6 to 8 inches. This comes from the cartridge case, from which small particles of metal are worn off by the expansion pressure. Large amounts of copper found in the dirt ring are considered a characteristic indication of a close shot. If, however, a copper-coated bullet has been used, then naturally no conclusion can be drawn regarding the possibility of a close shot, since in this case even a distant shot shows a distinct amount of copper.

*Traces from the barrel of the weapon.* Iron can be found in and around the entrance wound in a case of shooting with a weapon that has not been used for a long time, and the barrel of which may therefore be rusty. With automatic hand weapons, traces of iron can be detected up to a distance of 8 to 12 inches.

*Injuries from small shot.* With shotguns, the shot column can have a very concentrated effect at distances up to 1 yard. With a distance of up to 4 to 8 inches, the wound is practically circular. The greater the distance, the more irregular the wound. At a distance of up to 2 to 3 yards, there is generally a central entrance opening, and around it are single small holes from individual scattered shot. At a greater distance, the shot spreads out more into small groups; at 10 yards the scattering can amount to 12 to 16 inches.

*Damages to clothes from shooting.* If a shot has passed through clothes, the position of the bullet hole should be compared with the direction of the wound track in the body in the same way as described previously under the heading "Marks or Damage on Clothing."

## Modes of Death

### Death from Shooting

In suicide, the weapon is usually directed against the forehead, temple, or heart, and a shot fired upward and obliquely into the mouth is quite common. In deciding whether a case is one of suicide, an attempt should first be made to determine the extent to which the victim could have fired the shot in the approximate direction given by the track. In the case of pistol or revolver shots against the temple, it is necessary to know whether the deceased was right- or left-handed. It should be remembered that a person may fire a weapon with the left hand but be otherwise right-handed.

It is an essential condition for the assumption of suicide that the victim has been wounded by a close discharge, and that the weapon is lying in the proper position with respect to the body. If these conditions indicate suicide, the question should not, however, be considered as settled, since there is nothing to prevent some other person from firing the shot under the given conditions and then laying the weapon down in the proper position.

A more certain indication is available if injuries are found on the hand of the dead person that are produced when firing a shot, in the form of a mark on the thumb or forefinger or on the web of the thumb. Such marks may result from the recoil of the slide of an automatic pistol. The most certain proof of suicide is found in the form of fragments of tissue and blood spattered from the wound onto the hand of the dead person. Although, in cases of suicide, the hand of the deceased may be found to be blackened by powder, this cannot be taken as a proof since the weapon could have been pressed in the hand after the shot was fired. It is also necessary to decide whether the body is in a natural position under the circumstances. A fairly certain sign of suicide is when the person has taken off any hindering clothes or exposed some part of the body before firing. If the weapon is not present near the body, this is a very suspicious circumstance, but hasty conclusions should not be drawn from that fact alone. There have been cases in which a fatally injured person has traveled a long way before finally expiring or has thrown the weapon into a body of water. It has also happened that members of the victim's family have removed the weapon to deliberately create an appearance of murder, sometimes in the hope of escaping what they consider to be the disgrace of a suicide in the family.

It is a certain indication that a person died through the action of some other person when the discharge was beyond arm's reach. By arm's reach is meant the length of the arm plus possible assistance from an extension in the form of a stick or some other convenient means of reaching the trigger of a long-barreled weapon. It is true that it is possible to commit suicide by means of a distant shot, but this requires arrangements of such a type (string-pulls, etc.) that there should be no difficulty in revealing the truth. When the fatal shot was fired from behind, it is safe to assume that it is not suicide. An individual *could* fire a shot at the back of the head, but such a possibility is very far-fetched. The fact that the shot person has more than one injury cannot always be taken as a proof that death was caused by the action of some other person. Cases occur in which a person intent on suicide has fired two or possibly a number of shots, each of which producing a lethal wound, before becoming incapable of continuing the firing.

It is quite common for a person to be shot fatally either by accident or through personal fault. While hunting, it is possible to slip or stumble on rough ground, fall when climbing over a gate or other obstacle, or drop the weapon, whereupon a fatal shot may be fired. In such cases, there are generally marks at the scene of the accident or marks on the weapon that give a clear indication of what has happened. A fatal shot may also be fired accidentally when handling a firearm, e.g., when cleaning it. In such cases, the investigating officer should observe the greatest caution, and not assume from the start that the shooting was an accident. The victim may very well have committed suicide while giving the incident the appearance of an accident; a murderer may also simulate an accident. The police officer who carries out the investigation of a fatal shooting must not attempt to carry out any experiments that trespass on the sphere of activity of the pathologist or criminalist. However, it may be necessary to undertake precautionary measures in connection with evidence that for some reason may be exposed to destruction. It has been stated before that in and around a gunshot wound there may be found traces of incompletely burned powder residues, traces of metals from the primer, cartridge case, and bullet, grease and dirt from the bullet and from the barrel of the weapon, and other such evidence. These marks may be of decisive significance in determining, for example, the distance of the shooting, and they must therefore be protected as much as possible. In cases in which the bullet has gone through the clothes, there is always the risk that evidence may be destroyed by rain or by moving the dead body. The police officer should therefore protect such evidence against destructive action by any suitable means, for example, by covering the actual place or, in suitable cases, by fixing loose layers of clothing in a particular position by tying or pinning. If there is any risk that the bullet hole in the clothes may become soaked with blood when the body is moved, the police officer must find some method of preventing it.

The hand that holds the firearm at the instant of firing can become blackened by powder in the area of the web of the thumb and on the thumb and forefinger. The deposit of powder smoke produced in this way can be identified chemically. The hand of a dead body may, if necessary, be protected by wrapping in clean paper bags.

*Explosion injuries* are a variation of gunshot injuries. An explosive charge contains metal parts or is enclosed in a metal container that breaks up (e.g., a hand grenade). When it fractures metal objects, stones, or the like in the immediate vicinity, the fragments thrown off have an exceptionally great force that, however, quickly decreases. When such pieces from an exposion hit a nearby body, they can produce very severe damage. A small splinter of only a few millimeters diameter can perforate the brainpan. When it penetrates the body, it bores a wound channel that can easily be mistaken for a bullet track. The energy in a fragment from an explosion decreases so rapidly that generally it is not able to penetrate the body. At close quarters air pressure alone can cause fatal injury, thus the lungs may be ruptured if an individual has his mouth open during an explosion.

The fatal effect of an explosive charge is limited to the immediate vicinity; at a greater distance air pressure may cause injury from falling. Another way of committing suicide is to detonate dynamite in the mouth. The effect of such an explosion is generally that the head is torn away, while the skin of the back of the neck, with adhering bone and soft parts, is left on the neck. Suicide by explosion in the mouth can be carried out with nothing more than a blasting cap. In this case, the injuries are to the throat and organs of breathing. Generally, no damage is visible in the face; the lips and the skin of the face remain uninjured. Suicide has also been achieved by an explosive charge placed on the chest, in which extensive lacerations are produced.

The police officer should remember that wounds should be photographed, even when they are on a living person. The officer should therefore try to contact the doctor who has treated an injured person in order to discuss the possibility of photographing. This should not be delayed long, since a wound changes its appearance as it heals. Especially in the case of bite wounds, and wounds of which the form reveals the character of the weapon or instrument, it is important that photographing should be done before a scab forms or an operation becomes necessary. A scale should always be laid next to the wound.

## Death by Suffocation

The actual mode of suffocation death may be by hanging or strangulation, by hand or ligature, by covering the mouth or nose, blocking the larynx or windpipe, by crushing to death or drowning.

*Hanging.* A mode of death in which a cord is placed around the neck and tightened by the weight of the body constitutes hanging. The effect of hanging is that the blood circulation to the brain ceases very quickly, which produces immediate unconsciousness, while at the same time the air passages are closed up so that respiration ceases. The action of the heart may actually continue, so that death occurs only after some minutes. With violent modes of hanging, injury may be produced to the vertebrae and spinal cord. The noose need not be very tight, since only a small part of the weight of the body needs to be taken up for the hanging to be effective. The body does not, therefore, need to hang free. The effect is the same whether the hanging occurs with the body supported in a leaning, kneeling, sitting, or lying position. No one can escape from a tight-drawn noose once hanging in it, because vagal inhibition occurs rapidly. This has been shown by a number of cases of deaths of persons who wished to try the effect of a hanging without any intention of completing it—they found themselves unable to recover from their situation. Thus children have been killed by hanging when, from curiosity, they wanted to test a hangman's noose. Similarly, there have been cases in which a hanging situation has been arranged to obtain a perverse sexual stimulation. The commonly held view that death by hanging may be preceded by voluptuous sensations is, however, certainly incorrect.

In suicide by hanging, it quite frequently happens that the rope breaks and the individual falls down, but subsequently repeats the hanging with another rope and possibly at another place. This may necessitate tedious investigations, since the suicidal individual may have contracted bleeding injuries at the time of the fall or when, after the unsuccessful attempt, wandering around in a daze. In such a case, wounds, marks of blood, and disorder at the scene might be incorrectly interpreted as signs of a struggle.

The rope used is generally slender cord (e.g., a clothesline), but other objects may be used (e.g., belts, suspenders, towels, scarves, thick shoelaces, and the like). After hanging, there is usually found a typical mark on the neck—the so-called hanging groove. The broader and softer the noose, the less clearly the hanging groove shows. This is also the case when some part of the clothing comes between the noose and the neck. As a rule, however, the groove is distinct and full of detail, and it is often possible to distinguish marks of twisting, knots, and irregularities, and the width of the cord used can be calculated quite accurately.

The hanging groove generally has a typical appearance. The greatest pressure is exerted opposite the suspension point (i.e., if suspended from the back of the neck, the noose, if it is sufficiently thin or narrow, may have pressed in so deeply on the front side that it lies almost concealed by a roll of flesh. The groove then runs upward at an angle around the side of the neck, becomes less marked, and finally fades away as it approaches the back of the neck. The edges of the groove are generally puckered in the direction in which the cord slipped when the noose tightened. When hanging occurs in a lying or inclined position, the groove may be more horizontal, which gives it a certain similarity to a strangulation groove, from which it can easily be distinguished by the fact that the hanging groove is less marked and disappears at the back of the neck. In cases of strangling, in which the criminal's hands were held between the loop and the neck, the groove also disappears in the direction toward the hands. In general, however, the fingernails or knuckles produce such a great pressure against the neck that contusions appear in the skin. In rare cases the noose may be applied at an angle on the neck or right at the back of the neck, but the effect intended is still obtained, since the large arteries of the neck are compressed effectively even when this method of hanging is used. Sometimes the noose may slip upward after the first tightening, whereby two or more hanging grooves are produced. This may give rise to suspicion of a crime, but generally the pathologist finds no difficulty in elucidating the actual circumstances.

It can happen that a hanged person's fingers are found between the noose and the neck. This is not due to an attempt to loosen the noose, but rather to the fingers not having been removed when the noose tightened.

Dead persons may show, on the skin of the neck, marks that can easily be confused with hanging grooves. Such marks can be produced by articles of clothing pressing against the neck. On bodies that have been in water for a long time, or that are undergoing decomposition, the hanging groove may have disappeared.

Murder by hanging must be considered an extremely rare occurrence, and would be used only against children or persons who are unconscious or unable to defend themselves. In such cases it is to be expected that the victim will show injuries other than those that occur from hanging. A murderer may attempt to give the appearance of suicide by hanging up the body after the onset of unconsciousness or death. If this is done by hoisting up the body, distinct clues are usually present on the supporting object and on the rope. For example, a branch of a tree may show such a clear mark of rubbing on the bark that there is no difficulty in elucidating the actual circumstances—especially when the rope has also slipped sideways. On the part of the rope that has lain on and slipped against the support, the fibers are always directed upward against the latter.

Persons who have committed suicide by hanging sometimes show other injuries that in themselves could be fatal. In such cases, hanging has been employed after an unsuccessful attempt to kill themselves in some other way. Such cases are, however, easy to distinguish from those in which hanging is the final phase in a murder, since the local conditions generally give a clear picture of the course of events.

When a body is hanging free but there is no jumping-off point in the vicinity, such as a chair, table, step, stone, or stump, then there is every reason to suspect murder. In such cases the scene must be examined carefully in order to determine whether it was possible for anyone to have climbed up to the point of attachment. It is easy to find marks of climbing in trees (e.g., twigs broken off or leaves, bark, or moss torn away), and similar traces should be found on the clothing of the dead person. An easily removable starting point, e.g., a chair, may actually have been removed by mistake before the arrival of the police.

In cases of hanging, livid stains are strongly marked on the feet, legs, and hands, as well as immediately above the hanging groove. If such marks should be found (e.g., on the back of a freely hanging body), there is a question of the hanging having been done some time after death. The same question arises in a case when the arms or legs are bent, as it is possible that the body may have been hung up after the onset of rigidity. After the rigidity has relaxed and the limbs have become straight, in some cases the wrinkles remaining in the clothes can indicate that the limbs were previously bent.

The presence of dirt on the clothes (e.g., leaves, parts of plants, soil, dust, or other material) that is not present at the scene of the hanging should be noted especially, as should the presence of blood, saliva, or urine flowing in the wrong direction. Such observations may give rise to suspicion of a crime. If the knots and noose are formed in such a way that it is doubtful whether the dead person could have made them, this must be considered as a suspicious circumstance.

In suicide by hanging, right-handed persons usually place the knot of the noose on the right-hand side of the neck; left-handed persons place it on the left. Reversal of these positions is suspicious.

When investigating a case of hanging, the police officer should always have in mind that the autopsy can rarely decide between murder and suicide. As a rule, the course of events can be determined only from examination of the scene and from police investigation.

*Strangling.* This is usually done by hand or with a cord. In strangulation by hand, death sometimes occurs almost immediately from shock, but usually the squeezing of the neck arteries is incomplete, so that death results from interruption of the supply of air to the lungs (Fig. 16.18).

In strangulation by hand, there are typical fingernail marks on both sides of the throat—from the fingernails on one side and from the thumbnail on the other. If the criminal is right-handed the mark of the thumbnail is generally on the right side of the throat, and on the left side if the criminal is left-handed. There are often marks of several grips with the hands and abrasion of the skin where the fingers slipped. When death has occurred from shock, marks of nails may be missing. Strangulation is generally preceded by a struggle, so that other injuries may be found on the body, usually scratches or bleeding on the face, as well as marks on the clothes.

Strangulation by hand has nearly always resulted from extraneous violence (i.e., by another person), although individual cases of suicide

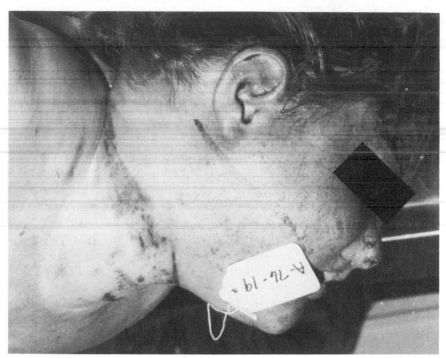

**A**

**B**

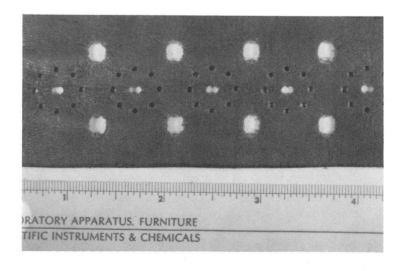

**C**

by strangulation by hand have occurred, the individual using a passive support for the hands so that the grip does not slip on the occurrence of unconsciousness. In strangulation by ligature, death occurs in the same way as with hanging, but the strangulation groove generally has a course and appearance different from that of a hanging groove. Usually, it goes around the neck in a horizontal direction, or its back part may be situated somewhat lower down on the neck than the front part on the throat. In some cases it can, like the hanging groove, be directed back and upward. The strangulation groove is usually located lower down on the neck than the hanging groove.

Strangulation with a cord can generally be considered as murder, and defense injuries are usually found on the victim. Such injuries may be absent if the victim was overcome from behind, or if strangled when sleeping, unconscious, or otherwise defenseless. In a case in which the cord is left on the throat after the crime, it is generally fixed tightly by means of a number of turns and knots.

Strangulation with a cord is a rare form of suicide. In those cases in which suicide can be presumed, the strangling has been carried out with a running noose or by a scarf, rope, or the like, laid around the neck and knotted with a half knot that is drawn so tightly that the neck arteries are compressed and unconsciousness supervenes. In both cases, one can expect that the hands will hold the noose fast after death, or that their position relative to it will give clear evidence of suicide.

*Investigating the scene of a hanging or strangling.* The procedure to be followed should be the same as described previously for the investigation of murder in general. It is important that the police officer learn something about how the knots and nooses that occur in hanging and strangling are made. The formation of knots and nooses of a certain type often indicates whether or not the person hanged could have personally made them. When a knot or noose is of such a type that it could not have been made by the victim, then this must cause suspicion. There is reason for being suspicious when, in a case of hanging or strangling, skillfully made knots and nooses have been found.

In describing knots and nooses, the usual names may be used, but it is not to be expected that everyone who reads the report will be familiar with them. Their construction should therefore be reproduced by a diagrammatic sketch or sketches, and they should also be photographed.

---

FIGURE **16.18.** Strangulation marks on the victim's throat (A) are similar to a suspect belt submitted for comparison (B) and (C). (*Iowa Department of Public Safety.*)

The noose should be examined immediately, and the origin of the material used should be determined as quickly as possible. If one or both ends of the cord have been recently cut and the corresponding pieces are not found at the scene, these circumstances must be eluci- dated. Cut-off portions of the material of the noose are often found at the scene, and in such a case scissors or another edged tool should be found in a likely place.

The ground under or around a hanged person must be investigated as soon as possible, so that any evidence that may be present will not be destroyed. If the individual was murdered and then hanged to give the appearance of suicide, it is to be expected that distinct evidence will be found, as considerable effort is required to hang up a dead body.

It is not uncommon for a person to commit suicide by hanging or strangling and, at the same time, to take measures to give the incident the appearance of murder. These measures may consist of binding the legs and attempts to bind the hands, but this, especially the attempt to bind the hands, is easily detected. The individual may also have used some kind of gag (e.g., a handkerchief), which is pushed in or bound around the mouth.

Knots in a hanging noose should not be undone or cut except in cases where the victim's life may still be saved. Where it is possible, cut the rope or cord some distance above the head, loosen the noose, and pull it over the head (Fig. 16.19).

The taking down of the deceased body must be done very carefully so that no new injuries are produced. A convenient way is to raise the body a little so that the cord slackens, and then cut the cord. The body is laid down and the noose is allowed to remain on the body. After the noose has been examined and photographed in its original condition, it is up to the pathologist to remove it during the autopsy.

The part remaining on the carrying object should be cut off at such a point that the knots are not altered or damaged, after which the cut-off parts are immediately bound together with string. If, for example, a cord is wound in several turns around the carrying object, a diagrammatic sketch of the arrangement is drawn as a reminder, after which the cord is cut and immediately wound around a similar object of the same diameter. When the line is composed of several parts (double or multi- ple), they are cut one by one and tied together in succession with cord or thread.

In cases in which it is suspected that an already dead body has been hung up, the fibers in the cord must be protected, most conveniently by placing the cord stretched out in a long box, so that it hangs freely. It can be held fast by loops attached by pins to the sides of the box.

What has been said about removing the hanging noose and strangling cord is the principal rule in all ordinary cases in which it is to be

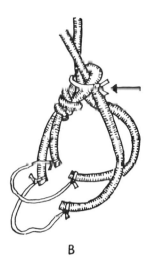

A                                    B

FIGURE **16.19.** When removing a noose from the neck of a body, the knots should not be disturbed or loosened. A fixed noose should be cut off and the ends immediately bound together (A). With a running noose, the position of the knot on the standing part (see arrow) is fixed, after which the noose is cut off. If the noose consists of a number of parts, they are cut, and the ends are bound together (B).

expected that the life of the individual can be saved. If, however, the body has been dead for a long time (certain signs of death being present, e.g., putrefaction), the noose or cord is left in an untouched condition. It is for the pathologist to examine it when making the postmortem examination. When, for any reason, the investigating officer has to remove the noose or cord from such a body, the knots must not be deranged or loosened. A running noose can be loosened so far that it can be slipped over the head, but before this the position of the knot on the fixed part should be marked in some way (e.g., with chalk), by sticking in a piece of wire or winding a thread around it. If the noose is tight and cannot be passed over the head, it is cut off at a convenient point, generally at one side of the neck, after which the ends are immediately tied together with string. The same method is used when conditions are such that for some reason the cord cannot be loosened and drawn over the head. In such a case, the position of the knot on the fixed part is marked, after which the cutting is done.

In cases of strangulation, the ligature should be removed in the same way as a noose in the case of hanging. Special care should be taken not to cut through knots that may not be visible from the outside. In general, the ligature should be removed in such a way that the manner of application may be reliably reconstructed. This may require photography and simple sketches to illustrate the various layers and knots that may be present.

As the knots in a cord may be required as evidence, they must be sealed in a suitable manner, and the circumference of the constructive loops should be measured and recorded.

*Blocking of the mouth or nose.* This is a rare cause of death and most commonly happens to newborn children. The stoppage may result either from a pillow or another soft object being pressed against the face or from a hand pressed against the mouth and nose, so that death occurs from suffocation. Suffocation may also result from the mouth and nose being stopped with, for example, cotton, a handkerchief, or piece of cloth. When a pillow or other soft material is used, there are no typical marks, but saliva or mucus may stick on the cushion in such a quantity and in such a way that it can give some information about the course of events. It should, however, be remembered that a number of cases may be accidents, such as happen when a child turns onto his or her face. When suffocation is done by hand, scratches may be produced on the face. If it is suspected that the mouth and nose have been stopped with cotton, for example, which was later removed, one should look for telltale signs (Fig. 16.20).

In exceptional cases, old persons may be killed by blocking the mouth and nose with a soft covering. Murder can also result when a criminal, without intending to kill, has attempted to silence the cries of the victim (e.g., in a case of rape).

*Blocking of the larynx and air passages.* Blocking can occur, for example, when food goes down the "wrong way," or vomited stomach contents are unable to get out through the mouth. Infanticide can be committed by a finger pressed down in the throat of an infant so that death results from suffocation. In this case, there will be serious injuries in the mouth and throat.

*Squeezing to death.* This can occur, for example, during panic in a crowd, when the victim is squeezed or trampled, or when a person comes under a heavy falling object or is buried by a fall of earth. The external injuries in such cases are generally considerable and easily interpreted. Squeezing to death can generally be considered as an accident, but the possibility should also be kept in mind that an earth slide was arranged with the intention of murder.

*Drowning.* This is death as a result of liquid entering the breathing passages so that access of air to the lungs is prevented. The liquid need not necessarily be water; it may be mud, sludge, or other viscous

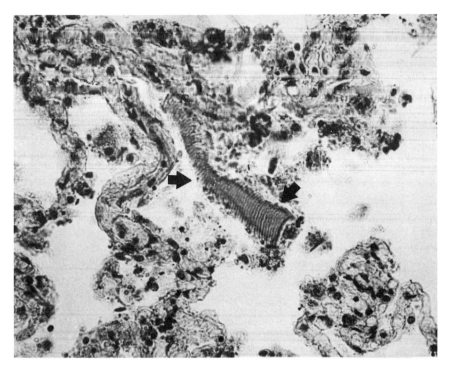

FIGURE **16.20.** A photomicrograph showing striated muscle fiber in the alveola. A man was found dead on a road. At autopsy, the trachea and bronchi were full of stomach contents, suggesting that he died from asphyxia caused from the vomiting. (*China Medical College, Shenyang, People's Republic of China.*)

material. Nor does the whole of the body need to be under the liquid. A person can drown when only the mouth and nose are under the surface. In a more general sense, the word "drowning" is used for every case of death in water, but this is incorrect since a death (e.g., while bathing) may be due to heart failure, cerebral hemorrhage, or shock (Fig. 16.21).

When a drowned person is drawn out of the water, a white foam often comes out of the mouth and nostrils, where it forms white spongy puffs that can remain for quite a long time, owing to the mucous contained in it.

When the cause of death is simply drowning, murder is comparatively rare and, as a rule, is committed only against children. If injuries are found on a drowned person that might have been produced by some other person, the drowning can generally be considered merely as the final phase of a course of events involving murder or manslaughter. It can also happen that a criminal attempts to conceal the discovery of the crime by sinking the victim under water.

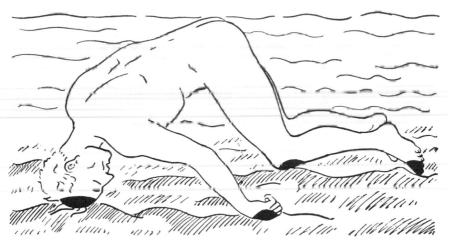

FIGURE **16.21.** The portions most exposed to injury when a body in water scrapes against a rough or stony sea bottom.

In cases of drowning, the question is generally whether it is suicide or accident. If the clothes have been removed or if it can be surmised that the location was chosen with the idea of avoiding the risk of bumping against a stony bottom, suicide is indicated. The opposite can indicate accident, as can marks of slipping found on stones at the edge of the water and injuries produced when the drowning person attempted a rescue (e.g., scraping of the skin of the hands and fingers or broken and torn nails).

The body of a drowned person may be tied in some way or have heavy objects attached to it to make it sink and remain on the bottom. In such cases, the police officer must proceed very cautiously with the investigation; the case may be judged as suicide, but suspicion of criminal acts should not be excluded.

A body lying in water is exposed to damage of many kinds. Propellers of boats may produce injuries. A body hit by a propeller can be cut right in half. Bodies in water are also often damaged in the breakers offshore, against rocks, or when they bump against a stony and uneven bottom.

## Death from Electric Currents

Death from electric currents can be caused by an electricity supply or by lightning.

Visible injuries may be present at the points of entry and exit of the current—and so-called current marks. If electric sparks or an arc touches the skin, there is a burn that often shows the same form as the object producing it. When the direct injury is slight, there are characteristically formed fissures and figures that indicate the passage of the current. Current marks are often round, sharply delineated, and light in color, or they may consist of edges or surfaces where the skin is charred. In severe cases, the injury penetrates the underlying tissues of the musculature and bones. The surface of the skin may be impregnated with fine metallic dust, which emanates from the current-carrying object, and this can be so great that it appears as a discoloration, sometimes gray or black, sometimes blue or bluish green. The metallic dust can be determined spectrographically. Considerable changes in the skin may also be produced at the point of exit of the current. At the points of entry and exit of the current, the clothing may be torn or charred; sometimes the damage consists of a number of small holes with burned edges.

Death from electric current may be either accident, suicide, or murder. There have been cases in which a trap has been set using house current, with the intention of murder.

Death from lightning is rare. When injuries are present on the body of a person who can be assumed to have been killed in this way, they may consist of current marks on the neck and soles of the feet; the clothes may be badly torn; metal objects in the clothes may be fused together, burned, or thrown away, even in cases where no injury is apparent on the body. So-called lightning figures on the skin are not burn injuries but result from changes in the blood vessels. These arboreal marks generally disappear very quickly after death.

## Violent Death in Fires

The cause of death and injuries on a person who has been burned to death can be determined only by a pathologist. Death may be due either to suffocation by smoke, carbon monoxide poisoning, or injury caused by falling beams, overturned furniture, falling walls, and so on. Generally, the person is already dead from such causes before the fire begins to attack the body.

Burned bodies usually lie in a distorted position, the so-called "pugilistic attitude,"which is caused by the contraction of the muscles under the action of heat. The skin and soft tissues crack gradually, and the cracks sometimes have quite even edges that can easily be confused with cut and stab wounds. The bones become more or less brittle, so that breakages occur. In the inner parts of the skull, the pressure may become so great that the bones of the cranium may shatter. The body is charred gradually by the head, the limbs being destroyed first. A greatly charred body sometimes has the form of a torso.

For complete combustion, very intense heat for a comparatively long time is required. A newborn baby can be burned away in an ordinary stove in 2 hours, but to consume an adult in the same time a temperature of 1250°C is needed, after which only certain bones remain.

Murder by burning does occur, but it can generally be assumed that the victim was subjected to other injuries before the fire was started. Disposal by fire after murder is, however, not uncommon. The criminal may, in both cases, have caused the fire with the object of destroying evidence. The pathologist can easily decide whether the victim of a fire was alive or dead when the fire started. If no signs of inhaled smoke or flakes of soot are found in the respiratory organs, that is a sign that the person was dead before the fire. Underneath a burned body there are often found parts of the skin that have escaped burning, as there also are on parts of the body where tight-fitting clothing has protected the skin. In such places, signs of external violence may show clearly. Traces of blood may be found on unburned portions of clothing under the body. Uninjured parts of the skin around the wrists and ankles may indicate that the victim was bound before the start of the fire. A ligature around the neck, destroyed in the fire, may leave a distinct strangling groove.

## Death by Freezing

Freezing to death does not, as a rule, produce any distinguishable injuries or changes in the body. At the autopsy, red spots may possibly be observed on those parts of the body where livid stains occur more rarely (e.g., the ears, tip of the nose, fingers, and toes). In most cases, only weak, helpless, insufficiently clothed, or drunken persons are frozen to death.

Freezing to death can occur as the result of criminal actions, e.g., exposure of newborn or delicate children. A person who has been rendered helpless by an assault can also freeze to death.

Persons who have died from freezing are occasionally found more or less undressed. This condition naturally gives rise to suspicions of murder. However, in some cases, it has been explained as an action by the victim who, at an advanced state of freezing, gets a sensation of heat.

## Death by Poisoning

The determination of death by poisoning is frequently a joint effort of the forensic pathologist and the forensic toxicologist. Only in certain instances will the investigating officer find the presence of physical evidence at the crime scene that indicates the death was caused by the ingestion of a poisonous substance.

Physical evidence located at the crime scene and noted upon gross examination of the deceased may sometimes be indicative of poisoning.

Evidence such as drugs, narcotic paraphernalia, markings on the body, or the presence of acids or caustic substances may provide an initial basis for forming an opinion about the case.

Corrosion around the mouth and face may be the result of consumption of acids or caustic chemicals such as hydrochloric acid, sulfuric acid, or lye. Odors of ammonia or burned almonds, or odor associated with cyanides can indicate certain poisons. In cyanide poisoning, lividity is a reddish color.

Certain drugs such as opium alkaloids and nicotine cause contraction of the pupils, whereas others such as atropine (belladonna) produce dilation.

In death from subacute and chronic arsenic poisoning, a large quantity of thin stool resembling rice and often containing blood may be found. Considerable excretion is also usual in the later stages of poisoning from corrosive sublimated or lead salts.

Strychnine causes convulsions. The corners of the mouth are drawn up and the face is fixed in a grin; the arms and legs are drawn together, and the back is severely bent backward because of contraction of the muscles.

Different-colored materials in the vomit can give clues to the type of poisoning. Brown material resembling coffee grounds indicates poisoning with strong alkalis such as sodium or potassium hydroxide; yellow indicates nitric and chromic acids; blue-green, copper sulfate; black, sulfuric acid; and brown-green, hydrochloric acid. A sharp-smelling vomit indicates poisoning with ammonia or acetic acid.

Murders by the use of a poison that must be taken internally to be effective are not numerous. Generally, it can be decided that murder by poison is committed only within a family or close group. In such cases, the criminal usually uses a poison that will not arouse suspicion by its color, odor, or taste. Murder or attempted murder by the use of poisonous gas occurs occasionally (e.g., carbon monoxide poisoning).

The police officer should know that in a case of death by poisoning only the investigation at the scene and examination of witnesses can determine whether the case is one of murder, suicide, or accident. The autopsy decides only the poison used and quantity.

It is not possible to go into a detailed description of different poisons and their actions. The boundary between poisonous and nonpoisonous substances is indefinite. A number of substances normally present in food can cause death by poisoning when they are taken in large amounts. Thus there is a case in which the consumption of 13 ounces of table salt caused the death of an adult.

A number of poisons should be mentioned, however, including those that have a powerful action and those that are responsible for most cases of poisoning.

*Gaseous and liquid poisons.* Although there are literally thousands, some of the more common ones are carbon monoxide, hydrogen cyanide, freon, methanol, toluene, benzene, gasoline, and chloroform.

*Heavy metals and other inorganic poisons.* Compounds and salts of antimony, arsenic, barium, chromium, lead, mercury, and thallium; strong inorganic acids and bases such as hydrochloric acid, nitric acid, sulfuric acid, sodium hydroxide, potassium hydroxide, and ammonia.

*Ethical, over-the-counter, and illicit drugs.* Ethyl alcohol; barbiturates; heroin; synthetically produced opiates (e.g., methadone); phencyclidine (PCP); minor tranquilizers such as Valium, Librium, meprobamate and over-the-counter medication when taken in excess. These drugs may be found in combination with each other and with alcohol.

*Other vegetable and animal poisons.* Atropine, cocaine, nicotine, scopolamine, strychnine, and snake poisons.

*Bacterial poisons.* Food poisoning (botulism).

The determination of poisoning as the cause of death can be made only by autopsy and chemical analysis. In a number of cases of poisoning, however, certain details in the appearance of the dead person or special circumstances in connection with the death may give some indication. The police officer who investigates the scene of a fatal poisoning can greatly assist the pathologist by recovering any evidence of poisoning.

The most usual indications are, first, residual poison in the form of tablets, powder, or residues in medicine bottles and, second, powder wrappings, boxes, tubes, ampoules, vials, and other containers. All such clues should be recovered, and each one should be packed separately in a tube or envelope. When the dead person is lying in bed, the bedclothes must be examined very carefully, since the poison may quite possibly have been in the form of powder and any that was spilled would be very difficult to detect.

All medicine bottles and tubes, including empty ones, should be kept, even if the stated contents are considered to be harmless. Even an apparently empty bottle may contain traces of powder, which can be identified by microchemical methods. The report of the investigation must state where such objects were found. Prescriptions can be useful guides for the pathologist.

Among the most important pieces of evidence in poisoning are cups, glasses, and other containers that are found in the immediate vicinity of the deceased or in such places and under such conditions that they can be placed in direct relation to the death. If any liquid left in a container is found, it should be transferred to an absolutely clean bottle, which is then sealed. When a container holds merely a sediment or undissolved residues, it should be wrapped in clean paper or preferably in a plastic bag. If there are finger or palm prints on it, these must be preserved. Spilled liquids can be collected by means of filter paper, which is then placed in a well-sealed clean glass jar.

When food poisoning is suspected, or it is possible that dishes may have conveyed the poison, the dishes used should be collected and packed in a suitable manner. Food dishes and remains of food are packed in clean glass jars that are well sealed. If such clues are not sent immediately to a public health laboratory, they should be kept in a refrigerator. If there is any suspicion of crime, remains of food should be looked for outdoors as well as indoors, in garbage cans, compost heaps, in the ground, and other such places.

Any hypodermic syringes that are found should be recovered and kept in such a way that they cannot become contaminated and the contents cannot run out or be pressed out. The needle of the syringe can be conveniently stuck into a cork to prevent its breaking. If there are finger or palm prints on the syringe, these must be preserved. When hypodermic syringes are found, ampoules and vials should be looked for in the vicinity.

Vomit, saliva, and mucous on or around the dead person may contain traces of poison and must be kept. Suspected stains on clothing and bedclothes are preserved by each of the articles being spread out on clean wrapping paper and rolled separately in the paper. Stains of urine and feces can sometimes give the pathologist a guide in making a decision, and should therefore be kept.

Cases of poisoning with methyl alcohol occur at times. It can usually be assumed that there are other persons involved; therefore, bottles and drinking vessels should be examined for possible finger and palm prints.

Chronic alcohol poisoning can cause sudden death, especially after bodily strain. In acute alcoholism, death occurs when the concentration of alcohol in the blood reaches 0.4 to 0.6 gram percent. The alcoholic subject can, however, provoke sudden death through various strokes of misfortune in a number of ways (drowning, falling, traffic accidents, freezing, suffocation from vomit that cannot be ejected, gagging from food in the windpipe). It has often happened that an alcoholic subject, while incapacitated, has died because of falling asleep in a position that made breathing difficult.

The pathologist when present at an investigation will decide which evidence should be collected; otherwise the investigating police officer should keep everything that might be suspected of being poison evidence, and should subsequently hand it over to the pathologist or toxicologist.

The presence of certain poisons in the human body can sometimes be confirmed a long time after death. Metallic poisons do not disappear with putrefaction. Arsenic can be detected in hair and bony parts hundreds of years after death, and lead also remains for a long time in the bone tissues. Scopolamine, atropine, strychnine, and morphine can be detected after several years; carbon monoxide poisoning, up to 6 months after death. Potassium cyanide is decomposed during putrefaction. Hydrocyanic acid and phosphorus remain for only a short time. Hypnotics are decomposed and disappear very quickly—some even in the time that elapses between their administration and the occurrence of death. An exception is barbitone (veronal), which can be detected in the body 18 months after death. In cases of exhuming a body of a person suspected to have died through poisoning with metallic poisons (especially arsenic), samples of the soil from the grave should always be taken. The soil itself may contain the poison.

## Carbon Monoxide Poisoning

Carbon monoxide is always produced when the combustion of carbonaceous matter is incomplete, and it is a normal constituent of smoke and explosion gases. It also occurs in mine gases, natural gas, and the like.

Carbon monoxide is a colorless and very poisonous gas with no odor or taste. The minimum concentration that can be injurious to human beings is 0.01% by volume, and 0.2% is dangerous to life. Continued exposure to such an atmosphere can produce death within an hour. If the concentration increases to 0.5% by volume, or more, then unconsciousness ensues after a couple of minutes and death follows quickly. With higher concentrations, unconsciousness comes on like a blow. Chronic poisoning by carbon monoxide is quite common, and is often due to prolonged exposure in shops, garages, traffic tunnels, and streets with high buildings and very heavy motor traffic.

The danger from carbon monoxide is due to the fact that the senses do not give warning in time. With acute carbon monoxide poisoning, there is headache, faintness, and nausea, with flickers before the eyes. This is usually regarded as a temporary indisposition, so that the individual in question may make the greatest mistake possible under the circumstances, that of lying down. Gradually, the person becomes sleepy and confused, and the limbs become numb. If the person finally begins to realize the danger, it is usually too late, since the body is so weak that the poisoned victim cannot move to safety. In a strikingly large number of cases of carbon monoxide poisoning, the victim is found close to a door, having been unable to open it, or by a window, having been unable to break—or even to think of breaking—the glass.

In cases of carbon monoxide poisoning, it is possible that the death was murder. The investigating officer should, therefore, not treat the investigation casually. To decide on suicide or accident immediately is wrong. The case should be considered as suspicious from the start and treated accordingly. The analysis of the situation and the result of the investigation must determine whether criminal action should be taken into account. At the autopsy the pathologist can determine only the cause of death.

Carbon monoxide poisoning from exhaust gases of internal combustion motors can occur when the engine of a vehicle is started up and allowed to run for a while in a garage with bad ventilation. Suicide may be committed in this way.

Because of the variety of chemical substances that can be fatal, the determination of the cause of death in suspected poisoning cases is no easy task. Toxicologists play a key role in these types of cases. In some instances the problem is compounded, because the human body is able to metabolize the poison into another related substance, or metabolite. Other problems (e.g., the small concentration of the poison in the body or the metabolite being naturally present) sometimes make these tests difficult ones.

## Rape-Homicide and Murders Related to Sexual Assault

Rape-homicides are murders committed in connection with rape and can be included with murders involving other sexual acts such as sodomy or anal intercourse. The methods employed in the investigation of such murders are, in general, the same as those techniques used in the investigation of an "ordinary" murder or suspicious death. The injuries found on the victim are often similar to those encountered in rape investigations, such as bruises on the arms and shoulders caused by forcibly holding down the victim, ligature marks on the wrists if the victim was tied, bruises on the back and buttocks caused by forcing the victim on the ground, marks on the inside of the thighs, knees, and around the genitalia. Physical evidence such as seminal fluid, hair, blood, skin and blood found under the victim's fingernails, and so on may also be present. Trace evidence found on the victim's clothing may be noted as well. The presence of alcohol or drugs should be determined from toxicological analyses.

The investigator should understand that the sexual aspects of these types of murders may manifest themselves in different and sometimes bizarre ways. Thus, sadism and other forms of sexual perversion may be observed, which may lead the inexperienced investigator to assume

that other than a sex-related murder is being investigated. Indications
such as feces or urine discovered at the scene of a murder may point to a
sex-related murder. Sadistic acts such as mutilation of the body, particularly the sex organs and breasts, and violent injuries such as biting,
strangulation, and multiple stab wounds are especially significant and
strongly suggest this type of murder (Fig. 16.22).

In investigating the crime scene, one should look for signs of a struggle. Evidence such as marks on the ground, pieces of torn clothing,
fragments of textiles, torn-off buttons, blood, semen, and the like
should be searched for and collected. Specimens of sand, soil, vegetation, and other materials should be collected for comparison with
debris found on the suspect's clothing.

When a suspect is apprehended, the clothing and body should be
examined immediately. Scratch marks on the hands, arms, and face,
bite marks, torn clothing, soiled clothing, hair, and blood may be important evidence.

A suicidal hanging is frequently associated with sexual homicide.
The victim may, for example, be dressed in the clothing of the opposite
sex (typically a man in women's clothing) or have pornographic literature present. Other signs such as the loose binding of the hands or legs
and binding of the genitals may be noted.

## Infanticide and Child Abuse

Homicide investigations of newborn and young children involve different circumstances than found in adult cases. The types of injuries
causing death in infants and children are often nonfatal to adults. In
many instances, the abandoned child has no means of identification
present. In cases resulting in death in the home, the crime scene may
show little or no physical evidence to associate the injuries with the
victim. Finally, when the young victim of beating or neglect is brought
to the emergency room for treatment, the child is almost always unable
to communicate the cause of the injuries. These are some of the problems to be addressed in murder investigations of children.

In cases of newborn death, the pathologist is required to determine
whether the child was viable, that is, capable of living. The infant is
considered to be viable when it has attained a stage of development
such that it would remain alive without any special care, e.g., in an
incubator. Babies with a length of 10 to 16 inches can certainly be born
alive, but as a rule are considered not to have reached such a stage of
development that they can continue to live.

Infanticide, or the killing of a newborn child, can be committed in a
variety of ways such as intentional neglect, killing with a weapon,
suffocation, forcing objects into the nose or mouth, or by drowning.

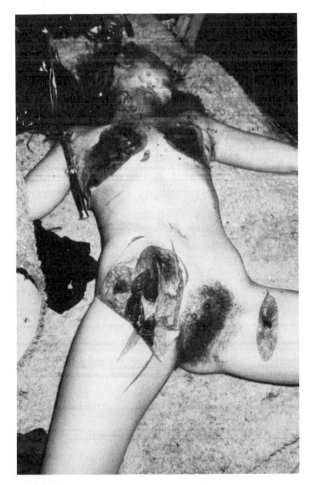

FIGURE **16.22.** A murder case showing sex-related mutilation. (*Los Angeles County Sheriff's Department.*)

Intentional neglect occurs when the parents fail to care for the child immediately after birth, in spite of being able to do so. Death may result from exposure, dehydration, or starvation. Heat regulation in the body of a newborn can be a significant factor in exposure-related deaths since the body temperature of the baby can drop rapidly.

Abandonment of a newborn child poses an additional problem. The child may be left without any means of identification. In cases in which the infant is left, wrapped only in a blanket or even without any clothes, it is frequently impossible to discover evidence to determine who the mother is.

Killing with a weapon may be carried out with blunt objects with the intent to injure the head or by striking the head against some hard object. Stabbing is also sometimes used in infanticide.

Strangulation is another possible cause of death. Strangling by hand leaves injuries and sometimes scratch marks about the neck.

Suffocation can be caused by placing a pillow or using a hand to cover the mouth or nose. If a hand is used, scratch marks may be found on the face. It should be noted, however, that suffocation may be accidental and caused by the infant's lying face down on soft bedding. Suffocation may also be caused by insertion of objects into the mouth. Items such as cotton inserted into the mouth may be the cause of death.

The so called battered child syndrome is another area of consideration in the deaths of children. Frequent beatings and cruel treatment as a means of punishment or discipline sometimes result in deaths of children. Poisoning, starvation, severe beatings, and scalding in very hot water are all means of injury and, often, death.

Examination by a pediatrician is required in suspected child abuse cases. In many instances, when the child is taken to the doctor or hospital emergency room, the parent may claim that the injury was the result of a fall or other unintentional injury. Careful examination of the injuries may show them to be inconsistent with the "accident" described. In addition, X-rays may show several broken and healed bones characteristic of repeated and severe beating.

## Trunk Murder, Dismemberment of the Body

Trunk murder is the name commonly used to describe murders in which the criminal, in order to dispose of the body of the victim, places it in a trunk, chest, large suitcase, box, or the like, that is either concealed or carried away (Fig. 16.23). Even more commonly, the victim is placed in a sack or covered with a blanket, clothing, or a tarpaulin. This crime is often associated with cutting-up of the body.

Dismemberment of a dead body may be offensive or defensive. The former is usually conditioned by passion and can be regarded as a form of sadism, whereas the latter is employed by a criminal who wants to conceal the body or to make it unrecognizable. The method used may give information regarding occupational experience (butcher or person with anatomical knowledge), and the surfaces of the wounds can indicate the implements used (knife, ax, saw). Dust and dirt from the body can, in favorable cases, give information of local conditions where the dismemberment was carried out. The murderer may conceal parts of the body at different places over a considerable area, with the object of making identification of the victim difficult or impossible, or may attempt to destroy the body (e.g., in an acid bath or by burning).

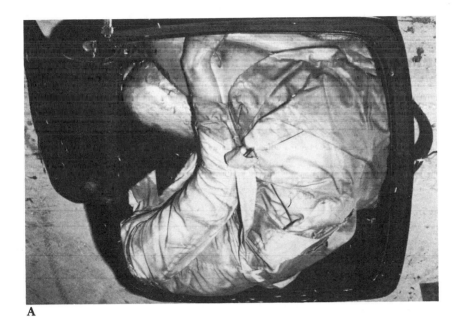

A

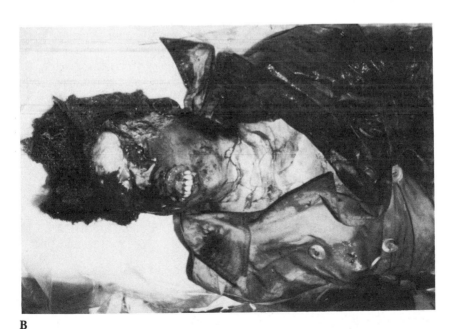

B

FIGURE 16.23. The body was discovered in a suitcase in the trunk of an abandoned car parked in a parking lot. The original condition of the body in the suitcase (A) and the deterioration of the face (B) are shown. (*Los Angeles County Sheriff's Department.*)

Frequently, the place where the body was found is not the same as the scene of the crime. If the murdered person is unknown, success in the search for the scene of the crime depends largely on the possibility of determining the origin of the containers or wrapping around the body or parts of the body. The first step is to determine whether labels, stamps, or writing can throw any light on their origin. These examinations involve such delicate procedures that they should be entrusted to an expert from the beginning. The crime scene investigator's preliminary examination should, therefore, not become too extensive.

Dirt or dust present in the wrapping may give direct information regarding what had been in it before. Fingerprints, hair, and other traces of the criminal should be looked for. When looking for fingerprints, no development media should be used until the laboratory expert has completed the examination. Bodies or parts of bodies found enclosed in a package are generally wrapped in a large quantity of paper, scraps of clothing, plastic bags, etc., obviously to prevent blood, other liquid, or odor from betraying the contents. The possibility that the fingerprints of the murderer will be found, in blood or blood serum, should be considered. Objects used to wrap the body or parts of the body can also be a useful guide in the search for the actual scene of the crime.

## Serial Murders

Serial murders are distinguished from multiple murders in that the latter are committed all at about the same time and the victims are in some way connected with one another (e.g., through family ties, so-

---

FIGURE 16.24. During the hot summer of 1985, the Los Angeles area was terrorized by one individual—the Night Stalker. Before his reign of terror was completed, at least 13 people were viciously murdered and numerous others were assaulted. His murder spree ranged from San Francisco to Orange County. A countywide task force was lead by Sergeant Frank Salerno and Deputy Gil Carillo of the Los Angeles County Sheriff's Department, Homicide Bureau. Evidence of a satanic link—upside down pentagrams (A, B) and an AC/DC cap were noted at early crime scenes and attributed to the Night Stalker. After his capture and during his trial, upside down pentagrams were found on the dashboard of his car and in his holding cell.
Based on a latent fingerprint from a vehicle used by the Night Stalker in an assault in Orange County, California, he was identified as Richard Ramirez on August 30, 1985. A mug shot photograph was released to the press the following morning. That same morning, as newspapers were being distributed, Richard Ramirez was on a bus returning to Los Angeles from Arizona. Within hours he was spotted and captured by citizens of Hubbard Street in East Los Angeles. Once in custody, he was positively identified as Richard Ramirez, alias the Night Stalker. Four years lapsed before Richard Ramirez was found guilty of all counts brought against him, which included 13 murders and 30 other felonies. He was sentenced to die in the California gas chamber. (*Los Angeles County Sheriff's Department.*)

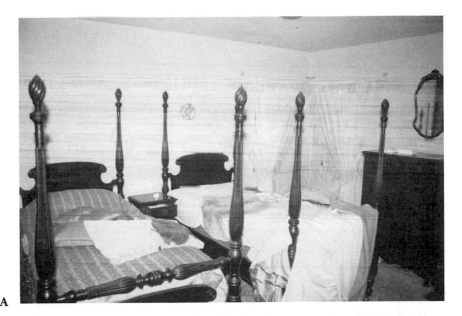

A

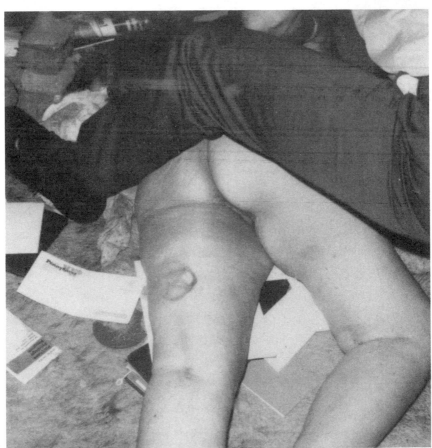

B

486

A

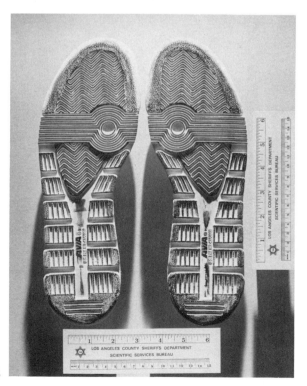

B

cially, or as neighbors). Serial murders occur over a period of time, sometimes years, and often over large geographic areas. Probably the most celebrated serial murderer in history was the infamous Jack the Ripper who terrorized London in the 1880s. Modern cases have occurred in New York, Los Angeles, Atlanta, Washington State, Florida, and elsewhere. Serial murders are among the most difficult types of homicides to investigate because of their complexity and a component unique to this type of crime—public alarm.

Serial murders follow an almost predictable course. Typically, investigators discover that the M.O. of a case they are working on bears similarities to that in other cases. As the investigation progresses, investigators from a variety of police agencies may become involved in the investigation, as well as may others (i.e., criminalists, pathologists, and so on). Once it becomes clear that the case involves a serial murder, communication with all others in the total investigation is imperative. Principal investigators, forensic scientists, and others who must take an active role in the case should be identified and the investigation coordinated from this point on. All suspected future cases should be reviewed and, if possible, the crime scenes should be visited. Because there is always a delicate balance between the public's right to know and the possibility of public hysteria, all press contacts should be handled from a centralized source, and specific details about the case should be withheld from the public so as not to hamper the investigation. (See Figs. 16.23 to 16.25.)

Once the news story breaks, enormous demands will be placed on those responsible for the investigation. Here "cool heads" must reign. Doubtless, there will be tremendous public pressure to solve case. Investigators will be deluged with telephone calls, yielding thousands of pieces of information (much of which is of little value). "Copy cat" cases, those with certain similarities to the serial murder cases, may develop.

There is usually little magic in the solution of cases of the size and

---

FIGURE 16.25. The crime scenes attributed to the Night Stalker started to show a grizzly pattern: restraints (i.e., cords, belts, handcuffs, and thumb cuffs) were found at many scenes, as well as various tools that were used to bludgeon his victims. A characteristic shoe impression linked several crime scenes. The unusual shoe pattern, identified as that of an Avia brand, was seen in soiled blood and dust. The impressions were preserved through the use of photography, plaster casting (A), and tape lifts. The shoe impressions were compared with each other and found to have similar class characteristics of the Avia aerobic, size 11 1/2 (B). After consultation with the owner of the Avia company, it was determined that the only one pair of size 11 1/2 shoes was distributed in the Los Angeles area, and 97 pairs in the entire state. The shoes were never recovered. (*Los Angeles County Sheriff's Department.*)

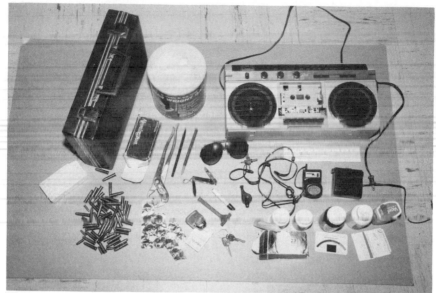

A

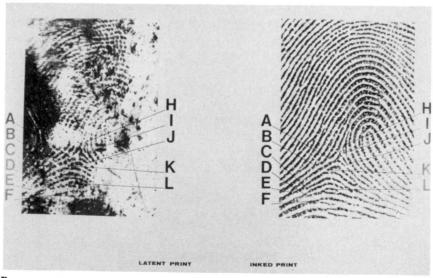

LATENT PRINT INKED PRINT

B

**FIGURE 16.26.** The Firearms and Latent Print Sections of the Los Angeles County Sheriff's Department, Scientific Services Bureau, played an integral role in Richard Ramirez's conviction by comparing the rifling marks from bullets recovered at different scenes. It was established that they were fired from the same handgun. This substantiated the feeling that the crimes were committed by the same individual. On the day of his arrest, items belonging to Ramirez were seized from a local Greyhound bus depot locker (A). Among these

C

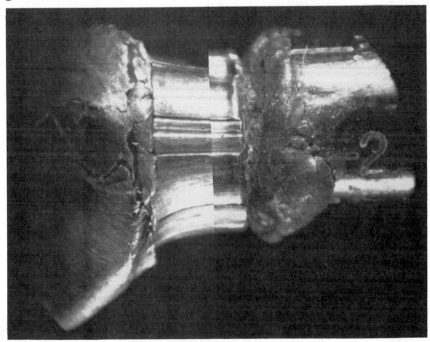

D

items were a yellow flashlight and live rounds of ammunition. A latent finger-print (B) on the flashlight was identified as belonging to Richard Ramirez, thereby linking him to the recovered property. More important, the live rounds exhibited a magazine signature identical to markings on expended cartridges found at four of the Night Stalker crime scenes (C, D). (*Los Angeles County Sheriff's Department.*)

scope of a serial murder investigation. Hard work, long hours, and attention to details solve these cases. The ability to sort through mountains of information, recognize behavioral patterns, and, above all, coordinate the efforts of scores of people associated with the various elements of the case, makes for a successful investigator.

One final talent for the investigator to master is worth mentioning—leadership. This know-how plays a part in serial murder investigations and may also affect other types of inquiries. The detective is ultimately responsible for running a police investigation. He or she has to rely on a host of professionals within the criminal justice system. Interpersonal skills really make a difference. Learning how to ask rather than demand, saying "thank you" for some extra effort, and establishing good, long-term cooperative working relationships distinguish the great investigator from the adequate one.

Homicide investigation brings together nearly all the skills and principles discussed throughout this text. It requires the coordination and cooperation of many disciplines and the capability of the investigator to assimilate large amounts of information. The skills needed to process the crime scene and the ability to recognize, collect, and preserve physical evidence are crucial. A mastery of the techniques of crime scene investigation is essential to modern law enforcement.

# APPENDIX

## Equipment for Crime Scene Investigations

The crime scene investigation officer needs special equipment to aid in the collection and preservation of evidence, photography, and sketching. Equipment should be flexible, portable, and arranged in suitable carrying cases. The following list of supplies and equipment suggests many items generally useful to have on hand at a crime scene investigation. Experience will suggest other materials in addition to those listed below that the investigator will find helpful:

### Basic Equipment

Flashlight and spare batteries

Disposable latex examination gloves

Coveralls or disposable clothing

50-ft steel surveyor's tape

12-ft steel tape measure

12-in ruler

6-in ruler

Writing paper and report forms

Graph paper

Clipboard

Writing and marking pens, pencils

Metal scribe

Chalk and crayons

Evidence tags

Evidence sealing tape

Stapler and staples

Adhesive and cellophane tape

Rubber bands

Scissors

Scalpel and replacement blades

Assorted large and small forceps

Spatulas

Paper towels

Hand magnifier

Disposable pipettes and rubber bulbs

Cotton-tipped applicators

Test tubes and corks

Compass

Magnet

pH paper

Antiputrefaction masks

Thumbtacks

## Evidence Packaging Supplies

Envelopes of various sizes

Paper bags

Plastic bags

Pillboxes

Metal paint cans and lids

Cardboard boxes

Screw cap glass vials of various sizes

Paper

## Photographic Equipment

Camera—35 mm and larger format such as 4 × 5

Lenses—normal, wide angle, and macro

Film—black and white, and color

Flash and batteries

Fresh batteries

Tripod

Level

Rulers and other devices to show scale of items

Light meter

Carrying case

Lens brush and lens tissue

## Fingerprint Equipment

Fingerprint brushes

Magna-Brush

Lift cards

Fingerprint powders

Lifting tape

Rubber lifters

Magnifier

## Hand Tools

Hammers

Hand or power saw

Screwdrivers

Pliers

Wrench

Pry bar

Vise grips®

Wire cutters

# BIBLIOGRAPHY

The following is a list of suggested further readings on many of the areas covered in the text. Because this book is written primarily for law enforcement personnel, material of a highly technical nature has been intentionally omitted. Thus, certain areas requiring a considerable level of scientific knowledge may be limited in this Bibliography. The references below serve as a starting point from which the reader wishing additional information may begin, but by no means represent an exhaustive bibliography on forensic science:

## Chapter 1

Bergman, R.A. "The Impact of Technological Advancement on Forensic Science Practice." *Canadian Society of Forensic Science.* 21(4):169–176, 1988.

Brown, C. "The Impact of Computer Technology on the Work of the Home Office Forensic Science Service in the U.K." *Canadian Society of Forensic Science.* 21(4):157–162, 1988.

Buckhout, R. "Eyewitness Testimony." *Scientific American* 231(6):2, 1974.

Delattre, E.J. *Character and Cops, Ethics in Policing.* American Enterprise Institute for Public Policy Research. Distributed by University Press of America, Inc., Lanham, Maryland, 1989.

Doyle, P. "The Role of the Expert Witness," *AFTE.* 21(4):639–642, 1989.

Giannelli, P.C. "Evidentiary and Procedural Rules Governing Expert Testimony." *J. Forensic Sci.* 34(3):730–748, 1989.

Hodgkinson, T. "Expert Evidence and Reasonable Doubt." *Law Quarterly Rev.* 104(4):198–202, 1988.

Hollien, H. "The Expert Witness: Ethics and Responsibilities." *J. Forensic Sci.* 35(6):1414–1423, 1990.

Knight, B. "Ethics and Discipline in Forensic Science." *J. Forensic Sci. Soc.* 29(1):53–60, 1989.

Peterson, J.L., and Murdock, J.E. "Forensic Science Ethics: Developing an Integrated System of Support and Enforcement." *J. Forensic Sci.* 34(3):749–762, 1989.

Saks, M.J. "Prevalence and Impact of Ethical Problems in Forensic Science." *J. Forensic Sci.* 34(3):772–793, 1989.

## Chapter 4

Bradford, L.W., and Biasotti, A.A. "Teamwork in the Forensic Sciences: Report of a Case." *J. Forensic Sci.* 18(1):31, 1973.

Dickinson, D.J. "The Aerial Use of an Infrared Camera in a Police Search for the Body of a Missing Person in New Zealand." *J. Forensic Sci. Soc.* 16(3):205, 1976.

Richards, G.B. "The Application of Electronic Video Techniques to Infrared and Ultraviolet Examinations." *J. Forensic Sci.* 22(1):53, 1977.

## Chapter 5

———. *Basic Police Photography.* 2nd ed. Eastman Kodak Co., 1968.

Collinson, J.G. "The Role of the Investigating Officer." *J. Forensic Sci. Soc.* 10(4):199, 1970.

Goddard, K.W. *Crime Scene Investigation.* Reston, Virginia: Reston Publishing Company, 1977.

Morse, D., Crusoe, D., and Smith, H.G. "Forensic Archaeology." *J. Forensic Sci.* 21(2):323, 1976.

O'Brien, M.W. "Scale Model Use in Criminal Trials." *J. Forensic Ident.* 39(6):359–366, 1989.

Scott, H. "The Role of the Photographer." *J. Forensic Sci. Soc.* 10(4):205, 1970.

Siljander, R.P. *Applied Police and Fire Photography.* Springfield, Illinois: Charles C. Thomas, 1976.

Single, A.K., and Jasuja, C.P. "Photographing Indented Impressions Under Oblique Light: A Simple Modification." *J. Forensic Sci. Soc.* 30(4):211–214, 1990.

West, M.H., Billings, J.D., and Frair, J. "Ultraviolet Photography: Bite Marks on Human Skin and Suggested Techniques for the Exposure and Development of Reflective Ultraviolet Photography." *J. Forensic Sci.* 32(5):1204–1213, 1987.

West, M.H., et al. "Ultraviolet Photography of Wounds on Human Skin." *J. Forensic Ident.* 39(2):87–96, 1989.

West, M.H., Barsley, R.E., Frair, J., and Hall, F. "Reflective Ultraviolet Imaging System (RUVIS) and the Detection of Trace Evidence on Human Skin." *J. Forensic Ident.* 40(5):249–255, 1990.

## Chapter 6

Abalos, A. "Regenerating Finger Pads on Burnt, Putrefied or Mummified Corpses." *International Criminal Police Review* 44(418):16–19, 1989.

Allen, M.J., et al. "The Dating of a Will." *J. Forensic Sci. Soc.* 23(3):199–203, 1988.

Allison, H.C. *Personal Identification.* Boston: Holbrook Press, 1973.

Knife

Shovels

Sifters

Rake

Bolt cutters

Power drill

Electrical extension cords

Hacksaw

Socket wrench set

Rope

Wood chisel

Ax

Cotton work gloves

Spatula

## Blood Collection Supplies

Orthotolidine

Acetic acid

3% hydrogen peroxide

Saline

Distilled water

Luminol reagent

Spray bottle

Cotton cloth

Spot plates

Cotton-tipped applicators

Disposable pipettes and rubber bulbs

Vacuum blood collection tubes containing EDTA

Syringes

Toothpicks

Rubber gloves

## Casting Materials

Dental stone

Rubber or plastic mixing bowls

Wooden spatula

Metal retaining bands

Wire or wooden splints for support

Baffle

Cardboard boxes to hold finished cast

Silicone rubber or dental impression material

Modeling clay for dam

Mixing bowl

Spatula

Ladder

Portable vacuum and filters

Portable generator

Metal detector

Hand-held tape recorder

Portable floodlights

Gunshot residue testing kits

## Safety Equipment

Hard hat

Coveralls

Heavy gloves

Access to breathing devices for clandestine drug labs

Hazardous chemical reference books

Arensburg, B. "Methods for Age, Identification on Living Individuals of Uncertain Age." *Canadian Soc. Forensic Sci. J.* 22(2):147–158, 1989.

Barton, B.C. "The Use of an Electrostatic Detection Apparatus to Demonstrate the Matching of Torn Paper Edges." *J. Forensic Sci. Soc.* 29(1):35–38, 1989.

Bettencourt, D.S. "A Compilation of Techniques for Processing Deceased Human Skin for Latent Prints." *J. Forensic Ident.* 41(2):111–120, 1991.

Black, J. "The Interaction of Visualization Fluids and Fingerprints." *J. Forensic Ident.* 40(1):28–30, 1990.

Breedlove, C.H. "The Analysis of Ball-Point Inks for Forensic Purposes." *J. Chemical Education* 68(2):170–171, 1989.

Brandt-Casadevall, C., et al. "Identification Based on Medical Data." *Canadian Soc. Forensic Sci. J.* 22(1):35–42, March 1989.

Brunelle, R.L., Breedlove, C.H., and Midkill, C.R. "Determining the Relative Age of Ballpoint Inks Using a Single-Solvent Extraction Technique." *J. Forensic Sci.* 32(6):1511–1521, 1987.

Brunelle, R.L., and Cantu, A.A. "A Critical Evaluation of Current Ink Dating Techniques." *J. Forensic Sci.* 32(6):1522–1536, 1987.

Buquet, A., et al. "The Application of Statistical Methods to the Analysis of Typewritten Documents: Regression and Covariance." *Int. Criminal Police Rev.* 44(420):10–16, 1989.

Burnes, K.R., and Maples, W.R. "Estimation of Age from Individual Adult Teeth." *J. Forensic Sci.* 21(2):343, 1976.

Campbell, B.M. "Separation of Adhesive Tapes." *J. Forensic Ident.* 41(2):102–106, 1991.

Camps, F.E. *Medical and Scientific Investigations in the Cristie Case.* London: Medical Publications, Ltd., 1953.

Cantu, A.A., and Prough, R.S. "On the Relative Aging of Ink—The Solvent Extraction Technique." *J. Forensic Sci.* 32(5):1151–1174, 1987.

Choudhry, M.Y., and Whritenour, R.D. "A New Approach to Unraveling Tangled Adhesive Tape for Potential Detection of Latent Fingerprints and Recovery of Trace Evidence." *J. Forensic Sci.* 35(6):1373–1383, 1990.

Conway, J.V.P., *Evidential Documents.* Springfield, Illinois: Charles C. Thomas, 1959.

Cowger, J. *Friction Ridge Skin.* New York: Elsevier, 1983.

Cowger, J.F. "Moving Towards Professionalization of Latent Print Examiners." *J. Forensic Sci.* 24(3):591, 1979.

Crown, D.A. "The Differentiation of Electrostatic Photocopy Machines." *J. Forensic Sci.* 34(1):142–155, 1989.

Dalrymple, B.E. "Case Analysis of Fingerprint Detection by Laser." *J. Forensic Sci.* 24(3):586, 1979.

Dalrymple, B.E., Duff, J.M., and Menzel, E.R. "Inherent Fingerprint Luminescence Detection by Laser." *J. Forensic Sci.* 22(1):106, 1977.

Day, S.P. "Evaluation of the Application of the Argon-Ion Laser to Document Examination: A Review of Casework and Experimental Data." *J. Forensic Sci. Soc.* 25(4):285–296, 1985.

Doherty, P.E., et al. "Deciphering Bloody Imprints Through Chemical Enhancement." *J. Forensic Sci.* 35(2):457–465, 1990.

Drake, W., and Lukash, L. "Reconstruction of Mutilated Victims for Identification." *J. Forensic Sci.* 23(1):218, 1978.

El-Najjar, M.Y., and McWilliams, K.R. *Forensic Anthropology: The Structure, Morphology and Variation of Bones and Dentition.* Springfield, Illinois: Charles C. Thomas, 1977.

Gamboe, T.E. "Small Particle: Developing Latent Prints on Water-Soaked Firearms and Effect on Firearms Analysis." *J. Forensic Sci.* 34(2):312–320, 1989.

Gilmour, C., et al. "The Effect of Medication on Handwriting." *Canadian Soc. Forensic Sci.* 20(4):119–138, 1987.

Glaister, J., and Brash, J.C. *Medico-Legal Aspects of the Ruxton Case.* Edinburgh: E and S Livingstone, 1937.

Gupta, A.K., et al. "Electrostatic Detection of Secret Writings." *Forensic Sci. Int.* 41(1,2):17–23, 1989.

Haglund, W.D. "A Technique to Enhance Fingerprinting of Mummified Fingers." *J. Forensic Sci.* 33(5):1244–1248, 1987.

Hall, R.F. "Latent Skin Print Identification Solves Homicide." *FBI Law Enforcement Bulletin* 48(10):9, 1979.

Haqua, F., et al. "A Small Particle (Iron Oxide) Suspension for Detection of Latent Fingerprints on Smooth Surfaces." *Forensic Sci. Int.* 41(1,2):73–82, 1989.

Harada, H. "A Rapid Identification of Black Color Materials with Specific Reference to Ballpoint Ink and Indian Ink." *J. Forensic Sci. Soc.* 28(3):167–177, 1988.

Harris, J., et al. "Characterization and Dating of Correction Fluids on Questioned Documents Using FTIR" *Canadian Soc. Forensic Sci. J.* 22(4):349–376, 1989.

Harrison, W.R. *Suspect Documents: Their Scientific Examination.* New York: Frederick A. Praeger, 1958.

Hart, L.J., et al. "Photographically Subtracting Interfering Images From ESDA." *J. Forensic Sci.* 34(6):1405–1407, 1989.

Hart, L.J., et al. "Typewriting Versus Writing Instrument: A Line Intersection Problem." *J. Forensic Sci.* 34(6):1329–1335, 1989.

Harvey, W. *Dental Identification and Forensic Odontology.* London: Henry Kimpton, Publishers, 1976.

Herod, D.W., and Menzel, E.R. "Laser Detection of Latent Fingerprints: Ninhydrin Followed by Zinc Chloride." *J. Forensic Sci.* 27(3):513–518, 1982.

Hilton, O. "History of Questioned Documents Examination in the United States." *J. Forensic Sci.* 24(4):890, 1979.

Hilton, O. *Scientific Examination of Questioned Documents.* New York: Elsevier North-Holland, 1981.

Hongwei, S., et al. "The Estimation of Tooth Age from Attrition of the Occlusal Surface." *Medicine, Science and the Law* 29(1):69–73, 1989.

Hooft, P.J., et al. "Fatality Management in Mass Casualty Incidents." *Forensic Sci. Int.* 40(1):3–14, 1989.

Horan, G.J., et al. "How Long After Writing Can an ESDA Image Be Developed?" *Forensic Sci. Int.* 39(2), 1988.

Jones, N. "Arson-for-Profit Investigations, Success or Failure? Recovering Water Damaged Business Records." *Fire and Arson Investigator* 40(3):50–52, 1990.

Katz, J.O., et al. "The Present Direction of Research in Forensic Odontology." *J. Forensic Sci.* 33(6):1319–1327, 1988.

Kerley, E.R. "Forensic Anthropology." *Legal Medicine Annual.* Wecht, C.H., Editor. New York: Appleton-Century-Crofts, 163–198, 1973.

Killam, E.W. "Is It Human? Differentiating Between Human and Animal Bones." *Crime Laboratory Digest* 16(1):9–22, 1989.

Kopainsky, B. "Document Examination: Applications of Image Processing Systems." *Forensic Sci. Rev.* 1(2):85–101, 1989.

Krauss, T.C. "Forensic Odontology in Missing Person Cases." *J. Forensic Sci.* 21(4):959–962, 1976.

Kremer, R.D., et al. "Paper, Its Material and Macro Structural Characteristics Relevant to Analytical and Diagnostic Test Development." *American Laboratory* 21(4 a):16 17, 1989.

Larson, C.P. "Unusual Methods of Human Identification Used in Three Cases." *J. Forensic Sci.* 19(2):402–405, 1974.

Lee, H.C., et al. "The Effect of Presumptive Test, Latent Fingerprint and Some Other Reagents and Materials on Subsequent Serological Identification, Genetic Marker & DNA Testing in Bloodstains." *J. Forensic Ident.* 39(6):339–358, 1989.

Lennard, C.J., et al. "Sequencing of Reagents for the Improved Visualisation of Latent Fingerprints." *J. Forensic Ident.* 38(5):197–210, 1988.

Lunt, D.A. "Identification and Tooth Morphology." *J. Forensic Sci. Soc.* 14(3):203–207, 1974.

Luntz, L.L., and Luntz, P. "Dental Identification of Disaster Victims by a Dental Disaster Squad." *J. Forensic Sci.* 17(1):63–69, 1972.

Marchand, P. "A Non-destructive Method for Determining the Grain Direction of Paper." *Canadian Soc. Forensic Sci. J.* 22(1):69–81, 1989.

Margot, P., and Lennard, C. *Manual of Fingerprint Detection Techniques.* Lausanne, Switzerland: Institut de Police Scientifique et de Criminologie, Universite de Lausanne, September, 1990.

MacFarlane, T.W., MacDonald, D.G., and Sutherland, D.A. "Statistical Problems in Dental Identification." *J. Forensic Sci. Soc.* 14(3):247–252, 1974.

McCarthy, M.M. "Evaluation of Ardrox as a Luminescent Stain for Cyanoacrylate Processed Latent Impressions." *J. Forensic Ident.* 40(2):75–80, 1990.

McCarthy, M.M., et al. "Preprocessing with Cyanoacrylate Ester Fuming for Fingerprint Impressions in Blood." *J. Forensic Ident.* 39(1):23–32, 1989.

Menzel, E.R. "Pretreatment of Latent Prints for Laser Development." *Forensic Sci. Rev.* 1(1):43–66, 1989.

Menzel, E.R. "Detection of Latent Fingerprints, Laser-Excited Luminescence." *Analytical Chemistry* 61(8):557A–561A, 15, 1989.

Menzel, E.R. "Comparison of Argon-Ion, Copper-Vapor and Frequency-Doubled Neodymium : Yttrium Aluminum Garnet (ND : YAG) Laser for Latent Fingerprint Development." *J. Forensic Sci.* 30(20):383–397, 1985.

Menzel, E.R. "Laser Detection of Latent Fingerprints with Phosphorescers." *J. Forensic Sci.* 24(3):582–585, 1979.

Menzel, E.R., and Fox, K.E. "Laser Detection of Latent Fingerprints: Preparation of Fluorescent Dusting Powders and the Feasibility of a Portable System." *J. Forensic Sci.* 25(1):150–153, 1980.

Menzel, E.R., Burt, J.A., Sinor, T.W., Tubach-Ley, W.B., and Jordon, K.J. "Laser Detection of Latent Fingerprints: Treatment of Glue Containing Cyanoacrylate Ester." *J. Forensic Sci.* 28(2):307–317, 1983.

Menzel, E.R., et al. "Fluorescent Metal-Ruhemann's Purple Coordination Compounds: Application to Latent Fingerprint Detection." *J. Forensic Sci.* 35(1):25–34, 1990.

Mittal, S., et al. "The Forensic Examination of Unfamiliar Scripts." *Int. Criminal Police Rev.* 44(418):11–15, 1989.

Morse, D., Duncan, J., and Stoutamire, J. *Handbook of Forensic Archaeology and Anthropology.* Tallahassee, Florida: Rose Printing Co., 1983.

Munson, T.O. "A Simple Method for Sampling Photocopy Toners for Examination, Pyrolysis Gas Chromatography." *Crime Laboratory Digest* 16(1):6–8, 1989.

Noble, H.W. "The Estimation of Age from Dentition." *J. Forensic Sci. Soc.* 14(3):215–221, 1974.

Olenik, J.H. "Cyanoacrylate Fuming: An Alternative Non-Heat Method." *J. Forensic Ident.* 39(5):302–304, 1989.

Osborn, A.S. *Questioned Documents.* 2nd ed. London: Sweet & Maxwell, Ltd., 1929.

Owen, T. "An Introduction to Forensic Examination of Audio and Video Tapes." *J. Forensic Ident.* 39(2):75–86, 1989.

Phillips, C.E., et al. "Physical Developer: A Practical and Productive Latent Print Developer." *J. Forensic Ident.* 40(3):135–147, 1990.

Pierce, D.S. "Tonally Reversed Friction Ridge Prints on Plastics." *J. Forensic Ident.* 39(1):11–22, 1989.

Plamondor, R., et al. "Automatic Signature, Verification and Writer Identification: The State of the Art." *Pattern Recognition* 22(2):107–131, 1989.

Reichardt, G.J., Carr, J.C., and Stone, E.G. "A Conventional Method for Lifting Latent Fingerprints from Human Skin Surfaces." *J. Forensic Sci.* 23(1):135–141, 1978.

Richardson, L., and Kade, H. "Readable Fingerprints from Mummified or Putrefied Specimens." *J. Forensic Sci.* 17(2):325–328, 1972.

Ruprecht, A. "Use of Direct Positive Photographic Paper in the Preparation of Fingerprint Exhibits." *J. Forensic Ident.* 39(4):244–247, 1989.

Sams, C. "The Role of the Fingerprint Officer." *J. Forensic Sci. Soc.* 10(4):219–225, 1970.

———. *The Science of Fingerprints: Classification and Use.* FBI, U.S. Dept. of Justice, 1973.

Sedeyn, M.J. "Handwriting Examination: A Practical Approach." *Forensic Sci. Int.* 36(3,4):169–171, 1988.

Seguss, R.K. "Altered and Counterfeit Travel Documents: A Canadian Perspective." *Int. Criminal Police Rev.* 43(413):11–17, 1988.

Sekharan, P.C. "Personal Identification from Skull Suture Pattern." *Canadian Soc. Forensic Sci.* 22(1):27–34, 1989.

Skinner, M.F. "Applied Archaeology and Physical Anthropology in a Forensic Context: A Review of Twelve Years of Forensic Anthropology in British Columbia." *Canadian Soc. Forensic Sci.* 22(1):83–88, 1989.

Skinner, M.F. "Method and Theory in Deciding Identity of Skeletonized Human Remains." *Canadian Soc. Forensic Sci. J.* 21(3):114–134, 1988.

Sognnaes, R.F. "Progress in Forensic Dentistry I." *New England J. Medicine* 296:79–85, 1977.

Sognnaes, R.F. "Progress in Forensic Dentistry II." *New England J. Medicine* 296:149–153, 1977.

Sopher, I.M. "Dental Identification of Aircraft-Accident Fatalities." *J. Forensic Sci.* 18(4):356–363, 1973.

Stewart, T.D. *Essentials of Forensic Anthropology.* Springfield, Illinois: Charles C. Thomas, 1979.

Stewart, T.D., Editor. "Personal Identification in Mass Disasters." *National Museum of Natural History.* Washington, D.C.: Smithsonian Institution, 1970.

Stewart, T.D. "What the Bones Tell—Today." *FBI Law Enforcement Bulletin* 41(2):1–5, 1972.

Taylor, L.R. "The Restoration of Water-Soaked Documents: A Case Study." *J. Forensic Sci.* 31(3):1113–1118, 1986.

Tolliver, D.K. "The Electrostatic Detection Apparatus (ESDA): Is It Really Non-destructive to Documents?" *Forensic Sci. Int.* 44(1):7–21, 1990.

Tucker, G. "A Modified Crystal Violet Application Technique for Black Electrical Tape." *J. Forensic Ident.* 40(3):148–150, 1990.

Twibell, J.D., Home, J.M., Smallson, K.W., and Higgs, D.G. "Transfer of Nitroglycerine to Hands During Contact with Commercial Explosives." *J. Forensic Sci.* 27(4):783–791, 1984.

Twibell, J.D., Home, J.M., Smallson, K.W., Higgs, D.G., and Hayes, T.S. "Assessment of Solvents for the Recovery of Nitroglycerine from Hands Using Cotton Swabs." *J. Forensic Sci.* 27(4):792–800, 1984.

Trowell, F. "A Method for Fixing Latent Fingerprints Developed with Iodine." *J. Forensic Sci. Soc.* 15(3):189–195, 1975.

Walton, A.N. "Laser Photography Using Laser Beam Painted Light Technique on Curved Surfaces." *J. Forensic Ident.* 39(3):177–180, 1989.

Wanxiang, L., et al. "A Study of the Principle of the Electrostatic Imaging Technique." *J. Forensic Sci. Soc.* 28(4):237–242, 1988.

Warren, C.P. "Verifying Identification of Military Remains: A Case Study." *J. Forensic Sci.* 24(1):182–188, 1979.

Weaver, D.E. "Photographic Enhancement of Latent Prints." *J. Forensic Ident.* 38(5):189–196, 1988.

Zugibe, F.T., and Costello, J.T. "A New Method for Softening Mummified Fingers." *J. Forensic Sci.* 31(2):726–731, 1986.

# Chapter 7

Blackledge, R.D. "Tapes with Adhesive Backings: Their Characterization in the Forensic Science Laboratory." *Appl. Polym. Anal. Charact.* 413–421, 1987.

Brasee, R.R. "Evaluation of Textile Fiber Evidence: A Review." *J. Forensic Sci.* 32(2):510–521, 1987.

Brunelle, R.L., and Reed, R.W. *Forensic Examination of Ink and Paper.* Springfield, Illinois: Charles C. Thomas, 1984.

Brunner, H., and Coman, B.J. *The Identification of Mammalian Hair.* Melbourne: Inkata Press Proprietary, Ltd., 1974.

Budworth, B. "Identification of Knots." *J. Forensic Sci. Soc.* 22(4):327–331, 1982.

Burd, D.O., and Kirk, F.L. "Clothing Fibers as Evidence." *J. Criminal Law and Criminology* 32:333, 1941.

Crown, D.A. *The Forensic Examination of Paints and Pigments.* Springfield, Illinois: Charles C. Thomas, 1968.

Dixon, K.C. "Positive Identification of Torn Burned Matches with Emphasis on Crosscut and Torn Fiber Comparisons." *J. Forensic Sci.* 28(2):351–359, 1983.

———. "Don't Miss a Hair." *FBI Law Enforcement Bulletin* 45(5):9–15, 1976.

Grieve, M.C. "The Role of Fibers in Forensic Science Examinations." *J. Forensic Sci.* 28(4):877–887, 1983.

Hicks, J.W. *Microscopy of Hair: A Practical Guide and Manual.* F.B.I., U.S. Government Printing Office, 1977.

Kirk, P.L. *Crime Investigation.* 2nd ed. Thornton, J.I., Editor. New York: John Wiley & Sons, 1974.

Longhetti, A., and Roche, G. "Microscopic Identification of Man-made Fibers from the Criminalistics Point of View." *J. Forensic Sci.* 3:303, 1958.

Murray, R.C., and Tedrow, J.C.F. *Forensic Geology.* New Brunswick, New Jersey: Rutgers University Press, 1975.

Nickolls, L.C. "The Identification of Stains of Nonbiological Origin." In: *Methods of Forensic Science.* Volume 1. Lundquist, F., Editor. New York: Interscience Publishers, John Wiley & Sons, pp. 335–371, 1962.

Petraco, N. "A Simple Trace Evidence Trap for the Collection of Vacuum Sweepings." *J. Forensic Sci.* 32(5):1422–1425, 1987.

Petraco, N. "Trace Evidence—The Invisible Witness." *J. Forensic Sci.* 31(1):321–328, 1986.

Pounds, C.A. "The Recovery of Fibers from the Surface of Clothing for Forensic Examination." *J. Forensic Sci. Soc.* 15(2):127–132, 1975.

Robertson, C.H., and Govan, J. "The Identification of Bird Feathers. Scheme for Feather Examination." *J. Forensic Sci. Soc.* 24(2):85–98, 1984.

Stratmann, M. "Identification of Textile Fibers." *Appl. Polym. Anal. Charact.* 387–411, 1987.

Strelis, I., and Kennedy, R.W. "Identification of North American Commercial Pulpwoods and Pulp Fibers." University of Toronto Press, 1967.

Suzanski, T.W. "Dog Hair Comparison: Purebreds, Mixed Breeds, Multiple Questioned Hairs." *Canadian Soc. Forensic Sci. J.* 22(4):299–309, 1989.

Suzanski, T.W. "Dog Hair Comparison: A Preliminary Study." *Canadian Soc. Forensic Sci.* 21(1,2):19–28, 1988.

## Chapter 8

Anderson, A. "DNA Fingerprinting on Trial." *Nature* 342(6252):844, 1989.

Becker, P.B., et al. "Genomic Footprinting." *Genetic Engineering* 10:1–19, 1988.

Bigbee, P.D., et al. "Inactivation of Human Immodeficiency Virus (HIV), Ionizing Radiation in Body Fluids and Serological Evidence." *J. Forensic Sci.* 34(6):1303–1310, 1989.

Cawood, A.H. "DNA Fingerprinting." *Clinical Chemistry* 35(9):1832–1837, 1989.

Cherfas, J. "Genes Unlimited." *New Scientist* 126(1712):29–33, 1990.

Cohen, J.E. "DNA Fingerprinting for Forensic Identification: Potential Effects on Data Interpretation of Subpopulation Heterogeneity and Band Number Variability." *Am. J. Human Genetics* 46(2):358–368, 1990.

Culliford, B.J. *The Examination and Typing of Bloodstains in the Crime Laboratory.* U.S. Government Printing Office, 1971.

Evett, I.W., et al. "DNA Fingerprinting on Trial." *Nature* 340(6233):435, 1989.

Gaensslen, R.E. "Blood sweat and tears . . . and, saliva and semen—The forensic serologist provides expert identification of body fluids." *Law Enforcement Communications* 23–30, February, 1980.

Gaensslen, R.E. *Sourcebook in Forensic Serology, Immunology and Biochemistry.* U.S. Department of Justice, National Institute of Justice, U.S. Government Printing Office, 1983.

Gimeno, F.E. "Fill Flash Photo Luminescence to Photograph Luminol Blood Stain Patterns." *J. Forensic Ident.* 39(3):149–156, 1989.

Graham, M.G., and Kochanski, J. "Move over Quincy." *NIJ Reports/SNI 182.* 4–8, November, 1983.

Grispino, R.R.J. "The Effect of Luminol on the Serological Analysis of Dried Human Bloodstains." *Crime Laboratory Digest* 17(1):13–23, 1990.

Hicks, J.W. "DNA Profiling: A Tool for Law Enforcement." *FBI Law Enforcement Bulletin* 57(8):1–5, 1988.

Klatt, E.C., et al. "AIDS and Infection Control in Forensic Investigation." *Am. J. Forensic Medicine and Pathology* 11(1):44–49, 1990.

Lander, E.S. "DNA Fingerprinting on Trial." *Nature* 339(6225):501–505, 1989.

Lee, H.E., et al. "The Effect of Presumptive Test, Latent Fingerprints and Some Other Reagents and Materials on Subsequent Serological Identification, Genetic Marker & DNA Testing in Bloodstains." *J. Forensic Ident.* 39(6):339–358, 1989.

MacDonell, H.L. *Bloodstain Pattern Interpretation.* Corning, New York: Laboratory of Forensic Science, 1982.

MacDonell, H.L. *Flight Characteristics and Stain Patterns of Human Blood.* U.S. Department of Justice, 1971.

Mills, P.R., et al. "The Detection of Group-specific Components from Urine Samples." *Forensic Science International* 43(3):215–221, 1989.

Neufeld, P.J., et al. "When Science Takes the Witness Stand." *Scientific American* 262(5):46–53, 1990.

Owen, G.W. *A Comparison of Some Presumptive Tests for Blood.* Aldermaston, England: Home Office Central Research Establishment Report No. 84, 1973.

Pizzola, P.A., Roth, S., and DeForest, P.R. "Blood Droplet Dynamics I" *J. Forensic Sci.* 31(1):36–49, 1986.

Pizzola, P.A., Roth, S., and DeForest, P.R. "Blood Droplet Dynamics II." *J. Forensic Sci.* 31(1):40–64, 1986.

Ross, A.M., et al. "DNA Typing and Forensic Science." *Forensic Sci. Int.* 41(3):197–203, 1989.

Saferstein, R., Editor. *Forensic Science Handbook.* Englewood Cliffs, New Jersey: Prentice-Hall, 1982.

Shell, E.R. "Sherlock Holmes Goes High-Tech—or the Case of the Telltale Enzyme Group." *Technology Illustrated.* April/May:74–79, 1982.

Stewart, G.D. "Sexual Assault Evidence Collection Procedures." *J. Forensic Ident.* 40(2):69–74, 1990.

Templeman, H. "Errors in Blood Droplet Impact Angle Reconstruction Using a Protractor." *J. Forensic Ident.* 40(1):15–22, 1990.

Thornton, J. "DNA Profiling: New Tool Links Evidence to Suspects with High Certainty." *Chemical and Engineering News* 67(47):18–27, 30, 1989.

Zweidinger, R.A., Lytle, L.T., and Pitt, C.G. "Photography of Bloodstains Visualized by Luminol." *J. Forensic Soi.* 18(4):296–302, 1973.

## Chapter 9

Beckstead, J.W., Rawson, R.D., and Giles, W.S. "Review of Bite Mark Evidence." *JADA* 99:69–74, 1979.

Benson, B.W., Cottone, J.A., Bomberg, T.J., and Sperber, N.D. "Bite Mark Impressions: A Review of Techniques and Materials." *J. Forensic Sci.* 33(5):1238–1243, 1987.

Bodziak, W.J. "Manufacturing Processes for Athletic Shoe Outsoles and Their Significance in the Examination of Footware Impression Evidence." *J. Forensic Sci.* 31(1):153–176, 1986.

Bonte, W. "Tool Marks in Bones and Cartilage." *J. Forensic Sci.* 20(2):315–325, 1975.

Cassidy, M.J. *Footwear Identification.* Royal Canadian Mounted Police, Ontario, Canada, 1980.

Cassisy, F.H. "Examination of Toolmarks from Sequentially Manufactured Tongue-and-Grove Fliers." *J. Forensic Sci.* 25(4):796–809, 1980.

Davis, R.J. "Systematic Approach to the Enhancement of Footwear Marks." *Canadian Soc. Forensic Sci. J.* 21(3):98–105, 1988.

Denton, S. "Extrusion Marks in Polyethene Film." *J. Forensic Sci. Soc.* 21(3):259–262, 1981.

Diaz, A.A., Boehm, A.F., and Rowe, W.F. "Comparison of Fingernail Ridge Patterns of Monozygotic Twins." *J. Forensic Sci.* 35(1):97–102, 1990.

Dinkel, E.H., Jr. "The Use of Bite Mark Evidence as an Investigative Aid." *J. Forensic Sci.* 19(3):535–547, 1974.

Ellen, D.M., Foster, D.J., and Morantz, D.J. "The Use of Electrostatic Imaging in the Detection of Indented Impressions." *Forensic Sci. Int.* 15:53–60, 1980.

Fawcett, A.S. "The Role of the Footmark Examiner." *J. Forensic Sci. Soc.* 10(4):227–244, 1970.

———. "FBI Laboratory Makes Tool Mark Examinations." *FBI Law Enforcement Bulletin,* Revised, 1975.

Glass, R.T., Jordan, F.B., and Andrews, E.E. "Multiple Animal Bite Wounds: A Case Report." *J. Forensic Sci.* 20(2):305–314, 1975.

Hamm, E.D. "The Individuality of Class Characteristics in Converse All-Star Footwear." *J. Forensic Ident.* 39(5):277–292, 1989.

Hueske, E.E. "Photographing and Casting Footware/Tiretrack Impressions." *J. Forensic Ident.* 41(2):92–95, 1991.

Hodge, E.E. "Guarding Against Error." *AFTE J.* 20(3):290–293, 1988.

Jungbluth, W.D. "Knuckle Print Identification." *J. Forensic Ident.* 39(6):375–380, 1989.

Lennard, C.J., et al. "The Analysis of Synthetic Shoe Soles, FTIR Microspectrometry and Pyrolysis-GC: A Case Example." *J. Forensic Ident.* 39(4):239–243, 1989.

Leslie, A.G. "Identification of Single Element Typewriter and Type Elements, Part I." *J. Canadian Soc. Forensic Sci.* 10(3):87–101, 1977.

Levinson, J. "Single Element Typewriters." *Forensic Sci. International* 13(1):15–24, 1979.

Mankevich, A. "Determination of Shoe Size in Out-of-Scale Photographs." *J. Forensic Ident.* 40(1):1–13, 1990.

MacDonald, D.G. "Bite Mark Recognition and Interpretation." *J. Forensic Sci. Soc.* 14(3):229–233, 1974.

Nielson, J.P. "Laser Enhancement of Footwear Marks on Brown Paper." *J. Forensic Ident.* 39(1):42–51, 1989.

Apolinar, E., and Rowe, W.F. "Examination of Human Fingernail Ridges by Means of Polarized Light." *J. Forensic Sci.* 25(1):154–161, 1980.

Ojena, S.M. "A New Improved Technique for Casting Impressions in Snow." *J. Forensic Sci.* 29(1):322–325, 1984.

Pierce, D.S. "Identifiable Markings on Plastics." *J. Forensic Ident.* 40(2):51–59, 1990.

Sperber, N.D. "Chewing Gum—An Unusual Clue in a Recent Homicide Investigation." *J. Forensic Sci.* 23(4):792–796, 1978.

Stone, I.C. "Fingernail Striations: An Unusual Toolmark." *AFTE J.* 20(4):391–395, 1988.

Rao, V.J., and Souviron, R.R. "Dusting and Lifting the Bite Print: A New Technique." *J. Forensic Sci.* 29(1):326–330, 1984.

Vale, G.L., Sognnaes, R.F., Felando, G.N., Noguchi, T.T. "Unusual Three-Dimensional Bite Mark Evidence in a Homicide Case." *J. Forensic Sci.* 21(3):642–652, 1976.

VanHoven, H. "A Correlation Between Shoeprint Measurements and Actual Sneaker Size." *J. Forensic Sci.* 30(4):1233–1237, 1985.

Von Bremen, A. "The Comparison of Brake and Accelerator Pedals with Marks on Shoe Soles." *J. Forensic Sci.* 35(1):14–24, 1990.

Von Bremen, U.G., and Blunt, L.K.R. "Physical Comparison of Plastic Garbage Bags and Sandwich Bags." *J. Forensic Sci.* 28(3):644–654, 1983.

## Chapter 10

Andrasko, J., and Maehly, A.C. "Detection of Gunshot Residues on Hands by Scanning Electron Microscopy." *J. Forensic Sci.* 22(2):279–287, 1977.

Barnes, F.C., and Helson, R.A. "An Empirical Study of Gunpowder Residue Patterns." *J. Forensic Sci.* 19(3):448–462, 1974.

Basu, S. "Formation of Gunshot Residues." *J. Forensic Sci.* 27(1):72–91, 1982.

Biasotti, A.A. "The Principles of Evidence Evaluation as Applied to Firearms and Tool Mark Identification." *J. Forensic Sci.* 9:428, 1964.

Burnett, B. "The Form of Gunshot Residue Is Modified, Target Impact." *J. Forensic Sci.* 34(4):808–22, 1989.

Dahl, D., et al. "Determination of Black and Smokeless Powder Residues in Firearms and Improvised Explosive Devices." *Microchemical Journal* 35(1):40–50, 1987.

Davis, J.E. *An Introduction to Toolmarks, Firearms and the Striagraph.* Springfield, Illinois: Charles C. Thomas, 1958.

DeGaetano, D., and Siegel, J.A. "Survey of Gunshot Residue Analysis in Forensic Science Laboratories." *J. Forensic Sci.* 35(5):1087–1095, 1990.

DiMaio, V.J.M., Petty, C.S., and Stone, I.C., Jr. "An Experimental Study of Powder Tattooing of the Skin." *J. Forensic Sci.* 21(2):373–377, 1976.

Fackler, M.L. "Ballistic Injury." *Annals of Emergency Medicine* 15:1451–55, 1986.

Fackler, M.L. "Wound Ballistics: A Review of Common Misconceptions." *AFTE J.* 21(1):25–31, 1989.

Fackler, M.L. "Wound Ballistics: A Review of Common Misconceptions." *JAMA* 259(18):2730–2736, May 13, 1988.

———. *Glossary of the Association of Firearm and Toolmark Examiners.* Augusta, Georgia: Fonville Printing Co., 1980.

Goleb, J.A., and Midkiff, C.R., Jr. "Firearms Discharge Residue Sample Collection Techniques." *J. Forensic Sci.* 20(4):701–707, 1975.

Havekost, D.G., Peters, C.A., and Koons, R.D. "Barium and Antimony Distributions on the Hands of Nonshooters." *J. Forensic Sci.* 35(5):1096–1114, 1990.

Hoffman, C.M., and Byall, E.B. "Peculiarities of Certain .22 Caliber Revolvers (Saturday Night Specials)." *J. Forensic Sci.* 19(1):48–53, 1974.

Josserand, M.H., and Stevenson, J.A. *Pistols, Revolvers and Ammunition.* New York: Bonanza Books, 1972.

Kilty, J.W. "Activity After Shooting and Its Effects on the Retention of Primer Residues." *J. Forensic Sci.* 20(2):219–230, 1975.

Klatt, E.C., et al. "Wounding Characteristics of .38 Caliber Revolver Cartridges." *J. Forensic Sci.* 34(6):1387–1394, 1989.

Krishnan, S.S. "Detection of Gunshot Residues on the Hands by Trace Element Analysis." *J. Forensic Sci.* 22(2):304–324, 1977.

Madea, B. "Determination of the Sequence of Gunshot Wounds of the Skull." *J. Forensic Sci. Soc.* 28(5–6):321–328, 1988.

Matricardi, V.R., and Kilty, J.W. "Detection of Gunshop Residue Particles from the Hands of a Shooter." *J. Forensic Sci.* 22(4):725–738, 1977.

McGuire, F.J., and Boehm, A. "Analysis of Gunshot Residue Test Results in 112 Suicides." *J. Forensic Sci.* 35(1):62–68, 1990.

Medich, M.G., et al. "Single Wound Produced, Simultaneous Discharge of Both Shells from a Double-barrel Shotgun." *J. Forensic Sci.* 35(2):473–476, 1990.

Nesbitt, R.S., Wessel, J.E., and Jones, P.F. "Detection of Gunshot Residue by Use of the Scanning Electron Microscope." *J. Forensic Sci.* 21(3):595–610, 1976.

Nichols, C.A., et al. "Recovery and Evaluation, Cytologic Techniques of Trace Material Retained on Bullets." *Am. J. Forensic Med. Pathol.* 11(1):17–34, 1990.

Petraco, N., and DeForest, P.R. "Trajectory Reconstruction I: Trace Evidence in Flight." *J. Forensic Sci.* 35(6):1284–1296, 1990.

Seamster, A., Mead, T., Gislason, J., Jackson, K., Ruddy, F., and Pate, B.D. "Studies of the Spatial Distribution of Firearms Discharge Residues." *J. Forensic Sci.* 20(4):868–882, 1976.

Simpson, K. "Identification of a Firearm in Murder Without the Weapon." *AFTE J.* 21(1):62–66, 1989.

Stone, I.C., DiMaio, V.J.M., and Petty, C.S. "Gunshop Wounds: Visual and Analytical Procedures." *J. Forensic Sci.* 23(2):361–367, 1978.

Wolten, G.M., Nesbitt, R.S., Calloway, A.R., Loper, G.L., and Jones, P.F. "Particle Analysis for the Detection of Gunshot Residue. I: Scanning Electron Microscopy/Energy Dispersive X-ray Characterization of Hand Deposits from Firing." *J. Forensic Sci.* 24(2).409–422, 1979.

Wolten, G.M., Nesbitt, R.S., Calloway, A.R., and Loper, G.L. "Particle Analysis for the Detection of Gunshot Residue. II: Occupational and Environmental Particles." *J. Forensic Sci.* 24(2):423–430, 1979.

Wolten, G.M., Nesbitt, R.S., and Calloway, A.R. "Particle Analysis for the Detection of Gunshot Residue. III: The Case Record." *J. Forensic Sci.* 24(4):864–869, 1979.

Zeichner, A., et al. "Improved Reagents for Firing Distance Determination." *J. Energetic Materials* 4(1–4):187–197, 1986.

## Chapter 11

Beveridge, A.O., Payton, S.F., Audette, R.J., Lambertus, A.J., and Shadick, R.C. "Systematic Analysis of Explosive Residues." *J. Forensic Sci.* 20(3):431–454, 1975.

Blackledge, R.D. "Methenamine—An Unusual Component in an Improved Incendiary Device." *J. Forensic Sci.* 36(1):261–263, 1991.

———. *Bomb Investigations.* Dover, New Jersey: National Bomb Data Center, Picatinny Arsenal, 1974.

Boudreau, J.F., et al. *Arson and Arson Investigation Survey and Assessment.* National Institute of Law Enforcement and Criminal Justice, Law Enforcement Assistance Administration, U.S. Department of Justice. U.S. Government Printing Office, 1977.

Brauer, K.O. *Handbook of Pyrotechnics.* New York: Chemical Publishing Co., 1974.

Brodie, T.G., and Gleason, A.W. *Bombs and Bombings: A Handbook to Detection, Disposal and Investigation for Police and Fire Departments.* Springfield, Illinois: Charles C. Thomas, 1973.

Carroll, J.R. *Physical and Technical Aspects of Fire and Arson Investigation.* Springfield, Illinois: Charles C. Thomas, 1979.

Davis, T.L. *The Chemistry of Powder and Explosives.* New York: John Wiley & Sons, Inc., 1941.

DeHaan, J.D. *Kirk's Fire Investigation.* 2nd ed. New York: John Wiley & Sons, 1983.

Dietz, W.R. "Improved Charcoal Packaging for Accelerant Recovery by Passive Diffusion." *J. Forensic Sci.* 36(1):111–121, 1991.

Ellern, H. *Military and Civilian Pyrotechnics.* New York: Chemical Publishing Co., 1968.

Evans, H.K. "An Unusual Explosive, Triacetonetriperxide (TATP)." *J. Forensic Sci.* 31(3):1119–1125, 1986.

———. *Introduction to Explosives.* F.B.I. Bomb Data Program, FBI/DOJ, 1975.

———. *Fire Protection Guide on Hazardous Materials.* 8th ed. NFPA, 1984.

Fisco, W. "A Portable Explosives Identification Kit for Field Use." *J. Forensic Sci.* 20(1):141–148, 1975.

Fitch, R.D., and Porter, E.A. *Accidental or Incendiary?* Springfield, Illinois: Charles C. Thomas, 1968.

Garner, D.D., et al. "The ATF Approach to Post-Blast Explosives Detection and Identification." *J. Energetic Materials* 4(1–4):133–148, 1986.

Henderson, R.W. "Fire Investigation from the Consultant's Point of View." *Fire and Arson Investigator* 39(2):23–28, 1989.

Hermann, S.L. *Explosives Data Guide.* Scottsdale, Arizona: Explosives Research Institute, 1977.

Hoffman, C.M., and Byall, E.B. "Identification of Explosive Residues in Bomb Scene Investigations." *J. Forensic Sci.* 19(1):54–63, 1974.

Jones, B.R. "Putting the Fire Scene in Perspective." *Fire and Arson Investigator* 38(3):59–60, 1988.

Jones, N. "Arson-for-profit Investigations, Success or Failure? Recovering Water Damaged Business Records." *Fire and Arson Investigator* 40(3):50–52, 1990.

Kempe, C.R., and Tannert, W.T. "Detection of Dynamite Residues on the Hands of Bombing Suspects." *J. Forensic Sci.* 17(2):323–324, 1972.

Keto, R.O. "Improved Method for the Analysis of the Military Explosive Composition C-4." *J. Forensic Sci.* 31(1):241–249, 1986.

Lenz, R.R. *Explosives and Bomb Disposal Guide.* Springfield, Illinois: Charles C. Thomas, 1965.

Loscalzo, P.J., DeForest, P.R., and Chao, J.M. "A Study to Determine the Limit of Detectability of Gasoline Vapor from Simulated Arson Residues." *J. Forensic Sci.* 25(1):162–167, 1980.

Meyers, R. *Explosives.* Essen Weinheim, Germany: Verlag Chemie, 1977.

O'Donnell, J.J. "Interferences from Backgrounds in Accelerant Residue Analysis." *Fire and Arson Investigator* 39(4):25–27, 1989.

Perr, I.N. "Comments on Arson." *J. Forensic Sci.* 24(4):885–889, 1979.

Phillips, S.A. "How Wood Chars and What It Means to the Fire Investigator." *Fire and Arson Investigator* 38(4):28–30, 1988.

Posey, E.P., et al. "Outline for Fire Scene Documentation." *Fire and Arson Investigator* 38(3):55–58, 1988.

Powell, G.L.F., and Spanswick, K.R. "A Case of Arson?" *J. Forensic Sci.* 24(3):627–630, 1979.

Price, T.A. "Appliances as a Fire Cause." *Fire and Arson Investigator* 39(3):30–34, 1989.

Stoffel, J.F. *Explosives and Homemade Bombs.* Springfield, Illinois: Charles C. Thomas, 1962.

Stone, I.C., Lomonte, J.N., Fletcher, L.A., and Lowry, W.T. "Accelerant Detection in Fire Residues." *J. Forensic Sci.* 23(1):78–83, 1978.

Townshend, D.G. "Identification of Electric Blasting Caps by Manufacture." *J. Forensic Sci.* 18(4):405–409, 1973.

Yallop, H.J. *Explosion Investigation.* Harrogate, England: Forensic Science Society Press, 1980.

## Chapter 12

———. *Alcohol and the Impaired Driver. A Manual on the Medicolegal Aspects of Chemical Tests for Intoxication.* Chicago, Illinois: American Medical Association, 1970.

Baum, R.M. "New Variety of Street Drugs Pose Growing Problem." *C&EN,* September 9, 1985.

Baumgartner, W.A., et al. "Hair Analysis for Drugs of Abuse." *J. Forensic Sci.* 34(6):1433–53, 1989.

Chung, B., et al. "Analysis of Anabolic Steroids Using GC/MS with Selected Ion Monitoring." *J. Analyt. Toxicol.* 14(2):91–95, 1990.

Cone, E.J. "Marijuana-laced Brownies: Behavioral Effects, Physiologic Effects, and Urinalysis in Humans Following Ingestion." *J. Analyt. Toxicol.* 12(4):169–175, 1988.

Cone, E.J. "Testing Human Hair for Drugs of Abuse. I: Individual Dose and Time Profiles of Morphine and Codeine in Plasma, Saliva, Urine and Beard Compared to Drug-induced Effects on Pupils and Behavior." *J. Anal. Toxicol.* 14(1):1–7, 1990.

Cravey, R.H., and Baselt, R.C. *Introduction to Forensic Toxicology.* Davis, California: Biomedical Publications, 1981.

Daigle, R.D. "Anabolic Steroids." *J. Psychoactive Drugs* 22(1):77–80, 1990.

———. *DOT Hazardous Materials Emergency Response Guidebook.* U.S. Government Printing Office, 1981.

Elsohly, M.A. "Morphine and Codeine in Biological Fluids: Approaches to Source Differentiation." *Forensic Sci. Rev.* 1(1):13–22, 1989.

———. *Fire Protection Guide on Hazardous Materials.* 7th ed. NFPA, Boston, 1978.

Fasanello, J.A., and Henderson, R.A. "Vacuum Searches in Narcotics Cases." *J. Forensic Sci.* 19(2):379–383, 1974.

Garriott, J.C., and Latman, N. "Drug Detection in Cases of 'Driving Under the Influence'." *J. Forensic Sci.* 21(2):398–415, 1976.

Garriott, J.C., DiMaio, V.J.M., Zumwalt, R.E., and Petty, C.S. "Incidence of Drugs and Alcohol in Fatally Injured Motor Vehicle Drivers." *J. Forensic Sci.* 22(2):383–389, 1977.

Graham, K., et al. "Determination of Gestational Cocaine Exposure, Hair Analysis." *J.A.M.A.* 262(23):3328–3330, 1989.

Harkey, M.R., et al. "Hair Analysis for Drugs of Abuse." *Advances Anal. Toxicol.* 2:298–329, 1989.

Hudson, J.D. "Analysis of Currency for Cocaine Contamination." *Canadian Soc. Forensic Sci. J.* 22(2):203–218, 1989.

James, R.D. "Hazards of Clandestine Drug Laboratories." *FBI Law Enforcement Bulletin* 58(4):16–21, 1989.

Kram, T.C., Cooper, D.A., and Allen, A.C. "Behind the Identification of China White." *Anal. Chem.* 53(12):1379A–1385A, 1981.

Lundberg, G.D., White, J.M., and Hoffman, K.I. "Drugs (Other Than or in Addition to Ethyl Alcohol) and Driving Behavior: A Collaborative Study of the California Association of Toxicologists." *J. Forensic Sci.* 24(1):207–215, 1979.

Mule, S.J., et al. "Rendering the 'Poppy-seed Defense' Defenseless: Identification of 6-Monoacetylmorphine in Urine, Gas Chromatography/Mass Spectroscopy." *Clin. Chem.* 34(7):1427–30, 1988.

Mason, M.F., and Dubowski, K.M. "Alcohol, Traffic and Chemical Testing in the United States: A Resume and Some Remaining Problems." *Clin. Chem.* 20:126, 1974.

McBay, A.J., et al. "Forensic Science Identification of Drugs of Abuse." *J. Forensic Sci.* 34(6):1471–1476, 1989.

————. *Narcotics Investigator's Manual.* U.S. Department of Justice, Drug Enforcement Administration, 1978.

O'Conner, D.L. "Developing a Standard Operating Procedure for Crime Scene and Identification Processing of Illicit Methamphetamine Labs." *J. Forensic Ident.* 38(6):299–302, 1988.

Turk, R.F., McBay, A.J., and Hudson, P. "Drug Involvement in Automobile Driver and Pedestrian Fatalities." *J. Forensic Sci.* 19(1):90–97, 1974.

Willette, R.E., Editor. "Drugs and Driving NIDA Pedestrian Fatalities." *J. Forensic Sci.* 19(1):90–97, 1974.

Willette, R.E., Editor. *Drugs and Driving NIDA Research Monograph 11.* U.S. Department of Health, Education, and Welfare, 1977.

## Chapter 13

Duenhoelter, J.H., Stone, I.C., Santos-Ramos, R., and Scott, D.E. "Detection of Seminal Fluid Constituents After Alleged Sexual Assault." *J. Forensic Sci.* 23(4):824–829, 1978.

Enos, W.F., Beyer, J.C., and Mann, G.T. "The Medical Examination of Cases of Rape." *J. Forensic Sci.* 17(1):50–56, 1972.

————. *Forcible Rape: A Manual for Sex Crime Investigators, Police Volume III.* U.S. Department of Justice, U.S. Government Printing Office, 1978.

Fraysier, H.D. "A Rapid Screening Technique for the Detection of Spermatozoa." *J. Forensic Sci.* 32(2):527–530, 1987.

Hazelwood, R.R., et al. "The Serial Rapist: His Characteristics and Victims, Part I." *FBI Law Enforcement Bulletin* 58(1):10–17, 1989.

Hazelwood, R.R., et al. "The Serial Rapist: His Characteristics and Victims, Conclusion." *FBI Law Enforcement Bulletin* 58(2):14–17, 1989.

Schiff, A.F. "Rape in the United States." *J. Forensic Sci.* 23(4):845–851, 1978.

## Chapter 14

————. "Building Material Evidence in Burglary Cases." *FBI Law Enforcement Bulletin*, 1973.

Fong, W. "Value of Glass as Evidence." *J. Forensic Sci.* 18(4):398–404, 1973.

Plumtree, W.G. "The Examination of Disc and Pin Tumbler Locks for Tool Marks Made by Lock Picks." *J. Forensic Sci.* 20(4):656–666, 1975.

Yallop, H.J. "Breaking Offenses with Explosives—The Techniques of the Criminal and the Scientist." *J. Forensic Sci. Soc.* 14(2):99–102, 1974.

## Chapter 15

Baker, J.S., and Lindquist, T. *Lamp Examination for On or Off in Traffic Accidents.* The Traffic Institute, Northwestern University, 1977.

Basham, D.J. *Traffic Accident Management.* Springfield, Illinois: Charles C. Thomas, 1979.

Clark, W.E. *Traffic Management and Collision Investigation.* Englewood Cliffs, New Jersey: Prentice-Hall, 1982.

Cousins, D.R., et al. "Data Collection of Vehicle Topcoat Colors. IV: A Trial to Assess the Effectiveness of Color Identification." *Forensic Sci. International* 13(2):183 197, 1989.

Dahdouh, G., et al. "The Identification of Domestic and Foreign Automobile Manufacturers Through Body Primer Characterization." *J. Forensic Sci.* 34(6):1395–1404, 1989.

Dolan, D. N. "Vehicle Lights and Their Use as Evidence." *J. Forensic Sci. Soc.* 11(2):69–82, 1971.

———. "Don't Overlook Evidentiary Value of Glass Fragments." *FBI Law Enforcement Bulletin.* 1976.

Drummond, F.C., and Pizzola, P.A. "An Unusual Case Involving the Individualization of a Clothing Impression on a Motor Vehicle." *J. Forensic Sci.* 35(3):746–752, 1990.

Hamm, E.D. "Locating an Area on a Suspect Tire for Comparative Examination to a Questioned Track." *J. Forensic Ident.* 38(4):143–151, 1988.

Lambourn, R.F. "The Calculation of Motor Car Speeds from Curved Tire Marks." *J. Forensic Sci. Soc.* 29(6):371–386, 1989.

Mackay, G.M. "The Role of the Accident Investigator." *J. Forensic Sci. Soc.* 10(4):245–254, 1970.

Monahan, D.L., and Harding, H.W.J. "Damage to Clothing—Cuts and Tears." *J. Forensic Sci.* 35(4):901–913, 1990.

———. *Photography in Traffic Investigation.* Kodak Publication M-21, Rochester, New York: Eastman Kodak Co.

Ryland, S.G., and Kopec, R.J. "The Evidential Value of Automobile Paint Chips." *J. Forensic Sci.* 24(1):140–147, 1979.

Zeldes, I. "Speedometer Examination: An Aid in Accident Investigation." *FBI Law Enforcement Bulletin* 49(3):11–15, 1980.

# Chapter 16

Adelson, L. *The Pathology of Homicide.* Springfield, Illinois: Charles C. Thomas, 1974.

Blanke, R.V. "Role of Toxicology in Suicide Evaluation." *J. Forensic Sci.* 19(2):284–291, 1974.

Burnham, J.T., Preston-Burnham, J., and Fontan, C.R. "The State of the Art of Bone Identification by Chemical and Microscopic Methods." *J. Forensic Sci.* 21(2):340–342, 1976.

Burton, J.F. "Fallacies in the Signs of Death." *J. Forensic Sci.* 19(3):529–534, 1974.

Chai, D.S. "A Study on the Standard for Forensic Anthropologic Identification of Skull-image Superimposition." *J. Forensic Sci.* 34(6):1343–1356, 1989.

———. "Classifying Sexual Homicide Crime Scenes—Interrater Reliability." *FBI Law Enforcement Bulletin.* August, 1985.

Copeland, A.R. "Multiple Homicides." *Am. J. Forensic Med. Pathol.* 10(3):206–208, 1989.

Copeland, A. "Suicide Among Nonwhites: The Metro Dade County Experience, 1982–1986." *Am. J. Forensic Med. Pathol.* 10(1):10–13, 1989.

——. "Crime Scene and Profile Characteristics of Organized and Disorganized Murderers." *FBI Law Enforcement Bulletin*, August, 1985.

DiMaio, V.J.M. *Gunshot Wounds—Practical Aspects of Firearms, Ballistics and Forensic Techniques*. New York: Elsevier Scientific Publishing Co., 1985.

DiMaio, V.J.M., and Zumwalt, R.E. "Rifle Wounds from High Velocity Centerfire Hunting Ammunition." *J. Forensic Sci.* 22(1):132–140, 1977.

Eckert, W.G. "The Pathology of Self-Mutilation and Destructive Acts: A Forensic Study and Review." *J. Forensic Sci.* 22(1):242–250, 1977.

Eisele, J.W., Reay, D.T., and Cook, A. "Sites of Suicidal Gunshot Wounds." *J. Forensic Sci.* 26(3):480–485.

Emson, H.E. "Problems in the Identification of Burn Victims." *J. Canadian Soc. Forensic Sci.* 11(3):229–236, 1978.

Fossum, R.M., and Descheneau, K.A. "Blunt Trauma of the Abdomen in Children." *J. Forensic Sci.* 36(1):47–50, 1991.

Gee, D.J. "A Pathologist's View of Multiple Murder." *Forensic Sci. International* 38(1,2):53–65, 1988.

Haglund, W.D., Reay, D.T., and Tepper, S.L. "Identification of Decomposed Remains by Deoxyrebonucleic Acid (DNA) Profiling." *J. Forensic Sci.* 35(3):724–729, 1990.

Haglund, W.D., et al. "Recovery of Decomposed and Skeletal Human Remains in the 'Green River Murder' Investigation." *Am. J. Forensic Med. Pathol.* 11(1):35–43, 1990.

Henssage, C. "Death Time Estimation in Case Work. I: The Rectal Temperature Time of Death Nomogram." *Forensic Sci. International* 38(3,4):209–236, 1988.

Henssage, C., et al. "Death Time Estimation in Case Work. II: Integration of Different Methods." *Forensic Sci. International* 39(1):77–87, 1988.

Hirsch, C.S., and Adelson, L. "A Suicidal Gunshot Wound of the Back." *J. Forensic Sci.* 21(3):659–666, 1976.

Howard, J.D., et al. "Processing of Skeletal Remains: A Medical Examiner's Perspective." *Am. J. Forensic Med. Pathol.* 9(3):258–264, 1988.

Klattet, E.C., et al. "Wounding Characteristics of .38 Caliber Revolver Cartridges." *J. Forensic Sci.* 34(6):1387–1394, 1989.

Kerley, E.R. "The Identification of Battered-Infant Skeletons." *J. Forensic Sci.* 23(1):163–168, 1978.

Kerley, E.R. "Forensic Anthropology and Crimes Involving Children." *J. Forensic Sci.* 21(2):333–339, 1976.

Kerley, E.R. "Special Observations in Skeletal Identification." *J. Forensic Sci.* 17(3):349–357, 1972.

Kintz, P., Godelar, B., Tracqui, A., Mangin, P., Lugnier, A.A., and Chaumont, A.L. "Fly Larvae: A New Toxicological Method of Investigation of Forensic Medicine." *J. Forensic Sci.* 35(1):204–207, 1990.

Malik, M.O.A. "Problems in the Diagnosis of the Cause of Death in Burned Bodies." *J. Forensic Sci. Soc.* 11(16):21–28, 1971.

Mann, R.W., et al. "Time Since Death and Decomposition of the Human Body:

Variables and Observations in Case and Experimental Field Studies." *J. Forensic Sci.* 35(1):103–111, 1990.

Muramatsu, Y., et al. "Concentrations of Some Trace Elements in Hair, Liver and Kidney from Autopsy Subjects—Relationship Between Hair and Internal Organs." *Science of the Total Environment* 76(1):29–40, 1988.

Murphy, G.E., Cantner, G.F., Wetzel, R.D., Katz, S., and Ernst, M.F. "On the Improvement of Suicide Determination." *J. Forensic Sci.* 19(2):276–283, 1974.

Masters, N., Morgan, R., and Shipp, E. "DFO, Its Usage and Results." *J. Forensic Ident.* 41(1):3–10, 1991.

Palmer, C.H., and Weston, J.F. "Several Unusual Cases of Child Abuse." *J. Forensic Sci.* 21(4):851–855, 1976.

Prouty, R.E. "The Zodiac: An Unsolved Serial Murder." *J. Forensic Ident.* 39(3):165–174, 1989.

Randall, B., and Jaqua, R. "Gunshot Entrance Wound Abrasion Ring Width as a Function of Projectile Diameter and Velocity." *J. Forensic Sci.* 36(1):138–144, 1991.

Rentoul, E., and Smith, H., Editors. *Glaister's Medical Jurisprudence and Toxicology.* 13th ed. London: Churchill Livingston, 1973.

Rhine, J.S., and Curran, B.K. "Multiple Gunshot Wounds of the Head: An Anthropological View." *J. Forensic Sci.* 35(5):1236–1241, 1990.

Rodriguez, A. *Handbook of Child Abuse and Neglect.* New York: Medical Examination Publishing Co., Inc., 1977.

Rodriquez, W.C., and Bass, W.M. "Decomposition of Buried Bodies and Methods That May Aid in Their Location." *J. Forensic Sci.* 30(3):836–852, 1985.

Rodriquez, W.C., and Bass, W.M. "Insect Activity and Its Relationship to Decay Rates of Human Cadavers in East Tennessee." *J. Forensic Sci.* 28(2):423–432, 1983.

Rumsch, B.J. "Medical Examiner Report of a Boeing 727-95 Aircraft Accident." *J. Forensic Sci.* 22(4):835–844, 1977.

Simpson, K. "Identification of a Firearm in Murder Without the Weapon (A Case Study)." *AFTE* 21(1):62–66, 1989.

Skinner, M.F. "Case Report in Forensic Anthropology: Animal and Insect Factors in Decomposition of Homicide Victim." *Canadian Soc. Forensic Sci.* 21(1,2):71–81, 1988.

Snyder, L. *Homicide Investigation.* 3rd ed. Springfield, Illinois: Charles C. Thomas, 1977.

Spitz, W.U., and Fisher, R.S. *Medicolegal Investigation of Death: Guidelines for the Application of Pathology to Crime Investigation.* Springfield, Illinois: Charles C. Thomas, 1973.

Stephens, B.G. "A Simple Method for Preparing Human Skeletal Material for Forensic Examination." *J. Forensic Sci.* 24(3):660–662, 1979.

Sundick, R.I. "Age and Sex Determination of Subadult Skeletons." *J. Forensic Sci.* 22(1):141–144, 1977.

Usher, A. "The Role of the Pathologist at the Scene of the Crime." *J. Forensic Sci. Soc.* 10(4):213–218, 1970.

Vieira, D.N. "Homicidal Hanging." *Am. J. Forensic Med. Pathol.* 9(4):287–289, 1988.

Warren, C.P. "Personal Identification of Human Remains: An Overview." *J. Forensic Sci.* 23(2):388–395, 1978.

Watanabe, T. *Atlas of Legal Medicine.* 2nd ed. Philadelphia: J. B. Lippincott, Co., 1972.

Watson, A.A. "Estimation of the Age from Skeletal Remains." *J. Forensic Sci. Soc.* 14(3):209–213, 1974.

Wertheim, P.A. "Investigation of Ritualistic Crime Scenes." *J. Forensic Ident.* 39(2):97–106, 1989.

Wright, R.K., and Davis, J. "Homicidal Hanging Masquerading as Sexual Asphyxia." *J. Forensic Sci.* 21(2):387–389, 1976.

# INDEX

# BIOGRAPHY

## BARRY A.J. FISHER

A native of New York City, Barry Fisher graduated from the City College of the City University of New York in 1966 with a B.S. degree in chemistry. He received an M.S. in organic chemistry from Purdue University in 1969 and an M.B.A. from California State University at Northridge in 1973.

In 1969 he joined the staff of the Los Angeles County Sheriff's Department, where he worked in nearly all sections of the laboratory. In 1979 he was promoted to Chief Criminalist, and in 1987 he was appointed the first civilian director of the Scientific Services Bureau.

The Los Angeles County Sheriff's Department's Scientific Services Bureau is accredited through the American Society of Crime Laboratory Directors, Laboratory Accreditation Board, and is one of the largest municipal crime laboratories in the United States. A scientific, technical, and support staff of over 160 people is involved in crime scene investigation, fingerprint identification, photography, polygraph, questioned documents, firearms, toxicology, narcotics analysis, forensic serology, and trace evidence examination.

The laboratory is headquartered in downtown Los Angeles and also operates three small regional labs around Los Angeles county. The Scientific Services Bureau provides forensic science laboratory services to the Sheriff's Department and all police agencies in Los Angeles County, except for the Los Angeles Police Department. Cases range from straightforward blood alcohol tests to complex serial murder investigations, as well as every other imaginable type in between. In 1990 the caseload for the laboratory was nearly 90,000, excluding breath alcohol cases.

Mr. Fisher is a member of several professional organizations. He is a member of the California Association of Criminalists and the California State Division of the IAI. He is past chairman of the Criminalistics Section and a fellow of the American Academy of Forensic Sciences, currently serving on its board of directors. He is past president of the American Society of Crime Laboratory Directors and is currently chairman of the Laboratory Accreditation Board. He is also a member of the Forensic Science Society, the International Association of Identification, the International Association of Chiefs of Police, the California Association of Toxicologists, and the California Association of Crime Laboratory Directors.

An author and lecturer, Mr. Fisher has delivered addresses on issues of forensic science at professional conferences in the United States, Canada, England, and Australia.